Composers of North America

Series Editors: Sam Dennison, William C. Loring, Margery Lowens, Ezra Schabas

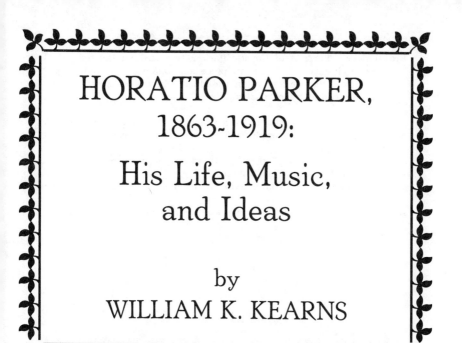

HORATIO PARKER, 1863-1919:

His Life, Music, and Ideas

by
WILLIAM K. KEARNS

Composers of North America, No. 6

The Scarecrow Press, Inc.
Metuchen, N.J., & London
1990

Frontispiece: Portrait of Horatio Parker from around the time of Hora Novissima, 1893. Frontispiece and photo on p. xviii from the Horatio Parker Papers in the Music Library at Yale University. Reprinted by permission.

Music example 7-4 is used by permission of Yale University Press.
Music examples 8-19 through 8-22 are used by permission of Boston Music Company.
Music examples 9-1, 12-7 through 12-12 are used by permission of the Music Library, Yale University.
Music examples 9-10 through 9-16 are used by permission of George Schirmer.
All publishers and libraries are acknowledged above each example.

British Library Cataloguing-in-Publication data available

Library of Congress Cataloging-in-Publication data

Kearns, William, 1928-
    Horatio Parker, 1863-1919 : his life, music, and ideas / by William K. Kearns.
        p.   cm. -- (Composers of North America ; no. 6)
    Includes bibliographical references (p.
    Discography: p.
    ISBN 0-8108-2292-X (alk. paper)
    1. Parker, Horatio W. (Horatio William), 1863-1919. 2. Composers--United States--Biography. I. Title. II. Series.
ML410.P163K4   1990
780'.92--dc20
[B]   89-70355

TABLE OF CONTENTS

Contents

FOREWORD

This series is designed to restore an almost forgotten part of our musical heritage. Few North American composers had their works performed frequently enough during their lifetimes to establish them in the standard repertoire of soloists, chamber groups, orchestras, or choruses. Their compositions, therefore, even when published, have tended to be forgotten.

Each volume begins with the life and works of a given composer, placing that person in the context of the musical world of the period and providing comments by contemporary critics. The authors note those compositions that today's listeners might enjoy. Each volume includes a catalog of the composer's works, complete with incipits, publication details, and locations of unpublished works.

The series will have served its purpose if it draws attention to the large body of work that has so long been treated with benign neglect. The editors believe that a number of these compositions are worthy of being performed today. They hope that those so indicated in text or catalog will be considered for performance by designers and conductors of concert programs and that performers will add some of these works to their repertoires.

Sam Dennison, William C. Loring,
Margery M. Lowens, Ezra Schabas,
Series Editors

For too many years, the name of Horatio Parker has remained almost unknown except to church musicians or those interested in American music of the late nineteenth and early twentieth centuries. If his name is at all familiar to others, it basks in the reflected glory of his famous pupil, Charles Ives.

In his own lifetime, however, Parker's name and music were well known and admired both at home and abroad. His *Hora*

Novissima became the most popular oratorio ever composed by an American, and his opera *Mona* won a $10,000 prize and performances by the Metropolitan Opera. A virtuoso organist, he held one of America's most prestigious positions in sacred music, at Boston's Trinity Church, and as professor and dean of Yale's School of Music, his influence on younger composers left an almost unmatched legacy. In England, he was honored by numerous performances of his choral music and by Cambridge University, which bestowed on him a doctorate of music, the first ever given to an American. In fact, Edward Elgar regarded him so highly that he wrote to his own music publisher in 1898: "[Parker's] *Hora Novissima* contains more 'music' than any of your other Englishmen have as yet managed to knock out. . . ."[1]

Parker was prototypical of a child born with a proverbial silver spoon in his mouth. His well-educated parents soon recognized his considerable musical gifts and continued to nurture them. Then, good luck again befell him in his late teens when he sought instruction from an up-and-coming, slightly older composer, George Whitefield Chadwick, who had just returned from a profitable sojourn in Germany with dozens of fascinating stories about music and musicians in the Mecca of tonal art. From that time forward, Parker would continue to be the luckiest--and, indisputably, the most industrious--American composer of his day until fate dealt him the nastiest hand of all, a premature death at the age of only fifty-six.

For well over twenty-five years, William Kearns has been engaged in a study of the life and works of Horatio Parker. Kearns's efforts first came to fruition in his monumental, two-volume doctoral dissertation (University of Illinois, 1965). Ever since, his continuing interest in both the man and his music has led him into even further research. This book, then, is the result of all those ongoing endeavors. In its first half, Kearns deals extensively with Parker's manifold pursuits as composer, organist, educator, and conductor, as well as his philosophy of music and reactions to the cultural issues and interests of his time. In the second half, the author traces Parker's overall development as a composer, discusses every major composition and most of the minor works, and provides numerous musical examples and a fair amount of contemporaneous critical commentary. Finally, Kearns challenges many of the commonly held, but uninformed, opinions about Parker's musical style and significance in a comprehensive attempt to establish the composer's rightful position in the history of American music.

---

[1]Michael Kennedy, Portrait of Elgar (London: Oxford University Press, 1968), p. 40.

Thanks to Kearns, a complete portrait of one of America's great masters of music has at last been limned, and Parker may now take his well-deserved place in the gallery of American creative artists. Few American composers ever merited a place of honor as much or more.

Margery Morgan Lowens
Baltimore, Maryland

PREFACE AND ACKNOWLEGMENTS

I am grateful to the editors of the series *Composers of North America* for asking me to write this study of one of the most important American composers of his generation. In keeping with the purpose of this series, I have tried to present the essential features of Horatio Parker's life, music, and ideas within the context of his society. Part I is the narrative of his life; however, I have interrupted the historical progression of events to examine critically his role as an educator in Chapter II and his philosophy of music and its relation to society in sections of Chapters IV and V. In Part II, I have dealt categorically with his music, and certain media--such as his large religious works, his operas, and his church music--have given me the opportunity to probe further into his ideas about music. The fact that each chapter reveals a different facet of his compositional activity should not obscure the essential unity of his style and its evolution. For this reason, I have tried to keep his basic line of development before the reader in each chapter, and, in the concluding chapter, I have summarized what I believe to be Parker's distinguishing features as a leading composer, musician, educator, and cultural leader in his day.

So much of Parker's music is now out of print and not easily available that I have included eighty-five examples of his music from all media. In many cases, I have drawn examples from the published vocal scores in order to include as much music as possible; however, I have frequently added orchestration and other annotations (framed with brackets) taken from the full scores of major choral works and operas. Throughout the text, appendices, and index, I have indicated complete works, published and unpublished, in italics and parts of composite works in quotation marks. The List of Works gives information about the type, size, and location of every complete composition by Parker known to me as well as approximate performance times for those works most suitable and available for revival. Throughout the text, I have also recommended specific works or parts of compositions worthy of present-day performance. Under Parker's name in the index can be found a complete alphabetical listing of the composer's works.

A characteristic feature of the history of American music has been how rapidly the music of some of its leading composers such as Parker has been set aside by following generations. The reasons are several, and I examine these in the final chapter. Certain people, however, have kept the flame burning for Parker throughout these periods of neglect. Foremost among these is the late Eva J. O'Meara, who became the music librarian at Yale during Parker's last years there and who, during the next forty years, assembled much of the present archive, which includes practically all of his extant compositions, writings, letters, and memorabilia. I refer the reader to the bibliography for other sources of Parker materials.

O'Meara worked closely with Parker's colleague George Chadwick, his successor at Yale David Stanley Smith, and his daughter Isabel Semler (all now deceased)--who did the principal studies about the composer preceding my own dissertation of 1965. Chadwick's monograph (1921) appeared shortly after Parker's death and is an affectionate tribute to his close friend. Smith's article in the *Musical Quarterly* (1930) is an excellent, succinct account of Parker's life and influence. Semler's *Memoir* (1942) is a compilation of some of Parker's letters and papers, family photographs, and a moving narrative of the composer's life based on this material and her own recollections. Although I have used these studies extensively, I have concentrated on Parker's professional life, particularly his music, and consider my purpose quite different from theirs.

Both O'Meara and Brooks Shepard, music librarian at Yale during the 1960s, were of inestimable help to me not only in my probe of the archive but also in providing help in locating other sources of information.

During the past decade, the Parker archive at Yale has virtually been completed with a few additional materials from the Parker family, specifically Parker's daughter, the late Isabel Semler; his nephew, the late Parker Bailey; and his grand nephew, George Semler Jr. Upon resuming my study in the archive in preparation for this book, I have been generously assisted by Yale music librarian Harold Samuel and Victor Cardell, who, until recently, was curator of the collection. In 1981, a definitive catalog of the archive was compiled by Adrienne Nesnow, and I have used this catalog (HP Papers) both in documenting my text and in preparing the List of Works.

I wish to acknowledge as well the help of my university community in the completion of this study. Dean Robert Fink of the College of Music, University of Colorado at Boulder, provided some released time from teaching and administrative duties. The Council on Research and Creative Work of the Graduate School granted funds for the preparation of the musical examples. Professor Karl Kroeger and my graduate students Melody Bedell and Kay Norton have graciously consented to reading portions of the text and have provided valuable suggestions. Professor emeritus William Reeves and my wife Sophia have spent countless hours helping me to prepare and proofread the text. Without their help, I could not have completed this study.

I would also like to recognize the support and encouragement of my associates in American music throughout the country who have known of my continuing interest in the life and music of Horatio Parker and who have shared their knowledge with me. They are too numerous to mention here, as are the many librarians, publishers, and others who have responded so generously to my inquiries. I have tried to recognize as many persons as possible at appropriate places in this study.

Finally, I must extend a special thanks to Dr. Margery Lowens, my editor, for sharing with me her extensive knowledge of this period in America's musical history and for her careful editing of my text. General editor William C. Loring has also been especially helpful in making suggestions upon his reading of the text and with editorial procedures.

Since the completion of my dissertation slightly over twenty-four years ago, American music scholarship has expanded greatly, and ideas about Parker and his role in American music have changed. Although I have drawn on the organization and ideas of my previous study, much has happened to make this book a somewhat different assessment of Parker's significance. During the intervening years, I have kept an annotated list of newer books, monographs, articles, and dissertations, now numbering well over one hundred items, which offer significant comment about Parker's career, and I have referred to several of these in the present study. The perspective of this more recent scholarship and a re-examination of my earlier work has caused me to crystallize my thinking into what I hope is a worthwhile appraisal of an important life in an important era of American music.

William Kearns
Boulder, Colorado
June, 1989

ABBREVIATIONS

A - alto voice
accom - accompanist, accompanied by
AMC - American Music Co., New York
APS - Arthur P. Schmidt , Boston
ASB - A. S. Barnes Co., New York
assn - association
arr - arranged, arranger, arrangement
[b] - bis - repeated opus number
B - bass voice
Bar - baritone voice
Bc - New England Conservatory Music Library
Be - Belwin
bibl - bibliography
BMC - Boston Music Co.
Bp - Boston Public Library
BpBr - Allen A. Brown Collection, Boston Public Library
bsn - bassoon
cb - contra bass viol
cf - compare
ch - choir
cl(s) - clarinet(s)
Cn - Newberry Library, Chicago
cond - conductor, conducted by
cresc - crescendo
CSE - Charles S. Elliot, New York
CT - Connecticut
CTW - C. T. Wagner Reprints, Washington, D.C.
CWT - C. W. Thompson Co., Boston
DC - Da Capo Press, New York
dept - department
ed - editor
EH - English horn
Eng - English language
ES - Edward Schuberth Co., New York
fl sc - full score
espr - espressivo

Ex(s) - Example(s)
Ga - Galaxy Music Co., New York
GBJ - George B. Jennings Co., Cincinnati
Ger - German language
GS - George Schirmer Co., New York
gt - great
HBS - H. B. Stevens Co., Boston
HL - Hall and Locke Co., Boston
hn - horn
HNE - Hinds, Noble, & Eldredge, New York
Ho(s) - holograph(s)
hp - harp
HP - Hope Publishing Co., Carol Stream, IL
HP Papers - *Horatio Parker Papers*, compiled by Adrienne Nes-
    now, see Catalogs under Bibliography.
HWG - H. W. Gray Co., New York
inc - incomplete
JBM - J. B. Millet Co, Boston
JC - John Church Co. Cincinnati
JF - John Fischer Co.,
Ks - William Kearns, see Catalogs under Bibliography
MA - Massachusetts
m - measure
med - medium
min - minutes
ML - M. Leidt Co., New York
mov - movement
Ms(s) - manuscript(s)
mS - mezzo-soprano voice
mm - measures
N - Novello Co., London
NE - Novello, Ewer, & Co. London, New York
NH - Library, School of Music, Yale University
Nw - Adrienne Nesnow, see Bibliography under Catalogs.
NY - New York
NYp - Music Division, New York Public Library
NYPL - New York Public Library
NYv - Music Library, Vassar, Poughkeepsie, New York
ob - oboe
OD - Oliver Ditson Co., Boston
op - opus, opera
orch - orchestra
p, pp - page(s), piano
ped - pedal
perf - performance, performed
pf - piano, performance

PHf - Fleischer Collection, Philadelphia Free Library
pizz - pizzicato
pseud - pseudonym
pt(s) - part(s)
pub, publ - published by
RB - Russell Brothers Co., Boston
rit - ritard
S - soprano voice
SB - Silver Burdett Co., Boston
sc - score
Sk - Oliver Strunk, see Catalogs under Bibliography.
stgs - strings
sw - swell
T - tenor voice
tbn - trombone
timp - timpani
TP - Theodore Presser Co., Philadelphia
trans - translator, translation
Ts(s) - typescript(s)
u - und (and)
unac - unaccompanied
v - voice
vc - violoncello
vc sc - vocal score
vn - violin
w - with
WAP - William A. Pond Co., New York
Wc - Library of Congress, Washington, D. C.
wo - without
ww(s) - woodwind(s)
YUP - Yale University Press, New Haven

Portrait of the principals for *Mona*, 1912. Front row left to right: conductor Alfred Hertz, mezzo-soprano Louise Homer. Back row left to right: composer Horatio Parker, Metropolitan Opera impresario Giulio Gatti-Casazza, librettist Brian Hooker.

PART I:
THE LIFE OF HORATIO PARKER

Chapter One

THE FORMATIVE YEARS

Childhood

Horatio Parker was born in the village of Auburndale, Massachusetts, on 15 September 1863.[1] Although it is now a part of Newton and metropolitan Boston, Auburndale was then isolated enough to afford what the nineteenth century considered the virtues of rural living. Horatio had the responsibility of caring for the family domestic animals,[2] but he also had the freedom to roam the Auburndale woods and to explore the banks of the Charles River.[3]

Parker's parents emphasized mental discipline, self-reliance, and self-improvement, which were to remain features of Parker's character throughout his life. Both parents were descended from English colonists who had come to the New World during the seventeenth century.[4]

Parker's mother, born Isabella Graham Jennings, probably exerted the greater influence on Horatio. The daughter of a minister, she was educated at Lasell Female Seminary, Auburndale. There she developed considerable linguistic and literary talent, and, at the time of her graduation in 1857, she held the title "Class Poet."[5] Thereafter, she remained at Lasell as "Assistant Instructor in English Branches and Music" for the few years preceding her marriage in 1859.[6] Her command of classical and modern languages as well as her poetic ability enabled her to maintain a strong professional relationship in later years with her son. She provided texts for many of his major works written before her death in 1904. Isabella was also a pianist and organist. She performed at the local Episcopal church and Lasell Seminary,[7] gave private lessons in the Parker home, and supervised Horatio's early musical training.

On 23 March 1859, not quite two years after her graduation from Lasell, Isabella married a local widower, Charles Edward Parker, an architect who practiced with some prominence in Boston until shortly before his death in 1890.[8] Sometime before the middle of the century, Charles Edward had established his residence in Auburndale. Here he lived with his first wife, who gave birth to four sons before she died in 1852. He also had four children by Isabella, of whom Horatio was the oldest. The other children by this second marriage were Cornelia Ellen (b. 1868), Edward (b. 1870), and Mary (b. 1875).[9]

The thirty-seven year difference in age between Horatio and Charles Edward may partially account for some diffidence in their relationship. The letters of Horatio to his father, written while Horatio was a student in Germany, show a respectful affection.[10] Charles Edward was a devout man, and some of this religious feeling must have carried over to Horatio who as an adult maintained the Episcopal affiliation held by his parents.

Horatio's full brother and sisters were several years younger, and throughout his life he carried responsibilities of the oldest child of the family. Cornelia ("Nellie"), who was five years younger, married Stephen A. Bailey, a teacher who later became a lawyer and moved to the West. In spite of their wide geographical separation, Parker and Cornelia remained close. They corresponded frequently, and Cornelia traveled with her family from their home in Salt Lake City to Los Angeles for the premiere of Parker's second opera, *Fairyland*, in 1915. Edward, who was seven years younger than Horatio, became a naval officer. Edward's premature death in 1919 affected Horatio deeply. Mary was thirteen years younger than Horatio. In an 1890 letter to Horatio, written only a year before her untimely death, Mary revealed her deep gratitude for his guidance and her strong admiration for his accomplishments as a rising young musician-composer in New York.[11]

There remains one other member of the Parker household with whom Horatio had a constant association, his spinster-aunt Alice Jennings. This deaf-mute sister of Isabella lived with the Parker family and performed most of the normal household duties, thus leaving Isabella, an "utterly impractical" housekeeper, free to indulge in her literary and musical activities.[12] Alice Jennings also seems to have had some literary ability in that she made an English translation from a German text for one of Parker's cantatas, *The Shepherds' Vision*.

For a man who moved with ease in the intellectual circles of his time, Parker's formal education was surprisingly haphazard. Among the records of schools in the area, only those of Williams Grade School in Auburndale contain his name. Anecdotes about Parker's early schooling are few. His impatience with academic study, a characteristic noted in his later work with Chadwick and Rheinberger, might be the basis for an observation by older residents of Newton to the effect that Parker was not considered "a bright or neat scholar."[13] Undoubtedly his mother supplied the story describing Horatio as a precocious five-year old reciting Browning's "Pied Piper of Hamelin" from memory at a school function.[14]

Parker's early musical training is not so shrouded in obscurity. His mother described his abrupt transformation from "positive dislike" to complete absorption in music:

> "In the month of October, 1877," writes Mrs. Parker, "Horatio suddenly began to take an interest in music, to ask all sorts of questions about it, and to spend literally whole days at the piano, beginning at daylight, and stopping only when his father sent him to bed, perhaps at 11 p.m. From this time onwards he had but one object. Sports and recreation were left out of his life, and the necessary education was with great difficulty imparted in the intervals of [between?] music study."[15]

In addition to instructing her son in piano and the fundamentals of music theory, Isabella had a set of organ pedals installed in the home so Horatio could receive instruction in organ.[16]

Hardly more than a year after beginning the study of music, Horatio had acquired enough theoretical knowledge to compose musical settings for fifty nursery rhymes by Kate Greenaway, the noted nineteenth-century illustrator and writer of children's verses.[17] Another youthful marathon was a set of "sixty-eight variations on a familiar theme."[18]

Approximately two years after that momentous October of 1877 during which he discovered music, Horatio secured his first professional position as organist at Saint Paul's, a small Episcopal Church in nearby Dedham, for which he was paid approximately $300 per year from September 1880 to January 1882.[19] He later confessed that his technique at that time was still quite limited: "The first simple hymns in church were played with fear and trembling, lest perchance the clergyman might change one laboriously prepared for another."[20]

Early Training in Boston

Parker's first professional position made him realize the necessity of seeking further musical instruction in neighboring

Boston. Most biographical sources list his teachers there as John
Orth in piano, Stephen Emery in theory, and George Chadwick in
composition at various times from 1880 through 1882. In one
interview, Parker also claimed W. F. Apthorp as a teacher.[21]

Among these teachers, Parker named Chadwick, only nine
years older, as most influential.[22] Chadwick noted that his student
demonstrated "remarkable facility in harmony and modulation," and
"a very fertile vein of lyric melody," concluding that "his melodies
and harmonies had a distinct and individual character of their own,
which may be detected in his later and more mature compositions."[23] Some of the truculence of Parker's schoolboy days carried over into these lessons, for Chadwick commented: "He was far
from docile. In fact, he was impatient of the restrictions of musical
form and rather rebellious of the discipline of counterpoint and
fugues. His lessons usually ended with his swallowing his medi-
cine, but with many a wry grimace."

This period of study saw the inception of one of the most
enduring of friendships. The two men continued to be in frequent
contact throughout the remainder of Parker's life. Their extant
letters in the Yale collection are convincing evidence of their close
relationship.[24] Loftiness of purpose and the most casual banter are
found side by side. Each shared the other's triumphs and tribula-
tions. Their discussions ranged from daily family activities to
professional and intellectual concerns. Both were highly discerning
men who were capable of appraising their own successes and disap-
pointments with detachment and occasional humor.

European Study

Parker evidently felt encouraged enough by his own professional advancement to take on European study. By 1882 he had left
his first church position at Saint Paul's for Saint John's in Roxbury,
where he played organ until June 25, the last Sunday before he
sailed for Europe.[25] Furthermore, Arthur P. Schmidt, the Boston
publisher who encouraged so many American composers, had
accepted Parker's *Three Songs* (1882) for publication a few months
earlier.

In his diary on 16 February 1882, Parker recorded: "Mother
conceived idea of borrowing from Mr. Carter--plan for me to go to
Europe. I think it is feasible, and hope sincerely that it both may
and will be carried out next fall." On June 6, he recorded that a Mr.
Burr had offered to lend him one hundred and fifty dollars for the
European trip, to begin on the first of July.[26] Parker was fortunate

in having a family who actively supported his European study both with encouragement and some funds. The financial resources of the Parkers were limited during this time, and Parker's letters from Europe describe how frugally he was living. However, they also express his gratitude for the periodic allowances from home.[27] Chadwick had talked with Parker about European study and was undoubtedly influential in Horatio's choice of teacher.[28] Originally Parker had planned to study with Joachim Raff at Frankfurt am Main, but Raff's death just before Parker's departure for Europe necessitated a sudden change to Munich and Rheinberger. Chadwick had studied briefly with Rheinberger, who had a close affinity to Raff and Liszt. Evidently Chadwick was more impressed with the exacting discipline of Rheinberger than what he considered the disorganization of Jadasson, another of his principal teachers.[29]

Parker arrived in Munich around the middle of July. Along with fellow American students Henry Holden Huss and Arthur Whiting, he settled in a local "Gasthaus." Before the opening of school, he traveled in Austria, Switzerland, and Italy. In company with Chadwick and Whiting, he first met Rheinberger at his summer home, Kreuth, near the Tegernsee in Austria. For the next three years, only very infrequent trips to scenic areas in Bavaria interrupted his steady routine of composing, studying, practicing, and concert going.[30]

The official records of Parker's activity at the *Königliche Musikhochschule*, found in the yearly reports from 1882 to 1885, contain lists of instructors, students, course descriptions, and records of concerts. They describe Parker as a student of Joseph Rheinberger in both composition and organ.[31]

Parker composed nothing before his Munich study to indicate that he would become America's leading choral composer by the mid-nineties. His compositions from study with Chadwick had been confined largely to short string quartet and orchestra pieces. At the *Hochschule* he turned to choral writing. In addition to several part songs, he composed three extensive choral works: *The Ballad of a Knight and His Daughter, King Trojan*, and a setting of Psalm 23. Undoubtedly his burgeoning interest in choral music is attributable in part to the church services with elaborate musical accompaniment at Saint Michael's and at other cathedrals which Parker attended in the Bavarian capital.[32] Three overtures and the *Symphony in C* are among the orchestral pieces that survive from this period. Some chamber music and organ pieces, mentioned either in the school catalogs or in Parker's letters, evidently are lost.

During the summer of 1884, Horatio was joined by his mother, his brother Edward, and his younger sister Mary--all remaining with him until the completion of his schooling the following summer. The letters Mrs. Parker wrote from Munich to the

remaining members of the family back in Auburndale provide a
vivid description of her son's last school year. From her first letter
we gain some idea of Parker's stature at the Conservatory:

> He has done a great deal of work this summer. His symphony
> is very fine, say those who know, and he has just written an
> arrangement of the 23rd Psalm . . . which is very nice indeed.
> Rheinberger asked him to play his (R's) new Organ Concerto
> [*Concerto for Organ and Orchestra in F*, Opus 137] for the
> first time in public, and he has offered to give him private
> organ lessons free of expense. A young German-American,
> who is in the house, told me last night, in Will's [Horatio's]
> absence, that he was confessedly far the best pupil in the
> school--that no one could compete with him in Organ-playing,
> in Conducting, or in Composition.[33]

Isabella later mentioned a visit to the Rheinberger home at which
she "could not help being gratified at the way they spoke of Will."[34]

A traveling Boston newspaper correspondent noted that
Parker "has been studying composition for some time under Rheinberger and . . . is now his master's favorite student."[35] A Boston
Evening Transcript reporter who visited Munich in the summer of
1885 wrote that, at the final concert of the season, Parker, along
with his fellow American students Huss and Whiting, "were offi-
cially and publicly congratulated, and each received a diploma.
These were higher honors than were ever before awarded to students in composition at this school."[36]

The exacting discipline that Rheinberger demanded made a
strong impression upon visiting Americans. Chadwick has called
him "a teacher, conservative, almost to the point of pedantry."[37]
David Stanley Smith, one of Parker's first students at Yale and his
successor as Dean there, also has commented on Rheinberger's
authoritarianism and demand for excellence which imbued Parker
with "the greatest respect for fineness of detail and the keenest
appreciation of the niceties."[38] Rheinberger's exactitude seems to
have been characteristic of the *Hochschule* in general. Nearly a
quarter of a century after Parker's time, the American composer
Mabel Daniels described the rigid classroom decorum that still
prevailed there.[39]

Tempering these descriptions of severity are the humorous
stories which Parker recounted to his friends and associates many
years after his Munich school years. H. E. Krehbiel, distinguished
critic of the *New York Tribune*, related that Parker disliked writing
counterpoint drills and would defer their preparation until immediately before they were to be submitted to Rheinberger. In one
instance, Parker, ever facile at working under pressure, was standing

at the classroom stove drying the ink on some exercises just completed. On entering the room, Rheinberger commented wryly that the exercises were probably already "dry enough."[40] The dean of Boston critics William Apthorp offered a similar description of Parker as a not completely docile student and of Rheinberger as a teacher with an inner core of warmth, even joviality:

> It is said of H. W. Parker that when he was a student in Munich under Rheinberger he was repeatedly introducing some new wrinkle, some unheard of effect in the modest compositions on which he was than laboring. Certain of these musical inventions were distasteful to the master, who detected in them an outrage against the canons of the Royal Conservatory, and others were railed at playfully but secretly endorsed and even imitated by Rheinberger himself.[41]

Contrary to prevailing opinion, Parker did not accept his German training uncritically. The so-called "German influence" which is said to have been dominant at Yale during his teaching career there was certainly not consciously fostered by him.[42] In fact, Parker, as a young professional musician in New York City, showed some skepticism about the inclusiveness of his German training. He commented in an 1893 interview that his study with Rheinberger was rather "a development of the seeds sown by his American teachers which contained most of the germs of art truth." He concluded then that "the largest mistake he would correct would be that of confining his musical education to Germany." He named France as having "the atmosphere most conducive to composition" and concluded that the musical environment of France had "an expansive, enthusiastic and romantic nature."[43] As a teacher at Yale, he continued to espouse France as the most favorable environment for training in composition, and many of his own students--including David Stanley Smith, Bruce Simonds, and Douglas Moore--did post-graduate work there.

While he was in Munich, Parker's activities had not gone unnoticed in America. Occasional news items concerning the activities of the American music colony in Munich served to remind the musical public that American students were not only acquiring competency there but were also even surpassing their European peers in some cases.

Parker showed no indication of staying on in Europe as some other Americans such as MacDowell did. In fact, Parker did not remain in Munich long enough during the summer of 1885 to attend his graduation exercises, so eager was he to begin his professional career at home.[44] He had what Van Wyck Brooks has called an "essential Americanism," which, although he admired things

European, precluded any thought of turning his back on his
own country.

Chapter Two

THE EARLY PROFESSIONAL YEARS

New York: 1885-1893

Upon returning to Boston in the summer of 1885, Parker sought employment as a private teacher. He is listed in the *Boston Directory* of 1886 as having a studio at 179 Tremont Street, a location for other music teachers, including John Orth and Arthur Whiting.

With the help of an influential Boston musician, Samuel Brenton Whitney, he soon moved on to a more secure means of employment as the music teacher at Saint Paul's Cathedral School, an Episcopal preparatory school for boys in Garden City, Long Island. The school offered a six-year curriculum designed to facilitate admission to the eastern colleges and has been described, along with Groton School, as highly imitative of the English educational system.[1] In the 1880s, all of the activities of the school were housed in an English-Gothic building which included a basement, three full stories, and some attic rooms in a mansard roof section. As was the case with many schools at that time, teachers and students shared both classrooms and living quarters within the same structure.

It is difficult to establish Parker's exact duties. The official school records from that period are lost, and the few surviving circulars and catalogues from that time do not contain his name. Evidently the major part of his work was private instruction on the piano, the only item concerning music listed in the 1886 circular.[2] A circular from 1888 lists a music faculty of three, a glee club of twenty-four voices, a small orchestra, an "artillery organization," and private instruction on piano, organ, violin, and banjo. Instruction in harmony is also mentioned. One would like to think that some of the increased emphasis on music here as compared to the meager offerings found in the earlier circular was a direct result of Parker's efforts; however, he was no longer a full-time employee of the school after the spring of 1887.[3]

Parker also taught during this time at the Cathedral School of Saint Mary, a sister institution to Saint Paul's, which is also located in the Garden City area. In the 1885-86 catalogue, the curriculum is described as consisting of six forms, each occupying a period of one year.[4] In the 1889-90 catalogue, music is listed as an optional course, along with drawing, painting, and dancing. Parker is designated as the music teacher from 1885 through 1890. His duties consisted largely of private piano instruction.

During his first year at Saint Paul's Parker worked on two major compositions, the *String Quartette* in F Major, Opus 11, and the cantata *Idylle*, Opus 15, based on verses by Goethe. The quartet was the more influential work in gaining an immediate reputation for its composer. On 7 December 1885, Parker wrote to Allen A. Brown, the well-known patron of music, concerning a performance of the work in Boston. Parker indicated that the work would be finished by Christmas and that the Dannreuther Quartet would perform it in Buffalo.[5] The *Quartette* was also played and favorably reviewed at Detroit in 1887.[6]

Parker also used his student compositions to become established as a composer. On 30 January 1886, Frank Van der Stucken conducted a performance of the *Scherzo*, Opus 13, at a New York concert in Steinway Hall.[7] Both a movement from the *Symphony*[8] and the overture *Regulus*[9] were reported to have received performances in Brooklyn by 1888. Parts of *King Trojan* were performed at the meeting of the Music Teachers' National Association held in Boston during the summer of 1886.[10] On 8 February 1887, Jules Jordan, the well-known oratorio tenor, directed a complete performance of the work with piano accompaniment by the Arion Club of Providence, Rhode Island, and, on November 24 of the same year, Frank Van der Stucken conducted the Choral Art Society of New York in a performance with orchestra.[11] The earlier *Ballad of a Knight and His Daughter* did not receive its premiere until 1891 when Jules Jordan and the Arion Club of Providence performed the work on February 23. G. H. Wilson listed the *Ballad* among his "Important Works by American Composers" in the *Yearbook* for 1892-93.

After a year of teaching at Saint Paul's, Parker returned to Munich in the summer of 1886 in order to marry Anna Ploessl, a young German piano student he had met at the *Hochschule*. They returned to Saint Paul's for the fall term of 1886 and set up housekeeping in an apartment within the school building itself. The adjustment for Anna from a secure, middle-class Bavarian home to crowded quarters of a boy's school was severe. Privacy was limited: the instructors and their families took their meals in the central dining hall along with the students.[12] By 1887, however, Parker had shifted the major part of his professional activity from teaching to church music, and the couple moved to more satisfactory living conditions in Manhattan.[13]

Although Anna was trained as a musician, she did not take an active role in her husband's professional life but rather contented herself with the duties of a *Hausfrau*--rearing children, cooking, housekeeping, and enforcing periods of quiet for the benefit of her composer-husband. The thirty-three years they spent together until Horatio's death are marked by domestic tranquility, happiness and a mutual dependence and respect--all of which are evident in their letters.[14] Of their four children, the three daughters, Charlotte, Isabel, and Grace, grew to maturity, married, and had families of their own. The boy William, born in 1891, lived only a few months.

The immediate reason for the move to New York in 1887 was a major position as organist and choirmaster of Saint Andrew's Church in Harlem.[15] (While teaching in Garden City, he had held a similar position at Saint Luke's in Brooklyn; however, there remains no official record of his service there.) Saint Andrew's was one of the oldest and most important Episcopal parishes in New York. Founded in 1828, when Harlem was still a village, it entered a period of troubled times during the seventies and eighties when the community was rapidly losing its rural identity and was merging into the vast metropolitan area of New York. The resulting population influx brought with it a diversity of ideas on church policy, including service music.

The particular issue that brought Parker to the Harlem Church, along with a new rector, was the use of a vested boys' choir as opposed to the quartet choir. The "high ritual" adherents carried the day; thus, Parker's choir consisted of nineteen boy sopranos, four boy altos, four tenors, and seven basses. Parker's duties were extensive. On Sundays, music had to be provided for four services: Holy Communion at 8:00 a. m., Morning Service at 11:00, Choral Vespers at 4:00, and Evening Prayer at 7:30. Parker stayed but one year at Saint Andrew's. Both the unsettled conditions there and the opportunity to move to a larger, more fashionable parish, the Church of the Holy Trinity at Madison Avenue and Forty-Second Street, are probable reasons for the change.[16]

The Church of the Holy Trinity was located across the street from Grand Central Station, its high tower and varicolored tile roof made it a landmark in the city and caused Parker to refer to it as "The Church of the Holy Oilcloth."[17] Here he served under the directorship of E. Walpole Warren,[18] an Englishman "known for his power of persuasion as a preacher and for his love of souls." Warren was one of the great "social gospel" preachers of the day,[19] and the "genial relationship" between rector and choirmaster mentioned by Isabel Semler was undoubtedly a factor in Parker's continued stay at Holy Trinity until he left New York in 1893.[20] Although the church has been described by one of its historians as a "pioneer place" and having had "a meteoric career in the years 1865-1880,"[21] the inevitable growth-and-decay patterns of a large city were having their effect during Parker's time there. In 1895 the church was razed to make room for commercial buildings on the site.

Parker's duties at Holy Trinity included Saturday choir rehearsals, three Sunday services, and a Wednesday evening service.[22] The musical conditions are described quite favorably in a contemporaneous newspaper account:

> His [Parker's] choir at Holy Trinity consists of forty men and boys of whom Mr. Burleigh [Harry Burleigh] tenor, Mr. Richtel, bass, Frank Fullen and Charles Snell are prominent soloists. The choir is in excellent condition; the choir room, large and orderly, bespeaks excellent discipline; and the singing is appreciated by all lovers of sacred song.[23]

Financially, the position, which paid approximately $375 per month, was certainly an improvement over the $2,000 per year offered by Saint Andrew's.[24] These figures probably do not represent net income but rather the gross amount the parishes spent on music. In most Episcopal Churches at that time, the musical director was expected to handle expenses such as a paid choir, soloists, and music. In addition to his regular church salary, Parker was able to earn extra, though irregular, income from such sources as weddings and funerals. These sums, varying from $15 to $35 dollars per month, are recorded in his diaries throughout his years as a church musician.

In addition to service duties, Parker gave recitals at Holy Trinity. Among his memorabilia at Yale is a set of five programs for the winter of 1892-93.[25] For these, he chose from among organ compositions by Bach, Rheinberger, and himself most frequently; however, works by Widor, Guilmant, Adolphe Hesse, and Sir Joseph Barnby were also included. Although Parker's recitals were primarily solo, he was assisted on some by violinists Gustav Dannreuther and Francis Fisher Powers, singer Harry Thomas, and cellist Paul Miersch.

Parker's position at Holy Trinity offered him sufficient time for composition, and during the early 1890s he wrote many hymns, anthems, art songs, piano and organ pieces, and part-songs. At no other time in Parker's career were his efforts channeled so extensively into smaller compositions. They had a waiting market in the vast numbers of American musical amateurs, church choirs, organists, and parlor pianists. He was writing to supply this strong demand as well as to establish a reputation. Most of this music was published as soon as it was written, and the money realized became, for the first time, an appreciable part of his income. The back of his diary for 1890 contains a list of seventeen instrumental pieces or sets, anthems, part and solo songs, together with fees totaling $610.

An ever-widening circle of musician-friends and increasing contact with organizations which devoted all or part of their activity to the cultivation of American compositions provided Parker with several opportunities for recognition during the late eighties and early nineties. Among these groups were the Music Teachers' National Association, the Van der Stucken Novelty Concerts, the New York Vocal Union, the various city and county festivals, and the Manuscript Society of New York.[26]

The Manuscript Society, which had been formed in the late eighties by American composers in order to perform and discuss their own works, had held a successful season of private meetings during the winter of 1889-90.[27] Thereupon, a series of public concerts was begun the following season, and, for the first concert on 10 December 1890 at Chickering Hall, Parker's overture, *Count Robert of Paris* was chosen as the opening selection. An elaborately printed program for this affair, containing incipits from each composition (Foote, Chadwick, Van der Stucken, Silas Pratt, and Harry Rowe Shelly were also represented), is preserved in the first volume of Arthur Foote scrapbooks, now in the Boston Public Library. Parker's diaries for the years 1891-93 mention other compositions of his performed in Manuscript Society meetings, among them the *Suite in A Major for Violin, Violoncello, and Piano* on 3 March 1893 and the *String Quartette* on 13 February 1894. His interest and activity in the group were necessarily restricted after he left New York, although he later served as an Honorary Corresponding Secretary and as a member of the Council[28] and was honored by a performance of his "The lamp in the west" for men's chorus at a 30 December 1901 meeting while he was on sabbatical in Europe.

Another of Parker's important associations during the New York years was with Frank Van der Stucken, whose many musical activities included composition, conducting, teaching, and the organization of various choral and instrumental groups. Van der Stucken not only included Parker's student compositions on his Novelty Concerts of the late 1880s, but, as a leading conductor of German singing societies, provided the composer with performance opportunities for several of his male choruses. Among these are the highly colorful cantata, *Normannenzug (Norsemen's Raid)*, Opus 16; the six secular part songs, Opus 33; and the four religious part songs, Opus 39. Parker's diaries (1890-93) contain numerous references to the Arion Club, a male chorus which Van der Stucken

directed from 1884 until 1895, and to various German-society
singing festivals which Van der Stucken organized. Parker's setting, *Blow, Blow, Thou Winter Wind*, Opus 14 (1891), may have
been written for the Arion Society European tour during the
summer of 1892.

In 1890 Parker set a portion of Bostonian Arlo Bates's
Albrecht as a cantata called *The Kobolds*, Opus 21, and the Norse
tale *Harold Harfager*, Opus 26, as a part-song, both with orchestral
accompaniment. *The Kobolds* was dedicated to the Hampden
County Musical Association, then conducted by George Chadwick,
and was performed at its annual festival at Springfield, Massachusetts, in May of 1891.[29] *Harold Harfager* was given its premiere
performance, 30 April 1891, at Chickering Hall in New York
City,[30] at a concert of the American Composers' Choral Association. The chorus of 126 voices was directed by Emilio Agramonte,
who later became associated with Parker at Yale.

In 1890, the Parkers made their first summer trip to Europe
as a couple. Parker's diaries reveal that they visited Munich and
several of the cathedral towns in England which later were to have a
significant role in his career. They continued making visits to
Europe and England approximately every two or three years until
World War I. Other summers were spent in American vacation
areas, such as Lake George, New York; West Chop and Vineyard
Haven, Massachusetts; and, after 1907, Blue Hill, Maine. Parker
often used vacations for sketching, scoring, copying, and proofread-
ing his compositions.

Although the early nineties brought professional recognition, they also were times of personal tragedy. Within the space of
a year, from August 1890 until July 1891, Parker's father, infant
son, grandmother, and youngest sister died. In the diaries for this
period, Parker recorded large medical bills, extended periods of ill
health, and the names of various health spas. The spring of 1892
seems to have been particularly difficult, with the words "sick,"
"mizzable," and "gout" appearing quite frequently throughout the
months of January through June. Having barely reached the age of
thirty, Parker was beginning a physical deterioration that would
progress steadily, ending in his untimely death at fifty-six years of
age.

Toward the end of his stay in New York, Parker once again
took on some institutional teaching responsibilities. During the first
half of 1892 he spent a part of most Mondays, Wednesdays, and
Fridays substituting for his good friend Edward Stubbs as Instructor
of Music at the General Theological Seminary in New York.[31] This
position was Parker's first experience in classroom teaching at the
college level and predates his frequently cited association with the
National Conservatory of Music by one-half year. Although neither

the Seminary Board nor Parker made explicit reference to his duties, he probably provided rudimentary musical instruction suitable to the training of priests and accompanied the students at Evensong.[32]

The terse statement "Conservatory Contract" in the diary for 19 November 1891 is the first reference to Parker's single year of teaching (1892-93) at the National Conservatory of Music in America. Parker was proud of this affiliation and later cited it frequently in references to his employment. In the six years since its beginning in 1885, the National Conservatory had grown from a school for the training of opera singers to include work in piano, orchestra ensemble playing, theory, composition, and music history. To become a member of a teaching faculty that included such illustrious names as Romualdo Sapio, Rafael Joseffy, Frank Van der Stucken, Gustav Hinrichs, Bruno O. Klein, Henry Finck, and the director, Antonín Dvořák, was a matter of prestige. At that time, the school's benefactor, Jeanette Thurber, appeared to be well on the way to her goal of making the National Conservatory into a school that might rival the Paris Conservatoire.

Generous tuition arrangements, a policy of accepting students regardless of race, creed, or color, and the high quality of instruction enabled the school to secure what were then enormous enrollments. One source mentioned that 207 students applied for piano instruction in 1890,[33] and another has estimated an average attendance of 600 students per year during the early part of the twentieth century.[34]

Most published biographical sketches about Parker claim that he taught music theory and composition at the Conservatory. In the Yale Collection are letters from former students which mention specifically harmony and counterpoint as his subjects.[35] A single entry for 1 November 1892, reading "Harmony, Conservatory," is the only reference throughout his diaries to the kind of work he was doing there; however, an advertisement for the school in the back of *Wilson's Musical Yearbook* for 1891-92 lists Parker as an organ instructor. The remaining diary references to the Conservatory (usually abbreviated as "Cons.") are scattered irregularly throughout the fall of 1892 to June 1893. Listed payments of around $80 per month indicate that the Conservatory position was a substantial activity.

Parker's year at the Conservatory coincided with the first year of Antonín Dvořák's directorship, and mention of Dvořák in the diaries is found in connection with a series of rehearsals culminating in a concert on 21 October 1892 in honor of the Bohemian master,[36] at which Parker played the organ for the performance of Dvořák's recently composed *Te Deum*, Opus 103. It is doubtful whether the two men had much contact in this urban school where the students commuted and the faculty of specialists worked part-time. Dvořák had been hired to bring prestige to the school. His duties were composing and teaching rather than the administration of the Conservatory faculty. Furthermore, he rather scrupulously avoided social functions.[37]

In one respect Parker's career was greatly influenced by Dvořák's presence. Mrs. Thurber, in order to honor her Director, had announced a composition contest shortly after his arrival. Prizes were offered in several types of composition, and Dvořák served as the principal adjudicator.[38] Parker submitted *Dream-King and His Love*, which took first prize in the cantata division. The diaries show that he had been working since 1891 on this piece along with *Hora Novissima*.

A gala concert of the prize compositions took place at Madison Square Garden on 31 March 1893. As the finale for the evening's program, Parker conducted his own work, with Anton Seidl's orchestra and the Conservatory Chorus performing. The *New York Times* reported that the affair was "dull" until the performance of *Dream-King*. Other critics were pleased with the cantata, their consensus raising Parker to a position of leadership in the younger generation of composers. Parker himself considered *Dream-King* as "among my favorite works. . . . It is very characteristic indeed."[39]

During the following month, Parker was engaged in preparation for what must be considered the most important performance in his career, the presentation of *Hora Novissima* on May 3 by the Church Choral Society and supporting instrumentalists, with the composer conducting.[40] Parker's concern for this performance is evident in the numerous diary notations about specific rehearsals. Only for the Metropolitan Opera production of *Mona* in 1912 did he record so many particulars leading to a performance.

Several reasons for the composition of this first and best-known of his oratorios have been given, one of which is that the setting of a Latin text was a popular exercise in accord with the eclectic spirit of the times. Many writers, including Semler, Chadwick, and Howard, have alluded to a connection between the impassioned level of the oratorio and Parker's own state of mind following the deaths of several of his family. The composer lent some credence to this suggestion by dedicating the work to the memory of his father.

Parker himself gave two other reasons for the composition of the oratorio. In an interview given during the spring of 1893, he said that it was written for the Chicago World's Fair,[41] and jottings in his diary at that time show that he had been corresponding about *Hora Novissima* with the Fair's musical supervisor, Theodore Thomas. Although the work was not performed in Chicago, Thomas did use the oratorio at the Cincinnati May Festival in the spring of 1894.[42] Approximately six months later, Parker indicated that the oratorio had been written expressly for the New York Church Choral Society which had given the premiere.[43] Evidently the work was written with several possibilities in mind.

The first performance of *Hora Novissima* was an inestimable success. The *Freund's Weekly* reporter captured the momentousness of the occasion:

> The rain descended and the winds beat, but did not succeed in keeping away a goodly audience, which nearly filled the building. Many of our leading church musicians were in the throng, and all who came were well repaid for their temerity, for they "assisted" at the production of a work remarkable for its boldness, originality and merit. A work of such magnitude, evincing so much musicianly knowledge allied to such charming melodic phrasing must take a high stand among compositions of its class.[44]

William J. Henderson left no doubt about the significance of the work:

> It was earnestly to be hoped that this one composition would establish his reputation as one of the most gifted of the rising American school. . . . The Oratorio made a deep impression and at once took rank among the best works written on this side of the Atlantic. . . . It will be received with praise in England.[45]

The thread running through many of the reviews is a sense of historical importance. Even before the premiere, several New York papers suggested that *Hora Novissima* was expected to be the major effort in the field of American oratorio up to that time. Henderson took pride in calling attention of the world to this composition but commented that the ultimate test lay in England, which, by the very nature of its musical institutions, was best suited to pass judgment. Thus, it was with some degree of pride, when, after the second performance of *Hora Novissima* in Boston approximately nine months later, a reviewer reported:

> It is a work that does not command consideration in estimating its value because of its origin on this side of the Atlantic, for it has already gained high commendation in England among the best judges of church music and has been accepted as a worthy contribution to the religious repertory of the day.[46]

The enthusiasm of this writer may have been caused by a mildly complimentary review of *Hora Novissima* which had appeared in

The Musical Times and was based upon an examination of the recently published piano-vocal score.[47] The first English performance of *Hora Novissima*, however, was still six years away.

The Boston critics were even more enthusiastic than the reviewers of the New York premiere. Louis Elson predicted that, if Parker could throw off more completely his "pedantic" proclivities, "he [would] be the greatest composer that America has produced."[48] Philip Hale made the most generous estimate of both Parker and *Hora Novissima* up to that time:

> I recognize his great talent, a talent that approaches genius, if it is not absolute genius. He has the natural gifts, he has the learning. He has the strength, his sensuousness is not eroticism. The conception of this impressive work is of noble proportions; the execution of which is an honor to our national art. Nor is it perhaps foolish to predict that the future historian of music in America will point back to "Hora Novissima" as a proof that, when there were croakers concerning the ability of Americans to produce any musical compositions save imitations of German models, a young man appeared with a choral work of long breath that showed not only a mastery of the technique of composition, but spontaneous, flowing, and warmly colored melody, a keen sense of values in rhythm and in instrumentation, and the imagination of the born, inspired poet.[49]

Boston: 1893-1894

In the fall of 1893, Parker moved to Boston in order to assume the position of organist and choirmaster at Trinity Church on Copley Square. His decision to leave New York had been announced earlier in March.[50] Among the reasons he gave for leaving Holy Trinity at New York was his increasing disenchantment with that part of the "Oxford Movement" which pertained to the use of boy choirs. The diaries from 1890 through 1893 contain occasional references to problems of discipline among the boys in the Holy Trinity Choir. Although Parker readily conceded the peripheral values of boys' choirs such as character building, he complained that they are a "burden" to the choirmaster and expressed the hope that the adult mixed choir at his new appointment would leave him more time for the important work of composition.

There were also personal reasons for the change: family, friends, and the many musical associations he had made as a youth in Boston. Furthermore, eight years in New York, where "the serious musician is treated as a mere entertainer,"[51] had not given Parker much hope for the future there. Henry Steele Commager cited the move from Boston to New York of America's then leading novelist William Dean Howells as symbolic of a change in the cultural Mecca of the United States.[52] If Commager is right, Parker was going against the grain by maintaining the superiority of New England not only in music but in all cultural matters:

> New England is the centre from which has radiated thus far a great part of all progress in Art, Literature, and other intellectual pursuits in America, and it seems perfectly fair to say that an History of Music in New England would practically cover the subject of the History of Music in America.[53]

Parker was returning to an environment which he had never left in attitude or outlook.

Finally, there was the very practical matter of financial remuneration. At least three contemporaneous accounts stress the fact that Trinity Church was paying Parker the largest income ever granted to any Boston church musician, a situation causing envy among the older, established organists and choirmasters such as J. C. D. Parker and Benjamin J. Lang.[54] The "princely salary," (the description used by the *Boston Journal*) was the approximately $650 listed in the monthly payments marked "church" in the back of the diary for 1895.

From 1869 until 1892 Trinity Church had been the parish of Phillips Brooks, one of the most influential preachers of the nineteenth century. He had been succeeded by Elijah Winchester McDonald, perhaps a less spectacular but nevertheless eloquent and persuasive minister, whose service at Trinity (1892-1904) nearly coincides with that of Parker. A typical Sunday at Trinity has been described as follows:

> There were big congregations, even the galleries being well filled. The morning congregations were made up, for the most part, of pew owners. In the afternoon at four, there was another large congregation in which men predominated--once more the galleries being well filled.[55]

In addition to providing service music, Parker found time during that fall to give an organ recital and to direct a performance of *Messiah*.[56]

The principal event of Parker's single year in Boston was the performance of *Hora Novissima* by the Handel and Haydn Society on 4 February 1894 in Symphony Hall. Parker conducted, and Emma Juch, Mrs. H. E. Sawyer, William H. Reiger, and Max Heinrich were the soloists. What should have been a crowning achievement up to that point in the young composer's career was marred by an unfortunate incident which occurred nearly on the eve of the performance. Madame Lillian Nordica, who had been hired to sing the solo soprano part, refused to participate because she was either sick or unwilling. Parker, stunned by what he considered a rebuke, made some intemperate remarks about Nordica which, in turn, drew a withering reply from the famous American diva. The affair was inflated by the newspapers into the *cause célèbre* of the Boston musical season; consequently, the reputation of neither principal was enhanced.[57]

Parker's sudden prominence as a composer coincided with a flurry of publications in 1893 equal to that other bountiful year of 1890. In addition to *Dream-King* and *Hora Novissima*, he finished work on the small church cantata *The Holy Child*, Opus 37, and also had published two sets of organ pieces (Opp. 32 and 36), a set of part-songs for men's voices (Opus 33), several pieces of sacred music, and six secular songs. The following year, another set of male part-songs (Opus 39), an anthem, and a few songs were also published.

Chamber music also occupied a significant part of Parker's time during this short Boston interlude. Some of his closest friends--Franz Kneisel, Timothée and Joseph Adamowski, Arthur Whiting, and Arthur Foote--were important chamber music performers in the area. On 20 February 1894, Parker appeared as one of the performers along with the Adamowskis in a performance of his *Piano Trio*, Opus 35. This trio was performed in Milwaukee on 17 May 1893 and again on 23 February 1896, the latter being an all-American music program which also included pieces by MacDowell and Van der Stucken.[58]

Parker's diary for 1895 reveals that two other pieces were performed by Boston Chamber groups: the *Suite for Violin and Pianoforte*, Opus 41, and the *String Quintette in D Minor*, Opus 38. Timothée Adamowski and Arthur Whiting presented the *Suite* in a public recital at Bumstead Hall on January 15 and later on January 20, in a private performance at the Saint Botolph Club. The following day the Kneisel Quartet, assisted by an additional cellist, presented the *Quintette*.

These performances took place after Parker had left Boston for New Haven, Connecticut. In May of 1894, the Corporation of Yale University elected him to the Battell Professorship of the

Theory of Music, a position that was being vacated by the retiring Gustave Stoeckel, Yale's first Battell Professor.

The decision to leave Boston must have been painful. Only a year earlier Parker had been emphatic in his desire to return to his native city, and the ensuing period had brought steadily increasing recognition. The daily, close association with relatives and friends would also have to be sacrificed. Furthermore, the prospect of his new environment must have caused him some concern. Yale University was only beginning to emerge from a conservative and moralistic approach to education and the arts.[59] In addition, the school was situated in the midst of a small, bustling, manufacturing city with a large immigrant population and little or no organized effort in cultural affairs.[60] Nevertheless, the prestige of a full professorship in one of America's important universities and the security and opportunity that go with such a position were overruling factors. Parker's resolution to accept the Yale post was the most significant professional decision of his life. It secured for him a permanent and important place in a wider spectrum of American musical activity. Hereafter, he was to be known not only as a composer and church musician but also as an educator. The consequences of his teaching career at Yale are examined in the following chapter.

Chapter Three

THE EDUCATOR

The Organization and Development
of the Music Curriculum at Yale

Although Parker never claimed to be a music educator and even disdained the role at times, he probably made a deeper impression and exerted a stronger influence on music education of the time than any other American composer. His persistent theme, the professional development of composers, was somewhat at odds with the philosophy of Yale College, which stressed mental discipline in a liberal arts curriculum;[1] however, Parker was backed by Yale President Timothy Dwight, who supported the co-equal existence of Yale College with the University's various professional schools such as music.[2]

Before Parker came to Yale, the music teaching staff consisted of one man, Gustave J. Stoeckel, who had arrived in New Haven in 1848 as a penniless German immigrant.[3] Stoeckel became connected with Yale in 1855 as "Instructor of Vocal Art, Organist, and Chapelmaster."[4] His rise in the academic world was even more retarded than that of his illustrious counterpart at Harvard, John Knowles Paine.[5] In 1864, Yale University conferred upon him the honorary degree, Doctor of Music, but it was not until 1890, the year in which a department of music was formally organized, that Stoeckel was awarded a professorship. He was then named Battell Professor of Music, the appointment to which Parker eventually succeeded.[6] Stoeckel developed and taught a two-year program consisting of *Harmony* (first year), and *Counterpoint, Canon, Fugue* (second year), with a third course, *Forms*, taught along with the first two courses. He also gave lectures on the history of music, esthetics, analysis, and biographies of composers.[7] Such was the status of music at Yale when Parker went there in 1894.

In keeping with President Dwight's dictum that "the Department might well be strengthened in its means of instruction and developed somewhat more fully in its courses and arrangements,"[8] several changes were soon effected. Parker's title was designated as the Battell Professor of the Theory of Music in order to distinguish his duties from those of Samuel Sanford, who was hired at the same time to develop a program of applied instruction.[9]

Parker expanded the course offerings from three to six: *Harmony, Counterpoint, The History of Music, Strict Composition, Instrumentation*, and *Free Composition*. These, together with a seventh course, *Advanced Orchestration and Conducting*, added in 1904, constitute the music curriculum during Parker's tenure and reflect his beliefs as to the essential components of college music training. *Harmony* remained basically the same course as Stoeckel's; however, the latter's composite *Counterpoint-Canon-Fugue* course was divided into two new courses: *Counterpoint* and *Strict Composition*.[10]

For the harmony course, Parker used one of the most famous nineteenth-century texts, Salomon Jadassohn's *Harmony*. In 1900, his erstwhile student, Harry Jepson took over the course and changed the text to George W. Chadwick's *Harmony* (1897), which nevertheless continued to follow Jadasson in many ways.[11]

Among the new courses, *The History of Music* was substituted for the previously informally scheduled "Lectures on the History of Music and Aesthetics." This course was conducted as a large lecture session varying from forty to seventy students and meeting once a week. As these lectures were intended for all students who wanted to gain a culturally broadening experience through music, no prerequisite was made for admission. The community was also invited to attend.

Parker taught *The History of Music* for the duration of his career at Yale. By observing his efforts to define the scope and purpose of the course, we gain some insight into his philosophy of music education, and from the lectures themselves we can form an impression of his attitudes toward composing, performing, listening to, and describing music. In addition, his opinions of composers and historical movements emerge more clearly here than perhaps from any other source.

Parker contrasted the history course with the professional music courses by stressing the role of "intelligent listening" in the former and the importance of composing in the latter.[12] Both functions, however, have a common base in "training students to understand music when they hear it." In the professional courses, his aim was to show students "by successive steps how to compose and to write music, bring them into contact with the methods and habits of composers, and enable them to express properly such musical ideas as they may have." For the History course, students should gain "a more intimate knowledge of the nature and structure of music than can be obtained through lectures or literature." To accomplish this goal, Parker augmented his lectures at the piano with numerous illustrations, and, for many students, his performances were a principal reason for electing the course.[13]

In an age of florid, poetic rhetoric about music, Parker confined his attention succinctly to the music itself:

> Although I am called the Professor of the Theory of Music, I am in every sense a practical musician. Theoretical in that the actual music I try to teach is on paper, but practical in that it is not meant to remain on paper alone but to be expressed in tones as well as notes.[14]

He thus regarded the usefulness of esthetics as being extremely limited:

> I must confess to a large ignorance of the metaphysical and aesthetic aspect of music. . . . I do not think that they have ever added to the sum total of purely musical knowledge. . . . The philosophers and scientists have never helped the practical musician in his search for new beauties. (Lecture I, p. 5)

Nevertheless, he spoke often on the matter of musical taste and used the course as a sounding board for his own ideas in this respect. A student should be taught "to respect, to satisfy, and to regulate his craving for the pleasure given by beautiful things.[15] In the manner of Emerson, Parker insisted that esthetics must, however, have its rational and spiritual as well as its sensual aspect.[16] The perceiver must do more than react to every and any artistic experience. He should select, control, and evaluate in a constant search for objective beauty: "A student is taught, therefore, in good schools what he should enjoy and why. He is taught to appreciate style and design and to compare the materials out of which different musical works are constructed."[17]

Although he protested that he was only a "practical" musician, Parker's lectures show a wide acquaintance both with the field of music history and then-leading contemporary texts and reference works. Much of his lecture material was drawn from the *Oxford History of Music* series. There are frequent references to important nineteenth-century European historians such as Lavignac, Ambros, Spitta, and Fétis, and the English scholars: Parry, Rowbotham, and Rockstro. At first no text was listed; however, Parry's *The Art of Music* was adopted for the 1902-03 school year and continued to be used until the first part of the second decade when Waldo Selden Pratt's *The History of Music*, was substituted for it.[18]

Parker's lectures did not merely parrot facts gleaned from histories and biographies. He voiced his own opinions, and he did not hesitate to disagree with his sources on occasion. Throughout his nineteen lectures in the history course, his own philosophy of history emerges as a coupling of linear progress and "great man" theories. He traced the course of music upward with emphasis on human pinnacles such as Guido d'Arezzo, Leonin, Franco of Cologne, Machaut, Landini, Dufay, Josquin, Palestrina, and Orlando di Lasso. His evolutionary point of view is reflected in such statements as "The imperfect work of Dufay improved and developed steadily and with wonderful rapidity until . . . it reached its culmination in Lasso" (Lecture VI, p. 2).

Parker admired the "colossal Baroque" as found in the music of Benevoli. His concluding remark on that composer is an observation which also served as a response to critics of his own music:

> The multiplying of contrapuntal devices was a weakness rather than a source of strength. Perhaps it indicates that too much learning is not good for composers, although I have found little to be frightened about in that direction (IX, 2).

In discussing Monteverdi, he revealed a conservative attitude toward church music which is not evident in his own larger sacred works. Here his belief in transcendental musical laws is evident:

> Monteverdi . . . was a bold thinker in dramatic music. . . . To my mind his greatest mistake was made not in his operatic writing but in his church music in which he tried to reconcile two things which can never go together. The more severe kinds of music are the only ones fit for use in the church. All musicians know that the only dissonances allowed in strict counterpoint are those of transition and suspension. . . . Unprepared discords are very beautiful and very necessary in our music but their introduction in polyphonic counterpoint is contrary to the nature of things. This, I believe, was Monteverdi's mistake and for this reason his church music compares unfavorably with that of his less progressive and perhaps less gifted contemporaries or predecessors. (IX, 3)

In his consideration of the ascetic attitude of the early Christians toward music, Parker sought an ethical basis for what he considered to be their aversion to chromaticism:

It is curious that this attitude of objection to chromatic music
which is quite common even at the present time should be
exemplified in so unfinished a state of development as that of
the early church music. I suppose the psychological basis of
this objection has always been a natural respect for simplicity
and directness which earnest people are apt to feel in artistic as
in other matters. (IX, 5)

In comparing the two masters at the close of the Baroque, he
found Bach more "modern" than Handel because of Bach's "infinite
carefulness" and his "indifference to outward effects" (X, 11). He
found the same conditions to be true of the more "modern" Brahms
when compared with Wagner. Parker invariably had the greatest
admiration for the more conservative composers.

What emerges from these lectures is not so much an objective history of music but the reactions of a keenly intelligent musician as he surveys the products of other composers throughout
various periods. Students were exposed to music as a living and
vital issue when they were treated to a lengthy diatribe against the
foreign control of opera in New York as a footnote to the history of
opera up to Gluck (XIV, 4-5).

Parker's lectures were not so erudite as those MacDowell
gave to a similar student population at Columbia. MacDowell gave
much more attention to theoretical discussions on the origin and
esthetics of music.[19] Nevertheless, Parker demonstrated an intelligence and enthusiasm that made his course one of the more important cultural offerings in American universities prior to World War
I.

The other two new courses, *Instrumentation* and *Free
Composition*, appeared in the *Catalogue* of 1894. *Free Composition*, in Parker's opinion, was the crowning achievement of the
music curriculum and the one he took the most delight in teaching.
Students took it after a careful disciplining in harmony, contrapuntal
techniques, orchestration, and creativity in the smaller forms. The
making of composers was the primary aim of a music school, and
they were the apex of a musical society: "I believe every nation's
musical life centers in and radiates from its own composers."[20]
Their nurturing during their academic years is a primary responsibility of a University: "I believe the finest thing which can result from
the study of music in our colleges is a composer."[21]

The seventh course for which Parker had a direct teaching
responsibility at one time or another is *Advanced Orchestration and
Conducting*. This course was offered infrequently: in 1908-09, two
students enrolled; and in 1916-17, ten students.[22] Parker insisted
that those taking the course be able to read from orchestral scores at

the piano, a requirement which evidently had a very limiting effect on enrollment.[23]

Aside from those for *The History of Music*, no other lectures or class notes are to be found among Parker's papers at Yale. Bruce Simonds, a former student who later became Dean of the School of Music, indicated that Parker did not use formal lecture notes for the professional courses. Rather, much of the time was spent in examining and correcting student assignments and in working out musical problems at the blackboard.[24] Isabel Semler wrote about the respect and affection that many students held for Parker as a teacher.[25]

Parker's teaching reputation, indeed, his place in history, has been increasingly altered by the growing reputation during the twentieth century of his most famous student, Charles Ives. The public has formed much of its impression of Parker from Ives's comments which are so ably drawn together by John Kirkpatrick in Charles E. Ives's *Memos* and from writers who have added their interpretations to Ives's remarks, a matter which I will examine further in the last chapter of this book. The courses that Ives took from Parker: *Counterpoint, Instrumentation,* and *Strict Composition,*[26] are of sufficient number for the teacher to have made a strong impression on the student.

The late Edwin Arthur Kraft, former organist at Trinity Cathedral in Cleveland, Ohio, has written about his impressions of the basic harmony course which he took with Parker:

> I studied Harmony, Counterpoint, and Fugue with Dr. Parker [ca. 1899-1901]. As I recall there were about thirty or more students in a class. Thus he was unable to examine the work of each student with any regularity, nor advise us from his vast storehouse of knowledge.
>
> I marveled at his ability to complete on the blackboard, with alacrity and skill, fascinating exhibitions of counterpoint.
>
> I always had the impression that he was a bit bored with the responsibility of teaching. It is quite possible of course, that we in the class were not sufficiently brilliant and responsive--also, he was undoubtedly eager to go off and compose! [27]

Perhaps unconsciously, Parker evoked the same commingled feelings of admiration and fear typical of the German academic tradition in which he was trained. For those students who thrived under his regimen, however, he was capable of giving genuine affection as well as blunt advice. Both are found in his letter to Douglas Moore on the eve of the latter's departure for Europe.[28]

Parker's General Concepts of Music Education

College Level. For over a quarter of a century, the philosophy of music education at Yale was dominated by one man. As is
evident from the review of courses above, Parker believed the
theory and composition sequence--harmony, counterpoint, composi-
tion--to be basic for all types of professional music activity. Just a
year after he had assumed the post at Yale, he made the following
contribution to a survey about college music teaching:

> But of course the chief study for the musician should be music.
> Not history or psychology or mathematics of music, nor acous-
> tics. Interesting as these things are, they are, in my judgment,
> no more useful than other things to a musician.[29]

In addition, he was distrustful of parallels drawn between even the
other arts and music, finding them "interesting and illuminating, not
often convincing."
     This "hard-headed" philosophy of music education which
emphasized a rigid, theory-dominated program of instruction was
not typical of all college music educators at the time. Many were
taking the position of Waldo Selden Pratt who, in the same survey,
urged a better general education for music students and a closer
affiliation with other areas of learning in order to end what he called
"the isolation of music." Pratt concluded:

> Music schools have sometimes ignored learning, strict scholar-
> ship and real character building. Other schools have too often
> ignored all aesthetic subjects and have underrated the sensi-
> tiveness of feeling and the dexterity of action that is indispens-
> able in art.

It is surprising that uncompromising emphasis on professional training was accepted at a liberal arts university with such
strong conservative leanings as Yale. The position that both Parker
and the Yale authorities held in common, however, was an emphasis on a disciplined course of instruction with specific objectives
and definite procedures for realizing these goals.
     An unusual opportunity to compare Parker's philosophy and
the program at Yale with those of other leading American universities came in 1904 with the rather sensational resignation of Edward
MacDowell from Columbia University. The circumstances of this
affair caused the *New York Times* to solicit opinions about the
academic status of music from four leading college music educa-
tors--MacDowell, Parker, Paine, and George C. Gow of Vassar.

The resulting article, "The Proper Place of Musical Study in Universities and Colleges," is a valuable commentary on varying attitudes at that time toward college music curricula.[30]

MacDowell, and Gow, to a certain extent, were skeptical about the professional benefits that a composer could derive from university and college training. Their interests lay in the development of closer ties between music and the general college program. Although Harvard had an exemplary record in training composers, Paine stressed the study of history as basic in higher music education. Only Parker mentioned the idea that the university has a primary obligation to the composer. He was to express this belief publicly and to act accordingly throughout his entire career as an educator.

Primary and Secondary School Level. In an address called "Music in our Public Schools," Parker outlined his most comprehensive statement regarding music education.[31] Here we find ideas encountered previously--the central position of the composer, the preference for the study of the music itself rather than related areas, and the treatment of music as an academic subject with definite skills and information to master--now molded into a pattern suitable for all stages of development. A single educational method is advocated for the "three functions which are called into action in the making of all music"--composing, performing, and listening:

> Now, I believe that the first steps for young people to take toward all three kinds of activity are absolutely identical, and that the performer goes the same road which the intelligent listener must travel, and the composer the road of the performer, only that the performer goes farther than the mere listener, and the composer farther than the mere performer. . . . I shall, therefore, in the beginning of training, teach every child exactly as if its object were to become a composer. . . . Ten in every dozen will arrive by the treatment at a more rational understanding and appreciation of the art than can be reached by any other method.

He found considerable discrepancy between his own view and current practices. At the elementary level, he deplored "singing-school" and "rote-note" methods, because they were taught more like extra-curricular activities rather than as solid, academic subjects: "Children should be taught to read and write music as they are in English. . . . The singing of patriotic and other songs is better suited to be a pastime than . . . continued study among grammar school children." In the high schools, he noted that the lack of any prescribed music was so widespread as to constitute a "missing link" between college and elementary music education. Here he called for three specific activities: the serious study of singing after thorough study in ear training and sight-singing, the development of taste, and the teaching of harmony.

Some inconsistency is evident among Parker's remarks on music education, particularly the idea that training for the three activities--composition, performance, and listening--should vary only in degree but not in kind, for in another place he declares the training of professionals and amateurs to be totally different:

> I am of the opinion that our Universities ought to teach advanced studies in music as well as furnish the equipment [for] intelligent amateurs. These two processes are totally different and neither should be neglected.[32]

Such a dualism did, in fact, exist between *The History of Music* and the professional music courses at Yale.

Parker's principal endeavor for elementary and secondary schools was a series of song and rhythmic activity books for the elementary grades called *The Progressive Music Series* which became an important school-music song set.[33] A purpose of this series was to include songs written by many leading composers of the day. In the four volumes of the original series (1914-16) and two additional volumes (1918-19), there are approximately forty compositions by Parker, including a few of his youthful settings of poems by Kate Greenaway.

Although the prestige of his name may have been a reason for Parker's being named editor, his function was certainly not merely an honorary one. He examined all of the material which went into the series and made suggestions. According to Charles E. Griffith, a former educational consultant for Silver Burdett:

> The Music Department archives [of Silver Burdett] included hundreds of so-called "mounts" on which Dr. Parker indicated his "grading" as to the musical quality of the music score so mounted. It also includes photostatic reproductions of personal letters to Dr. Parker from composers in Europe who expressed their pleasure in anticipation of his call on them and their interest in his project to have composers whose names were household words represented in a series of school books for children of the United States.[34]

Parker did his editorial work by mail and had no opportunity to consult directly with his co-editors.[35]

Parker's major function as editor was his acquaintance with nearly every major composer of his day, both European and American. Much of his sabbatical in Europe during the winter of 1912-13 was spent holding personal interviews with composers, many of whom he persuaded to contribute to the series.[36] Parker received substantial financial remuneration for this series. The diaries for 1912 and 1914 show $500 each, and a total of over $6,000 is recorded for 1917-1919.

Parker also served as editor of *Music and Drama*, a volume in a vocational series for young people.[37] This project was much smaller than his work for Silver Burdett. According to the chief editor, Parker would receive $200 for "two days work."[38] This "work" consisted of a ten-page introduction (largely pieced together from parts of his earlier essays) to an anthology of miscellaneous articles by various writers. The editorial function here appears to be honorary. Parker was sent the previously selected articles to "look over" before their publication, and he specifically disclaimed any responsibility for those in the volume which were not concerned with music.

Toward the end of his career, Parker wrote some part-songs for secondary school groups. These include "Springtime Revelries," "The Storm," both on texts by Nixon Waterman, and "Freedom, Our Queen," the poem by Oliver Wendell Holmes. The Holmes text was a popular one for American composers, having been set by George Templeton Strong and John Paine at the time of the Columbian Exposition in 1893. Two other school part-song settings are "Triumphal march," the text by David Kilburn Stevens, and "I remember the black wharfs and ships," the poem by Longfellow.

Some songs and choruses, two editorships, and an address, constitute Parker's tangible contributions to elementary and secondary school music. His major concern was the development of a discerning appreciation for good music among the public. Getting composers to write songs for school children, suggesting revisions of elementary and secondary curricula to produce better listeners, performers, and even composers instead of just rote singers--all of these ideas reveal his belief in the importance of primary and secondary music training.

Parker's interest in these areas are part of the more inclusive view of music and its role in society that he adopted during the last decade of his life. The choral societies, festivals, chamber music concerts, and church music activities which had constituted his professional life as a young man no longer bounded his thoughts about music. Just as opera was an important new compositional activity, so did music education become a new interest during the period 1909-1919. Parker acted on this concern by initiating the short-lived Public School Music Curriculum at Yale (1917-21), one of his last administrative acts.[39]

The Administrator

Parker shared the administration of the Department of Music at Yale with Samuel Sanford at first. As late as 1900, the music section of the *Report of the President of Yale University* was signed by both men. Nevertheless, Parker had been called the "director" or "head" of the Department from the time he had come to Yale, and he had in fact carried out such responsibilities. Nevertheless, the official delegation of authority was not made until 1904 when he was appointed "Dean."[40]

Undoubtedly, Parker considered administrative tasks a nuisance; however, notable strides were made during his tenure in the development of the School's resources and prestige. During his administration, the number of courses for the Bachelor of Music degree was increased from three to seven, numerous prizes, awards, and scholarships were instituted, entrance requirements were strengthened, a separate library for the School of Music was established, and annual series of chamber music concerts, solo recitals, orchestra concerts,[41] and lectures[42] were offered.

In each annual *Report of the President*, Parker stressed the needs of music performance. During his administration, the number of applied music instructors was increased from one for piano to over eight teachers for piano, organ, violin, cello, and voice. The greatest single boon for applied music during Parker's administration was the granting of credit for such instruction in 1900.[43]

The lack of adequate physical facilities was a persistently nagging problem and a recurring theme in each *Report of the President*. Makeshift arrangements in scattered buildings were the norm for well over half of Parker's administration. Some rooms in a former church were authorized for Practical Music in 1895. After 1900, the theory courses outgrew their rooms in the Treasury building and were moved to the former home of President Dwight. The building of Woolsey Hall, a large, attractive auditorium, and the installation of the famous Newberry Organ there, both in 1903, were important gains for the School; however, they did not alleviate the problems of inadequate classroom and practice space and equipment. The completion of Albert Arnold Sprague Memorial Hall in 1917, a gift from the widow of a Yale alumnus, finally made possible a permanent location for most music instruction and activities.

Parker's role as an administrator is perhaps the most inadvertent aspect of his career. He was not asked to come to Yale because of any demonstrated administrative ability. None of his addresses mention administration, and the few references that he made to his deanship in his correspondence show his frustration over its many time-consuming details. Nevertheless, Parker had a clear vision of the kind of school he wanted and the energy and determination to accomplish his goals through his own hard work and the ability to enlist the support of others. Luther Noss, a former music Dean at Yale himself, concluded:

> The Yale School of Music will probably never again be in a position to compile a record of growth and progress comparable to that which it achieved in these 25 years [1894-1919]. . . . By far the greater part of [the credit] . . . must be given to Horatio Parker.[44]

The Conductor

Along with the heavy teaching load Parker carried when he first came to Yale, he found time to take over the directorship of the fledgling New Haven Symphony Orchestra, an activity that had far-reaching consequences for the Department of Music. By combining the activities of this group with those of the music school, Parker formed a university-community orchestra which soon received national attention as an academic innovation.

The orchestra's nucleus was composed of New Haven members of a New York musical organization called Dorscht Loge. These men had been giving local concerts in New Haven for about ten years with the assistance of their New York colleagues.[45] During the winter of 1893-94 Parker, then in his first year at Yale, was asked to attend some of the rehearsals and was soon invited to become their conductor. He accepted and moved almost immediately to effect the liaison between the newly organized orchestra and Yale University. In a Yale *Catalogue*, Parker outlined the nature of this connection:

> The New Haven Symphony Orchestra, under the direction of the Professor of the Theory of Music, gives four concerts during the winter. This organization is a complete and well-equipped orchestra of about fifty players, and is a valuable adjunct to the Department of Music.
>
> Students of orchestration are afforded an opportunity to hear their work actually performed, and any composition which is original and of sufficient merit may be performed publicly.

The same orchestra affords an opportunity to acquire
orchestral routine for those students of the violin who are able
to pass the examination for admission to the orchestra.[46]

News of the experiment in a university-community orchestra
reached Boston almost immediately. A reporter for the *Boston
Herald* commented:

It represents the first attempt it is said in this country of a
University to foster and develop a high class of musical
talent. . . . Professor Parker has started out under the patronage
of Yale to develop another Boston Symphony."[47]

The subscription concerts soon were increased to five per
year to which were added such events as an annual student composition concert, a commencement performance, an occasional program
with the Oratorio Society, and a children's concert. The number of
concerts remained the same until World War I caused a reduction to
three subscription concerts for the 1918-19 season.

An examination of the programs for the New Haven
Symphony Orchestra during the twenty-five years that Parker was
its conductor and musical director shows that he was not deterred by
the technical limitations of his amateur players. The repertory
consisted of those pieces heard on the programs of major orchestras
of the time, and the roster of guest artists who performed with the
orchestra included many leading performers of the day.[48]

On every occasion where he was given an opportunity,
Parker emphasized the importance of the Symphony Orchestra as a
laboratory for student composers. The final orchestra concert of
each season was devoted to the presentation of student compositions. After one such program, Parker commented that his student
Roger Huntington Sessions's work, *Symphonic Prelude*, was "a
creation of considerable originality and power."[49]

Educational activities of the orchestra also included direct
efforts to raise the level of music appreciation in the community at
large. During the 1903-04 season, a successful attempt was made to
bring teachers and students of local public schools into the concert
audience. Special ticket prices were offered and schools were
dismissed early on concert days.[50] Parker also tried to broaden the
appreciation of the inexperienced listeners at the regular concerts,
for Louis Elson reported that he introduced "the orchestra work with
a short lecture, analyzing the compositions and playing different
themes and figures on the piano."[51]

It is now difficult to assess the musical achievements of this
orchestra, although its function as a laboratory for composition
students and as a means of acquainting the New Haven public with

the orchestral literature is beyond dispute. Parker made no exaggerated claims of musical artistry for his orchestra. He did acknowledge that visiting professional orchestras might present programs of higher quality but maintained that a permanent local orchestra would be of inestimably greater musical value to the community.[52]

The New Haven Symphony was thus a pioneer in the field of the community orchestra, a type which has now proliferated in the United States. Many of its practices, such as numbers of concerts per year, appearances of artist-celebrities, rehearsal procedures, financial arrangements, emphasis on music appreciation, arrangements with public schools, and hiring of players from other, more musically established communities, have since been adopted by other orchestras.

Although the directorship of the New Haven Symphony was Parker's most extensive conducting activity, the organization of the New Haven Oratorio Society in 1903, enabled him to realize an even more cherished goal. Having recently returned from English choral festival performances, he was taken with the idea of transplanting this tradition to New Haven. Unfortunately, the Oratorio Society did not achieve the permanent success of the Symphony Orchestra. For some years, the group was able to give as many as three performances a year; other seasons, not a single concert was attempted because of lack of funds. The Society ceased to function by the time of World War I. Nevertheless, it did, in the course of its irregular existence, perform several monumental works under Parker's direction: Handel's *Messiah*, (1903), Bach's *B Minor Mass* (1904) and the *Passion According To Saint Matthew*(1912), Verdi's *Requiem* (1905), Elgar's *Dream of Gerontius* (1908), Rossini's *Stabat Mater* (1908), Gounod's *Redemption* (1909), Mendelssohn's *Elijah* (1910), and two of his own works: *Saint Christopher* (1905) and *Hora Novissima* (1908).

Finally, Parker's conducting of various choral societies outside of New Haven and his occasional guest appearances as a conductor of his own music must be taken into account. Reviewers generally found his conducting to be creditable. As with administration, however, he seems to have had no strong interest in conducting *per se*. It was another duty he naturally assumed as one of the country's musical leaders. Only the Philadelphia choral groups which he directed during the years before World War I, made conducting a significant part of his income.

Parker's own reminiscence about the early struggles of his New Haven Symphony perhaps best summarizes his main commitment as a conductor:

> So we made an orchestra for household use. It was rather
> funny sometimes, but the conductor was young at the time and
> did not mind work. . . . The orchestra grew in numbers and in
> grace; concerts were given to gain experience, assurance and
> money. Student exercises were played at rehearsals. The
> authorities were shown that the orchestra was a necessary
> adjunct to the department.[53]

To make the performance of classical music an essential part
of a community's activity rather than an exotic import appears to
have been his main purpose as a conductor, and this role, at the
same time, enabled him to demonstrate his own musical vision.

Chapter Four

NATIONAL AND INTERNATIONAL RECOGNITION

Activities 1894-1899

Teaching duties at Yale University were only part of the proliferating number of activities in which Parker was engaged during the last years of the nineties. He continued to hold his position as organist and choirmaster at Trinity Church in Boston, to which he commuted each weekend excepting summers until the beginning of the twentieth century. He also traveled to Springfield, Massachusetts, during the spring of 1895 in order to direct a choral group there.[1]

In his second year at New Haven, Parker organized a women's choral group known as the Euterpe Society. The rehearsals were held on Friday evenings, thus replacing his previous conducting activity in Springfield. The Euterpe Society became an important social as well as musical activity in the community life of New Haven. Contemporary newspaper reports reveal that the concerts were not only of high musical quality but also were visually impressive, with much attention given to costuming and floral arrangements.[2] This women's group continued to be active under Parker's direction during the waning years of the century until it was superseded by other choral groups such as the Oratorio Society and the People's Choral Union.

Parker also gave occasional organ performances in New Haven and in the surrounding communities. On one such occasion, the *New Haven Evening Leader* reported that a "large and fashionable" audience heard him give a dedication recital on the new instrument at Christ's Church.[3] He performed music by Bach, Guilmant, Rheinberger, and some of his own compositions, closing the program with an improvisation on the Saint Anne hymn-tune.

Between 1895-1899 Parker gave an increasing number of talks throughout the country.[4] A lecture which eventually came to be called "Music in America" had its inception during this period,[5] and may have been given in March 1897, when Parker spoke on American music at the Peabody Institute in Baltimore, Maryland. He was severely criticized by the *Baltimore Sun* for taking the position that there is no "indigenous" American music.[6] This speech is his earliest known public statement in the controversy then raging over Dvořák's recommendation that American composers consider using Negro and Indian themes in their music.

In addition to these many activities, Parker kept doggedly at his primary interest, composition. Among the smaller works from this period are organ and piano pieces, songs, part-songs, and anthems. A larger composition is the highly colorful rhapsody for baritone voice and orchestra, *Cáhal Mór of The Wine-Red Hand*, which was dedicated to the well-known singer Max Heinrich and was sung by him at its initial performance, a Boston Symphony Orchestra concert on 29 March 1895.[7]

One of the composer's better occasional cantatas, *Ode For Commencement Day At Yale University, 1895*, followed *Cáhal Mór* by only a few months. Parker received the text from his colleague Edmund Clarence Stedman on April 1 and, according to his diary, finished the composition by May 10. The *New Haven Register* used the occasion of its performance at the commencement exercises that year to take note of Parker's accomplishments at Yale:

> Few first-year professors could show so much for one year's work--a large, well-trained chorus, a fine original composition, well worthy to commemorate a great day, and an excellent orchestra to render it.[8]

A brief lull in the production of major works occurred during the summers of 1895 and 1896, both of which Parker spent in England and Germany; however, during the summer of 1897, he was occupied with his largest work from that period, *The Legend of Saint Christopher*. This second oratorio is the result of a commission from the Oratorio Society of New York, which gave the work its first performance under the direction of Walter Damrosch in Carnegie Hall on 15 April 1898. In this work, Parker blended the traditional structural arrangements of his earlier *Hora Novissima* with dramatic elements such as the use of leading motives and fluid orchestral connections from one section to another. Although *Saint Christopher* did not attain the popular success of *Hora Novissima*, it nevertheless should be recognized as one of Parker's most imaginative compositions.

Laus Artium, the only composition for which Parker ever used a pseudonym was composed during the summer of 1898 at Vineyard Haven.[9] This homage to art by one of its faithful servants, Artium Lauditor, as he chose to call himself, is a substantial work modeled after the more conservative, self-contained sections of *Hora Novissima*. The work evidently never received a public performance.

A more important composition from 1898 is the motet for unaccompanied choir, *Adstant Angelorum Chori*, which won the $250 prize offered by the Musical Art Society of New York. The piece was presented by that group under the direction of Frank Damrosch on 16 March 1899. Although *Adstant* was hailed at that time by the New York critics for its loftiness and its evocation of the Renaissance choral tradition, it really is inclusive of many different choral styles.

A Northern Ballad was written during the winter of 1898-99. This symphonic poem is Parker's most important composition for orchestra alone and the most frequently played of his instrumental works. It was first performed by the New Haven Symphony under Parker's direction on 7 April 1899 and again at the Springfield (Massachusetts) Festival on May 4.[10] Subsequent important performances are those by Gericke and the Boston Symphony (1899), Theodore Thomas (to whom the work was dedicated) and the Chicago and Cincinnati orchestras (1900), the New York Philharmonic (1901), and by groups at both the Saint Louis World's Fair (1904) and the Panama-Pacific Exposition (1915).

The Years of the English Festivals: 1899-1902

On 17 January 1899 the terse notation, "Letter from Atkins--Worcester Festival--Hora Novissima!!," is recorded in Parker's diary. The correspondent, Ivor A. Atkins, was then the newly appointed organist at Worcester Cathedral in England. He became one of Parker's most enthusiastic supporters and was largely reponsible for creating the interest that English musicians showed in Parker's music at the turn of the century. Atkins had invited Parker to participate in one of the most venerable English choir festivals. Commonly known as the Three Choirs Festivals, these annual meetings of the choirs from Gloucester, Worcester, and Hereford had rotated among those respective cities for nearly two hundred years. Parker's elation is apparent if one realizes that the invitation was an unprecedented honor for an American composer.

It is uncertain why Atkins, who was making his debut as an organizer of activities for the Worcester Festival, selected a work from across the Atlantic. The American singer David Bispham took credit for introducing *Hora Novissima* in England by giving a copy of the score to Hans Richter, director of the Birmingham Festival, who then may have shown it to others.[11]

Bispham exaggerated the importance of his missionary effort, since both Parker and his music were already known in England. *The Musical Times* had published an analysis of *Hora Novissima* immediately after its first performance in New York in 1893,[12] and Parker had toured English cathedral towns during his summer trips of 1890 and 1895. Also, his letters and diaries indicate that he was in the habit of leaving copies of his own compositions and those of fellow American composers wherever he thought there might be a possibility of a performance.

Some of the English press had called for a performance of *Hora Novissima* immediately following its 1893 American premiere,[13] and Parker even mentioned in an interview shortly afterwards that an English performance was then imminent.[14] The oratorio did not receive an English presentation until the Worcester Festival of 1899, so perhaps Bispham's efforts may have helped to renew interest in the work.

Parker, who had been invited to conduct the performance, arrived in England for the September Festival on Saturday, August 12. The five weeks before the Worcester performance were a busy round of sight-seeing and concert-attending. He also traveled to and from the constituent towns rehearsing the various participating choirs. The *Worcestershire Chronicle* recorded the following account of one such rehearsal:

> On the reassembling of the Worcester contingent of the Festival Chorus, this week, Mr. Parker, the composer of "Hora Novissima," attended to conduct a rehearsal of his work. He was accompanied by two other American professors of music--Messrs. Sanford and Jepson. Mr. Parker is not in appearance like the traditional American. Young looking, stoutly built, clean shaven, with black moustache, and gifted with a charming manner, he commended himself at once to the choir, every member of which, it may be averred, did his or her best to show the composer that good music is appreciated and worthily rendered over here. The first chorus went so satisfactorily as to evoke from Mr. Parker the exclamation: "Well, it does me good to hear you sing"; and all three visitors, in the course of the evening, expressed themselves delighted with the quality of the chorus. They thought the work had the prospect of a finer representation than it had yet received. Stress was

laid upon the accuracy and good tone of the singing after a
holiday break.

Mr. Parker is a resourceful conductor, especially strict
as to marking light and shade, but helpful in his methods, and
adept in the art of lightening toil by occasional touches of
humour.

On entering the room Mr. Parker was very warmly
received, and there was hearty applause at the close of the
rehearsal of his work, which occupied about an hour.[15]

The report concluded with the observation that, because of interest
in *Hora Novissima*, a larger number of visitors than usual was
expected.

On Monday, September 4, ten days before the performance,
Parker traveled to London to rehearse the participating orchestra. In
an interview after the rehearsal, he gave his impressions of English
orchestras to a reporter from the London *Morning Leader*:

Prof. Parker is very enthusiastic about English orchestras. "The sensation yesterday while conducting for the first
time an English band," said the professor to a *Leader* representative, "was delightful."

"The massing of bands," he added, "is much the same
all the world over. But the English band seems to work with
greater harmony with the choir. One is the natural complement
of the other."

"Although I am naturally proud," he continued, "of
our high class American orchestras, I must say I am charmed
with your English style. I won't go so far as to say that in
England the music is rendered much better than it is at home,
but I have been most favorably struck with the conduct and
playing of your big bands."[16]

The Worcester Festival was a four-day affair filled with both
older, established works and contemporary pieces by British
composers Charles Wood, Samuel Coleridge Taylor, and Worcester's own Edward Elgar. *Hora Novissima* was performed on Thursday morning, September 14, the next-to-last day of the festival, with
soloists Emma Albani, Ada Crossley, Edward Lloyd, and Plunket
Greene--all distinguished opera and oratorio singers. This presentation was one of the principal attractions of the entire Festival. Over
two thousand persons attended, a number which was exceeded only
by the opening concert of the Festival when Mendelssohn's *Elijah*
was heard.[17] Parker noted in his diary: "splendid performance,"
and sent a message to the choir expressing the opinion that he had
never heard anything of his so excellently rendered.[18]

The consensus of English criticism was favorable with the exception of the London *Daily Chronicle* which found it lacking in originality:

> With the performance in the cathedral this morning of Professor Horatio Parker's "Hora Novissima," interest in the Festival attained its culminating point. . . . When it was announced that the Professor of Music at Yale University had been invited to conduct a Three Choirs' Festival of his oratorio, "Hora Novissima," both curiosity and expectation were kindled, notwithstanding the knowledge that his musical training had not been wholly and solely American.
>
> Professor Parker may therefore be looked upon as one of the most representative composers of the superior class of which America can at present boast. This being the case it is with regret I am compelled to say that the score of "Hora Novissima" offers nothing remarkable, except the appearance of being much older than it really is. In the matter of production in public it dates from six years back, but its style and method are those of a more distant period. The music oscillates between Gounod and Dvořák, with a decided preference for the former, and occasionally there are suggestions of Mendelssohn. Of Wagner or of the lesser lights in "advanced" composition there is scarcely a trace. From beginning to end the work lacks individuality.
>
> It is pleasing to the ear, it is acceptable to the understanding, but at no point does it stimulate. The thoughts contained have been previously expressed, and in somewhat similar language.[19]

The Three Choirs Festival presentation became a catalyst for other performances of *Hora Novissima* in England during the subsequent winter. On 26 November 1899, a London presentation was given at Queen's Hall by a chorus and orchestra of three hundred, conducted by Churchill Sibley.[20] Parker's first important oratorio had finally achieved recognition in England, something that American critics had predicted for it at the time of its New York premiere in 1893.

In the diaries for the winter of 1899-1900 there is only one brief mention of *A Wanderer's Psalm*, which was commissioned for the following Three Choirs Festival of 1900 at Hereford.[21] Parker had also been invited to conduct a performance of *Hora Novissima* at Chester, England, earlier that summer. He left New Haven in July, arriving at Chester in time for the final rehearsals and the performance on July 27. His diary comments show that his stay in this picturesque cathedral town was just as pleasant as the previous year's visit to Worcester. He noted being entertained by the director of the festival at supper on two nights and by the mayor at a luncheon.

English compositions on the Chester program included Hubert Parry's *Blest Pair of Sirens* and Arthur Sullivan's *Overture, In Memoriam*; both are short works.[22] Another contemporary work of greater length heard at Chester was Dom Lorenzo Perosi's oratorio, *The Transfiguration*, which had been the subject of some controversy after a performance the preceding year in London. At Chester, the solid, traditional workmanship of *Hora Novissima* made a much more favorable impression on British reviewers than did what they considered the insipid style of Perosi.

The Hereford performance of *A Wanderer's Psalm* took place on Thursday morning, September 13.[23] Slightly over one-half hour in length, it was performed first on a program which also included excerpts from *Parsifal* and Beethoven's *Ninth Symphony*. Parker conducted his own work and the solo quartet included Madame Albani, Ada Crossley, Plunket Greene, and Andrew Black. The reaction of the English press was mixed, with the provincial papers quite laudatory and the London journals mildly critical.[24] London critics found the work conservative and lacking in originality, judgments which the London *Daily Chronicle* had made concerning its prototype *Hora Novissima*. *A Wanderer's Psalm* was reviewed more unfavorably when it was performed in Boston at People's Temple on December 17 of that same year.[25] Thereafter, the work received no other performances.

During the winter of 1900-1901, Parker began working on two major compositions, the *Concerto for Organ and Orchestra*, his most ambitious work in a purely instrumental medium, and *A Star Song*, a choral work which was not only commissioned for the Norwich (England) Festival of 1902 but also received the 1901 Paderewski Prize in the division of choral composition. He also started work on his edition of *The Hymnal* (Episcopal), a project which took over two years to complete.

The following summer, Parker and his family left for Europe, where they spent the next fifteen months, his sabbatical year. Although most of this time was spent in Munich near the home of his wife's family, he made trips to England, France, and even one journey back to the United States for a professional commitment.

He found it necessary to return to New Haven during the fall of 1901 to participate in the commemoration of the bicentenary of the founding of Yale College, for which he had composed a commissioned work *Hymnos Andron*, or *Greek Festival Hymn*, the preceding summer. He rehearsed the student chorus of 150 voices and the New Haven Symphony Orchestra and conducted the performance, the highlight of the two-day celebration, on October 23. The preceding day, Parker had conducted the Gounod Society and the New Haven Symphony in a performance of *Hora Novissima.*

November found Parker back in England, where he visited Atkins in Worcester and heard his *Service in E* sung at the cathedral there.[26] He conducted the Worcester Choral Society in a performance of his part song *Come Away* and the unaccompanied chorus "Jam sol recedit igneus," from *Saint Christopher.*[27]

Traveling elsewhere in the British Isles, Parker appeared to be carrying out a campaign to create a favorable image of the American composer. He wrote to Mrs. Chadwick:

> I went to Birmingham, Leeds, Glasgow, Edinburgh, Cambridge, Hereford and other places, mending fences, and roaring when called upon to do so. . . . Please have him [Chadwick] send me without delay a few copies of his "Lovely Rosabelle" and his "Phoenix." I have promised some people copies of them and it will do no harm at all.[28]

On returning to Munich he attended performances of *Die Meistersinger, Siegfried, Die Zauberflöte, Hänsel und Gretel* and *Aïda.* He also recorded visits with conductor Felix Weingartner and musicologist Adolf Sandberger. On a visit to Paris in March, 1902, he heard *Manon, Le Roi d'Ys,* and *Samson et Dalila.* In May he attended the Lower Rhine Festival at Düsseldorf, where he saw Elgar and heard the *The Dream of Gerontius* in its first Continental performance.[29]

Parker then went to England, where he received an honorary Doctor of Music degree from Cambridge University on June 10. He had been corresponding with the University officials and faculty as early as December 1901 concerning the degree. Charles Villiers Stanford, who nominated Parker, had then requested a list of important works after admitting that he was familiar with only two of Parker's compositions, *Hora Novissima* and the *Greek Festival Hymn.* Stanford commented: "the Council mind is impressed by quantity as well as quality."[30]

In March 1902, R. C. Jebb, an official of Cambridge University, confirmed the decision to honor Parker:

> The council of the Senate agreed this morning on my motion, to offer the Honorary Degree of Doctor in Music to Professor Horatio Parker. It may be of interest to you to know that the decision was unanimous, every member present voting in the affirmative.[31]

Following the ceremony, Parker spent the remaining summer on the Continent. He returned to England, where the third part of *Saint Christopher* was given at Worcester on September 10. It was also performed in its entirety later in the month at the Bristol Festival. At both performances, the oratorio was received with more enthusiasm than at any of its earlier presentations in the United States.

Parker was unable to secure an extension of his sabbatical leave in order to attend the performance of his *A Star Song* at the Norwich Festival, October 23. The work was given an excellent presentation, according to one report, with Kirby Lunn, Kate Moss, Plunket Greene, and Robert Redford singing the solo roles.[32]

The summer of 1902 marked the peak of Parker's recognition by the English. Scattered performances of his works, such as that of *Hora Novissima* in Birmingham on 23 February 1905, occurred during the following years; however, England failed to become permanently interested in his music. Nevertheless, Parker had made noticeable progress in gaining recognition for American composers outside of their own country. He had no fewer than four major works performed in England (two of them more than once) in addition to the part songs, *Come Away* and "The lamp in the west," (composed for choruses at Worcester and Bristol respectively), and *The Kobolds* at Birmingham and Bishop Auckland.[33] His service music was used in some English cathedrals, and his *Six Old English Songs*, particularly "The lark now leaves his watery nest," had substantial sales in England.[34]

Perhaps the most significant result of the English performances was Parker's determination to create in New Haven a singing society comparable to those he had directed in the cathedral towns. The New Haven Oratorio Society, which he organized the year following his return to America, and the impressive group of oratorios that they performed prior to World War I are his strongest identification with English choral music practice.

The Composer and His Society

During the early years of the twentieth century, Parker gave some important addresses which outline his conception of the relation between the composer and society. The first of these was given in 1900 before the prestigious National Institute of Arts and Letters, to which he had recently been elected. Although he covered a wide range of other musical subjects, the most important is his discussion of the American composer.[35] Here he stated that the level of musical sophistication in society is dependent upon its composers:

> A nation's musical life must always center in and radiate from
> its composers. They are the only real producers; singers and
> players are reproducers. The composers alone show unmistak-
> ably the real degree of musical cultivation which obtains in any
> country.

Parker noted that American composers had not as yet made any appreciable impression upon Europeans, although the latter had come to respect "our mechanical achievements and natural posses-sions" as well as our literature and painting. America, he felt, was too apologetic about and protective of its composers. He insisted that success in composition should be measured against European standards: "We can learn the true value of our own work only by comparing it frankly with what is produced by other nations."

Parker had some very specific ideas as to how America could support its composers, "not, I think, by encouraging all sorts of people to go into music as a profession or occupation, but rather by encouraging heartily and intelligently those only who have proved that they cannot keep out of it." He thought that a composer should be an ascetic. Among the dissipating affects in a composer's environment are "money getting early in life . . . too social inclina-tion, too admiring friends, too much information on other subjects, [and] too great reliance in the efficacy of 'taking lessons.'" "Sympathy and understanding" are the primary needs of the young composer. Society's obligation is not simply "free education, scholarships, prizes, etc.," but also the more difficult task of "secur-ing greater intelligence among the mass of the people toward creat-ing a natural demand for those things which the artist alone can supply." Public taste had to be elevated to an "intelligent, intellec-tual enjoyment" of music: "But merely to please or amuse, to soothe and gratify is a very modest aim, and quite insufficient to my thinking for any art which is to be taken seriously." A sense of responsibility toward music would lead the public from mere pleas-ure to the more significant area of appreciation:

> I think it their manifest duty as it surely is to their greatest
> advantage to bring to the enjoyment of music the most intelli-
> gent, enlightened, and cultivated sympathy and understanding it
> is within their power to encompass.

Edward MacDowell found what he considered to be the platitudes in this address so offensive that he nearly declined an invitation to join the Academy the following year. He wrote to Hamlin Garland:

Parker, who has neglected his duty in connection with the
Society [of American Musicians and Composers]. . . , still finds
time to come down to New York and spout such discouraging
twaddle to a lot of distinguished and representative men, who,
for lack of knowledge of the subject, must take it on trust.[36]

A second address of major importance during this time is an
accounting of his European sabbatical leave of 1901-02 to a group
of his colleagues at Yale.[37] Called "Impressions of a year in Europe," the paper is not only a repository of Parker's opinions on the
music he had heard while on the Continent and in England but also
contains some valuable discussion of how the American composer
should react to European trends.

Germany was his principal point of comparison. There he
found "a natural reaction from the intense paternalism under which
the Germans live" in the music of Richard Strauss. Strauss was the
epitome of a new, individualistic tendency, "a shriek for the recognition of his own personality. It is plainly removed as far as he can
get it from the impersonal, abstract serenity of the great classic
masters." Parker viewed Strauss's "direction" with some apprehension:

> I have great doubts as to whether Anglo-Saxons can
> ever adopt this tendency. It seems to me anti-pathetic to our
> character, and I think there is a better direction in which music
> can be guided. We profit enormously in technical details from
> Strauss and his long train of followers, but I do not think that
> we, the Anglo-Saxon race, need be among them. We can
> admire but we need not imitate them.

He found the trend in both England and America to be
toward a more impersonal, abstract style--a healthy antidote to
musical tendencies on the Continent:

> It may be that the art of absolute music is exhausted.
> Strauss thinks so, but I am loath to believe it. On the whole, I
> am inclined to think that music among the Anglo-Saxons is
> built upon a more solid foundation, one better calculated to
> sustain the weight of an imposing superstructure, than the
> music of the Germans. The music of the Germans is now so
> colored by externals that it has hardly a separate existence.
> That of the French seems not to come from deep enough, not to
> go deep enough--superficial. That of the Italians is opera--a
> form with such manifest limitations that one may also regard it
> as outside the sphere of reasonable activity among Anglo-
> Saxons. For the present English and American music is surely

> as a whole more impersonal, more abstract than thin, and if it
> remains untainted by these [qualities] seems sure to bring forth
> results of great beauty and value. German, French and Italians
> unite in one grand scramble to dodge the obvious ways of
> putting things. They are all trying to create an entirely new
> vocabulary. So much so that they frequently lose sight of form
> and substance. The old vocabulary will do very well if one has
> but new ideas to express. Not that I object to addition to our
> means of expression--but the new vocabulary must always
> remain a means, and never become an end of expression.

Parker's emphasis on "form and substance" as the "more solid
foundation" for "Anglo-Saxon" music follows that line of American
philosophy which can be traced back to such transcendental statements as that of Ralph Waldo Emerson, who said: "The question of
Beauty takes us out of surfaces to thinking of the foundations of
things."[38]

In another address, given at the end of the first decade,
Parker again defended his belief in an absolute music free from
analogies to language and other explicit meaning:

> Serious critics and essayists have made vigorous
> attempts to oust the music of the future from separate existence
> and to relegate it to the position of a human language which is
> to be used when it is quite grown up to express, more or less
> pictorially, ordinary or extra-ordinary human happenings or
> emotions. . . . The application of pure reason to such emotional
> phenomena as our pleasure in music results occasionally in
> something very like nonsense.[39]

Here again Parker reflects transcendentalist ideas by maintaining
that pleasure from music is a distinctive reaction, one which cannot
be comprehended or analyzed by logical means.

In Parker's time, the age-old question of studying an art
object by breaking it down into component parts was being raised
anew by German psychology, which advocated a scientific, analyti-
cal view of the art experience. Parker rejected such analysis not
only for esthetic response but also for composition itself:

> A composer must be bad at logic, for his life work is the ex-
> pression of something which is beyond [that] which words can
> hardly touch or enlighten, charmingly as some of our gifted
> critics and literati have spoken and written, for music is the
> expression of feeling and not of [ordinary] feeling, but of
> musical feeling, and progress is made not by reasoning in the
> usual sense but by intuition, instinct, and mostly by practice.[40]

Parker thought that the composer must submit his "intuitions" to
public test. No formula or process can be outlined to insure success: "For instance we now can show in words how and why it is
that Beethoven symphonies are made aright. Beethoven himself
could not have done so nor could any one living at his time."[41]

 To summarize, Parker can be considered a formalist in his
"Anglo-Saxon" approach which maintained a "separate existence"
for music exclusive of any verbal or logical means of description.
"Form and substance" are the most evident features of this music.
The impression on the listener should be impersonal and abstract,
and any feelings aroused should be purely "musical" ones. Furthermore, the composer has only his own feeling and intuition,
developed through practice, to guide him in writing such music.

 Rejection of analysis and insistence that a work stand only
for itself were characteristic of much American thinking about
music at this time. The pragmatic approach, the act of doing,
whether composing or performing, is substituted for speculation and
reflection. That it is frequently antagonistic to intellectualism is
evident in Parker's hyperbole: "It is consoling to think that all the
words written and spoken about art have never yet influenced creative artists to any discernible extent."[42] The musical environment at
Yale University during Parker's tenure there--with emphasis on
composition and performance to the virtual exclusion of disciplines
allied to music--is clearly an application of his ideals.

Various Events: 1902-1914

 During the winter of 1902-03, the *Organ Concerto* was
performed by the Boston Symphony Orchestra on 26 and 27
December 1902, and by the Chicago Symphony Orchestra on 2 and
3 January 1903. The Boston critics could not overlook the novelty
of the instrumentation (organ, brass, timpani, and strings) sufficiently to consider seriously the musical value of the work, but Chicago
critics were quite enthusiastic about the piece. Parker was the soloist with both orchestras, and most writers support the conclusion
that he was a masterful and polished performer. Louis Elson described his playing as musicianly.[43] The Chicago reviewers were
less reserved:

> Being an organ virtuoso of first rank, it must have been a
> temptation for Professor Parker to have written something to
> display his powers in full. It is always evident that he is play-

ing easily and that his reserve power is great. [*Chicago Record Herald*]

Parker played with ease, finish, breadth, certainty. [*Chicago Evening Post*]

The Bach fugue [encore] was played with great clarity, fine attention to the dynamic proportions, and splendid musicianship. [*Chicago Tribune*][44]

In spite of Chicago's enthusiasm, the *Organ Concerto* received few subsequent performances.[45]

Two other major compositions were written in the two years following Parker's return from his sabbatical leave. The manuscript score at Yale for the first work carries the title *Vathek*, and on the final page is the inscription: "Sept. 1903, Vineyard Haven: Based on William Beckford's tale." *Vathek* equals Parker's other symphonic poem, *A Northern Ballad*, in size and excellence, although it seems not to have been performed during Parker's lifetime.

The second composition is *Crépuscule*, a concert aria for mezzo-soprano and orchestra on which work was begun during the summer of 1904,[46] but not completed until 1907.[47] In 1911 the piece won a prize in the solo voice-with-orchestra category of a contest sponsored by the National Federation of Music Clubs. It was performed by the Philadelphia Orchestra under the direction of Karl Pohlig on 27 March 1911 at a biennial meeting of the Federation held in Philadelphia.

Summers gave Parker his best opportunity for serious composition, while the winters continued to be filled with teaching, conducting, and church duties. Early in 1904, he accepted the directorship of a women's chorus in Bridgeport, Connecticut, a position that lasted only for the duration of that spring.[48] He traveled there regularly on Monday evenings for rehearsals and for a concert on April 11.[49]

The following autumn, Parker became the director of the Choral Club in Derby, Connecticut, a position he held until the year of his death in 1919. The Derby Choral Club had been organized by a group under the leadership of Mrs. Frances E. Osborne, who became a close friend of Parker. It grew to some 250 members drawn from several of the small communities surrounding New Haven. At least one major choral program with orchestra and soloists was performed each year in addition to two other less ambitious programs.[50] Parker received approximately $300 a season for weekly rehearsals and occasional concerts.[51]

For some time before 1903 Parker had considered the possibility of finding a church position in New York City. While he was
still on his sabbatical in Europe, certain of his friends among church
officials were seeking an opening for him.[52] His increasing administrative duties at Yale along with the long weekly journeys to Trinity Church in Boston made a change quite desirable. After returning
from Europe, Parker entered into correspondence with a Charles
Ives, an alderman of the Collegiate Church of Saint Nicholas in
New York City, concerning the position of organist and choirmaster
there.[53] Parker recorded in his diary: "Saw committee, engaged for
church" on 6 February 1904. This position was to be his last as
organist and choirmaster.

The Collegiate Church of Saint Nicholas, one of the Dutch
Reformed group of churches, was a brownstone edifice on the
northwest corner of Fifth Avenue and Forty-Eighth Street. It boasted of one of the oldest congregations in Manhattan, dating back to
1628, and, at the time of Parker's service there, many of New
York's most prominent families, including that of Theodore Roosevelt, were members of the congregation.[54] The church was later
razed to make room for Rockefeller Center.

The Saint Nicholas position was the first major one that
Parker, a devout Episcopalian, had taken outside his own church.
He must have accepted the appointment with reluctance and only
after it was evident that no opportunities were available at that time
in New York Episcopal churches. The reaction from his own
denomination was immediate. They were reluctant to see America's
foremost church composer whose edition of *The Hymnal* was just
then being published leave the Episcopal fold. Winchester Donald,
of Boston, who had helped Parker in looking for a New York position, chided him for leaving the Episcopal Church to accept this
"lucrative and distasteful position."[55] But leave he did. In May,
1903, he began his new duties at Saint Nicholas.

One tie which had held Parker close to Boston in the nineties dissolved the following year with the death of his mother on 16
October 1904.[56] Isabella had never become reconciled to her son's
leaving the Boston area. As late as 1902, she still entertained such
aspirations for him as the Harvard chair of music or the directorship
of the Boston Symphony Orchestra.[57] She had maintained residence in the family home at Auburndale after the death of her
husband in 1890 and continued her literary activity almost to the
end. In fact, her most productive collaboration with her son came
during the last decade of her life with the book to *The Legend of
Saint Christopher*. Her final years were clouded by the uncertainty
of insufficient income. The family letters in the correspondence at
Yale reveal the worry and financial burden concerning Isabella that
Parker and his sister Cornelia carried during the years 1900 to 1904.

With the death of his mother and the transfer of church positions removing two important reasons for his frequent appearances in Boston, the focal point of Parker's weekend activities now became New York. The diaries for the period 1904-1910 contain many entries of New York activities far too numerous to record in any detail here. Certain items do stand out because of their recurrence. The spring examination of the American Guild of Organists was a regular event in which Parker participated. He also gave organ recitals at Columbia University, and these were normally scheduled within a few weeks of similar annual recitals at Yale. Lectures and performances of his own compositions in New York are also listed.

The trips to New York also gave Parker an opportunity to participate in the artistic and social life of that city. Plays, operas, symphony concerts, chamber music recitals, and choral concerts are crowded into the schedule of these busy years. He also had an opportunity to renew old friendships and make new ones. Henry E. Krehbiel, who had reviewed many of his compositions in the *Tribune*, became an intimate friend around this time. Parker was often a guest in the Krehbiel home, and the two men frequently attended operas and concerts together. Other close friends living in New York City included Arthur Whiting, Franz Kneisel, Gustav Dannreuther, Frank Damrosch, Thomas Tapper, and the Toedt family. Parker's capacity for abiding friendship is evident in the series of strophic songs which he wrote as Christmas presents from 1903 to 1916 for the concert tenor Theodore Toedt, his wife Ella, who had sung in the first performance of *Hora Novissima*, and their children.

Among the New York professional, social, and honorary groups in which Parker participated are the Dorscht Loge, the MacDowell Club, the Century Association, and the American Academy of Arts and Letters. The Century Association, which maintained quarters at 7 West Forty-third Street, was Parker's favorite social club.[58] Here some of the best literary and artistic minds of the day gathered in an informal social atmosphere to attend programs, hold meetings, entertain friends, or read in the club library. Parker spent many hours between rehearsals, concerts, and church services in this stimulating atmosphere.

Certainly Parker's most distinguished association was with the American Academy of Arts and Letters. The American Academy was newly created at that time, an exclusive group of fifty members selected from the larger parent organization, the National Institute of Arts and Letters. Parker's election took place on 13 May 1905. Such was his rising stature during these years that only one other musician, Edward MacDowell, preceded him in election to the Academy.[59]

The important commissions that Parker received during the early years of the twentieth century are the most convincing evidence of his eminence as a composer. The first of these is the part-song with band accompaniment *Union and Liberty*, a setting of verses by Oliver Wendell Holmes, written for the inauguration of Theodore Roosevelt. Parker traveled to Washington, D. C., to conduct the Marine Band and Inaugural Chorus of 500 voices in the presentation of his work.[60]

A second commission during this spring was the composition of music to a dedication ode, *Spirit of Beauty*, for the new Albright Art Gallery in Buffalo. The poem was written by Arthur Detmer, a high school principal in Lafayette, Indiana. Parker attended the dedication program on May 1905, at which President Eliot of Harvard was principal speaker. The Forty-Seventh Regimental Band and a male chorus of about 180 voices performed *Spirit of Beauty* outdoors before the large neoclassic building.[61]

The best kept secret of Parker's entire professional career was his composition of incidental music for two rather sumptuously staged plays, one of which was given on the New York stage. He did not include these compositions in lists of his own works that he provided for such publications as *Grove's Dictionary*.

The first of these two ventures was a drama in four acts, *The Eternal Feminine*, by Frances Nathan, written for Margaret Anglin, a leading actress of the time.[62] The action takes place on an island in the Aegean Sea around 400 B. C., and the plot centers around the theme of women controlling the destinies of men. The play was intended for production in New York during the season of 1904-05. According to one news release, Parker had nearly completed his first work for the dramatic stage, consisting of "fourteen orchestra pieces with several female choruses," by the early fall of 1904.[63] This work is evidently lost. Press notices in the theater collection of the New York Public Library reveal that performances were given in New Haven, Detroit, Indianapolis, Chicago, and San Francisco, but, as no reviews of New York performances are among the clippings, it is probable that the work did not reach the stage there.

The earliest mention of the second of these stage works, is found in the diary, 28 June 1905: "Made bargain about Prince of India." This "bargain" refers to an agreement to compose incidental music for an elaborate Broadway setting of Lew Wallace's historical novel. Although the book did not achieve the spectacular popularity of *Ben Hur*, it was nevertheless well-known enough at the time to be dramatized on the New York stage.

Parker's diary indicates that he worked on the score during the summer of 1905, which he spent in Bavaria. The play was given its premiere performance at the Broadway Theatre in New York on 24 September 1906. The dramatization was done by J. I.

C. Clarke, and the principal role of the Prince was played by the actor Emmett Corrigan. The *New York Times* called the play the most spectacular production on the New York stage that season:

> Sumptuous entertainment . . . a feast for the eye, if not always exactly for the mind and ear. For the whole, Prof. Parker's music, however, provides an admirable and atmospheric accompaniment.[64]

Although Parker's growing interest in dramatic music may have been a factor in his writing music for these two plays, the fees he received were probably the most important reason. In the income entries at the back of the diaries for those years, he recorded $450 for *The Eternal Feminine* and $800 for *The Prince of India*.

During the first decade of the twentieth century, Parker also came into contact with an important organization of the time for the advancement of contemporary music, the Litchfield County Choral Union. The Choral Union consisted of singing societies from several communities in the northwestern part of Connecticut which, after rehearsing singly throughout the winter in individual groups, combined to give a festival of contemporary music each spring at Norfolk. The Norfolk Festival was sponsored by and held on the estate of Carl and Irene Stoeckel, respectively the son of Yale's first Battell Professor and the daughter of the donor for the Battell chair at Yale. The Stoeckels hired conductors to drill the various singing groups and a symphony orchestra to perform at the Festival. They commissioned much of the music and provided the concert facility called the "music shed." The Norfolk Festival was closely modeled on the English festivals, and commissions were given almost entirely to English and American composers.

Parker's association with the Norfolk Festival goes back as far as 1902, when Carl Stoeckel notified him that he had been made an honorary member of the Litchfield County Choral Union, along with John Knowles Paine of Harvard.[65] Isabel Parker Semler dated the family trips to the Norfolk Festival from about 1905,[66] but the earliest mention of these affairs in Parker's diaries is found in June, 1908, when his ballad *King Gorm the Grim* was performed there. From then on, notations concerning the Festival are found nearly every year. Mrs. Semler has vividly described the concerts, the excitement of premiere performances, the dinners and social gatherings in the Stoeckels' home, and the loveliness of that country setting. The site is now the summer home for the Yale School of Music.

The three Parker compositions commissioned by Stoeckel cover a span of ten years, from 1908 to 1918, They vary considerably. *King Gorm the Grim*, for chorus and orchestra, is a musical setting of a tale drawn from that body of Norse and Celtic legends which had served so frequently as inspiration for the composer during the nineties. The second commission, *Collegiate Overture*, also for chorus and orchestra, was composed for the Festival of 1911, and is a setting of college songs. Finally, *The Dream of Mary*, a religious work combining solo, choral, and instrumental settings with melodramatic recitation, congregational singing, and tableaux of Biblical scenes, was composed for the Festival of 1918.

In the fall of 1907, Parker took on conducting positions which were to be among his most important activities for the next several years. He had been approached the previous spring about the possibility of becoming the director of one of Philadelphia's best known and wealthiest male singing societies, the Orpheus Club, and its sister organization, the Eurydice Chorus.[67] He made arrangements to be absent from Yale on Mondays so that he could go on to Philadelphia each week after he had completed his Sunday duties at Saint Nicholas Church in New York. He was to rehearse the Eurydice Chorus on Monday afternoon and the Orpheus group in the evening, returning to New Haven by night train in order to resume his teaching obligations on Tuesday.

The Orpheus Club had been founded in 1872 by a few disgruntled members of an older singing group called the Abt Society.[68] Under the direction of Michael H. Gross, the Club had concentrated largely on English part-songs rather than the more usual German repertory. Frank Damrosch succeeded Gross as the Club's director in 1897 and probably suggested Parker as his own replacement in 1907.

The Eurydice Chorus had been organized around 1886 and thereafter established a local reputation for performances of high quality.[69] As was the case with their legendary namesakes, the Eurydice Chorus and the Orpheus Club were closely connected. They shared the same conductor and occasionally gave joint concerts, such as a production of *The Legend of Saint Christopher* on 18 April 1912.

When Parker accepted the position as director of the Orpheus Club, the *Philadelphia North American* commented: "The advent of Dr. Parker is an important step in the advance of musical affairs which has been made in Philadelphia in the past few years. Like Carl Pohlig, leader of the Philadelphia Orchestra, he is a man of international reputation."[70] Parker soon entered into the musical life of Philadelphia. Activities with the Manuscript Society, the Art Club, and at the Penn Athletic Club are recorded in the diaries for the spring of 1908.

During Parker's tenure the Orpheus Club maintained comfortable social quarters at 1520 Chestnut Street. The usual membership numbered about seventy men. Although the group stressed social as well as musical activities, their concerts were of high quality, and they maintained a tradition of participating in many of Philadelphia's important musical events. Three concerts a year were usually performed at the Academy of Music. The first usually consisted of part-songs for male voices; the second, larger works with full orchestral accompaniment; and the last concert, light works with more popular appeal.

One of the more ambitious works Parker chose was a version of Sophocles's *Antigone* with incidental music by Mendelssohn. David Bispham did the recitation.[71] Because much of the repertory was lighter, however, one writer remarked that "many of the Club's functions . . . have been charming rather than musically significant."[72] The Orpheus Club was undoubtedly the incentive for many of Parker's arrangements and compositions for male chorus from this period; *The Leap of Roushan Beg* and the revised *Norsemen's Raid* are the most important pieces. *Alice Brand* and the *Seven Greek Pastoral Scenes* are major works composed for the Eurydice Chorus.

Parker was well paid for these services. He listed in his diaries amounts of $500 for each Orpheus Club and $250 for each Eurydice Chorus concert. This compensation, compared with $500 which he was receiving at the time for an entire season's directorship of the New Haven Symphony and $300 for the Derby Choral Club season, was a probable factor in keeping him active in Philadelphia long after his physical strength was insufficient to maintain such a strenuous commuting schedule. Entries for the Orpheus Club are listed in the diary for as late as 1916, although Philadelphia historians list his tenure as conductor from 1907 to 1914.[73]

As Parker increasingly used his composing time after the turn of the century to write larger works, the number of his smaller works decreased. He continued to write only one or two anthems per year from 1900 to 1905. Thereafter he published only two before his death. He stopped composing music for piano altogether but did complete nine short pieces and one major work for organ, the *Sonata in E-Flat*, during the last part of the first decade. Only in the area of the art song did Parker's productivity in short compositions continue at the pace he had maintained in the 1890s.

Beginning with the summer of 1907, the Parker family spent most of their summers at Blue Hill, Maine, a favorite vacation area for several American musicians during that time. Here they enjoyed social activities with members of the Kneisel quartet, who rehearsed their winter programs there, the well-known editor Thomas Tapper and his wife Bertha Feiring Tapper, a concert pianist, and critic H. E. Krehbiel. In nearby Mount Desert were Ethelbert Nevin's widow, Anne Paul Nevin; Harold Randolph, director of the Peabody Institute, and the Damrosch families. In addition to clambakes, poker, and other informal pastimes, which are frequently recorded in Parker's diaries, the Kneisels usually gave a concert each year.[74] The restfulness of Blue Hill was conducive to creative work, for here he wrote a large part of his opera *Mona* during the summers of 1909 and 1910.

Chapter Five

THE FINAL YEARS

The Production of Mona

The years of Parker's life between 1909 and 1912 were dominated by the composition and production of his first opera *Mona*. On 15 December 1908, the Metropolitan Opera Company announced its sponsorship of a contest for an opera in English written by a native-born composer. A cash prize of ten thousand dollars and a production at the Metropolitan were the proffered incentives. The contest announcement created considerable interest among American musicians, for, up to this time, the Metropolitan had shown little interest in producing any American opera with the exception of Frederick Converse's *The Pipe of Desire*, the production of which was delayed until 1910.[1]

There can be no doubt that Parker's incentive for writing *Mona* came directly as a result of the contest announcement. Just before the first performance in 1912, he told an audience in Ansonia, Connecticut, that he had contemplated writing an opera for some time and had asked Brian Hooker, an erstwhile colleague in the English department at Yale, to write a suitable libretto for him. Hooker, he related, had taken no definite action on the proposal until the announcement of the contest.[2]

Parker recorded in his diary that he received the "Brian Hooker Scenario" on 12 February 1909, approximately two months after the Metropolitan Opera management had announced the contest. By summer's end, he had finished Act I and had sketched Act II. On 28 March 1910, he noted that he had "sent opera to Brian Hooker."

That same winter held no respite from the usual round of engagements. The diaries show that, in addition to his church position, he conducted the New Haven Symphony, the choral groups of

Philadelphia, the Ansonia Society, and did a production of Coler-
idge-Taylor's *Hiawatha* with the New Haven Oratorio Society.
Parker also made several guest appearances both as conductor and
organist.

Some extraordinary events made this particular winter
unusually busy. Samuel Sanford, Parker's long-time associate at
Yale, died, and the necessary reorganization of the teaching staff
had to be made. Furthermore, Parker's father-in-law became seriously ill, and Anna, who so scrupulously enforced quiet periods for
composition at home and otherwise managed the domestic affairs,
left for Munich, Germany. There was now the added responsibility
of looking after the children. Letters to his wife during the spring of
1910 reveal the tremendous strain under which the composer was
working. One lists the many daily details which left him no time
for rest. In another he indicated that he was "mentally exhausted"
and resigning his church position in New York.[3] On 24 August
1910 at Blue Hill, only a few weeks before the close of the contest,
Parker recorded in his diary that he "finished scoring Mona."

The winter of 1911-12 must have been one of anticipation
for the several American composers whose scores were being
evaluated in the contest. In spite of the attempts of the Metropolitan
management to keep the contestants anonymous even to the judges,
the *New York World* reported that operas had been submitted by
Albert Mildenberg, Arthur Nevin, E. R. Kroeger, Arne Oldberg,
Alfred G. Robyn, and Charles Wakefield Cadman.[4] The judges
were George Chadwick, Charles Martin Loeffler, Walter Damrosch,
and Alfred Hertz, who was at the time conductor of German opera
at the Metropolitan.

On 3 May 1911 the unanimous decision of the judges
awarding Parker the prize was announced. Parker traveled to New
York the following day to receive the congratulations of the Metropolitan Opera's manager Giulio Gatti-Casazza and to make plans
for the production. When asked by reporters if he was surprised at
the decision, Parker answered equivocally: "It would be immodest
to say that I was not."[5]

Reaction of the press to the announcement of the prize-
winner varied from full approbation to surprise. William Henderson applauded the decision, commenting that "the winner is one in
whom every connoisseur of music can unhesitatingly accept as the
incarnation of American Scholarship and accomplishment in the
field of the lyric art."[6] Philip Hale traced Parker's interest in opera
to the "dramatic element" in *Hora Novissima* and *Saint
Christopher*.[7] Emilie Frances Bauer, however, was incredulous that
an oratorio composer would attempt opera.[8]

The period between the announcement of the prize in May
1911 and the performances of *Mona* in March 1912 was one of

intense strain. Parker had to endure both a general disgruntlement
with the handling of the contest as well as opposition to the selection of his opera. The *Tribune* disparaged the quality of the entries,
quoting Hertz as saying that ten of the scores were "absolutely
worthless."[9] The *New York World* also quoted the conductor as
having said: "Some scores should never had been sent to the
committee."[10] Yet another source contradicted this assertion, indi-
cating that Hertz thought all of the operas to have been worthy of
consideration.[11] The *New York World* groused that the restriction to
entries by native-born composers was like "a race to be open only to
thoroughbreds bred in Alaska."[12]

The most malicious barbs came from *The Musical Courier*.
This periodical, which had been critical of Parker as far back as the
New York performance of *Saint Christopher*, now became more
acerbic. Among other things, it questioned Parker's ability, his
motivation for writing the opera, the contest procedures, and particularly the fact that judges Chadwick, Loeffler, and Damrosch were
Parker's personal friends. The *Courier's* comments became increasingly vituperative as the day of the first performance approached.

Parker inadvertently fanned the flames of the controversy by
some casual but indiscreet remarks about Italian opera and Giuseppe Verdi. *The Musical Courier* seized upon these and, in a
report called "Exit Verdi"[13], and in other articles, ridiculed Parker
for daring to compare his work with those of the Italian master.
Noting the *Courier's* diatribe, a writer for *Musical America* concluded: "I do not feel certain that everybody is praying for its
[*Mona's*] success."[14] The sizable amount of favorable press reaction preceding the production, however, is an indication that *The
Musical Courier's* attitude was not shared by many.

Shortly after the prize announcement, Hertz, who was
scheduled to conduct the performance the following season, left for
a summer in Europe. Parker wrote to him several times concerning
details of the production. The contents of these letters deal largely
with the composer's preparation of the work for publication, proof-
reading, helping to select principals, and modifications of the original score for performance. These letters also make evident Parker's
complete confidence in Hertz.

There are many references to "Madame Olive," Olive
Fremstad, the Metropolitan soprano originally designated to sing the
principal part of the heroine. The choice of Fremstad created many
difficulties, since she was generally unavailable for discussions and
made demands for rather drastic revisions of her part.[15] From his
summer vacation spot at Blue Hill, Parker sent Hertz an altered
copy of the title role for "Olive" but indicated that he "would rather
not do it to suit a singer's whim."[16] When Fremstad was later re-

placed by Louise Homer, Parker was still somewhat perturbed. In spite of the difficulties that he had experienced with Fremstad, he was apprehensive about Homer's ability to sing the part. He wrote to Hertz:

> Perhaps Mrs. Homer will do it well. She is virtuous and admirable in many ways but not peppery and allows her chin to interfere with perfect pronunciations. I once heard her sing the Finale of Götterdämmerung and the top notes were just a little fishy at times, but she is a fine woman and I hope for the best.[17]

He later wrote that he had been working with Homer and indicated that she was well prepared.[18]

By the end of the year he showed the strain of anticipation:

> Frankly, I very much dread having the performance put off until the very end of the season, and should like, if possible, to do something to keep up interest and circulation during the next three or four weeks.[19]

He was soon given numerous opportunities to do so. On 10 January 1912, he appeared before the MacDowell Club of New York to give a resumé of his opera. Following the talk he played several excerpts at the piano. From this performance, one observer concluded: "Dr. Parker's music showed itself to be a free post-Wagnerian weave, fluent in style, exhibiting personality rather than marked individuality, and always with a sustained quality of distinction."[20]

Parker's diary reveals that he soon became directly involved in the Metropolitan production. He attended weekly rehearsals, which began shortly after Christmas, 1911. A large number of the changes were reported to have been made during these rehearsals. The conductor's score, now at Yale University, shows several but not an unduly large number of cuts. The *Boston Evening Transcript* reported: "Time and again the need of more rehearsals has deferred the performance."[21] *The Musical Courier* hinted in a much less complimentary way at the confusion during rehearsals: "Parts of Mona are so funny . . . that listeners and participants were joined in laughter by the composer himself who told the principals to make whatever changes they thought necessary."[22] A writer for *Musical America* reported warily after the dress rehearsal: "There seemed little dissent regarding the exceptional poetic beauties of Brian Hooker's text, but Mr. Parker's music entailed wide and radical divergencies of opinion."[23]

If Parker was upset by the inordinately large amount of preperformance criticism and even abuse, he remained outwardly unperturbed. He expressed his complete satisfaction with the preparation shortly before the first performance:

> Nothing has been left undone to make a success of Mona by Mr. Gatti-Casazza. . . . It will be presented to the public with the greatest possible advantage. The work has been beautifully put on the stage. No composer could reasonably ask for a better list of artists. Then I am most grateful to Mr. Hertz for the tireless enthusiasm that he has shown in the preparation of the work. It is now ready for the verdict of the public.[24]

The first performance on the evening of 14 March 1912, was attended by a capacity audience. The ovation appeared to be genuinely enthusiastic, with twelve curtain calls at the end of the first act, and Parker receiving an ovation in a solo bow on the eleventh call.[25]

The opening night plaudits were not reflected in the reviews of the opera. The critics generally found the libretto undramatic and the music unmelodic. Even Parker's most enthusiastic supporters did not concede to *Mona* enough appeal to be included in the permanent repertory of the Metropolitan. Only three performances, on March 23 and 29 and April 1, followed the opening night production.[26]

The Period of Fairyland: 1912-1916

Although Parker must have been deeply disappointed by the reviews of *Mona*, his confidence in his own ability to write dramatic music remained unshaken. Before the excitement of *Mona* had subsided, he was settled in Munich for the sabbatical winter of 1912-13 and was hard at work on his second opera, *Fairyland*, for which Brian Hooker again provided the libretto.[27] By Christmas of 1912, Parker had progressed far enough in his writing to ask for suggestions from Hertz:

> Now I have made sketches for a new one as different from "Mona" as anything can be. It is better theatrically--not better music I fear--and I am going to keep it liquid--that is unfinished and in sketch form until I can show it to you. It is far sweeter and more cheerful than "Mona" but not without serious moments.[28]

In this letter, Parker revealed some sensitivity to criticism about the unremitting gloom of *Mona*. He continued:

> I haven't seen or heard anything to make me more discontented with "Mona" than I have been all the time and I hope you too have some affection left for her after all your care and trouble last season. There seem to be good spots as well as the other kind and I believe that if we had as many opera organizations in America as there are here it would go the rounds and perhaps please the serious part of the public. On rereading it all I think that there is some definite character to the music and that it is really personal.

The composition of *Fairyland* was well under way when another opera contest with a large cash prize was announced. It was sponsored by the National Federation of Music Clubs, which suggested that some Western city offer a prize for an American opera and undertake its production in conjunction with several West Coast events being planned for the summer of 1915 to celebrate the opening of the Panama Canal. Fred W. Blanchard, a member of the Federation and a native of Los Angeles, was responsible for the choice of that city to sponsor the contest, and the Federation then agreed to hold its biennial convention there.[29]

Arrangements were worked out during the winter of 1912-13, and news of the contest was made public at the Federation Convention held in Chicago during May, 1913. At that time the Los Angeles group announced that it had raised $10,000 for the prize-winner and would support its production with an additional $40,000 to $50,000. Los Angeles also agreed to supply a chorus, ballet corps, and an orchestra.[30]

Parker left no indication that he knew of the Federation contest before the public announcement was made, although he had finished sketching two acts before that time. Composing progress is recorded in the diaries from 1912 to 1914, with the sketch of Act III completed by 11 July 1913. Later that summer, Parker wrote that he had shown the piano score to Hertz. Orchestral scoring was begun that fall. By 8 February 1914, Act I was finished; by April 14, Act II; and by July 4, the entire work was completed. Parker then held final consultations with Hooker before sending the score off to the contest on July 29. This diary indication is the first that *Fairyland* was destined to be an entry. On October 12, a few days before the formal announcement that *Fairyland* was the prize-winning opera, Parker recorded in his diary that he "heard about Fairyland."

The National Federation of Music Clubs had created a special committee, the American Opera Association, headed by

Blanchard, to handle the contest and the opera production.[31] The three contest judges were Adolf Weidig, professor at the American Conservatory in Chicago; Charles Louis Seeger, professor at the University of California, Berkeley; and Wallace Arthur Sabin, an organist and glee club director in San Francisco. None were from the East, nor were they friends of Parker, as had been the case in the Metropolitan Opera contest. Their task was immense, since they had, by one account, fifty-six scores to examine.[32] Although they had no previous experience in opera, their work was perceived to be satisfactory, for the controversy surrounding the Metropolitan Opera contest did not recur.

Sizable extant correspondence pertaining to the Los Angeles presentation reveals just how active a part Parker took in many of the arrangements. Since the local committee at Los Angeles was inexperienced, the composer participated in making decisions concerning the hiring of a conductor, singers, and even the procuring of a theater and stage properties--duties that would normally be handled by an impresario. He wrote several letters to Blanchard during the winter of 1914-15 concerning these details, stressing particularly the need for a good conductor. His first recommendation was Alfred Hertz, although pressure was evidently being exerted to select an American conductor:

> If you feel that you must have an American conductor,
> I should think that the choice would lie between Mr. Walter
> Damrosch of N. Y. and Mr. Henry Hadley of San Francisco.
> The former has wide experience, but I know less about the
> latter.[33]

Parker was pleased in the eventual choice of Hertz.

Still later, the composer was alarmed that the performance might be given in a small theater. He reminded Blanchard: "The work is not an operetta but a serious opera."[34] Blanchard replied that the American Opera Association might have difficulty in securing the opera house known as Clune's Auditorium because of the "'awful' motion picture success."[35] This difficulty was also surmounted and the work was eventually given in the large auditorium. The first performance was scheduled to take place on July 1 at the conclusion of the biennial convention activities for the National Federation of Music Clubs.

The convention was planned with an especially strong emphasis on American music in order to attract large numbers of native musicians to the West Coast. The outbreak of World War I had also engendered more than usual enthusiasm for the idea that the United States could take over the role of international cultural leadership from Europe. The proclamation that American music

had finally "come of age" seemed at no time to be so ripe for affirmation as at Los Angeles, so far removed from the Eastern seaboard
and cultural subservience to Europe. Exuberant municipal pride
abetted the confidence of the delegates that this convention would
be a historic one for the cause of American music. Los Angeles
officials had planned one of the most extravagant conventions in the
history of the Federation, including musical activities by the Los
Angeles public schools, an American choral music program sung by
massed Los Angeles choirs of some 1,000 voices, the greeting of
Parker, his wife, and Federation delegates with a huge floral flotilla
upon their arrival by a special train,[36] and a gigantic "electrical
pageant" consisting of some sixty-five floats of flowers, choirs,
celebrities, and California girls.[37]

   Upon arrival to begin rehearsals of *Fairyland*, conductor
Alfred Hertz professed to be extremely impressed by the enthusiasm
of the local participants: "When the public hears the 180 voices in
the 'Fairyland' choruses and the orchestra of nearly 100 pieces, it
will properly concede that never has there been such a production in
the West."[38] Aside from the principals and the newly organized
orchestra, the performing forces were amateur, and Hertz found
some twenty-five rehearsals to be necessary. He drilled the orchestra and principals in three-hour daytime sessions and the chorus
during the evenings. His ability and prestige gave the large number
of inexperienced participants the stability they sorely needed. If the
attention he received from Los Angeles newspapers is any indication, the conductor soon became the focal point of the production.
His success was such that he decided to remain in the Far West, for
the following winter he accepted the directorship of the San Francisco Symphony Orchestra.

   The dress rehearsal took place on Tuesday evening, June 29.
The presence of nearly one thousand invited guests made this final
rehearsal in reality a first performance. The opening, two nights
later, on July 1, was a gala occasion for Los Angeles society. The
Los Angeles Examiner and other papers devoted a large amount of
space to photographs of prestigious guests arriving and leaving the
opera house. The police had to break up a crowd which had formed
in front the theater to view the celebrities. Three more performances were given during the following two days. Extensive publicity resulted in near capacity crowds for the first four performances
and made necessary the scheduling of two more performances on
the following Thursday and Friday evenings, July 8 and 9. The enthusiasm which had engulfed Los Angeles during the suspenseful
weeks before the premiere seemed to disappear with hardly a trace
after the July performances. Although the critics found more in
Fairyland to their liking than they had in *Mona*, they were not
sufficiently enthusiastic to encourage other productions. Rumors

during the summer of 1915 that other American cities were interested in producing *Fairyland* came to nothing. The Panama-Pacific Exposition did request a presentation in San Francisco that summer, but Hertz insisted that the performing groups be the Los Angeles Orchestra, chorus, and ballet troupe, a condition that neither the pride nor the finances of the San Francisco Exposition officials would permit.[39] Thus *Fairyland*, like *Mona*, blazed a rather spectacular but short-lived path across the horizon of American opera.

The production of *Fairyland* was not Parker's sole activity during the summer of 1915, for he had also agreed to lecture during the summer session at the University of California, Berkeley. He spent the early part of the summer commuting between rehearsals of the opera in Los Angeles and classes at Berkeley, teaching there three mornings and two afternoons per week. A group of lectures, "Church music since Bach," at Yale is marked as having been delivered in this series.[40] He also gave a paper, "The art of listening," which he had already delivered a few weeks before to a meeting of the California Music Teachers' Association in Oakland.[41] On July 12, Parker attended the Music Teachers' National Association meeting in Berkeley. The patriotic fervor so evident at Los Angeles was carried over into the Association meetings. In a burst of nationalistic sentiment very rare for him, Parker noted in his diary, "America for American Musicians."

Parker was one of several composers honored at the Panama-Pacific Exposition in San Francisco on August 1, "American Composers' Day." The principal feature of this commemoration was an orchestral concert held in Festival Hall for which he conducted his tone poem, *A Northern Ballad*.[42] Other American composers represented on the program included George Chadwick, Mabel Daniels, Frederick Stock, Ernest Kroeger, Carl Busch, and W. J. McCoy.

The Parkers returned home via Oregon, Washington, Canada, and Lake Superior. They arrived in New Haven on August 11 to the good news that money had been granted for a new building to house the School of Music, a facility for which Parker had persistently pleaded ever since he had become a professor at Yale. The remainder of the summer was spent at Blue Hill. Here he worked on an orchestral suite to *Fairyland*, later performed at the December concert of the New Haven Symphony Orchestra.

The excitement of the *Fairyland* production and summer on the West Coast nearly overshadows another important musical event for 1915. Earlier, on April 13 of that year, Parker's third oratorio, *Morven and the Grail*, commissioned by the Handel and Haydn Society for its centennial celebration, was performed in Boston. Parker's diary has only one notation about *Morven*, that it was completed on 29 November 1914. It is probable that he was working on the oratorio during the summer of 1914, during which time *Fairyland* was scored. Although the work is the least effective of Parker's oratorios, the composer nevertheless took into account the significant changes that this medium was undergoing during the early twentieth century. The criticisms of *Morven* following its performance were yet another disappointment the composer had to accept during the final decade of his life. Older critics, such as H. T. Parker, Philip Hale, and Louis Elson, continued to find some significant qualities in Parker's music, but Olin Downes, who represented a new generation of critics, found little to praise.[43]

During 1916, Parker composed two works for occasions at Yale University. The first was a commission from the School of Fine Arts in commemoration of the fiftieth anniversary of its founding. Parker was asked to provide music for a play, *Cupid and Psyche*, by John Jay Chapman. The *Masque*, as the work came to be called, was produced on June 19 as a part of the three-day celebration and was repeated the following October 20.[44] The commission is notable for having brought Parker together with one of America's foremost men of letters. Chapman also collaborated with the composer on Parker's final large-scale work, *The Dream of Mary*.

The other major composition of 1916 was written for the bicentennial celebration of the moving of Yale College to New Haven. *An Allegory of War and Peace*, as this work is called, consists of several choruses with band accompaniment. According to one Boston newspaper, it was the principal musical composition for a huge pageant "visualizing two hundred years of progress of college and city and vitalizing the many great episodes of their history."[45] Nearly seventy-thousand observers were expected to attend the affair in which about seven thousand persons were to participate. Parker's students and former students, Seth Bingham, Douglas Moore, Harry E. Jepson, Walter Ruel Cowles, David Stanley Smith, and William B. Haesche, composed other sections of the pageant. The text was supplied by the pageant director, Francis M. Markoe, a 1906 graduate of Yale University who had made a career of organizing such spectacles. The extravaganza took place on Saturday afternoon, 21 October 1916, in the Yale Bowl.

The Place of Music in Society

Parker's comments made during the second decade of the twentieth century about the role of music in American society show a marked transition from the earlier, restrictive principles to a tolerance which allowed almost every kind of musical activity. He had always been pragmatic in insisting that the "empirical process" is a composer's only effective guide,[46] and he now applied that idea to the diversity of musical activity around him. Whereas formerly he had concerned himself only with classical music, he now attempted to define a purpose for all kinds of music and somehow or other to find a philosophical position that embraced a much wider musical spectrum.

The change becomes apparent after 1915, both in his statements about music generally and in his own compositions. *Fairyland* is a concession to provincial American operatic tastes, which at that time did not extend much higher than the operetta or musical comedy. Thereafter, each of his compositions reveals a withdrawal from the highly chromatic period of *Mona* in a deliberate attempt to widen the appeal of his music. *Cupid and Psyche* embodies the clarity and incisiveness of the Baroque style; *An Allegory of War and Peace*, the massiveness of the ceremonial cantata; *The Dream of Mary*, the simplicity of the congregational hymn and the dramatic appeal of the melodrama; and the World War I pieces, the overt emotion of patriotism. Finally, *A. D. 1919*, not only is inclusive of the patriotic, the massive, and the sentimental, but also contains some of the composer's most effective artistic elaborations.

His growing interest in the public's musical receptivity is evident in the address, "The art of listening" (1915), a topic which he had earlier dismissed with a few platitudes. Music listening is now treated as a skill which can be developed through practice in the recognition of musical components: melody, harmony, rhythm, dynamics, tone color, and form, as well as style recognition, listening, and amateur performances. He also called for an appreciation of "the spirit in which it [music] is conceived and executed" and the exercise of "discriminating musical patriotism" through support of national musical enterprises.

In his concern for broadening the base of musical appeal, he did not compromise with his earlier position regarding the hierarchy of composer, the performer, and listener, in descending order of importance. Nor were his earlier opinions on the relative significance of various kinds of music changed. As befitting one whose reputation was based in large measure on his skill as a contrapuntist, he considered polyphony as the apex of serious music: "Counterpoint is the study of melody. . . . Polyphony is melody carried to its ultimate development, and polyphony is what differentiates Folk music from Art music."[47]

No doubt Parker's many activities during the last decade of his life--conductor of amateur performing groups, consultant for church hymnals and music text books, editor of a leading songbook series for the elementary grades, teacher of music history for the

layman, and administrator for a public school music course at
Yale--caused him to be concerned with the many varied social
functions of music. In the extremely conservative atmosphere of
the American Federation of Arts meeting at Washington, D. C., in
1916, he made a speech which marked him as a radical in his call
for federal aid to the arts, an appeal which must have been viewed
with apprehension by many of the delegates. He envisioned "a
department of arts in Washington, occupying the same relation to
the psychic needs of the nation as the Department of Agriculture to
its physical needs." He also stressed the need for a "national conservatory" which "would set a standard for the whole country." On
the lighter side, he defended ragtime music, which did not "distress"
him " by "its vulgarity." He concluded whimsically: "There is a
great deal of virtue in honest vulgarity. Think of fried onions."[48]

In his final set of pronouncements, "Our Taste in Music,"
written in 1918 for *Yale Review*, his earlier dogmatism concerning
higher musical standards had completely disappeared. He took on
the demeanor of an elder statesman who is indulgent with the
musical variety found throughout the land. "Negro music" (meaning jazz), revival singing, fox-trotting, and the use of serious music
in a popular idiom (Parker noted the practice combining *Swanee
River* with a foxtrot arrangement of Dvořák's *Humoresque*.)--all
met with his sympathetic appraisal. He concluded approvingly that
popular music was moving toward "increasing euphony" and
harmonic complexity, with such tunes as *Poor Butterfly* replacing
more elemental types, such as *Champagne Charlie*. He also expanded his earlier comments on "vulgarity":

> In truth there are two very different kinds of taste.
> May I call them high and low to save space? I am tempted to
> suffix "brow" to each adjective for entire clarity. Each inclines
> resolutely to ignore and despise the other. "Stupid and dull as
> ditchwater," says Mulvaney of a symphony; "Hopelessly trivi-
> al and vulgar," is Mr. Endicott's comment on an insinuating
> waltz. Perhaps both are right. I think an enormous part of our
> national common progress is made by breaking down barriers
> between such types. Training the lowly to enjoy exalted music
> is known to be meritorious. I never heard anyone commend the
> reverse process of training the fastidious to recognize vulgar
> excellence. . . . Good and bad are relative terms in music as
> well as in life.[49]

Although Parker had mellowed considerably toward popular
music in these late addresses, one detects in them a wistfulness for
his own cherished personal ideals. He had always been committed
to a program of elevating mankind morally and spiritually by means

of art. In spite of his call for a tolerance of all kinds of music, he may yet have been fearful of the dissipating effect that "vulgar excellence" might have on these higher standards. Such a possible conflict was to remain unresolved. In the few remaining months of his life, he had no opportunity to expand on the subject.

The War Years and Their Aftermath: 1917-1919

The final three years of Parker's life were ones of failing health and severe curtailment of activities. The United States's entry into World War I in April, 1917, and the resulting reduction of cultural events helped to push him toward a restriction of the punishing schedule he had kept all his life. After the Spring of 1916, he stopped his trips to Philadelphia, although he did continue to conduct the New Haven Symphony Orchestra and the Derby Choral Club through the spring of 1919. The new music building, Sprague Memorial Hall, was opened during the fall of 1917, but the elaborate series of recitals which he had helped to plan in observation of the occasion had to be drastically reduced because of the war.

The military conflict itself deeply affected Parker.[50] He was concerned for his two sons-in-law who were in the armed services on the Allied side as well as for his wife's relatives who were in Germany. He also must have felt the profound disillusionment of his generation, which had been thoroughly rooted in nineteenth-century optimism. Nevertheless, "the proper course of action," as he expressed it, was to preserve those ideals which had been the mainstay of his own youth and manhood:

> Serious music is not without its value in such times as these. Perhaps the need of it is felt by some even more keenly than in periods of greater tranquility. In any case, our immediate duty requires that we neglect no opportunity of upholding and raising those aesthetic standards which are committed in some measure to our keeping.[51]

Although much of the normal musical life of the country was severely disrupted, Parker found several ways to make his own contribution to the war effort. Even before the involvement of the United States, he had instructed the firm of Novello to divert royalties from sales of his publications in England to relief agencies.[52] Three of his compositions from this period stem from the war: *Hymn for the Victorious Dead*, *The Red Cross Spirit Speaks*, and *A. D. 1919*.

The music for *The Red Cross Spirit Speaks*, the poem by John Findley, was written for Louise Homer at the request of Mrs. Richard Aldrich, wife of the music critic.[53] Homer used the number throughout her concert tour during the winter of 1917-18. At a concert in Carnegie Hall, she is reported to have sung it dressed in "a red satin gown, arms outstretched, making a Red Cross.[54] Parker directed that all proceeds for the song be donated to the Red Cross.[55]

Parker's diaries for his final years show a variety of activities. The remaining summers were spent at Blue Hill among old friends such as the Krehbiels, the Whitings, and the Kneisels. In 1916, Parker had the opportunity to become well-acquainted with Fritz Kreisler, who was also vacationing there. After one visit with the violinist, he noted in his diary (July 4), "a most interesting and well-informed chap." During the winters he traveled occasionally to Boston and New York. He recorded in his 1917 diary having attended a performance of Loeffler's *Hora Mystica* in Boston on March 3 and of DeKoven's opera, *The Canterbury Pilgrims*, at the Metropolitan Opera House on May 1. Additional notations for 1917 show lectures at the American Academy, New York, and in Hartford and Norfolk, Connecticut; and concerts in Derby, Hartford, and Springfield. Entries in the 1918 diary indicate that Parker found time to take private lessons in Italian.

During the spring of 1918, Parker completed his final commission for the Norfolk Festival, *The Dream of Mary*.[56] This Morality, as Parker and the librettist, John Jay Chapman, chose to call the work, was the kind of artistic enterprise that would have appealed to the adventuresome Carl Stoeckel, the Festival's patron. This musical dramatization of the life of Jesus in a series of tableaux with accompanying narration varies from meager chordal support of melodramatic recitations to fully self-contained choral and orchestral sections. A reviewer of a later performance at the Opera House in Brooklyn on 29 March 1920 described the staging as follows:

> The story is told by a narrator called the Angel of Communication and all the principals are in costume. A curtain is hung between the performers and the orchestra and chorus, and, as the Angel describes the miracles, the various characters form a group on the stage.[57]

Stoeckel personally supervised the details of staging and costumes in addition to his usual tasks of hiring soloists, orchestra, and making arrangements for the chorus. His relations with Parker seem to have been amiable enough, judging from the extant correspondence about the Norfolk production.[58] Chapman, on the other hand, expressed some dissatisfaction with the producer's meddling.

He wrote to Parker: "People wouldn't give such things at all if the impressarii weren't allowed to set them up there after their own fancy."[59]

The production was given on 4 June 1918. Helen Thompson, who sang the principal role of the Angel, was supported by musicians from New York and by members of the Litchfield County Choral Union. Following the premiere in Norfolk, *The Dream of Mary* was given three additional performances within the next few years: in New York by the Columbia Festival Chorus under Walter Henry Hall in August, 1919; in Scranton, Pennsylvania, at the Century Club on 11 and 12 March 1920; and at Brooklyn, as mentioned above.[60]

At the end of the war, Brian Hooker urged Parker to work with him on a "paean of victory" in anticipation of a performance at a victory celebration at New York's Madison Square Garden.[61] Although this particular event did not occur, Yale University did commission both men to write an ode for the 1919 commencement in honor of the Yale men who had lost their lives in the war.

A letter from Anson Phelps Stokes, then Secretary of the University, asking Parker to "comply with the suggestion of the University that you cooperate with Brian Hooker in setting to music a poem suitable for the commemorative exercises at Yale this Spring" suggests a certain reluctance on the composer's part.[62] The letter also stipulated with apologies the sum of $250 as an honorarium. The composer's failing health may have been a reason for his hesitation to begin yet another sizable work. His daughter has suggested that his reluctance stemmed from the deep impression the text made on him and an awareness of the emotional and physical drain its musical setting would demand.[63] Once he agreed to accept the commission, however, he worked with characteristic speed. Having received the poem *A. D. 1919* from Hooker on May 5, he finished the music (probably the piano-vocal score) on May 15.[64] The manuscript full score is dated June 1, 1919. The piece calls for soprano solo, four-part chorus and full orchestra.

Isabel Parker Semler has described poignantly its first performance at the Yale commencement exercises on June 15:

> There was no doubt about the understanding and emotion of those who first heard it. . . . The seats were filled with many students returning from France or the high seas, my husband among them. I . . . can still hear the lift and fall of the voices at the words "Friends with the hearts of strangers, Boys with the eyes of men." This was a moment, indeed. Clad in the crimson robes of a Doctor of Music of the University of Cambridge, England, Father conducted the first performance of this tender,

stirring work, and I think he may have known it was the last
time he was ever to conduct.[65]

This performance, which really brings Parker's career to a
close, is charged with the symbolism of the changing order. *A. D.
1919* is both a farewell and a salute to the rising post-war generation. Shortly after commencement, Parker and his wife left New
Haven for Blue Hill. Entries in his diary for the summer of 1919
became increasingly infrequent as his health steadily deteriorated.
On September 12 he was taken to a hospital in Bangor, Maine,
where he underwent an appendectomy. He then returned to New
Haven in October much too ill to resume his teaching duties but
nevertheless able to make one last public appearance on November
29, to witness the marriage of his youngest daughter, Grace.

On December 9, Parker and his wife left New Haven for a
recuperative cruise to Santo Domingo and other points in the West
Indies. They got only as far as New York when Parker was stricken
with pneumonia. He was taken to the home of his daughter Isabel
in Cedarhurst, Long Island, where he died on 18 December 1919.[66]
The funeral was held in Saint Mary's Church at Newton Lower
Falls, very close to his boyhood home of Auburndale, on 20
December 1919. Among the pallbearers were his professional
associates at Yale and his closest friends.[67]

A life such as Parker's, touching nearly every phase of
American music, elicited, upon its cessation, tributes from many
different sources. President Hadley of Yale commented upon him
as an educator, noting that he successfully combined the qualities of
"a productive scholar, an exacting teacher, and a successful organizer."[68] The Reverend Winfred Douglas spoke most eloquently of
Parker's significance in the religious field, "a setter-up of lofty
standards . . . of truth, sincerity, of steadfast faithfulness to lofty
ideals of nobility and of intellectual beauty, of loyalty to the
Church, and of loving and humble service to God."[69]

Among the leading American critics who had evaluated
Parker's compositions for years, William J. Henderson called the
choral works "his true heritage," describing them as "dignified,
scholarly, aristocratic . . . adhering to the finest ideals of the purity
of taste."[70] Henry E. Krehbiel summarized Parker's achievements
as technical proficiency, eclecticism, and "unswerving, high ideal-
ism."[71]

Oddly enough, some minor music journalists and writers for
smaller newspapers were less perfunctory and more revealing in
their comments. *The Christian Science Monitor* noted that in Parker's later career, "he grew into favor with his friends as a man and
out of favor with them as a composer"; nevertheless, the writer
conceded that he had earned "a permanent niche" in the history of

oratorio and church music.[72] The *Springfield Republican* described
the composer's music as appealing to a more highly specialized
group than the works of MacDowell and Chadwick.[73] Other small
newspapers described Parker as intellectual, esoteric and idealistic.
The *Lowell* [Massachusetts] *Courier* called *Hora Novissima* and
Mona as "pretty 'high brow' for this country," but noted that Parker's death "brings to an untimely end one of America's most notable
outgivings of original music."[74] Also paying him tribute as an intellectual composer, the *Hartford Post* commented: "He was in the
realm of artistic creation and performance, apart, in a measure from
the common man."[75] The *Hartford City Times* wrote: "His
music . . . is roundly, robustly, and nobly American. It has a dignity
of harmony, a soundness of technique which command for it respect
of all those who know. Against the tendency to the light and frothy
and ephemeral . . . Professor Parker stood as a noble mountain
peak."[76]

Approximately seventy obituaries from papers throughout
the country among the memorabilia at Yale (there are undoubtedly
many more) are significant testimony to the nation's high regard for
Parker and the loss it felt at the time of his death.

PART II:

THE MUSIC OF HORATIO PARKER

Chapter Six

SECULAR CHORAL MUSIC

Overview

Rheinberger must be given some credit for Parker's interest in secular cantata composition, for Parker has no pre-Munich works even remotely suggesting the complexity and dramatic intensity of his two student cantatas, *The Ballad of a Knight and His Daughter* (1884) and *King Trojan* (1885). Rheinberger composed no fewer than five large-scale secular choral works, in addition to ballads for male choir and numerous part-songs, a substantial number of which were written during the time of Parker's study in Munich.

The rejuvenation of English choral music was also a factor guiding Parker's compositional activity. The English festivals of the seventies, eighties, and nineties featured both continental and native works. Among the leading English composers were Charles Hubert Hastings Parry and Charles Villiers Stanford, whose careers parallel that of Parker. All three were professors whose music commanded considerable interest and respect during their lifetimes but is neglected today. During his English trips, Parker chose to identify himself with these conservative composers rather than with the more progressive Elgar.

We can also look closer to home for reasons why Parker wrote cantatas, for nearly every American composer of his time found the cantata to be an important *genre*. His immediate forebears who composed in this idiom are Dudley Buck, Frederick Grant Gleason, John Knowles Paine, and George Whiting, and his contemporaries include Arthur Foote, George Chadwick, George Templeton Strong, and Amy Beach. Three other contemporaries-- Arthur Whiting, Edward MacDowell, and Charles Martin Loeffler-- did not compose cantatas but wrote choral music in other forms.

79

Finally, several groups which Parker directed or with which he was associated--the German singing societies of New York, the Euterpe Society of New Haven, the Derby Chorus, the English cathedral-town choirs, the Norfolk Festival, the Philadelphia glee clubs, and his public school music enterprises--became incentives for one or more choral compositions varying in size from simple part-songs to elaborate cantatas.

Parker's secular choral music falls into three chronological periods. Of these, only the first (1882 to 1893), during which time he resided first in Munich and then in New York, plays a paramount role in his overall growth as a composer. The works of this period include the student cantatas mentioned above and the New York works: *Idylle* (1886), *Normannenzug* (*The Norsemen's Raid*, 1888), *The Kobolds* (1891), *Dream-King and His Love* (1893), and several part-songs, mostly for men's chorus.

The second period (1894 to 1906) covers the time when Parker moved to Boston, then to New Haven, and subsequently became involved in the English festivals. As he was preoccupied with the larger sacred choral forms, he wrote only a few part-songs and some arrangements for such groups as the Euterpe Society of New Haven, the Manuscript Society of New York, and the English choral societies. They show less preoccupation with Germanic literature and a turning to subjects drawn from English literature.

The final period, after 1907, is diversified and reflects largely the commissions he received because of his standing as a national figure. A commission for the Norfolk Festival elicited the retrospective ballad *King Gorm the Grim* in 1908. Parker's interest in public school music during the last decade of his life is apparent in some part-songs, published both individually and in school song books. A few arrangements and some original compositions, among which the cantata *Alice Brand*, the ballad *The Leap of Roushan Beg*, and the *Seven Greek Pastoral Scenes* are outstanding, were done for the Orpheus Club and the Eurydice Chorus of Philadelphia between 1907 and 1913. As in the case of the second period, this music only incidentally reflects the composer's more serious intentions, for his major efforts were then expended on the operas *Mona* and *Fairyland* and his last oratorio, *Morven and the Grail*. In this final period, Parker chose almost exclusively literature from English or American poets.

The Part Songs

Most of the part-songs are not strongly indicative of any stylistic period in the composer's development. Their utilitarian function is quite evident in the fact that they display little artifice. They are usually set in simple strophic or ternary forms with prevailingly homophonic texture, regular four-bar, antecedent-consequent phrasing, and rather simple diatonic melodies and harmonies with some chromatic embellishment. The earlier part-songs, those written in Munich and New York, are exceptions to these generalizations, for their elaboration indicates that Parker had not yet made a strong distinction between the more elemental part-song and the more complex cantata.

The earliest part-song, *Mountain Shepherd's Song* (1884), is for four-part men's chorus with piano accompaniment. It consists of five stanzas and is long for the strophic type. The guileless theme and its chordal accompaniment are nearly unvarying for the first three strophes. Only the quickening pace of the piano accompaniment for each strophe provides a sense of gathering momentum. By the fourth strophe, more radical alterations occur with a change to the parallel minor mode and a more independent, descriptive accompaniment suggestive of the approaching storm. The last strophe is climactic, with the choral theme, now in augmentation, sung in unison against motivic figures in the accompaniment.

Two Part Songs for women's chorus, "The Fisher" and "The Water Fay" (1892), are rather ornate. Both songs vary from unison to four parts, and soprano solos are prominently featured. Their melodies shift frequently between parallel major and minor modes, and their harmonies are strongly tinted with chromatic passing tones in the inner parts. Frequent harmonization of the melodies in thirds, harmonic progressions rich in secondary tonal movements, rhythmically varied accompaniments, several climactic points, and extensive modulatory schemes are among the more sophisticated features of these pieces.

Harold Harfager (1891) is Parker's most ambitious part-song. The poem is a brief description of Norse troops and their leader, Harold, as they prepare for the "glories" of battle and sacrifice. The musical treatment is dramatic, with homophonic choruses evolving from germinal phrases into extended sections and descriptive effects in the orchestral accompaniment. A short solo for alto voice contributes further to the diversified features of this piece.

By the 1900s, the distinction between Parker's part-songs and cantatas is clearly evident. His *Three Part-Songs* (Opus 48) for male chorus are harmonized melodies with little or no elaboration. The first song in this group, a setting of Ella Higginson's poem,

"The lamp in the west," was the most commercially successful of all
Parker's works in this medium.[1] As the opening phrase shows, it is
quite unpretentious, with its direct appeal in the manner of the more
popular song writers of the time such as Ethelbert Nevin and Carrie
Jacobs Bond (Ex. 6-1A). The piece is not without harmonic complexity as can be found in its third phrase (Ex. 6-1B).

Example 6-1. Excerpts from "The lamp in the west,"
       Op. 48, No. 1, JC, 1901.

A. p. 3, mm. 1-4.

B. p. 3, mm. 8-12.

The Secular Cantatas: Nineteenth Century

The larger, multifarious cantata, in which the composer can manipulate materials more freely, was more conducive to Parker's compositional temperament than the part-song. In these cantatas he developed the craft which enabled him to write *Hora Novissima* and continued to serve him well in many of his later choral works.

Nature, unrequited love, chivalry, and heroism are the themes of the texts, most of which are by obscure German authors. Among these works, *The Ballad of a Knight and His Daughter*, *King Trojan*, and *The Norsemen's Raid* have a preponderance of dramatic action, whereas *Idylle* is largely predisposed towards sentiment. *The Kobolds* and *Dream-King* combine both the dramatic and the sentimental.[2]

The two student works, *The Ballad of a Knight and His Daughter* (1884) and *King Trojan* (1885), are remarkable achievements in view of Parker's other compositions up to that time. *The Ballad* has a tripartite arrangement, and each section, in turn, is divided into three parts. The entire narrative is sung by the chorus; however, some variety is achieved by the alternation of mixed voices with male or female choruses. The choral writing is almost entirely homophonic, except for a point of imitation on the first line of the second stanza in the opening chorus (vocal score, p. 5) and, later, a canon at the octave between the male voices and the orchestra, (p. 9, mm. 2-4). A prevailingly homophonic style with infrequent short points of imitation is also a characteristic of the later cantatas.

The music for *King Trojan*, the most ambitious of all the cantatas from either the Munich or New York years, shows some of the ponderousness of the story. A particularly slow-moving Part I contains sundry expository narrative threads: Trojan's fascination with the night, his aversion to daylight on pain of death, and his regular nocturnal visits to the castle of his beloved. Each concept is given an independent, complex musical organization consisting of a variety of solos and choruses. The pace of Part II is much faster, for the music pushes quickly to the climax: Trojan's fateful ride and his destruction by the rays of the dawning sun. Notable are the intense dialogue between Trojan (baritone) and his page (tenor), the rhapsodic orchestra interludes, and the fluctuating tonal scheme--all features of the composer's dramatic writing in his later cantatas.

The first New York cantata, *Idylle* (1886), was evidently composed in great haste during Parker's first year of teaching at Saint Paul's Cathedral School. It does not have the expansiveness, variety, and occasional dramatic technique shown in the student cantatas, but rather it relies upon structural symmetry, antecedent-consequent phrasing, lyrical writing, conservative harmonic modulation, and restricted tone color.

On the other hand, the second New York cantata, *The Norsemen's Raid* (1888), cast in a large ABA form, is Parker's most imaginative composition up to this time. The opening section has two choruses, the first largely unison and the second in four-part, homophonic style. In the cantata's extended and highly varied middle section, the sea voyage, raids, and victory celebrations of the Norsemen are depicted in the fluid, dramatic style evident in parts of the earlier *King Trojan*. Motives or key phrases become germinal points from which melodies evolve, as in the opening chorus of the middle section, where the key melodic figure in the first tenor, an octave leap followed by the drop to the dominant level, is repeated and then developed at some length. The original figure returns at midpoint and, in the ensuing section, the other voices, which have given the first tenor harmonic support up to this point, now disperse into a short, imitative figure which leads to the cadence (Ex. 6-2).

The next major work, *The Kobolds* (1890), was composed for the Springfield Festival and, like *The Norsemen's Raid*, is entirely choral. The outer sections have the lyrical, sectional style of *Idylle*; however, in the middle section, variety is evident in an emphatic unison declamation (vocal score, p. 14), in scherzo-like, detached eighth notes (p. 17), and in a few short imitative figures (p. 12).

The final cantata of the New York period, *Dream-King and His Love* (1891), is the most artistic in its blending of areas showing continuous dramatic flow with those written in a more traditional sectional style. The overall design is ternary, with close attention paid to internal key relationships. Two large E-flat-major sections of over one hundred measures each frame a middle section quite complex in its tonal and textural organization. The first tenor solo is one of the most conservative parts of the cantata, with a single expressive idea, lyrical lines, antecedent-consequent phrasing, and a repe itive "rocking" accompaniment figure, which continues for fully half of the aria (vocal score, pp.8-9). The choral technique in this cantata is quite varied, including the usual four-part, homophonic, lyrical style (in the opening and closing choruses) and declamatory sections over a continuous motivic thread in the orchestra. *Dream-King* also contains unison writing and the longest instance of imitative writing (twenty-one measures, pp. 10-12) in any cantata to date.

The cantatas from the first period show steady growth in techniques which were later to become Parker's stock-in-trade: the use of harmony and the manipulation of rhythm for expressive purposes, frequent instances of word-painting and pictorial effects,

Example 6-2. Tenor, "The morning dawns," *The Norse-men's Raid*, Op. 16, vc. sc., JC, 1911, p.11, m. 8-p. 15, m. 4.

and mastery in the handling of the orchestra, not only in imaginative accompaniments to the solo and choral sections, but also in independent instrumental preludes, interludes, and postludes. These instrumental elaborations of thematic material become one of the most important aspects of the composer's style.

    Throughout these cantatas, Parker sought unity through thematic repetition: the introduction of a motive in an opening or

early section and its reappearance either as a head motive to following sections, or in orchestral interludes, or as part of the accompaniment. At times these recurrences are almost imperceptibly woven
into the texture of the piece. *Dream-King* has such a unifying feature in the motive which first appears as a phrase in the tenor solo of
the middle section (Ex. 6-3A). It recurs at the conclusion of the
tenor solo and in the choral refrain, harmonized more ornately with
a descending chromatic line in an inner part (Ex. 6-3B). In the final
chorus, it is heard in a yet more complex setting, with an added
chromatic ascending line in the inner strings (Ex. 6-3C). Finally, it
appears at the close of the cantata in the violins over a sustained
dominant pedal (Ex. 6-3D). This type of thematic recurrence is
frequently used in the later cantatas and ceremonial works.

　　Although the Munich and New York cantatas quite under-
standably did not receive the critical attention bestowed on Parker's
later large choral works and operas, some evidence exists to show
the regard his contemporaries held for this music. *The Ballad of a
Knight and His Daughter* was listed in Wilson's *Yearbook* for

Example 6-3. Unifying refrain, *Dream-King*, Op. 31, vc. sc.,
　　GS, 1893

A. p.8, mm. 13-20.

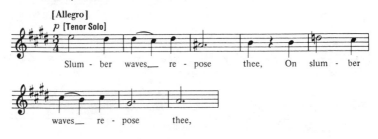

B. p. 9, mm. 8-15.

C. p. 23.

D. p.31, mm. 4-11.

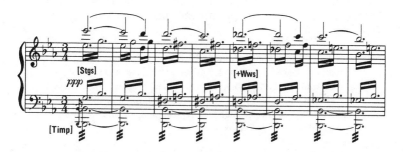

1892-93, together with a few of his other works, under the heading, "Important Works by American Composers."[3] *Dream-King* not only won the prize of the National Conservatory in the cantata division, but it seems to have been the unofficial favorite among all the prize-winning compositions performed at the Conservatory concert on 30 March 1893. *The Boston Evening Transcript* was enthusiastic about the work:

> It is a cantata of sterling merit, superbly melodious and throughout containing some of the most effective and masterly voice writing that has yet appeared from the pen of its gifted composer.[4]

King Trojan received the most numerous and extensive reviews. At its initial performance in Munich (1885), the American correspondent for the *Boston Evening Transcript* commented:

Both chorus and orchestra are treated with the skill of the
master and the self-possessed musician. It impressed me as the
most important and effectual work for mixed chorus and orchestra yet produced by an American, always excepting those
by Payne [sic].[5]

A New York performance by the Choral Art Society in 1887 elicited only mildly favorable responses. Henry Krehbiel reflected the
opinion of most in finding it to be "a smooth and melodious composition, capitally scored so far as the instrumental combinations are
concerned, but monotonous in color and feeling."[6] By the time
King Trojan was performed at the Worcester (Massachusetts) Festival in 1899, Parker was already recognized as a leading American
composer, and the Boston critics had the benefit of hindsight in
their evaluations. The critic for the *Boston Evening Transcript*
commented:

The work has unbounded melody, ingeniously expressed; has
many passages of genuine beauty and imaginative power, and
in instrumentation is both picturesque and graphic. Here Mr.
Parker hints at what was more broadly indicated in "Hora
Novissima", his independence of typical phrasing and his ability to work out conceptions of his own.[7]

The cantatas of the Munich and New York periods received
several important performances and, at least during the nineties,
were the principal medium in Parker's rise as an important composer. After the New York performance of *Dream-King*, most critics
were ready to award him the position of America's leading choral
composer if he could then produce a work of sufficient size, complexity, and originality to merit the distinction. They had only to
wait a little over a month when, in May 1893, the premiere performance of *Hora Novissima* confirmed their expectations.

Secular Cantatas: Twentieth Century

Fifteen years elapsed following the 1893 performance of
Dream-King before Parker again took up the secular, dramatic
cantata. By the time his *King Gorm the Grim* was produced at the
Norfolk Festival of 1908, he was a nationally acclaimed composer
and had extended his associations far beyond the German influence
of the early years. Nevertheless, he returned to Germanic and
Nordic legends which had dominated his early cantata period, for

King Gorm the Grim is the story of an aging Danish monarch who, to his profound grief, loses his only son in battle. Many musical features of the earlier cantatas are present; however, *King Gorm* is much more advanced in its colorful orchestral writing, the use of motivic association, and in the intensity of its tragic theme. For these reasons, it is an important forerunner of the opera *Mona*.

The two leading motives of *King Gorm*, those of the old King and his son Harald, form the melodic substance of the orchestral introduction and are evident throughout the entire cantata. The Gorm motive has a disjunctive rhythm characterizing the gruff, wizened ruler. It is the basis of the chorus for the first stanza and is fully realized in its concluding lines (Ex. 6-4). Harald's motive is heard in the orchestra passage concluding the chorus for the second stanza (Ex. 6-5), in the following orchestra interlude (vocal score, p. 7), and in the orchestral figures accompanying the next two stanzas. With its smooth rhythms and chromatic harmony, representing a comely, frail youth of fifteen upon whom his parents dote, it contrasts strongly with Gorm's motive.

Example 6-4. Gorm's motive, *King Gorm the Grim*, Op. 64, vc. sc., GS, 1908, p. 15, mm. 6-9.

The proportion of this short ballad given over to orchestral development of motivic figures is greater than that of even *St. Christopher* and *Mona*, two of Parker's most dramatic works. In a particularly effective interlude, the orchestra is called upon to represent the departure of Harald and the Danes and the ensuing battle with a distant enemy. The laconic march theme, beginning softly and building to a fortissimo, is followed by an abrupt dynamic change to piano and the sounding of Harald's motive, a musical premonition of the prince's death in this expedition (vocal score, pp. 17-20 .

Example 6-5. Harald's motive, *King Gorm the Grim*,
           Op. 64, vc. sc., GS, 1908, p. 15, mm. 6-10.

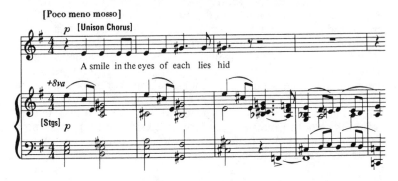

The closing chorus is a masterful dirge (pp. 23-26). King Gorm's queen prepares the hall for Harald's funeral, and Gorm finally accepts what all fear to tell him, that his son is dead. Parker sustains this pathetic mood right up to the closing chords of the orchestra.

King Gorm is depersonalized in that most of the story is related in third person and is sung entirely by the chorus, even the few spoken lines of Gorm and his queen. Nevertheless, by maintaining the focus of the tragedy on Gorm and his reaction to events, poet Theodor Fontane created a powerful and unified emotional impression which Parker was able to match musically.

Parker's positions as conductor of the Orpheus Club and Eurydice Chorus of Philadelphia (1907-16) enabled him to produce a number of original choral works and transcriptions which show his complete emancipation from the Germanic ballad. The part-song *Piscatrix* is based on a poem from the collection *A Peddlar's Pack*, by D. H. Holmes; *The Leap of Roushan Beg* is from Longfellow; *Alice Brand*, from Sir Walter Scott; and the *Seven Greek Pastoral Scenes*, from antiquity.

The Leap of Roushan Beg, for men's chorus, and *Alice Brand*, for women's chorus, follow closely the stylistic features of previous cantatas. Here, simple, homophonic choruses frame more dramatic inner segments, and concluding sections recapitulate parts of the opening choruses and material from the inner portions. These works have prominent, lengthy solos and divide into four rather than the usual three sections.

The Leap of Roushan Beg is a narrative of an Arab bandit's great love for his horse, which carries him to safety by jumping a chasm thirty feet wide in full view of his pursuers. This adventurous tale gave Parker an opportunity for the kind of bravura he had not indulged in since *The Norsemen's Raid* (1888) and "Cavalry Song" (1891). The climax of *Roushan Beg* occurs in the chorus of pursuing soldiers singing their melismatic chant to Allah (vocal score, pp. 12-13) as Roushan Beg and his horse leap over the chasm. The jump is illustrated musically in the accompaniment by an ascending, three-octave glissando followed by a descending, whole-tone scale (pp.19, m. 8, to p. 20., m. 3).

Alice Brand is a longer cantata with a more involved story. Sir Walter Scott's setting of the old Scottish narrative includes magic, chivalry, highly exalted womanhood, dwarfs, elves--numerous elements found in the many folk legends which had become the settings for many nineteenth-century cantatas. *Alice Brand* lacks opportunities for the colorful accompaniment and descriptive effects of *Roushan Beg*, but it does contain more solos and a more carefully integrated structure through the use of a head motive and refrains. Its pentatonic melodies, elemental harmony, Scotch-snap rhythms, and dance meters suggest folk-song features. *Alice Brand* and the symphonic poem, *Northern Ballad*, are the most explicit among Parker's compositions in reinforcing his "Anglo-Saxon" image.

While neither *The Leap of Roushan Beg* nor *Alice Brand* are major compositions, both have careful workmanship and fluent technique. Notable are the frequent interaction of choral and solo sections, the use of chorus both in refrains and as a dramatic agent, the ever-varying profiles of the associative melodic figures, and the vitality of the solos, from the self-contained aria to the flexible arioso.

The *Seven Greek Pastoral Scenes* for women's chorus have no dramatic continuity but rather are a group of short love poems drawn from the classic poets Meleager and Argentarius. The common subject is the salutation to spring. The timeless beauty of these lyrics inspired Parker to do some of his finest work.

Four short choral sections, each displaying considerable individuality, alternate with three equally brief but exquisite solos. The accompaniment consists of oboe, harp, and strings, a combination which the composer increasingly favored in his twentieth-century works such as *The Shepherd's Vision* and *Cupid and Psyche*. Piano is suggested as the alternate accompaniment and is quite adequate considering the relatively restricted writing for the orchestra.

In the three solo sections, an impressionistic atmosphere is maintained by undeveloped fragments of melody, tonal ambiguity, and coloristic rather than functional chord progressions. The first solo (No. 2), a tender dialogue between soprano and oboe can serve as an illustration. The simple chordal accompaniment is tonally ambivalent throughout. The first half of the song wanders from the tonic G minor, touching on but never confirming the tonalities of C major, E-flat major, and F minor (vocal score, p. 12, mm. 1-15). Although the melody, with its emphasis on the tonic and fifth scale steps, is strongly indicative of G minor, the diatonic descent through the lowered second degree suggests the Phrygian mode and creates an exotic atmosphere (Ex. 6-6). Finally, the piece ends on a C major chord, the subdominant of G minor.

Whereas the choruses of previous dramatic cantatas tend to be conservative, those of the *Seven Greek Pastoral Scenes* have fairly involved melodic, harmonic, and tonal structures and are quite different from one another. Aside from the stable, D major theme with which it begins and ends, the opening chorus is rhapsodic and modulates freely. The second chorus (No. 3) has a strong pulse and moderate-to-fast tempos. The unaccompanied chorus (No. 5) has the pervasive chromatic style found in the concert aria *Crépuscule*, also composed during this period. Both this and the last chorus have considerably more independent linear and imitative writing than Parker's other cantata choruses.

Three of the choruses are unified by a theme which, having evolved from foregoing melodic fragments, becomes fully evident at the climactic point near the end of the opening chorus (Ex. 6-7). The theme returns in the unaccompanied chorus (p. 24, m. 6), where it is freely treated, and again in the final chorus in more nearly its original form.

Example 6-6. *Seven Greek Pastoral Scenes*, Op.74, vc. sc., GS, 1913, p. 12, mm. 1-7.

The secular cantatas from the Philadelphia period are distinctive in that Parker returned to a *genre* that he had largely abandoned after his New York years. Following *Hora Novissima*, his principal growth as a composer can be traced through a number of increasingly dramatic larger sacred works which are capped by his two operas. Nevertheless, he continued to compose with great facility in a medium related to the cantata, the ceremonial or occasional work. The latter pieces are more lyrical than dramatic, and it is to these that we now digress briefly in the following chapter before resuming our study of his main line of development.

Example 6-7. *Seven Greek Pastoral Scenes*, Op.74, vc. sc., GS, 1913, p.8, mm. 3-6.

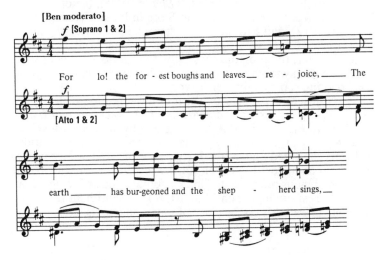

Chapter Seven

THE CEREMONIAL MUSIC

The Texts

As did many composers of his generation, Parker devoted an appreciable amount of time composing music for specific ceremonies. Nine compositions can be grouped under the heading of ceremonial works. Of these, four--*Ode for Commencement Day At Yale University 1895*, *Greek Festival Hymn* (1901), *An Allegory of War and Peace* (1916), and *A. D. 1919*--were written for celebrations at Yale University. The other five occasional works reveal the variety of events during Parker's lifetime that called for the writing of such cantatas: the presidential inauguration of Theodore Roosevelt (*Union and Liberty*, 1905); the dedication of the Albright Art Gallery in Buffalo, New York (*Spirit of Beauty* 1905); the opening of the present Wanamaker Department Store in Philadelphia (*A Song of Times*, 1912); and a tribute to an international service organization (*The Red Cross Spirit Speaks*, 1918). Judging from its size and subject matter, the remaining composition, *Laus Artium* (1898), must have been written for an important, but as yet unknown, occasion honoring some cultural endeavor.

Nowhere is the eclectic spirit of the times more clearly reflected than in the texts of *Laus Artium*, *The Greek Festival Hymn*, and *Spirit of Beauty*. *Laus Artium*, the text by an unknown writer, is a eulogy to art, particularly music. After a listing of the various art forms sheltered under "the lofty portal of Art's supreme domain" and an appeal to heaven for the restoration of "the age of gold," an obvious reference to Greek antiquity, music is singled out as "the fairest, youngest child of art." This sentiment reflects a statement of Parker's on the place of music among the arts:

> Although music is quite the youngest and probably the
> subtlest of the arts, it seems also the most democratic in com-
> parison with painting, sculpture and architecture, and I believe
> that for one person who will glow with enthusiasm for a beauti-
> ful painting, statue, or building, you can easily find a dozen
> who grow very warm about musical enjoyment.[1]

In addition to being the longest of the ceremonial texts, *Laus Artium*
is also the most diverse. Some of its passages also deal with patriotism and the waste and futility of war.

The poem, *Spirit of Beauty*, by Arthur Detmer, is yet another
appeal for a return to the spirit of classical Greece, an invocation to
"bring again the age of gold," the "splendor of the far-off days,"
when "great Apollo laughed" and "nymphs by hidden rills leaped
and danced."

Thomas Goodell's poem, *Hymnos Andron* or *Greek Festival
Hymn*, written and sung in classical Greek to commemorate the
two-hundreth anniversary of the founding of Yale College, is an
allegory on the importance of a university in society and a significant indication of the role that the classics played in university life
at the time. The opening strophe gives us an idea of the elevated
poetic style in these cantatas:

> Worthless appears the brief span of time
>> the stern hand of Fate on mortals bestoweth;
> Yet by noble and wise benefaction
>> man to the highest state is exalted.
> Then by will of Zeus
>> his work of devotion abideth,
> And he who hath wrought it
>> wins immortal renown.[2]

The earlier *Ode for Commencement Day, 1895*, has a similar
but less eloquent text written by another Yale colleague, Edmund
Clarence Stedman.

The poem for a *A Song of Times*, by John Luther Long,
departs from that *fin de siècle* yearning for a rebirth of classical
antiquity. It is, rather, based on another theme prevalent in American literature of the time--the exaltation of man in his present state
and a prediction for an even more glorious future. The role of
commerce is given special attention, thus making the poem a fitting
tribute for the refurbishing of a major retail store.

The remaining texts deal with patriotic and war themes. The
inaugural hymn for President Theodore Roosevelt, Oliver Wendell
Holmes's *Union and Liberty*, is a singular and fervent patriotic
sentiment. That portion of the Yale Pageant of 1916 with which

Parker was concerned, *An Allegory of War and Peace* (written by the pageant director, Francis M. Markoe), was described as "one of the most dramatic scenes . . . depicting . . . mothers who have given their sons for both war and peace."[3] The poem, like *A Song of Times*, is a paean to man's ingenuity in the manner of much pre-World War I literature. *The Red Cross Spirit Speaks* (1918) by John Findley is hardly more than a trite verse describing the activities of the International Red Cross Organization. For the poem to his last work, *A. D. 1919*, Parker had special affection. He is said to have declared that there was nothing he could add to its significance by way of music.[4] Written by Brian Hooker, the librettist of most of his major works in the twentieth century, it does have more literary merit than texts for the other ceremonial works. Nevertheless, the topical features of this ode to the Yale men who lost their lives in World War I outweigh its esthetic value, and this highly emotive poem has failed to create interest beyond its own time.

Musical Features

The musical structures of the ceremonial works have some variety within a consistent general plan. As the texts are not narrative, the musical organization tends to be more sectionized than much of Parker's other choral music. These pieces consist of three or four major parts which usually can be divided further into two to four sections and sometimes, in the case of the larger works, into further subsections. The final parts nearly always involve some type of recapitulation, usually of the opening part but occasionally of important themes in the center of these works. The middle parts usually introduce contrasting themes and meters and modulate more frequently than the flanking sections, but occasionally development of material from the opening section occurs.

Some works are exceptional. *The Red Cross Spirit Speaks*, for soprano and orchestra, is in modified strophic form, consisting of six stanzas. *The Greek Festival Hymn* has an orchestral introduction followed by six odes (each divided into a strophe sung by male chorus and an antistrophe sung by full chorus), and a postlude. *Laus Artium* is an extensive work and is divided into sections along the lines of *Hora Novissima* with full choruses, a solo, and a quartet. *An Allegory of War and Peace* is another large work with two self-contained Latin choruses as well as more fluid, descriptive episodes.

Key relationships are more conservative than in the dramatic cantatas and operas. One notable feature, the change from minor to major mode, usually accompanies a shifting of sentiment from a troubled to an exultant mood. For example, *A Song of Times* has an opening, D minor section, "Time was," a period of want and avarice, which contrasts with the final, D major, *maestoso* chorus, "Time shall be," a vision of man conquering the earth and reaching out into the universe with limitless ingenuity.

The melodies of these ceremonial cantatas are on the whole simpler than those in Parker's other choral works. The first strophe of the *Greek Festival Hymn* is illustrative of unadorned writing in which the composer nevertheless captures the exalted sentiment of the text. The diatonic melody has a somber nobility with the alternation of dactyl and spondee supported by nonchromatic harmony and a persistent quarter-note accompaniment in the bass line (Ex. 7-1).

Example 7-1. *Greek Festival Hymn*, Op. 53, vc. sc., GS, 1901, p. 2, mm. 1-8.

In these works Parker uses his full panoply of unifying devices. In addition to large recapitulations, we find the recurring refrain or phrase motive, the head motive, and ritornello themes. The opening motive of *Union and Liberty* can serve as an illustration. It is heard in two different forms in the first chorus (Ex. 7-2A & B), is further transformed in the middle section of the work, and is sung in augmentation against its original form in the recapitulation. Furthermore, the motive is also heard both as a fanfare in the introduction and in rhythmic diminution as an orchestral accompaniment (Ex. 7-2C) against the broad, chordal, cadential progressions in the coda.

Example 7-2. Unifying theme, *Union and Liberty*, Op. 60, vc. sc., GS, 1905.

A. As first theme, p. 5, mm. 2-5.

B. Transformation, p. 14, mm. 1-4.

C. Rhythmic diminution, p. 44, mm. 3-4.

An even more flexible motivic treatment is found in *Spirit of Beauty*. The principal motive, the most distinctive feature of which is the descent of a fifth (see brackets, Ex. 7-3), is heard in the instrumental introduction (Ex. 7-3A), in the opening choral statement (Ex. 7-3B), and in the subsequent interlude (Ex. 7-3C). In the third section, the principal motive again is used, underlining the appearance of the title words in the text (vocal score, p. 15, mm. 1-6).

Whereas in Parker's art songs, operas, major choral works, and parts of the dramatic cantatas, a fairly involved harmonic system seems to govern melodic contours, the plainer melodies of the ceremonial music are supported by a simplified and subordinate harmonic structure relatively free of chromaticism. There are

Example 7-3. Principal motive, *Spirit of Beauty*, Op. 61,
vc. sc., GS, 1905.

A. p. 1, mm. 11-15.

B. p. 2, mm. 16-17.

C. p. 2, mm. 18-19.

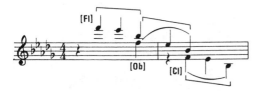

exceptions in some of the more ambitious works such as *Laus Artium* and even in such glorified hymns as *The Red Cross Spirit Speaks*. In the latter, the diatonic, opening melody undergoes a drastic change by the beginning of the third stanza as a result of increasing harmonic sophistication. The chromatic motion upward in the bass line from the tonic to the dominant of B-flat major in the opening measures of the third stanza (vocal score, p. 5, mm. 3-6) is a reversion to the harmonic mannerisms of the nineties; however, the sudden modulation one-half step upward to B major in the third measure is clearly a twentieth-century effect.

Parts of *A. D. 1919* are complex despite Parker's avowal that "it was written so that every man Jack in the audience might understand it."[5] Although the piece opens with a banal march theme, the middle section contains some of the composer's more advanced writing, a lyrical, triadic motive unfolding in sequences over an accompanying rhythmic figure consisting of a quarter followed by two eighth notes (Ex. 7-4). Frequent modulation, florid orchestral accompaniment, and free interchange of the lyrical motive between chorus and orchestra are reminiscent of the operas *Mona* and *Fairyland*.

Example 7-4. *A. D. 1919*, Op. 84, vc. sc., p. 14, m. 7-p. 15, m. 1. Copyright 1919, 1946, Yale University Press. Used by permission.

Polyphonic writing is less evident in the ceremonial works than in the larger choral pieces, although there are short fugal sections in both *Laus Artium* and *A Song of Times*. A favorite contrapuntal device, already noted in *Union and Liberty*, is the recapitulation of the opening theme, augmented to twice its normal time value, against motivic fragments in the original time value. The largely lyrical, homophonic, four-part writing is occasionally relieved by unison and two-part passages. Most unusual is the *Greek*

Festival Hymn, in which the choruses are written almost entirely in unison, with division into parts only at a few climactic points.

Solos are less numerous than in any other type of larger choral work. They are generally more elaborate than the choral melodies and appear in the middle portions of the *Ode for Commencement Day, Laus Artium, Greek Festival Hymn, A Song of Times*, and *A. D. 1919*. Several works such as *Union and Liberty, Spirit of Beauty*, and *An Allegory of War and Peace* are without solos. *The Red Cross Spirit Speaks* exists in both solo and choral arrangements.

Most of the instrumental accompaniments are conceived largely in terms of rhythmic and harmonic support for the voices. Independent, contrapuntal lines are unusual, and descriptive writing is greatly reduced from that of Parker's other choral works. The introductions, usually about twenty-four measures in length, present themes which are used later in the body of the work. Less frequent are those motivic-saturated interludes of the dramatic cantatas and oratorios which are such a distinctive feature of Parker's style. Most interludes are simple transitions from four to eight measures in length. *Spirit of Beauty, Union and Liberty*, and *An Allegory of War and Peace* have wind band as well as orchestral accompaniments. *A Song of Times* is almost a *tour de force*, calling for an accompaniment consisting of a bugle corps and organ in addition to band or orchestra. At the Philadelphia performance, Parker is said to have declared the combined effect "the most thrilling he had ever heard."[6]

The *Greek Festival Hymn* has colorful, nineteenth-century orchestration which contrasts with its neoclassic melodies, restricted harmonies, and simple form. The alternation of brass, woodwinds, and strings in the introduction to the first strophe, the choir of lower brass instruments at the beginning of the second section of the same strophe (vocal score, p.3, beginning. m. 17), the use of clarinet, bassoon, cello, and horn at various times to double the baritone solo line (p. 6), and the use of *pizzicato* (p. 1) show that variegated tone color is an important ingredient of the work.

The ceremonial cantatas are a musical type which had strong appeal during the late nineteenth and early twentieth centuries. In the eighties, George P. Upton had called Paine's *Oedipus Tyrannus* "the most important and scholarly work an American composer has yet produced."[7] Later, H. E. Krehbiel, a critic who knew Parker's music intimately, considered the *Greek Festival Hymn* as one of the composer's very best pieces and made repeated laudatory references to it at various times. At the time of the initial performance during the Yale Bicentennial, he wrote:

> They [Goodell and Parker] have attempted for modern purposes
> and with modern agencies to reproduce the spirit and to some
> extent also the body of antique choral art. . . . The *Greek
> Hymn*, for its successful mediation between the ancient art of
> music and the modern art of music, is simply masterful.[8]

As in the case of *A Wanderer's Psalm*, in which Parker used Gregorian chant as one of the themes, the blending of the old with the new fascinated critics like Krehbiel; however, immersion in the past had to be tempered with "modern agencies." Actually, cultivated musicians and music lovers at the turn of the century were easily satisfied with just a few general allusions to older music. An interest in historical styles for their own intrinsic merits was still far ahead in the twentieth century.

The ceremonial works reflect the changing social and political issues of the times. The turn-of-the-century pieces deal with lofty esthetic, patriotic, and ethical themes, while those of the 1910-20 period are concerned with industrial progress and war. Parker set these texts with restraint, using formulas which he had developed in his cantata writing during the eighties and nineties and occasionally injecting newer, twentieth-century features; however, his significant growth as a composer did not occur in this *genre*. His early development had been in the medium of the secular cantata, and, beginning with the composition of *Hora Novissima* in the early 1890s, the large sacred work was to become his principal vehicle of expression for the next decade. These compositions are examined in the following chapter.

Chapter Eight

THE LARGE SACRED CHORAL WORKS

Overview

The most ambitious of Horatio Parker's choral works are his three oratorios--*Hora Novissima* (1893), *The Legend of Saint Christopher* (1898), and *Morven and the Grail* (1915)--each coming from a different style period and each reflecting a distinctive phase in the evolution of the oratorio at the turn of the century. Two Psalm settings, *Psalm für Soprano Solo, Frauenchor, Orgel und Harfe* (1884) and *A Wanderer's Psalm* (1900), are from the Munich and the English periods respectively. The two Christmas cantatas, *The Holy Child* (1893) and *The Shepherds' Vision* (1906), were written for church rather than choral festival performance; accordingly, they are discussed in the chapter on church music. The remaining large works of a religious character are single essays in various types. These include the prize-winning, unaccompanied, eight-part chorus *Adstant Angelorum Chori* (1898); another prize-winner, the highly individualistic "Choral Rhapsody" *A Star Song* (1902), from the English period; and the "Morality" *The Dream of Mary* (1918), commissioned for the Norfolk, Connecticut, Festival.

Parker's large sacred works are impressive in both number and scope when compared with those of other nineteenth- and early twentieth-century American church composers. Although Chadwick and Foote made significant contributions to religious choral music, neither were identified as church musicians to the degree that Parker was. Among Parker's immediate Boston forerunners, J. C. D. Parker had written some modest religious cantatas (*Redemption Hymn* and *Saint John*) and an oratorio (*The Life of Man*), which were popular in the eighties and nineties. The facile Dudley Buck, on whom the mantle as America's foremost church composer had rested prior to its assumption by Horatio Parker, wrote several reli-

103

gious works of cantata length and a single large oratorio, *The Light
of Asia*. This oratorio, a setting of Sir Edwin Arnold's famous epic
depicting the life and teachings of Buddha, was first performed at
one of Novello's oratorio concerts in London (1885), the only major
American composition to receive such attention in England prior to
Hora Novissima. Buck is, however, remembered today more for his
tuneful quartet anthems.

Another predecessor was the Philadelphia organist, William
Wallace Gilchrist, who attracted some attention when, for his setting of Psalm 46, he was awarded a $1,000 prize offered by the
Cincinnati May Festival in 1882. Among the features of this piece
are a dynamic, highly descriptive orchestral accompaniment and
nearly the gamut of prevalent choral styles, from the opening choral
hymn through the demonic heathen's chorus to the final fugue.[1]

During the early eighties, Gilchrist probably was on the
periphery of young Horatio Parker's musical environment, but John
Knowles Paine was definitely near the center. This erudite Harvard
professor was a pioneer in the field of American oratorio, as he had
been in so many other areas of musical activity. His *Mass in D*
(1865) is one of the few large choral works by nineteenth-century
American composers to have a twentieth-century renascence,[2] and
his *Saint Peter* (1873) not only holds the distinction of being the
first full-length native oratorio but is comparable to many continental and English oratorios of the time. *The Nativity*, written about ten
years later, is less distinctive.

But it was the European tradition which actually provided
primary inspiration for young Parker. Both his Boston youth and
study in Germany gave him the opportunity to become thoroughly
acquainted with this repertory which forms the background for his
own works.

The Lord Is My Shepherd

Parker's single religious essay of cantata proportions before
Hora Novissima (1893) is a setting of the Twenty-third Psalm
(*Psalm für Soprano Solo, Frauenchor, Orgel, und Harfe*), composed at Munich during the summer of 1884. Whereas his contemporaneous secular cantata, *Ballad of a Knight and His Daughter*, is
restricted to choral writing, *Psalm* has both choral and soprano-solo
sections, and the soprano voice is also used as an obbligato in the
final chorus. *Psalm* has a more complex modulatory scheme than
Ballad. The sacred piece attracted some attention at its first performance in Munich on 13 December 1884:

More recently a setting of Psalm XXIII was given, of which the Munich *Fremdenblatt* speaks as follows: "Mr. William Parker (from Rheinberger's class) has repeatedly shown his talent as a composer. The Psalm XXIII . . . has not, to be sure, the character of a church composition, but it is a stout piece of work for the concert room, where it will always win applause." The *Allgemeine Zeitung* calls the psalm a "work which bespeaks a great and vigorous talent."[3]

Parker's mother Isabella provided a more intimate account of the concert:

> I wish all my friends could have heard the 23rd Psalm which was sung at the last concert. . . . It was the most beautiful composition of his that I have ever heard. The harp was played by a nice young German girl, and the whole sung in German. Mr. [Henry Holden] Huss played the organ and Will directed. The piece was received with great enthusiasm. They called Will back after it was over and shouted Bravo! Bravo!--and the paper, whose criticisms mean something, spoke of it next day as "a grand and talent-showing work."[4]

Twenty years later in 1904, the work was published with a few revisions and English text as *The Lord Is My Shepherd.*

Hora Novissima

The nine years between the performance of *Psalm* and that of Parker's next major religious work *Hora Novissima* (1893) were ones of considerable compositional growth. The several secular cantatas composed during the Munich and New York periods helped him to acquire the technique necessary to deal with large choral structures, expressive harmony, and colorful orchestration. His early art songs gave him a chance to develop skill and subtlety in handling the solo voice. Finally, his organ pieces provided the opportunity for polyphonic writing. On the other hand, his many anthems and sacred songs from this time have the least direct bearing on his increasing skill and artistic sensitivity. Their utilitarian purpose necessitated a more simplified approach to composition.

Parker's intimate associations with New York choral organizations in the late eighties and early nineties and the abundance of oratorio performances in both New York and Boston were incentives for choral composition. Not only was the established repertory frequently heard, but newer works such as Alfred Gaul's *The Holy City*, Gounod's *Redemption*, Max Bruch's *Arminius*, and Edgar Tinel's *Franciscus* were given American performances shortly after their premieres at the English choral festivals.

Equally important to Parker's development were his visits to the English festivals themselves in 1890 and 1892, from which he made first-hand acquaintance with the extensive revival of choral music that Great Britain was experiencing. The well-rehearsed, amateur choirs of the cathedral towns provided opportunity for performance of many works by both continental and English composers.

Thoroughly steeped in this choral tradition, Parker, nevertheless, bypassed the usual dramatic Biblical plot of the typical Victorian oratorio and chose as a text for his first major choral work one of the contemplative, medieval Latin poems. Rather than adding to the already numerous settings of the *Requiem*, *Stabat Mater*, or *Te Deum*, he turned instead to a portion of the less well-known *De Contemptu Mundi* by Bernard de Morlaix, a medieval monk from the French monastery of Cluny, whose work was then enjoying popularity largely as a result of a translation by the nineteenth-century English scholar and theologian, J. M. Neale.[5] Although the complete poem is a discourse on the sinfulness of the world, that section beginning with the line "Hora Novissima" is a joyful vision of eternal life in the celestial city.

Chadwick claims that Parker first considered a setting of the poem, *Vita nostra plena bellis*, but had abandoned it "on account of the monotony and inflexibility of the text".[6] Parker gave the following account of his choice of the *Hora Novissima* text:

> I selected that poem, not because it is particularly the best one of its kind, but because it best suited my purpose. It occurred to me that, as the "Stabat Mater" had been made so beautiful in the musical setting, this could be made as well. At the same time, my uncle, a Professor of Latin and Greek at Dartmouth, to whom I wrote a description of what I wanted, also recommended this poem.[7]

The carefully planned structure of *Hora Novissima* is an important part of the impression it makes on the listener. Parker's division of the poem into eleven sections gives the oratorio the approximate size of Rossini's and Dvořák's settings of *Stabat Mater*, which are divided into ten parts each. Three elaborate choruses (I, IV, VI) serve as an opening, middle, and closing for Part One, and two other complex choral movements constitute the middle (VIII) and closing (XI) sections for Part Two. The quartet (II) and unaccompanied chorus (X) are balanced as the second and penultimate numbers respectively. The solos, one for each member of the quartet, are evenly distributed--those for bass (III) and soprano (V) in Part One, and for tenor (VII) and alto (IX) in Part Two.

Parker used many unifying devices throughout *Hora Novissima*. Frederick Burton's comment that it should be called a "choral symphony" may have been prompted not only by the manner in which the larger choruses have the character of symphonic movements, but also because of the way certain themes pervade the entire work in the manner of the cyclic symphony.[8] These unifying devices will be noted in the discussion which follows, first of the choruses, then the quartet, and finally the solo sections.

The tripartite opening chorus has, in addition, an orchestral introduction and a coda. The exposition (vocal score: p. 2, m. 27, through p. 6) and recapitulation (p. 11, m. 6, through p. 14) follow sonata-form key relationships. The middle section (p. 7, m. 1 through p. 14) is one of contrast rather than development. The coda is very lyrical with its slower-moving choral line over a new legato orchestral motive (p. 15, m. 1, through p. 18).

The principal theme of the introduction and opening chorus (Ex. 8 -1A), is germinal for many other themes in the oratorio and is based on a pattern of descending fourths. It possesses a distinctiveness and solemnity whether it sounds alone, as in the introduction, or later against the declamatory lines of the opening chorus (p. 8, mm. 27-31).

Example 8-1. Themes from *Hora Novissima*, Op. 30, vc. sc., N. 1893.

A. Germinal motive, p. 1, mm. 11-15.

B. Fugue subject, p. 37, mm. 1-4.

The second chorus "Pars mea, rex meus" (IV) is subtitled "Introduction and Fugue." The subject (Ex. 8-1B) is a free inversion of the principal theme from the opening chorus, suggesting that this movement could be considered developmental in the overall structure of the oratorio. One must turn to the recital pieces for organ to find other cases of such extended polyphonic writing among Parker's earlier works, although a few scattered points of imitation are present in the secular cantatas. The "Introduction" is a thematic reservoir from which material is drawn for both the subsequent fugue subject and the episodes. It also serves as a modulatory section from the previous bass aria in D minor to the fugue proper in E-flat major. The fugue itself is divided into three tonal areas, the two larger E-flat sections flanking a C minor section. The subject is heard in its entirety twelve times in a symmetrical arrangement of four times for each of the three sections. The first two sections are devoted to the subject and its answer, which occupy all but seven of thirty-eight measures (pp. 37-41). The strict imitative texture is then relaxed in the final section to permit a working out of the subject along the lines of sonata-form development procedures (pp. 41-47). The fugue reaches its climax as the chorus sings the subject in augmentation against its original metrical version in the orchestra (beginning p. 47, m. 4). With a strong bass line consisting of repeated eighth notes and an organ added to the already considerable orchestral resources, the effect is overpowering. Such writing as "Pars mea" fully justifies the high opinion Parker's contemporaries held concerning his contrapuntal skill.

The third chorus "Tu sine littore" (VI), which closes Part I, is largely a recapitulation of materials found in the opening chorus and is similarly organized. A new, hymnlike melody, derived from and used in counterpoint to the principal theme from the first movement (now simplified to half notes) again reminds the listener of the carefully established thematic relationships in the oratorio (Ex. 8-2).

The massive double chorus "Stant Syon atria" (VIII), from Part II, was compared by Philip Hale to the scherzo movement of the Beethoven *Choral Symphony*.[9] Hale jokingly added that the piece is suggestive of "waltzing in the Holy City." The composer's skill in handling the two choruses is evident in the variety of textures he is able to achieve, from massive homophonic to intricate polyphonic writing. As usual Parker's counterpoint is essentially harmonically oriented, with thematic fragments that fit together and are easily exchanged among the orchestral and voice parts.

This "scherzo" is interesting rhythmically through the use of occasional hemiola and irregular phrase lengths in the first and third subsections. In the second and fourth subsections, the principal cyclic theme appears majestically against the rhythmic scherzo

Example 8-2. "Tu sine littore," *Hora Novissima*, Op. 30,
    vc. sc., N, 1893, p. 57, mm. 7-10.

motive (Ex. 8-3). The relation of this cyclic theme to the principal
motive (Ex. 8-1) is apparent in their similar harmonic support and in
the prominence of the fourth as a melodic interval. The cyclic
theme first appears in the coda to the earlier bass aria (p. 34, mm. 2-
5) and in the final chorus (p. 154, m. 4-p. 156, m. 3).

Example 8-3. "Stant Syon atria," *Hora Novissima*, Op. 30,
    vc. sc., N, 1893, p. 95, mm. 1-2.

The unaccompanied chorus "Urbs Syon unica" (X) immediately precedes the final chorus and serves as a serene section, much
in the manner of penultimate slow movements in many romantic
symphonies. The chorus was highly praised in its time by W. J.
Henderson as being derived from "Holbrecht, Brumel, and Josquin
DePres," a statement which has since been criticized as being "very
wide of the mark."[10] There are superficial resemblances to the
Netherlands motet style. Parker chose a four-two meter, which
gives the music the appearance of the older music editions available

at that time. The steady rhythmic flow, the arched curve of the melody and the use of successive points of imitation based on thematic fragments all allude to the Renaissance style (Ex. 8-4). Even a few archaic mannerisms such as the use of open-fifth and open-octave intervals are present (p. 120, m. 10; p. 126, m. 12). On the other hand, the tonal scheme, chord progressions, points of climax, and constant dynamic fluctuations belong to the nineteenth century. Perhaps Parker was aware of the enthusiasm which English festival audiences had shown for Gounod's unaccompanied chorus "Requiem aeternam," in the "old style," from *Mors et Vita*.[11] American audiences were equally impressed by Parker's neo-Renaissance writing, even those who criticized other parts of his oratorios.

Example 8-4. "Urbs Syon unica," *Hora Novissima*, Op. 30, vc. sc., N 1893, p. 116, mm. 1-5.

The final chorus "Urbs Syon inclyta" serves as a culmination of important themes in the work much in the manner of the typical romantic symphony. Like many of the previous choral themes, the principal theme of the last movement is derived from the germinal motive of the first movement, the original descending fourth patterns now inverted to ascending fifths (Ex. 8-5). The choral writing varies from unison to extended antiphonal and homophonic sections. The orchestra is given an important function in the unfolding of the musical ideas by means of a lengthy introduction and two substantial interludes. Finally, the breadth provided by the *maestoso* tempo and the weight of the brass and organ make the concluding chorus a grand finale.

    Hora Novissima's choral writing was considered its most impressive feature. William Henderson spoke of it as "superb in its treatment of parts."[12] The *Musical Courier* compared the fugue subjects with those of J. S. Bach and concluded: "All is noble, dignified, serious, and earnest."[13] Philip Hale commented: "Poly-

Example 8-5. "Urbs Syon inclyta," *Hora Novissima*,
Op. 30, vc. sc., N, 1893, p. 128, mm. 13-16.

phony does not become a mere answer to a self-imposed
problem. . . . Mr. Parker has a peculiar facility in contrapuntal
writing, in expressing his thoughts in the severe style." Howard
Malcolm Ticknor conceded that Parker's craftsmanship kept the
vocal ensembles "interesting even when a long and fully wrought
fugue is present." Another writer declared rhapsodically: "We felt
ourselves seized hold of and borne up by a very strong hand. . . .
His choruses grow stronger, more vital and impressive as they go
on; little by little they wrap their tentacles about you and carry you
away unresisting." The English critics were later to recognize
Parker's mastery in choral writing. *The Musical Times* called it
"massive and effective."[14] Vernon Blackburn, in his review of the
Worcester Festival performance of 1899 for *Pall Mall* magazine,
commented favorably on the "broad swing of many of the
choruses," although he considered the part-writing "not oversubtle"
in its ingenuity.[15]

With frequent instances of *fugato* treatment, of double
counterpoint and use of augmentation, the choral polyphony of
Hora Novissima is based upon the Handel-Mendelssohn tradition.
In spite of their retrospective nature, such choruses as "Pars mea,"
"Stant Syon atria," and "Urbs Syon inclyta" compare favorably in
design and amplitude with polyphonic choral sections from well-
known nineteenth-century works such as the "Liber scriptus,"
"Sanctus," and "Libera me" from Verdi's *Requiem*, and the choral
fugues from the third and seventh sections of Brahms' *German
Requiem*.

In the discussion of the choruses above, we have noted
Parker's concern with establishing thematic unity in his oratorio.
Before proceeding to a discussion of the quartet and solo arias, we
should consider other unifying features which contribute to the
remarkable cohesiveness of this oratorio.

A pervasive if subtle unifying feature is the rhythmic pattern
of nearly every theme: a pattern consisting of long notes flanked by
those of shorter value and marked by either a stressed or an agogic
accent at midpoint. This rhythmic motive is evident in the choral

sections described above as well as in the solos and the quartet (see brackets in Ex. 8-6); yet, each theme has its own individuality. As with the choral themes, fourths and fifths frequently act as pivotal intervals in the melodic contours of the solo and quartet melodies. Another group of themes has a lyricism which resembles the style of the nineteenth-century Anglican hymn. They are set to arpeggiated or repeated harmonic-rhythmic accompaniment patterns and usually appear as introductory orchestral material, as counterpoint to the first and more basic group of themes, as second-subject themes in the sonata-form sections, and as contrasting themes in the solos. Two themes of this group recur in cyclic manner, thus providing yet another unifying feature for the oratorio. The first appears as the second theme in the opening chorus (Ex. 8-7) and is heard later as the orchestral accompaniment to the middle section of the alto solo (p. 12). The second, an orchestral theme from the coda of the opening chorus (Ex. 8-8), reappears as the head motive to the soprano aria (p. 49, m. 3), and then as the orchestral accompaniment to the double chorus in the finale (p. 142).

Finally, another recurring passage serves as a connecting device rather than a theme. It nevertheless is striking and consists of an ominous sounding, descending chromatic line followed by an appoggiatura figure. It appears twice in the opening chorus (p. 2, mm. 5-12 and p. 9, m. 8 through p. 10, m. 8), in the closing chorus to Part I (p. 68, mm. 6-15), and in the finale (p. 141, mm. 9-15). The appoggiatura figure alone recurs briefly in the tenor solo (p. 76, m. 15).

The texture of the quartet and solo portions of the oratorio contrasts with the polyphonic severity of the choral sections. A more sensuous musical style is evident in lyrical writing, a richer harmonic palette, and highly colorful orchestration where incidental solos for woodwinds are abundant. The quartet "Hic breve vivitur" resembles closely another quartet "Quis est homo," from Dvořák's *Stabat Mater*: in position as the second number of each work; in structure, with imitative openings followed by full, homophonic sections; and in texture, with a lyrical melody (Ex. 8-6E) supported by a persistent but subdued rhythmic accompaniment.

Although their principal themes do share a common rhythmic basis (Ex. 8-6), each solo aria is highly individualistic. The bass solo "Spe modo vivitur" has the foreboding if not the wrathful sentiments common to the English oratorio tradition. The pentatonic outline of its principal theme is a feature common to composers of the Boston group.[16] The soprano solo "O bona patria" is the least complex with its relative tonal stability, angular melody, and repeated accompaniment figures.

Example 8-6. Themes from solo sections and quartet of *Hora Novissima*, Op. 30, vc. sc., N, 1893.

A. Bass aria, p. 29, mm. 9-13.

B. Soprano aria, p. 49, m. 19-p. 50, m. 2.

C. Tenor solo, p. 75, mm. 9-14.

D. Alto solo, p. 110, m. 22-p. 111, m. 2.

E. Quartet, p. 19, mm. 5-6.

Example 8-7. Second theme from opening chorus, *Hora Novissima.* Op. 30, vc. sc., N, 1893, p. 4, m. 8-p. 5, m. 5.

Example 8-8. Theme from coda of opening chorus, *Hora Novissima*, Op. 30, vc. sc., N, 1893, p. 16, mm. 5-11.

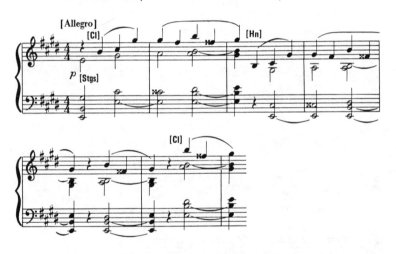

    The alto solo "Gens duce splendida" contains a variety of moods: a martial orchestral introduction, a joyous first section, and a sentimental middle part. The use of the orchestra to echo fragments of thematic material in the solo voice (Ex. 8-6D) and the militancy of the orchestral accompaniment again reminds one of Dvořák's *Stabat Mater*, specifically his treatment of the alto voice in the opening to the quartet "Quis est homo" and the solo "Inflammatus."

    The style and melodic contour of the tenor solo "Urbs Syon aurea" is reminiscent of "Ingemisco," from Verdi's *Requiem* . Its freely evolving melody, pervading chromaticism, and kaleidoscopic orchestral figures make it the most ornate section of the work. One writer exuded: "[The tenor] will be so enraptured that he will possibly want to scream it rather than to sing it restrainedly."[17] In the solo sections, Parker overcame to some extent the rigid two-measure phrasing which dominates so much of this oratorio. Phrase extensions by means of repetition and sequences are frequent; however, even more freedom in rhythmic flexibility and melodic growth is occasionally found, such as in the middle section of the bass aria, where the normal two-measure, six-beat phrase is expanded into phrases of seven beats (4/4 plus 3/4 time) and then into a climactic phrase of eleven beats (Ex. 8-9).

Example 8-9. Excerpt from bass aria, *Hora Novissima*, Op. 30, vc. sc., N, 1893, p. 31, mm. 9-11.

In the conservative 1890s, the alto and tenor solos appeared to be quite forward-looking, enough so that one critic considered them "the weakest portions of the work" because of their "exuberant instrumentation, unsettled tonality, and continual modulations." Today, these solo portions appear to be an attempt to follow the Italian tradition of sensuous religious writing. Although Parker professed to disdain Italian opera, he did admire the religious works of Pergolesi, Rossini, and Verdi. The blending of sacred and secular so characteristic of Italian oratorio is, after all, compatible with the ideas of many esthetically inclined American Protestant churches at the turn of the century.

The social gospel of the nineties encouraged the use of secular ideas in church music, but this tendency did not go unchallenged. Although little discussion regarding the "secular" aspects of

Hora Novissima occurred after the New York premiere, the Boston performance the following year (1894) elicited considerable argument. Philip Hale cited certain sections which he considered to be too operatic:

> In the very first chorus the phrase "Recta remuneret" might be sung by any chorus in any half dead Italian opera, while the conductor is stamping the time and the atmosphere of the stage is heavy with garlic. In the quartet, in the soprano solo, and in the choral passages, as in the "Spe tamen ambulo" . . . there is an opera house in sight. (*Boston Journal*, 5 Feb 1894)

On the other hand, Howard Ticknor took umbrage with Hale and defended what he called the "florid-ecclesiastic" tradition:

> We cannot coincide in the opinion of the learned and able critic of the Journal [Philip Hale, above] that Mr. Parker has oscillated or fluctuated between the church and the opera house. It seems to us that Mr. Hale does not allow full weight for the disposition of Catholic music to take to itself all brilliant secular forms, provided there be contained within them a spirit serious enough to accord with the services of a ritual which appeals to the eye through costume and processional and lights, and to other senses by priestly intonings and by the diffusion of incense and perfume. (*The Musical Courier*, c. 1894).

In a revealing letter to the *Boston Evening Transcript*, the composer and organist Homer A. Norris noted: "One can hardly meet an average harmony student who does not call the work thoroughly interesting and enjoyable, but too operatic." He concluded that oratorios should evolve just as other musical forms and insisted that "Puritanical prejudice" caused many to insist on "self-suppression" in writing religious music. Morris did not put the matter to rest, for, at each subsequent performance of the work in Boston, the argument was renewed.

Hora Novissima reached the apex of its popularity during performances at Boston in 1897 and Worcester, Massachusetts, in 1898. Reviews of these events treat the oratorio not with the usual curiosity which accompanies a novelty, but rather with the sort of accolades accorded a well-established work. Nearly a decade after its composition, Frederick Burton called it "one of the few oratorios with which the musical world is familiar," and noted that it was then being performed in the United States more frequently than any other oratorio.[18]

Hora Novissima maintained its popularity well into the first part of the twentieth century. By 1918, however, qualifications such as this one following a Handel and Haydn Society performance, were finding their way into usually favorable reviews:

> Under the test of the years, the finer, the inner qualities of "Hora Novissima" endure and retain all their freshness. At the same time the episodes obviously constructed to "fill in," the casual musical ideas incompatible with the theme and the text, the Wagnerian influence which a quarter of a century ago were to be expected in orchestra writing, are rapidly aging.[19]

If this review suggests that *Hora Novissima* might become a "period piece" rather than hold a permanent place in the standard repertory, the years following World War I saw its importance as the leading American oratorio fade considerably. The reviews of these performances show that the part of *Hora Novissima* which retained its vitality was its conscious association with contrapuntal religious music of the past. The remainder--soaring melodies, opulent harmonies, frequent modulations, and colorful orchestration--seemed no longer to be new and exciting but, rather, stereotypes of a period that had suddenly become unfashionable.

Some critics of today discount even the polyphonic sections as "academic" and stress the lack of originality of the work as a whole. Gilbert Chase has noted the frequency, even in Parker's time, with which certain passages or sections of *Hora Novissima* were said to resemble those in the works of other composers from the Renaissance masters to the European Romantics, "all of which," he concluded, "adds up to a rather disconcerting hodgepodge of influences."[20] Certainly today's listener is surprised by nearly direct quotations such as the ascending contour of the "Dresden Amen" in the coda of the first chorus (p. 17, mm. 1-7) and the sudden appearance of a fragment of the "Wedding march" from Mendelssohn's music to *A Midsummer Night's Dream* at the climax of the closing chorus to Part I (p. 72, mm. 4-11). Most critics of Parker's day casually acknowledged but were not very concerned about reminders of other composers' music. Perhaps Vernon Blackburn expresses this point of view best in his discussion of the 1899 Worcester, England, performance:

> To say that he had pieced his work together . . . from other composers' ideas would be the wildest injustice, and would show indeed that the whole spirit and genius of "Hora Novissima" had been absolutely missed. . . . The man was full of ideas and imagination, and, perhaps with lack of stern criticism and careful sifting, but certainly with perfect gaiety, good

humor, and courage, he set them all down in due order. To
deny the thing originality is to avoid the work altogether. It has
the best originality in the world, that of being alive in itself, of
possessing liberality, freedom, extraordinary openess of sentiment. I do not know where else to look in quite recent music
for just these qualities.[21]

Hora Novissima had captured the taste of the pre-World
War I musical public, but its popularity waned in the more ascetic
atmosphere following the Great War. As we approach the cente-
nary of its creation, a recognition of its inventiveness and craft,
coupled with a more tolerant attitude towards its eclectic features,
should re-establish it as a monument both in the history of the oratorio and in American music.

The Legend of Saint Christopher

Parker's second oratorio, *The Legend of Saint Christopher*
(1898), followed *Hora Novissima* by about five years. Its libretto is
the longest and best of those that Isabella Parker wrote for her son.
In choosing the medieval legend of the Syrian giant Offerus who,
after serving both royalty and the devil, finally turned to Christianity and, in the act of carrying the Christ child across a swollen river,
earned both his name ("Christ-bearer") and sainthood, Parker
embraced a theatrical subject typical of those found in many nineteenth-century oratorios.
   The most direct precedent for *Saint Christopher* is Rheinberger's cantata, *Christophorus*, on the same subject, written in
1880, only two years before Parker went to Munich. In place of
Rheinberger's division into two parts, Parker's book has a "prologue" and three "acts," each of which deals, in order, with the
temporal, demonic, and religious phases of the story. In Rheinberger's cantata, the incidents of the story unfold in a rather contrived
manner: for instance, a "voice" speaks to the giant dissuading him,
first, from service to the King, and then, from service to Satan. In
Parker's work, these incidents grow from more plausible dramatic
situations showing Offerus's disillusionment with his earlier masters: first, the sight of the King trembling by a haunted wood, and,
later, of Satan cowering before the cross. Parker also relied to a
greater extent than Rheinberger upon more plastic musical tech-
niques--dialogue, arioso, and motivic orchestral interludes--to por-
tray the various stages of the giant's conversion to Christianity.

The most progressive features of *Saint Christopher*, those which most clearly justify its classification as a "dramatic" oratorio, are symphonic interludes, continuously unfolding music in long sections of each act, and the prominence of leading motives. Parker had previously given some attention to matching text with appropriate music, but, in *Saint Christopher*, he suddenly demonstrated a mastery of fully developed Wagnerian premonitory, associative, and reminiscent devices.

The fanfare which opens the oratorio reappears in Act II, where it is identified with the giant Offerus's conversion to the Christian faith (vocal score; cf. p. 1, mm. 1-3 with p. 91, mm. 5-7; Ex. 8-10). King Oriens's motive, another fanfare first heard in Act I (p. 6, m. 23-p. 7, m. 2), later becomes associated with the religious hermit of Act III in an orchestral interlude (p. 112, m. 15-p. 113, m. 2), and the listener realizes that this impoverished ascetic was once the proud king.

Example 8-10. Offerus fanfare motive, *St. Christopher*, Op. 43, vc. sc., N, 1898, p. 91, mm. 5-9.

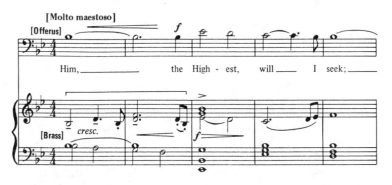

Satan's motive is the most varied and frequently used of the short fanfare group. It first appears as a premonition in the second scene of Act I when King Oriens, having acquired Offerus as a servant, expresses the fear that the giant might be lost to a greater master (Ex. 8-11A). In some of its several transformations, the motive is found as a succession of legato quarter notes in one of the orchestral interludes (Ex. 8-11B) and in waltz rhythm in the second of Satan's arias (Ex. 8-11C).

Whereas these and other call-type motives occasionally punctuate the texture of *Saint Christopher*, the lyrical motives, with their greater adaptability to lengthy sequential treatment, make up a

Example 8-11. Satan's motive, *St. Christopher*, Op. 43, vc. sc., N, 1898.

A. p. 37, mm. 10-12.

B. p. 52, mm. 12-14.

C. p. 87, m. 26-p. 88, m. 1.

larger portion of the work. One of the most poignant is the descending figure signifying Offerus's search for the greatest master (Ex. 8-12), rich in augmented, minor, and diminished chords and suspensions. Another motive, a descending scale pattern treated sequentially, refers to Offerus's obeisance (Ex. 8-13). Yet another motive portraying the character of Offerus is that associated with the giant's conversion to Christianity (Ex. 8-14); it is similar to the obeisance motive in its linear descent and approaches the expansiveness of Wagnerian treatment in the conclusion of Offerus's aria and the following orchestral interlude (pp. 77-78).

The ten orchestral sections which are scattered throughout the work contain the greatest concentration of leading motives. Suggestions of this kind of orchestral writing are found on a smaller scale in the secular cantatas as far back as the student period. Essentially, motivic material is amplified in elaborate sequential patterns. Particularly notable are the interludes between the scenes

Example 8-12. Offerus search motive, *St. Christopher*,
Op. 43, vc. sc., N, 1898, p. 7, mm. 12-15.

Example 8-13. Offerus obeisance motive, *St. Christopher*,
Op. 43, vc. sc., N, 1898, p. 21, mm. 3-7.

for Act I in which the Offerus and King Oriens motives are developed (pp. 18-19, 24-25, 37), the introduction to the hunting scene
(Act I, Scene 3) with its numerous calls and other rustic motives
(pp. 38-41), and the preludes to the first and last scene of Act III in
which motives associated with Christianity and the storm are heard
(pp. 103-107, 159-163).

Other parts of *Saint Christopher* blend these newer dramatic
techniques with the older sectional structure. The processional
scene in Act I is divided into men's, maidens', soldiers' choruses,
and finally a double chorus. Nevertheless, a continuous musical
flow from one chorus to the next is present, and the various choruses are unified by a "processional" motive which is first heard in
the orchestral introduction (p. 6, mm. 1-4). This motive is expanded
into a theme which becomes a principal musical idea in the maid-

ens' chorus and the double choruses (p. 11, mm. 5-8; p. 15, mm. 3-6).

Example 8-14. Offerus conversion motive, *St. Christopher*, Op. 43, vc. sc., N, 1898, p. 77, mm. 9-16.

The newer musico-dramatic techniques are absent in some choral and solo sections. The Queen's aria from the middle scene of Act I (pp. 25 -31) is illustrative of the symmetry so apparent in *Hora Novissima*. Its AB-AC structure is interrupted by the King's shorter, more dramatic arioso, and a brief choral refrain is used to conclude each half of the aria. An *Andante* tempo, a lyrical melodic line, chromatically moving inner parts, and the smooth rhythmic patterns of this section contrast with the more turbulent, angular style of the surrounding scenes. Another aria, that of the hermit from the opening scene to the last act (pp. 114 -116), with its sweeping melody and sensuous harmonies, is also self-contained.

Among the independent choruses, the homophonic prologue and its considerably modified recapitulation as the closing chorus of the oratorio (cf. p. 1 with p. 180) give the oratorio a more traditional cast. Another independent section, the affirmation of Christian faith in Act II, "On the cross the Lord of Heaven died" (pp. 80-84, 93-99), is impressive, with its imitative choral writing against a contrapuntal accompaniment in the orchestra.

The most extensive choral writing is found in the set of three consecutive "ecclesiastical" choruses of Act III (pp. 124-140). The dramatic justification for these lengthy, independent sections is Offerus receiving instruction in the lessons of the church. Each chorus follows a traditional setting: "Gloria in Excelsis Deo" is festive, employing incisive rhythms and florid orchestration; "Agnus Dei" is placid with its homophonic choral style; and "Quoniam, Tu solus sanctus" is an imposing fugue, the subject being the accompaniment figure from the previous "Gloria." One of the outstanding examples of traditional writing in the work, the fugue was reported to have "caught the fancy of the house" at the Carnegie Hall premiere and interrupted the performance of the work long enough for the composer "to bow his acknowledgements from a first tier box."[22]

The foregoing choruses suggest that Parker wished to retain in *Saint Christopher* the choral style for which he was so highly praised in *Hora Novissima*; therefore, one is not surprised to find an unaccompanied chorus, "Jam sol recedit," near the conclusion of *Saint Christopher* (pp. 149-154). It serves as a reflective moment before the final chorus and invokes a superficial allusion to the Palestrina choral style like its prototype, "Urbs Syon unica," from *Hora Novissima*.

Late nineteenth-century oratorio composers rarely passed up the opportunity to contrast the sacred and the profane musically. George McFarren's *John the Baptist* and Edgar Tinel's *Franciscus*, (The latter was heard in New York in 1893) stress such a duality. In *Christophorus*, Rheinberger had used a highly turbulent chorus describing the wandering giant who becomes ensnared by Satan and followed it with a reposeful, religious section. In *Saint Christopher*, these sacred-profane contrasts are given the most conservative musical settings: the sections are clearly defined, and the thematic material is ordinary. Excepting the more contemporary harmony, Satan's first aria (pp. 59-62), with its dotted rhythms, disjunct melody, and subordinate orchestral accompaniment, recalls the standard "furious" oratorio solo for bass, such as Polyphemus's aria from Handel's *Acis and Galatea*. The musical ideas and structure, modified strophic form, and concluding chorus, give the aria even the somewhat comical aspect of a Gilbert and Sullivan operetta. Satan's second aria, in which he tries to dissuade Offerus from leaving, is less stereotyped (pp. 86-90). Here temptation is suggested by waltz time. The accompaniment is more flexible, with the occasional use of Satan's motive (Ex. 8-11C) and some text painting such as a fanfare on the word "call" (p. 89, m. 29). The conflict between church and the devil reaches its climax in an antiphonal section (pp. 70-74) which dovetails the conclusion of the lengthy male chorus representing Satan's legions (pp. 62-73) with the beginning of the religious chorus for women, "Asperges me, Domine" (pp. 74-76).

As the character of Offerus is constantly evolving, his several dramatic arioso sections contrast with the fixed portrayals of the King, Queen, Satan, and the hermit. Parker was to use this same relationship in his last oratorio, *Morven and the Grail*, in which the restless, ever-searching figure of Morven is given a fluid, evolving setting as opposed to the set forms for other characters and ideas.

In *Hora Novissima* Parker had achieved a remarkably unified oratorio, in spite of diverse musical elements, not only by the rather obvious means of using some recurring principal melodies but also by establishing subtle intervallic and rhythmic relationships among the large body of themes. Such integration does not appear to be the goal of *Saint Christopher*, which emphasizes inclusiveness rather than unity. All of the elements of the nineteenth-century oratorio are present, the newer, dramatic techniques along with the older, architectonic ideas. The result is a work which lacks the sharp definition of *Hora Novissima*, in spite of Parker's earnest purpose and some of his best writing in places.

Because of its variety, critics of the first American performance were diverse in their reactions. Although Henderson, Krehbiel, and Elson were generally complimentary and admired the "ecclesiastical" portions of the work the most, some of their comments makes one wonder if they were discussing the same work. For instance, Henderson found "no traces of modernity," claiming that it could have been written fifty years previously "by the contemporaries of Mendelssohn." Likewise, William Apthorp complained of a Puritanical tendency and implied that Parker might have taken his church a little too seriously. "He may have a sort of chasteness of artistic feeling that renders ordinary music-dramatic methods repugnant to him, as unworthy of being associated with a sacred subject"[23] On the other hand, Elson described Parker's dramatic style as overbearingly modern and containing "sections where modulations pursue each other into a tonal jungle, where enharmonic changes grow thick as blackberries in August. . . . Hell is full of syncopation and diminished seventh chords."[24] Those closest to Parker reserved their praise largely for the more conservative sections of the oratorio. Chadwick called "Jam sol recedit" "an unsurpassed masterpiece,"[25] a judgment echoed by David Stanley Smith, who noted that the "slightly Wagnerian treatment" did not interfere with "clarity and reserved elegance and formalism."[26]. Smith described the "Gloria in excelsis" and "Jam sol recedit" sections as "Parker's finest."

Saint Christopher never achieved the popularity of *Hora Novissima* in the United States, which was not willing to accept such extensive Wagnerian dramatic trappings in a religious oratorio;

however, it appears to have been more favorably received in England. When Parker first went there in 1899 to conduct *Hora Novissima*, he left the impression that he considered *Saint Christopher* the superior work.[27] His good friend, the Worcester organist Ivor Atkins, was also very enthusiastic about it.[28] *Saint Christopher* was given a single full performance at Bristol and a presentation of the third act only at Worcester, both in 1902.

After the Bristol performance, the London *Telegraph* reacted in a manner quite different from that of the earlier American critics by showing its preference for the dramatic portions and complaining of the "lengthy choruses without sufficient dramatic justification." The London *Times* also approved of *Saint Christopher's* operatic qualities:

> The whole seems to be contrived operatically as if it were designed for Bayreuth, or some stage where religious subjects could be presented without offending pious susceptibilities. . . . It is probable that an opera from his pen would obtain great results.[29]

Undoubtedly Parker drew sustenance from such an evaluation when, in middle age, he turned to opera.

Adstant Angelorum Chori

The consensus of the critics was that the unaccompanied sections of *Hora Novissima* and *Saint Christopher* were among the best parts of those works. The judges for the New York Musical Art Society competition for an a cappella work (1898) may therefore have been predisposed toward recognizing Parker's excellence in this medium by selecting his *Adstant Angelorum Chori*, for eight-part chorus, as the winner.

Based on the medieval poem attributed to Thomas à Kempis, the subject of *Adstant* resembles that of *Hora Novissima* in that it is another ecstatic vision of the celestial country--a chorus of angels standing with "bells resounding" and "garments blazing," singing praise to the "Sovereign Deity." The English translation, by Parker's mother and frequent collaborator, Isabella, captures the rapture of Thomas's poem.

Although a lengthy unaccompanied choral composition was unusual for American composers of the time, the form was also essayed by Arthur Foote, with his *Vita Nostra Plena Bellis*, and Charles Martin Loeffler, with *One Who Fell in Battle*. Both Foote's and Parker's works are similar in that they contain a wide variety of choral devices and are organized into expository, contrasting, and recapitulating sections. Foote's composition is divided into eight parts and tends to be homophonic throughout. Parker's work has five musical sections (parts of the four stanzas of poetry are repeated in the fifth musical section) and contains a fugue, antiphonal and canonic writing, short points of imitation, some pictorial effects, and large climaxes built by means of sequential patterns and extended cadences.

The opening melody of *Adstant* is written in the style of an Anglican hymn. The clarion-like theme of the antecedent phrase and the contrasting, conjunct motion of the subsequent phrase provide the basic musical materials for the first section of the piece (Ex. 8-15).

Example 8-15. Opening period, *Adstant Angelorum Chori*, Op. 45, GS, 1899, p. 1, mm. 1-10.

The first four lines of the second stanza (pp. 14-24) are set as a sturdy, four-voice fugue. For the last part of the section, the E-flat minor "Sanctus" theme from the first stanza returns in E-flat major (tenors) and is joined with the musical material of the second stanza (Ex. 8-16).

Example 8-16. Excerpt, second section, *Adstant Angelo-rum Chori*, Op. 45, GS, 1899, p. 22, mm. 3-7.

The change of meter (from 4/4 to 3/8 time) and pace (from *Allegro* to *Allegretto*) clearly mark the third stanza as the contrasting section of the motet. Its rich harmonic texture is less bound to conventional church style. The fourth stanza of the poem is transitional, and, in the fifth and last section of the motet, parts of the fourth, second, and first sections are recapitulated in a reversal of thematic succession, a practice Parker was to use later in the *Organ Concerto* of 1902.

A few instances of text-painting are evident, the most obvious being a detached, quarter-note figure sung antiphonally on the words "Tympanizant, citharizant" (pp. 2-3). A more significant compositional feature is the impressive series of climactic points scattered throughout the work. Each section reaches its momentary peak; however, the recapitulation sustains a musical loftiness throughout that matches the exalted poetry.

Following its initial performance by the Musical Art Society of New York in 1899, the work was given a very favorable review in *The Monthly Musical Record*:

> The work is decidedly modern in its general harmonic plan,
> though ecclesiastical harmonies are frequently employed in it.
> The polyphony is uncommonly rich and varied. The voice
> parts are brilliantly written and are very effective.[30]

The writer considered the finest part to be the fugue but concluded that the chief obstacle to its popularity would be its difficulty. He noted: "Few choruses would be able to sing it."

Although the *Sun* criticized the motet for its "slightly monotonous" tendency and commented that it "occasionally strays from an ecclesiastical character," the remaining New York newspapers expressed very favorable opinions.[31] Most reviewers followed the lead of Krehbiel, who highly esteemed what he called the blending of the old with the new. With *Hora Novissima, The Legend of Saint Christopher*, and *Adstant Angelorum Chori*, Parker had established an eclectic style to which responsible criticism in America reacted favorably. He was to continue this manner of writing in the immediate years ahead with *A Wanderer's Psalm* and *Hymnos Andron*.

A Wanderer's Psalm

A Wanderer's Psalm was commissioned for the Three Choirs Festival held at Hereford, England, in 1900. Parker worked on the piece during the winter of 1899-1900 following the well-received performance of *Hora Novissima* the previous summer in Worcester, England. Not surprisingly, the new work is a somewhat condensed version of the earlier oratorio.

The independent sections of *A Wanderer's Psalm* (reduced to seven from the eleven of *Hora Novissima*) and cyclic treatment of themes are obvious similarities. The choruses show further evidence of modeling. The first chorus has a broad and dignified opening followed by a quieter, more lyrical section, as does its prototype. The large, choral third movement, with its opening fugato and lyrical, homophonic middle section, combines elements found in the extensive middle choruses of Parker's first oratorio. Also the use of a penultimate unaccompanied chorus had by this time become a hallmark of Parker's choral writing. Finally, the last chorus introduces a new closing theme and also serves as a general recapitulation of several thematic elements from the entire work in the manner of *Hora Novissima*.

Turning to the solos, one finds those for alto (No. 2) and soprano (No. 5) to be self-contained ternary forms with florid orchestral accompaniments reminiscent of the clearly marked structures and sensuous writing in solo sections of *Hora Novissima*. Although far from literal, the principal theme of the alto solo (No. 2) is closely modeled after the earlier oratorio's bass aria, "Spe modo vivitur," in contour, pentatonic structure, tonality, and accompanying texture.

A *Wanderer's Psalm* does have some features different from its model. In the central movement, the bass solo and chorus beginning with the text "They that go down to the sea in ships," Parker turns to associative writing more characteristic of *Cáhal Mór* and *Saint Christopher*. The short orchestral introduction has an undulating eighth-note figure descriptive of the heavy, rolling motion of the seas, and the bass solo line dips to a low A on the words, "His wonders in the deep" (vocal score, p. 57, m. 14). The orchestra continues with several pictorial devices depicting the storm in the following chorus. Among these are a sixteenth-note figure (p. 58), which doubles the previous rhythmic motion, a rising and falling chromatic line (p. 60), a careening melody for the words, "They reel to and fro" (p. 65, mm. 1-4), and a sudden climax for "at their wit's end" (p. 65).

The London *Times* found this descriptive writing excessive, complaining: "In the necessity of providing picturesque musical illustration . . . the composer . . . has not paid due regard to the necessity of preserving a dignified style." The reviewer called the aforementioned "reeling" figure "a really ludicrous bit of realism."[32]

The actual use of the Gregorian peregrine psalm tone is surprisingly incidental considering that the piece bears the subtitle, "Tonus Peregrinus." A rhythmic paraphrase of the first part of the plain song is intoned by the trombones in the orchestral introduction (Ex. 8-17) and in the opening and closing choruses. The plainsong also appears in another place, the orchestral accompaniment to the soprano solo (p. 82). H. E. Krehbiel praised Parker's embellishment of the chant:

> He [Parker] blends the learned forms proper to sacred music with the modern descriptive style. . . . The Peregrine tone contains no suggestion of the monotonous chant. It never occurs in its baldness, but is presented in a variety of phrases, changed in rhythm, changed in harmony, changed in feeling.[33]

Parker did not confine his borrowing of melodies to the peregrine tone. One cannot fail to be reminded of the familiar English horn solo from the slow movement to César Franck's *Symphony in D Minor* on hearing the opening measures of the soprano solo (p.80, mm. 8-12). Parker may not have known Franck's symphony; however, he must have been aware of the resemblance of his choral motive in the storm scene (p. 59, m. 4) to the well-known horn call which opens *Der Fliegende Holländer*.

The provincial English press was quite laudatory after the 1900 Hereford performance. The London papers, however, were

Example 8-17. Use of peregrine tone in orchestral introduction, *A Wanderer's Psalm*, Op. 50, vc. sc., N,
1900, p. 2, mm. 14-17.

considerably more discerning and spoke out decisively against the
conservative style as well as the apparently blatant borrowing of
themes from other composers' works. At the same time, some
admired Parker's handling of the orchestra and the "boldness" of his
conception. Practically all were favorably impressed by his skill as
a contrapuntist.[34]
   The reviews of the Boston performance the following
December were decidedly more unfavorable. Philip Hale reflected
the majority opinion in writing: "This Psalm was written to order,
and I regret to add that it makes the impression of perfunctory
labor." He found the work "labored," "unimaginative," and "disappointing."[35]
   Peter C. Lutkin's favorable opinion stands in contrast to the
others. In a review of the published vocal score, he lavished on the
piece such descriptions as "heroic mold," "practiced hand of a
master," and "keen sense of rhetorical and aesthetic values." He
continued with a flattering assessment of Parker's position in
American music and his role as the model for a distinctively American style of composition:

> That America can produce such a work is a matter of great
> encouragement and congratulations. Professor Parker's
> choral works rank worthily beside the very best of modern
> compositions in that line. They seem to foreshadow an Ameri-
> can school of composition--one which we hope will be based on
> directness, condensation and diatonic strength.[36]

This concept of the "American school" resembles Parker's
own ideas on the matter; however, Lutkin's admiration for *A
Wanderer's Psalm* appears to be singular. The work disappeared
from the concert stage after the Boston concert of 1900.

A Star Song

The difference between *A Wanderer's Psalm* and *A Star Song*, written during the following winter of 1901, is so major as to indicate a great deal of soul-searching during that time. Whereas *A Wanderer's Psalm* is a backward glance, a reworking of techniques already utilized in *Hora Novissima*, *A Star Song* shows an awareness of the transformation that English choral music was undergoing at the turn of the century.

Parker's travels during this period gave him an opportunity to be an observer of both English and continental activities. Upon arriving in England for the summer of 1900, he received the following communication from A. G. Jaeger, a representative for Novello:

> Will you stay over for the B'ham [Birmingham] Festival? It will be the most memorable Festival to *English* Art since Festivals began: *two real creations, original, strong, beautiful*: Taylor's "Hiawatha" and Elgar's extraordinary, inspired "Gerontius," the biggest thing *any* English composer has ever done--you don't think much of E. E., I know, but wait till you hear this "Gerontius."[37]

Parker was unable to stay in England long enough to attend the Birmingham Festival that fall, but he heard the second and much better presentation of *The Dream of Gerontius* at Düsseldorf in June of 1902.[38] A short time later, he led the New Haven Oratorio Society in performances of both works.

The revolutionary nature of *Gerontius* is two-fold. First, the entirely personal nature of John Henry Cardinal Newman's text replaces the stereotyped Biblical figures which had been the subject of so many nineteenth-century oratorios. Second, the dramatic organization of the music, a continuous unfolding of associative themes, is substituted for the traditional sectional structure. Rubinstein's "sacred opera," *The Tower of Babel*, and Parker's own *Saint Christopher* are forerunners in the attempt to weld the newer dramatic style onto the oratorio. What effect *Gerontius* may have had on the composition of *A Star Song* is pure conjecture; however, some newer features of the latter--expansiveness in melodic line, a more subtle harmonic conception, and greater freedom in phrase structure--suggest that Parker was advancing along the same musical path as Elgar.

The poem by H. Bernard Carpenter, on which Parker based his *Lyric Rhapsody* (the subtitle for *A Star Song*), is an effusive allegory in which the permanence and strength of universal love are symbolized as the morning star shining from the heavens. The use of simile and metaphor is so profuse as to render the meaning obscure. Consider the following verse from Part II:

> Lo, the moon sinks dim As a bead on a goblet's rim
> Whence the feaster has drained, the last
>   spark of its life resplendent,
> And the sky's deep cup downturn'd With light unadorned,
> Hangs hollow, unjewel'd with stars
>   Above earth impendent;

The stilted elegance of such lines in an extended poem caused one of England's most respected critics, Vernon Blackburn, to react rather strongly:

> The poem is weak. . . . A riot of words, an almost unmeaning piling of phrase upon phrase, a most amazing disregard of metaphor--these are the characteristics of the poem which Dr. Parker has taken for his inspiration. The result is literally something like chaos.[39]

The musical setting is divided into four parts, one for each section of the poem. To English audiences, accustomed to ample choral sound in opening movements, Part I of *A Star Song*, titled "Introduction, Choral Recitative, and Tenor Solo," must have been disappointing, for its proportions are miniature rather than massive. The "Introduction" is scored for the extremely high registers of the flutes and violins as background to the opening motive in the clarinets, bassoons, and cellos, which is spun out with an expansiveness quite different from the hymnlike compactness of opening themes from Parker's earlier oratorios.

The "Choral recitative" proceeds, but not by the usual accumulation of polyphonic lines; rather, each of the four vocal parts in turn is given a line drawn either from the opening motive or a countertheme. The sopranos sing the first line of verse, occasionally joining with the violins (Ex. 8-18). The basses then enter, accompanied by pizzicato strings and percussive brass chords, followed by the tenors and then the altos--each accompanied by a characteristic orchestration. In no voice, however, does the theme take on a memorable contour. A more conventional tenor solo then completes the movement. The structure and melodic style, radically different from the traditional oratorio opening, elicited scathing denunciation from Blackburn: "He [Parker] has chosen to be daringly modern. . . . The old melody has shivered into space; even the old *soupçon* of imitativeness has given place to a singularly hard and dry sentiment."

Example 8-18. Excerpt, opening chorus, *A Star Song*,
   Op. 54, fl. sc., JC, 1902, p. 9, mm. 4-11.

As *A Star Song* progresses, the more familiar elements of
Parker's choral style appear. Parts II and III have clearly etched
choral and solo themes and ternary forms. Part IV, a quartet and
chorus, "When night goes abroad," begins as a general recapitulation of the introduction to Part I, continues with a homophonic
quartet (full score, p. 73), then antiphonal writing between the

quartet and the chorus (p. 94), and finally, a large climactic choral section (p. 96)--all usual procedures in Parker's previous works. Parker used cyclic devices to unify the work. In the middle section of Part II the languid rhythmic and melodic style of the opening movement returns, and in Part III, the vaporous principal motive from the opening movement is heard. It also reappears in Part IV as a point of imitation in the quartet (p. 83) and later as orchestral accompaniment to the antiphonal section.

Although Parker did fall back on some of his time-tested devices in choral writing, the piece never quite recovers from its daring opening and leaves the listener with a remote, indefinite impression. The tonal organization also contributes to its strangeness. For example, the climax of Part IV is effected on an E major chord (p. 96), an augmented fifth above the final A-flat cadence.

The single performance of *A Star Song* at the Norwich Festival received the most unfavorable criticisms of any of Parker's presentations in England. Vernon Blackburn, who had admired *Hora Novissima*, commented: "Professor Parker has taken an excursion to the stars, and none will be more happy than his English admirers when he finally decides to return to earth." The *London Standard* described much of the piece as "a series of sound patterns," and the *London Telegraph* evaluated the work as scholarly but lacking in inspiration: "Effects are sought; they do not come [naturally]. . . . Less elaboration in structure, and more spontaneity in expression, less study and more impulse would be a change for the better."[40]

A Star Song is a pivotal work, a change in direction which now can be followed mostly in the dramatic music that was to command his most fertile creative energy for the next decade, for Parker would not write another large religious work for nearly fourteen years. In the concert aria *Crépuscule* and in the opera *Mona*, he would continue to discard many of the stylistic elements with which he had been identified during the nineties and concentrate on an increasingly chromatic language to serve the poetic or dramatic idea.

Morven and the Grail

Thirteen years, two major operas, some incidental music to plays, some secular cantatas, art songs, and a few instrumental compositions separate *A Star Song* (1902) from Parker's next major religious work, *Morven and the Grail* (1915). Much had happened in the field of oratorio while he had been otherwise diverted.

Following *Gerontius* (1901), Elgar had written *The Apostles* (1903) and *The Kingdom* (1906). Frederick Delius had drawn on Nietzsche for his *A Mass of Life* (1904), and Sir Granville Bantock had composed some of his most important oratorios and unaccompanied choral works. Americans were also writing different types of choral pieces: among them, Frank Van der Stucken's *Pax Triumphans* (1906), Frederick Converse's *Job* (1907), George Chadwick's *Noël* (1908), and George Henschel's *Requiem* (1913). *Morven* takes into account some of the philosophical conceptions found in these works, particularly those of Elgar.

Morven also shows some relationship to Parker's earlier works, particularly *Saint Christopher*, written nearly seventeen years before. *Morven* contains three parts; *Saint Christopher* is divided into three acts. Morven, the hero, searches for the Holy Grail; Offerus (Saint Christopher) seeks the greatest master. On the other hand, a significant difference exists between Isabella Parker's pictorial libretto to *Saint Christopher* and Brian Hooker's symbolic text for *Morven*. Morven passes through various phases: sensuality (Part I), heroism and then asceticism (Part II), only to discover that the Holy Grail is not to be found in any one of these but rather followed through all (Part III). The quest is completed by the end of Part II, and Part III is devoted to the meaning of that search. In *Saint Christopher*, Offerus's search continues until the final chorus, thus sustaining the dramatic action almost to the end.

Morven falls short of that elemental dramatic motion which propels *Saint Christopher*. The quaint, humanized Satan of *Saint Christopher* is replaced in *Morven* by a more abstract conception of man's struggle to overcome evil. This modern interpretation of the Christian message has neo-Hegelian trappings: a continual process of self-renewal and a striving for more perfect self-realization are substituted for the older concept of attaining an ultimate, blissful repose in Heaven. The ideas in *Morven* are so recondite that Hooker felt it necessary to insert explanations between the various sections of the poem printed at the head of the vocal score.

Although Cardinal Newman's verse, *The Dream of Gerontius*, is also philosophical, its dramatic setting is contemporary, whereas *Morven*, carries the accessories of many medieval tales. Like *Saint Christopher*, the dramatic resolution of *Gerontius* occurs near the end of the oratorio, when the spirit of Gerontius is brought before the throne of the Almighty to the great chorus "Praise to the Holiest." The following dramatic scene with the "Angel of Agony" almost exactly balances the previous epic statement of the chorus, and a short, meditative choral section closes the work. With Hooker's Protestant story, Parker is denied a Roman Catholic composer's opportunity to picture the terrors of Judgment. Because Morven completes his search in Part II, Parker must make his supreme choral effort, "Saints in Paradise," shortly after the middle of the oratorio. He has little dramatic action to set musically for the third and final part.

As he had done for each Act of *Saint Christopher*, Parker maintained a continuous musical flow within each Part of *Morven*; however, the subsections of the three Parts are more self-contained, their connection sometimes being so tenuous as a single sustained note. Within each Part, Parker contrasted architectonic sections, such as the large choruses "Dwellers in Avalon," "Heroes of Valhalla" (Ex. 8-19), "Saints in Paradise," and the final "On earth," against more fluid, dramatic areas, much as Elgar had done in *Gerontius*.

Example 8-19. Excerpt, "Heroes in Valhalla,"
            Morven, Op. 79, vc. sc., p. 69, m. 13-p. 70,
            m. 6. Copyright 1915, 1942, Boston Music Company,
            116 Boylston St., Boston, MA 02116. Used by per-
            mission.

Parker also uses dramatic-musical associations, although certainly not to the extent of his contemporaneous opera *Mona*. The most striking association is the "call" motive (Ex. 8-20), which is sung by the Angels of the Grail following the orchestral introduction and at several places throughout the oratorio. In its function as a summons for Morven to continue his quest, this motive undergoes several transformations throughout the work. Its most distinctive feature is a sudden, lurching chordal progression from F-sharp to B-flat at the cadence point. Such advanced harmonic writing places *Morven* clearly in the style of *Mona*, although the sectional structure of much of the oratorio suggests a transition to Parker's final, simpler style.

Example 8-20. Call motive, *Morven*, Op. 79, vc. sc., p. 12, mm. 1-5. Copyright 1915, 1942, Boston Music Company, 116 Boylston St., Boston, MA 02116. Used by permission.

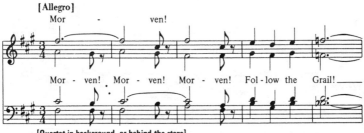

As with Gerontius and Offerus, the character of Morven is usually treated in the dramatic, arioso style. At times descriptive devices are used in the orchestra, such as the florid violin part accompanying Morven's singing about the sea early in the oratorio (Ex. 8-21). These instances are not nearly so frequent as in previous works such as *A Wanderer's Psalm*.

Parker's use of antiphonal writing in the manner of a litany for the quartet against the slower melody of the chorus (Ex. 8-22) may have been influenced by *Gerontius*. The lovely theme which turns on a descending seventh interval is the principal motivic material for much of Part III.

Parker's attempt to revitalize the overworked Victorian oratorio style received some recognition from critic Philip Hale. Writing in the *Boston Herald*, he described Parker's new style as an "enriched harmonic idiom," a "new sense of the delineation and

Example 8-21. Arioso, *Morven*, Op. 79, vc. sc., p. 18,
    mm. 1-5. Copyright 1915, 1942, Boston Music
    Company, 116 Boylston St., Boston, MA 02116.
    Used by permission.

emotional suggestion of instrumental timbres," a "new freedom of
modulation," and the subservience of "form and procedure" to "the
imaginings and the emotions, the picture, the vision and the impulse
that are the real content of the music."[41]

Writing for the *Boston Advertiser*, Louis Elson expressed his
approval of the more traditional parts of *Morven* but cautioned:

> Mr. Parker has departed in a great degree from the learned
> ecclesiastical school of which he was such a master, and is
> entering more and more into the dramatic field, in which he is
> much weaker. He does not seem to have the operatic instinct.

Example 8-22. Excerpt, "On earth," *Morven*, Op. 79,
   vc. sc., p. 181, m. 8-p. 182, m. 5. Copyright 1915,
   1942, Boston Music Company, 116 Boylston St.,
   Boston, MA 02116. Used by Permission.

H. T. Parker, of the *Boston Evening Transcript*, approved of
the craft shown by the composer in "the manipulation of choral
masses," "a sense of large and ordered design," "artful procedure,"
and "ingenious detail." Nevertheless he concluded: "The music
never transports the hearer out of himself and into the fullness of
illusion. . . . [Parker's] severity of ideal seems to deprive his music
of vitality, to make it only semi-articulate on the emotional side."

Among the newer generation of critics, Olin Downes was most severe, going so far as to call the work "mawkish," "uninspired," and "barren of ideas."
Morven and the Grail was the last of Parker's compositions to receive a premiere in Boston during his lifetime. In the twenty-one years between the Handel and Haydn Society performances of *Hora Novissima* (1894) and *Morven* (1915), the composer's works had run the gamut from acclamation to rejection there. Whether or not the critics approved of a particular composition, they usually applied such adjectives as "scholastic," "intellectual," and "austere" to his music. These words dogged Parker throughout his career.

The Dream of Mary

Parker's last major composition on a religious theme, the "Morality" *The Dream of Mary* (1918), was written after the composer was well into his final stylistic period. This phase of his writing can be described as having two essential characteristics: that of recalling some idiomatic features which predate his dramatic period and of making an effort to overcome his reputation for complexity by writing in a plain, more accessible manner. *The Dream of Mary* is yet another manifestation of Parker's great interest in the religious-dramatic forms of the past (in this case the medieval morality play) and his attempt to embody them with contemporary techniques. Chadwick, who shared this interest, said of the style: "Parker returned to a simple form of expression appropriate to such an art form."[42]
The work is divided into ten parts and covers the various seasons of the church year. The music consists of congregational hymns, solos, ensembles, choral sections, melodramatic recitations, and orchestral interludes. In constructing the libretto, John Jay Chapman, the noted American writer, selected appropriate Biblical passages, arranged their order, and added some sections of his own. The dramatic thread is the dream in which the Virgin Mother foresees the birth, life, death, and resurrection of Christ.
Chapman had treated the same subject before, in 1911, when he wrote a text for a *Christmas Cantata*, with music by Philip Goepp, the Philadelphia organist, composer, and critic.[43] Except for a few minor changes such as locale (Goepp's work has a present-day setting), the two stories are practically identical. Nor does the similarity end there. Many of the structural features of *The Dream of Mary* which were considered "novel" by the critics--the congregational hymn singing, the trios of shepherds and of kings, the

melodramatic recitation--are also present in Goepp's cantata.[44] An antecedent to both Parker's and Goepp's works, however, is Chadwick's *Noël*, which preceded *The Dream of Mary* as a commissioned work for the Norfolk Festival by ten years and which has the same story and a similar structure.

Undoubtedly the most impressive feature of *The Dream of Mary* is its performance plan. The piece has an unusual degree of audience participation. Parts I ("The first Christmas"), II ("The Doxology"), IV ("The Advent"), and VI ("The children"), all open with hymnlike melodies sung in harmony by the chorus, children's choir, and "congregation." The audience also participates in sections of Part V ("The miracles of faith"), Part VIII ("The burial"), and joins in the finale of Part X ("Christmas once more") to bring the entire piece to an impressive close. The esthetic appeal of the work is further enhanced with melodramatic recitation and tableaux, devices then very popular in post-war America. For a performance at the Brooklyn Opera House on 29 March 1920, the staging was described as very effective.[45]

Although the *The Dream of Mary* has the usual solo and choral sections that the public had come to expect in a standard oratorio, emphasis on an impersonal, relatively unadorned writing causes some monotony. Such striking ideas as the crucifixion and the resurrection are treated in the same mildly chromatic style as the less sentient parts. Some individuality can be found in hymn harmonizations, solo sections, and in the orchestral writing, particularly the postludes that conclude some of the sections, but, only with the single fugue closing Part IV does Parker achieve the grand effects of his earlier oratorios. With anthem and hymn styles alongside sections exhibiting more compositional artifice, *The Dream of Mary* is inclusive of both Parker's mundane and festive religious music styles. Herbert Sanders described the work as a superior one of its type, noted the excellent blend of text and music, and commented on its lack of performing difficulty.[46]

Such works as Chadwick's *Noël*, Goepp's *Christmas Cantata*, and Parker's *The Dream of Mary* are musical relics of a religious-esthetic bond which, although an important feature of American culture during the early years of the twentieth century, has largely gone the way of the multifarious Victorian oratorio. *The Dream of Mary* was one of the last attempts Parker made to appeal to a wide public, but the work, almost from the moment it was written, was outmoded by swiftly changing styles during the second decade.

From *Saint Christopher* to *The Dream of Mary*, most of Parker's major religious compositions display in varying ways considerable concern for dramatic textual treatment. The main line of his evolution as a composer was guided by his increasing concern

for dramatic values, a condition which became clearly evident shortly before the turn of the century. The most direct manifestation of
this interest, the incidental music, the operas, and the masque, is the
subject of the next chapter.

Chapter Nine

MUSIC FOR THE STAGE

Parker's Music for the Stage Before Mona

Throughout most of his life, Parker reflected the image of a scholastic composer whose musical interests were too narrowly confined to include the dramatic stage. Many composers of his generation viewed opera with distrust, even hostility, and many of his own public utterances convey the impression that he considered the medium an unsatisfactory art form. For the most part, he probably would have agreed with Sir Hubert Parry's wry observation that opera's "invariable associates are dirt and tinsel; its history is falseness, intrigue, shallowness, levity, and pretension."[1]

Actually Parker had shown strong dramatic tendencies in many of his major choral compositions, even as far back as his student days in Munich. The sections of larger choral works from this period are frequently connected by a continuous flow of music, and their themes often recur for dramatic as well as musical reasons. The orchestral accompaniments reveal a great sensitivity to the text, and the interludes often make thematic references to the dramatic substance of the vocal sections. As early as 1898, a fully developed leading-motive technique is evident in the dramatic oratorio *The Legend of Saint Christopher.*

The following year, Parker, in a reversal of his characteristic anti-operatic stance, is reported to have expressed the desire to write an opera. In an interview with Vernon Blackburn following the production of *Hora Novissima* at the Festival of the Three Choirs in Worcester, England, the composer professed a deep feeling for the music of Puccini, especially *La Bohème.* He confided to the English critic: "I think it is very, very great."[2] In response to Blackburn's question as to why he did not compose in that *genre,* Parker replied: "Give me a book, and I will write an opera."

His sabbatical leave of 1901-02, spent in Europe, seems to have intensified Parker's interest in opera. His diary for that winter contains numerous references to the many operas he saw in Berlin, Paris, Munich, and London. On 21 March 1902, he recorded a visit in Berlin with Richard Strauss, whose *Feuersnot* had been produced in Dresden the previous November. Strauss had just turned from the writing of symphonic poems to operas. In Parker's talk "Impressions of a year in Europe," given to "The Club" at New Haven the following winter, Strauss loomed as the composer of the moment. Even though Strauss's reputed thesis "that the art of absolute music is exhausted," seemed to be extreme, Parker could not conceal his admiration for the German composer: "His figure occupies the largest part of the musical horizon of the present day in Europe. . . . He is thoroughly educated, naturally most gifted, and original to a degree which is sometimes positively painful."[3]

Before Parker's growing operatic ambition was fulfilled, he was given the opportunity to gain some theatrical experience by writing incidental music for two plays, *The Eternal Feminine* (1904) and *The Prince of India* (1906). Unfortunately, no score for the first work survives, only the meager description from newspaper items of the time that it contained several orchestral pieces and some women's choruses.

The holograph full score for the second work is not so finished as those of Parker's other major works. Doubled parts and repeated melodic figures are usually indicated as such in musical short-hand rather than written out. The score calls for tenor solo, chorus, and a theater orchestra consisting of flute, oboe, two clarinets, bassoon, two horns, two trumpets, trombone, harp, percussion and strings.

Lew Wallace's novel *The Prince of India*, as adapted for stage by J. I. C. Clarke, offered Parker an opportunity for great variety and color in his incidental music. *The Theatre* magazine described the spectacle as follows:

> The "Prince of India" compels respect with its great sweep of idea and circumstance, apart from the commensurate elaborateness of the production. Worthy intention is there, and it is noteworthy to what small extent theatricalism intrudes. . . . In this drama we have an abundance of the pictorial, views of Constantinople and the Golden Horn, a panorama of the Bosphorus, a storm with the waters rushing by lashed by the tempest, the assault on the walls and their crumbling, the interiors of the church of Sancta Sophia (that which nothing more impressive and beautiful has ever been seen on our stage, the like of which Henry Irving never attempted), the striking of the

Prince of India with a bolt of lightning as he stands on a crag of
barren rock, etc.[4]

The sheer amount of music is one indication of how important Parker's contribution was. In a rambling organization consisting of a Prologue and five acts, there are no fewer than fifty-nine
sizable segments of music in addition to numerous brief fragments
of a few measures sandwiched between spoken lines. The larger
instrumental sections include an overture, preludes and postludes to
the various acts, incidental solos (mostly for flute, oboe, clarinet),
trumpet fanfares, and dances calling for a large battery of percussion instruments.
    Aside from a single tenor solo, the vocal sections are choral.
These include a chorus in the Prologue, and, later, a soldiers' chorus, a chorus of maidens, a religious chorus singing a *Kyrie*, and
finally, a triumphal choral paean which brings the play to a finish.
    In order to enhance dramatic action, Parker used a rudimen-
tary leading motive for the Indian Prince. The composer also
adopted some exotic musical devices intended to suggest the near-
Eastern setting of the story. These are elaborate melodic ornamentation (Ex. 9-1A), emphasis on the harmonic minor scale (Ex. 9-1A
& B), and "sing-song" melodies with their repeated, narrow-range
intervals (Ex. 9-1C).
    Beyond providing Parker with some experience writing for
the theater, *The Prince of India* has little relation to the operas
which were to follow. Its pleasing, uncomplex choruses, coloristic
devices, and occasional motivic associations do not compare with
the dramatic problems the composer set for himself in *Mona* and
Fairyland. Nevertheless, this substantial work for the Broadway
stage and the earlier *Eternal Feminine* serve to alter the general
impression that he had no dramatic experience when he turned to
opera composition.

Mona

    Mona illustrates Parker's artistic convictions about dramatic
music more completely than any of his other compositions. We
find many of these ideas in his address on French opera (1916).[5]
He had little patience for Italian opera, much of which he considered "a dull affair," but great admiration for reformers such as
Gluck and Wagner, whose purposes he considered identical to his
own. He called Gounod "Victorian, intensely so, and popular
Victorian at that," and he expressed surprise that *Faust* was still

Example 9-1. Excerpts, *The Prince of India*, ms., 1905,
from the Horatio Parker Papers in the Music
Library at Yale University. Used by permission.

A. p. 50.

B. p. 94.

C. p. 197.

popular in Germany. On the other hand, he had a grudging admiration for Bizet's *Carmen*, noting that it was "too brutal for the Victo-

rian age." He concluded: "Beauties grow old and fade but strength does not." He also liked *Le Joungler de Notre Dame* but considered Massenet "rather superficial and thoroughly theatrical. His style is almost too sugary and, except for dramatic purposes, will hardly outlast our own time, but it reflects contemporary taste very faithfully." Although he objected to the realism of *Louise*, he considered Charpentier's opera to be "good theatrically . . . a few steps beyond Massenet." The common thread running throughout these evaluations is Parker's admiration of strength and his aversion to sentimentality.

Shortly after he had begun work on *Mona*, Parker read his address on "Contemporary music" (1909) to the American Academy of Arts and Letters in which he noted that "opera is just now the largest figure on our musical horizon."6 Here, too, he deprecated Italian opera, calling it "suave," even "popular," and not nearly so important as parallel movements in Germany and France. From these countries he singled out Strauss and Debussy and concluded that "it seems impossible to find any notable work of our own day which does not show the influence of one or the other of these two men." He cited *Salome* and *Pelléas et Mélisande* as their significant works, commenting that, in both works, "the voices declaim; the orchestra sings." Parker admired Strauss and Debussy as having "a rich, individual, personal melodic and harmonic vocabulary" and making "new and satisfying rhythmic discoveries" as well as showing "a wealth of new and beautiful color."

He showed his preference for Strauss, "the most consummate master of musical expression the world has ever seen." He admired Strauss's power: "Most people want a healthy bellow from time to time to show that the orchestra is alive, and in *Salome*, we have an orchestra with its lid entirely removed." *Pelléas et Mélisande*, on the other hand, contains "a preponderance of white blood corpuscles," and "the orchestra has its mouth stuffed with cotton-wool lest it should really make a noise."

Parker preferred the music of Strauss to that of Debussy also on purely theoretical grounds, calling "the six-tone scale" and the "augmented triad . . . a definite negation of tonality or the key sense." "The continual evasion of the obvious" caused him to become annoyed with Debussy, whereas Strauss had a "greater directness." The matter of clarity in key relationships was no mere whim with Parker but rather the very basis of his musical thinking as is clearly evident from his summation of the point:

> Harmony [in Debussy] has become an attribute of
> melody, and our harmonic sense--a recent growth--furnishes
> the only means we have of definitely localizing formal portions
> of musical structure. Total absence of form is inconceivable in

music, and form implies inevitably some degree of formality. This element is always clearly present in Strauss and always purposely absent in Debussy. . . . At great climaxes Strauss ordinarily seeks a simple triad; Debussy, some more than usually obscure and refined dissonance. The harmonic element in Strauss is, perhaps, less refined, but less subtle. In Debussy it is less direct and less beautiful, but quite distinctly less obvious, if less varied.

Parker turned to polyphony, "the ultimate development" of melody and rhythm, in concluding his comparison of the two composers: "There seems to be infinitely more polyphonic and rhythmic vitality in Strauss's work than in that of Debussy." In making this elaborate comparison, Parker was actually revealing his credo as a composer. He was completely dependent upon the harmonic principles that were an outgrowth of the common practice period, and he recognized Strauss to be a composer of the same, more conservative bent. Debussy's modality, pentatonicism, use of chord streams, distortion of normal harmonic functions, and fragmentary melodic style were alien to him, and, although he occasionally used some impressionist devices, he leaned more often toward the full-bodied orchestra and the broad, tuneful climaxes of Strauss. *Mona* shows these preferences, for it is stylistically more akin to the early operas of Richard Strauss.

Parker approached the composing of his first opera seemingly with the full weight of the long and complex history of the *genre* upon his shoulders. In his "French opera" address, he recognized that opera is "a perpetual problem, the nature of which changes from one generation to another."[7] Furthermore, he felt this problem to be an insoluble one "on which the best of musical minds have sharpened themselves ever since it was first offered." He defined three aspects of the problem as "striving for better dramatic habits," "for better declamation," and "for more eloquent orchestral expressions." Here we also have Parker's expressed goals for *Mona*, objectives which sound distressingly lofty for a composer making his initial attempt at music drama. Even more unfortunate is their apparent incompatibility with the expectations of the American operatic public of the time, as are evident in the numerous articles that preceded the performance of *Mona*. Philip Hale wrote:

> We may expect to find in "Mona" an opera veering away from the complexities of the ultra-modern school. It is impossible to think of Parker as a disciple of Richard Strauss or even of Puccini.[8]

The *Christian Science Monitor* hinted that Parker would extend the English oratorio style into opera.[9] Likewise, H. T. Parker concluded that *Mona* would incline toward a "lyric" rather than a "dramatic" style.[10] The *New York Evening Post* used the occasion of the Metropolitan Opera contest announcement to issue rather blunt advice for "budding American opera composers" to follow examples of Victor Herbert, Arthur Nevin, and Frederick Converse, none of whom, it said, "has shown a disposition to understate the value of melody."[11] It noted that *Salome, Electra,* and *Pelléas* "deliberately taboo melody," and concluded that the American composer should turn to *Carmen* and *Die Meistersinger* for models.

Parker felt that he had made considerable progress toward his first goal, "the striving for better dramatic habits," in his choice of literary collaborator Brian Hooker. Hooker was a young intellectual who had only recently left teaching posts at Yale and, subsequently, Columbia, and was beginning to make his way in the literary world as a free-lance writer.[12] As an undergraduate at Yale, he had won practically every literary prize (an achievement that probably did not go unnoticed by Parker) and had served as an editor of literary publications there.

The story of *Mona* is set in southwestern Britain, the seat of the Druidic religion during the Roman occupation around the end of the first century.[13] Although Hooker disclaimed reference to any actual historical incident, his libretto was undoubtedly influenced by an uprising of native tribes against Roman rule in 61, A. D.[14] The Druids, angered by the political and social interference of the Romans in their affairs, were led by a woman, Boadicea, in a series of battles but were eventually suppressed. Hooker probably derived the name of his heroine from that of the geographic locality Mona, a stronghold of the rebellious Druids.

The Mona of Hooker's plot is a young Briton girl who has visions that she is to assume the role of her ancestor Boadicea and lead the Britons in another rebellion against Rome. Her mission is somewhat complicated by the fact that she is engaged to Gwynn who, unknown to her and the other Britons, is the son of the Roman governor, although he was born of a British mother and has lived among the Britons as one of them most of his life. Gwynn hopes to establish a permanent peace between the Britons and the Romans and sees in his forthcoming marriage to Mona a union of the two antagonistic peoples. However, Mona--strongly persuaded by her superstitious foster parents, Enya and Arth; by their son Gloom, who secretly loves Mona; and by Caradoc, the chief bard of Britain--finally breaks away from her lover and leads her people in a rebellion against the Romans. Another important character is Nial, a supposedly half-witted changeling among the Britons, who plays the role of a bystander and commentator. His innocent but perceptive comments upon the circumstances which drive Mona and her people to destruction provide the opera with a continuing philosophical commentary. Eventually the Britons are defeated, and Mona, in anger, kills her lover Gwynn, who she believes has betrayed her. Mona has neither Salome's erotic sensuality nor Electra's unwavering fanaticism. Rather, the Druid queen wavers between love and duty, and her indecisiveness triggers the tragic events of the opera.

From today's vantage point, the deficiencies of the story are much easier to see than they were to those concerned with the production of the opera. Parker was very pleased with the book. In a revealing interview with his friend H. E. Krehbiel, the composer described Hooker's work as "exceedingly beautiful, a poem rather than a libretto."[15] But, in his choice of Hooker as a "poet" rather than as a "librettist," Parker unintentionally had a competitor as well as a collaborator. The libretto to *Mona* was published in the fall of 1911, nearly six months before the actual production of the opera, and most leading critics echoed Parker's sentiment that the book was an art work in itself.[16] Amid the praise for the libretto, only a few doubts were expressed. Philip Hale asked if there were "sufficient action" and "truly dramatic situations" and wondered if the text might restrict the composer and the singers.[17] Hale's skepticism was prophetic, for the irony of the situation should have been evident long before the first performance: a press, which was liberal in its praise of the libretto for its modern, subtle poetic qualities, at the same time had shown itself hostile to the modern music dramas emanating from Europe. It expected Parker's operatic style to lie somewhere between the English oratorio and Bizet with just a touch of Wagner.

After the first performance of *Mona*, most major writers reversed themselves concerning the merits of Hooker's libretto.[18] Charles Henry Meltzer offered the most succinct and accurate analysis of the libretto, calling the plot and the literary style "too diffuse, too erudite, too literary."[19] Certainly Hooker's choice of Elizabethan English and his sometimes convoluted sentences do not lend themselves to instant aural intelligibility, no matter how fine they appear on the printed page. For example, Nial asks why a Roman soldier was killed by one of the Britons: "What hath he done, the Roman, wherefore Arth / Should slay him?"[20] In the same scene, Mona inquires as to the meaning of the initials on the hilt of the murder weapon: "What mean these runes / Here graven?"[21] The choice of such archiac expressions impeded the comprehension of the basic plot.

Parker must have been aware that a "literary" text would not necessarily make a good libretto, but, in view of the criticism of the poor quality of texts for previous American operas, he may have felt it necessary to have an especially good one.[22] Furthermore, several contemporary European operas, among them *Pelléas et Mélisande* and Paul Dukas's *Ariane et Barbe-Bleu*, had poetic texts which were also considered to be outstanding librettos. Perhaps these factors encouraged him to attempt what he thought was the difficult task of mixing "utterly irreconcilable arts."[23]

Provided with a text which was generally acclaimed before the first performance as having fulfilled the necessary dramatic requirements, Parker turned to the second goal of establishing a suitable kind of declamation. Following the traditions of the Florentine *camerata*, Gluck, and Wagner, he proceeded on the assumption that the text was to be the paramount consideration in the choice of musical materials. In parts of *Mona*, the usual considerations of balance, repetition, and contrast in musical phrasing are made subordinate to a vocal writing which attempts to follow and intensify the natural variations of speech in its modulation, accent, and pitch. Since the libretto is treated as if it were prose, and vowel quantities rather than metrical accents become the rhythmic guide, the regularity of meter and prominence of pulse are also considerably weakened.

A typical section from the Act I monologue, in which Mona tells Gwynn of her recurring dream, can serve as an illustration (Ex. 9-2). The voice appears to be written in a manner which follows almost exactly the normal speech-rhythm for these lines, the important emotive words being emphasized by higher pitches. In only the first measure does Mona join the orchestra by singing one of the motives (identified in brackets). Not all, nor even a major part, of *Mona* reaches this extreme use of heightened declamation, but Parker's intention in this and other parts of the opera is supported by both his and Hooker's expressed belief that the words and the music had been perfectly matched.[24] Parker's overly zealous application of these principles of text setting caused H. E. Krehbiel to grumble: "How much more wisely did Wagner, the founder of the constructive system used by Professor Parker, build! Even in 'Götterdämmerung,' when the occasion warranted it, he let Gunther's men sing like a 'Leidertafel.'"[25]

There can be no doubt but that the critics of the time considered *Mona* to be historically unique because of Parker's application of the principles of heightened declamation to grand opera in English. William Henderson, H. T. Parker, and Richard Aldrich used much space in their columns explaining this fact; however, they all agreed more or less with Krehbiel's laconic summary: "There is too little melody in it, and much too little concerted music."[26]

Example 9-2. Excerpt, Mona's monologue, *Mona*, Op. 71,
vc. sc., GS, 1911, p. 7, m. 9-p. 8, m. 11.

But the impression gained from these reviews that the whole of *Mona* is unbroken recitative is exceedingly misleading. Actually the structure, far from being a "fluid stream of recitative," can be broken down into easily discernible sections, such as the monologues of Mona in the first and last acts, her duet scenes with Gloom and Gwynn in the second act, the solo sections of Gwynn, Nial, and Enya, and the dialogue between the Governor and Gwynn in the second act, and the Druid chorus in second act. Lyrical points are reached at some place in practically every scene. Considering the esthetic problem the composer had set for himself, the voice parts contain a surprising amount of melodic writing. Certainly Gwynn's solo and the following love duet of Act II, Mona's monologue in Act III, the oath scene in the first act, and the Druid chorus from the second act have sections of extended melody. The technical difficulty of the solo parts was another focus of criticism. The ranges for both Mona and Gwynn were described justifiably as "cruelly high."[27] The several unprepared entries above high Gs in both parts make the love duet a major obstacle. The declamation in dramatic scenes, such as that in which Gwynn describes the Roman army, contains several sudden leaps to high notes which may have their expressive reasons, but musically they are awkward and disconcerting.

   Still another problem, particularly in terms of the goal that Parker and Hooker sought, was the generally unsatisfactory diction of most of the singers. There is a touch of irony in the fact that Albert Reiss (Nial), the only foreign-born member of the cast, was alone in receiving praise for his enunciation. The native-born principal artists, Louise Homer (Mona) and Riccardo Martin (Gwynn), had particular trouble in conveying the meaning of a text that the audience had been led to believe would be comprehensible much in the manner of a play. The reviews show that this expectation was hardly fulfilled. Henderson commented:

> For those who believe that the performance of opera in English
> is to be the final solution of all the aesthetic problems surround-
> ing the hybrid art form called opera, it may be recorded that
> only in driest parts of the recitative could every syllable be
> understood.[28]

   Charles Henry Meltzer thought the problem to be in the orchestration: "He [Parker] has scored his opera rather richly and rather heavily, forgetting that the words of the librettist should be heard through (or above) his orchestration.[29]

   Meltzer points to the relationship between the second and third goals that the composer established. Of the three--dramatic veracity, improved declamation, and orchestral expressiveness--Parker was best equipped, by reason of his previous writing for orchestra in his more dramatic choral and solo works to handle the orchestra as an expressive medium through which the emotional impact of the opera would be conveyed. It is the orchestra as a dramatic agent which is the most successful feature of *Mona*, and, as a result, those sections where the voices depart from their constraining, declamatory role and join the orchestra in performing the lyrical motives, such as those of the love duet from Act II, are the most intense and satisfying moments of the opera.

The orchestra is a large one of approximately one hundred players. By reinforcing the woodwind, brass, and percussion families, Parker had the means at his disposal to follow the lead of Strauss, and the tumultuousness of Strauss's orchestration is approached in *Mona's* climactic sections. On the whole, Parker showed little advancement in instrumental color over that of *Crépuscule*. The woodwinds and horns handle many of the lyrical themes, the brass and percussion, the weightier moments, and the strings remain the backbone of the orchestration. The incidental solos, while spread among all the families (the oboe is usually favored), are usually fragmentary and fall short of being striking. Little emphasis is given to the heterogeneous mixtures that give such opulence to the music of some of Parker's contemporaries such as Elgar.

The critics' reactions to the tone color of *Mona* were mixed. Some writers were impressed, calling the score "richly transparent," "incessantly varied and contrasted," "dramatically expressive," "solid," "rich," and "masterly." Others called it "gray and misty," "sombre, dark, and noisy," and "monotonous." Parker had tried to write idiomatically and with some variety; however, the pervading gloom of the plot, the lack of sufficient orchestral interludes, and the tying of his orchestration so closely to leitmotives were limiting factors and dampened somewhat his usual effulgence.

In spite of its conservative taste, the musical public undoubtedly assumed that Parker would use some type of associative device as other American composers had done,[30] and he did not disappoint them:

> I have employed leitmotives in *Mona*, of course. For I can't conceive of anyone's writing an opera nowadays without them. You can't expect the public to unlearn what Wagner taught it. I have, however, taken care not to use so many motives as to confuse the listener with their complications.[31]

In his address to the MacDowell Club shortly before the performance, Parker mentioned using "fifty or sixty" leading motives, a large number for even the most diligent listener to retain.[32] Although he left no list, an examination of the score makes the association between music and idea obvious.[33]

The character of Mona is portrayed by a group of themes. Among those associated with her leadership of the Druids are her destiny to fulfill a great mission (vocal score, p. 12), her attachment to her insidious half-brother, Gloom (p. 133), and her role as the successor to Boadicea. The last-named, a sweeping theme, is developed in an orchestral interlude following the scene in which Mona's relationship to Boadicea is revealed (Ex. 9-3; violins).

Example 9-3. Boadicea motive, *Mona*, Op. 71, vc. sc., GS,
1911, p. 62, mm. 11-14.

Mona's feminine nature is described in motives of doubt
about assuming leadership of the rebellion (p. 7, m. 8; p. 10, mm. 1-
3), and of longing to fulfill a mother's role (Ex. 9-4). The last-
named motive is illustrative of the progressive, non-functional
harmonic procedure found in parts of *Mona*. Seventh chords followed by alternating major and minor chords (E-flat 7/B-flat minor
7/F minor/C-flat major/B-flat minor) unfold over a pedal B-flat
pitch. At the beginning of the excerpt, the augmented triad (B-
flat/D/F-sharp), which Parker had criticized in the music of Debussy, is quite prominent.[34] Closely related to Mona's feminine
motives are those describing her love for Gwynn: ecstasy (p. 6),
beauty (p. 150), and contentment (p. 14).

Gwynn also has a number of musical associations. The one
most frequently used has an elasticity which makes it easily adapt-
able to various tempos and styles. In one of its most distinctive
presentations, the monologue of Act I in which Mona describes a
recurring dream, the motive serves as a premonition identifying
Gwynn as the "white-shrouded figure" who attempts to wrest from

Example 9-4. Femininity motive, *Mona*, Op. 71, vc. sc.,
     GS, 1911, p. 14, mm. 5-7.

her the sword, the symbol of her leadership (Ex. 9-5; oboe and
violin part). Here the augmented triad (E-flat/G/B-natural) occurs
in even bolder fashion than in Example 9-4, although the B-natural
eventually resolves to an A-sharp. Another, quite different, motive,
represents Gwynn as a man of peace, and resembles a hymn-tune
with its tepid, two-bar sequences and chromatic appoggiaturas on
the strong beat of every other measure (Ex. 9-6).

The character of Gloom, Mona's half-brother and the principal antagonist in the drama, is developed through a number of
circumstances such as the British revolt, Gloom's love for Mona,
and his hatred for Gwynn--each with appropriate musical material.
Gloom's most distinctive motive is heard at his initial entry (Ex. 9-
7). It is tonally ambiguous with a half-diminished arpeggio on E
progressing to a B-flat augmented triad, both over an F-sharp pedal.
The resolution to B minor in the fourth measure establishes momentarily a firm key center which immediately gives way to the side-
slipping sixth chords (E-flat/D) of the death motive as Gloom pre-
dicts Gwynn's death. Again, tonality is maintained tenuously by
the pedal point on B natural.

There are also associations that depict ideas or objects.
One of the most impressive is the "unspeakable name," a reference to a Druid god (Ex. 9-8). In this massive, half-note figure,
the upper and lower parts of the orchestra proceed in contrary
motion. The chord progression is tonic major/mediant
minor/subdominant minor for each of the transposing sequences, which are connected by a woodwind, sixteenth-note
embellishment. The sword motive (Ex. 9-9), as found in Mona's
monologue from Act I, has a similar harmonic motion upward
to the mediant chord (D-flat major/F minor; woodwinds and
trumpets), and is accompanied by a Roman motive (sixteenth

Example 9-5. Gwynn's motive, *Mona*, Op. 71, vc. sc., GS, 1911, p. 29, mm. 1-6.

Example 9-6. Gwynn's peace motive, *Mona*, Op. 71, vc. sc., GS, 1911, p. 115, mm. 6-11.

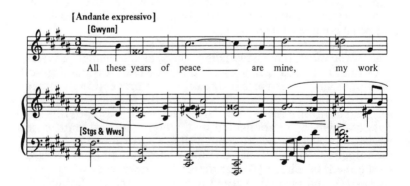

Example 9-7. Gloom and death motives, *Mona*, Op. 71,
   vc. sc., GS, 1911, p. 51, mm. 1-5.

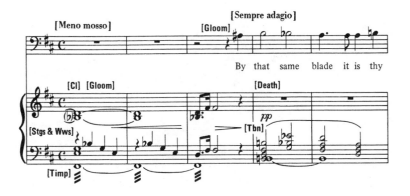

Example 9-8. Unspeakable name motive, *Mona*, Op. 71,
   vc. sc., GS, 1911, p. 15, mm. 13-16.

notes in the strings), the latter providing much of the rhythmic
substructure throughout the monologue.

In his MacDowell Club address and elsewhere, Parker made
considerable mention of assigning certain tonalities to given characters and situations. Thus Gwynn's motives are frequently in B
major; Mona in her "womanly" aspect, E-flat major; and Mona as
the Druid queen, E minor. The composer quipped that he had written the love music in G-flat major, "the legitimate offspring of B
major and E-flat major."[35]

Since Parker's earlier works show impressive use of motivic
expansion in elaborate orchestral interludes, one is surprised to find
this technique suppressed in *Mona*. He seems to have been reluc-

Example 9-9. Sword and Roman motives, *Mona*, Op. 71,
   vc. sc., GS, 1911, p. 27, mm. 8-10.

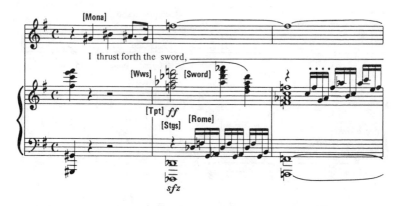

tant to allow sufficient pause in the stage action so that the orchestra
might elaborate upon some of the important ideas. Only in a few
places--such as motives of the "unspeakable name" (p. 16),
"Gwynn's love for Mona" (p. 18-19), "Mona, the Queen" and
"Boadicea" (p. 65, p. 133), and the love music of the second
act--does the composer dwell on these themes sufficiently to bring
out their lyrical qualities. A second flaw is the large number of
motives and their sometimes rapid, fleeting use. Mona's declamation (Ex. 9-2) is illustrative of such crowding. Finally, some of
these leading motives, such as the British army and war motives
(Ex. 9-2), are not sufficiently distinctive to command attention on
their own.

We have already noted in the foregoing discussion of the
excerpts that advanced harmonic ideas are found in an appreciable
part of *Mona*. The chromatic texture from which the many themes
and colors well up is composed of altered chords, frequent use of
ninths and elevenths, chains of sevenths, and other unusual progressions. The degree of complex vertical organization, intricate key
relationships, fluctuating and deceptive tonal movements, and
occasional bitonal sections are matched nowhere else in Parker's
writing.[36] Yet, chromaticism is rarely used as an end in itself but
rather as a means of moving quickly from one key to another in an
opera where tonality, as well as motive, is a means of character- and
idea-identification.

For an explicit example of how Parker's harmonic concept
works in a more extended manner, let us return to Mona's monologue (Ex. 9-2; p. 152 above), which has also served above as an
example of Parker's declamation concepts. Here, the flow of

motives overburdens the listener. The approximate clock-time of this excerpt is slightly over a minute. At first Mona tells Gwynn how much she has missed him. Starting in E-flat minor (Mona's womanly aspect), with Mona joining the oboe in the doubt motive, the music turns to a strong cadence in C major (one of the love music keys) in measures 3-4 of the excerpt. But other visions, those of Britain, crowd Gwynn out, and measures 5-7 effect an unstable turn to E minor, the key of Mona as queen. Over an altered dominant chord in E minor, Gwynn's motive is heard in the oboe (m. 8), but this fleeting statement is lost in the group of British motives which follow. Just how ambivalent Mona's state of mind is at this moment is evident with the altered dominant chord, which, with the change of one note (B-natural rising to C), becomes the dominant of B-flat minor (m. 9), and the British army motive takes over at the strong cadence in B-flat (m. 10). A war motive follows (m. 12). Mona's thoughts momentarily return to Gwynn, supported by the lyric line of the oboe (m. 11-12) and the deceptive cadence to a G-flat major chord (end of m. 12). An ambivalent diminished chord (m. 13) leads to a strong cadence in B-flat minor and a British war motive (m. 14-15), as Mona's thoughts return to those of duty. Finally, Mona asks Gwynn why he has been away so long. The music passes weakly through E minor, but the E minor chord is treated as a II7 of B followed by a V of B, (m. 17; Gwynn's key), as Gwynn is about to speak.

The critics of the day were naturally disconcerted by the strange harmonic progressions of *Mona*. H. T. Parker said, "He stops at nothing in endlessly recondite and daring harmonic device."[37] Max Smith found in the harmony "a willful search for ugly dissonance which apparently has no psychological or dramatic point."[38] Such comments do not do justice to the scope of harmonic usage, from a relatively conservative style in a few places to a more progressive style. In a review of a 1961 concert performance of the love duet, one of the most lyrical portions of the opera, critic John Freeman noted a resemblance to the music of Vincent d'Indy,[39] incidentally, a composer whom Parker admired.

That *Mona* might not win popular acclaim was a distinct possibility in the minds of many at the time. A few days before the first performance, H. T. Parker wrote: "*Mona* . . . rejects all the easy means to winning success; it . . . will be a test not only of the American composer but also the American audience," which he expected to be challenged by the newer methods of contemporary music drama it employed.[40]

Although *Mona* has been generally described as an opera too advanced for its audience, some critics appear to have noted a start in realizing H. T. Parker's ideal. W. B. Chase reported that the audience did not restrain itself by observing the Wagnerian custom of applauding only between acts but rather "broke into applause . . . during the love duet on the opening night."[41] Krehbiel also observed the "enthusiasm of the crowd" and "intense listening" at the second performance.[42] Both critics, who had written unfavorable reviews after the opening night, described their own increased pleasure at the later performances.

The four performances at the Metropolitan during the spring of 1912 were to be the only opportunities for audiences to accustom themselves to the complexities of *Mona*. It surely would not be so perplexing to today's listeners, whose concept of lyricism is considerably broader than that of Parker's time. Although a revival of the complete opera is not likely, concert performances of excerpts can demonstrate that much of the opera has a beauty of its own. Krehbiel and Chase sensed this quality at the time of the Metropolitan performances, and, throughout the 1920s and 1930s, A. Walter Kramer and Paul Rosenfeld also maintained that *Mona* was an important but neglected opera.[43] The work remains a significant phenomenon--a bold, experimental approach to opera in English. *Mona* can readily claim its historical place as a harbinger of a new, more flexible, manner of treating both music and text, an ideal which has continued to be influential on the American lyric stage.

Fairyland

In turning from *Mona* to *Fairyland*, the second opera on which Parker and Hooker collaborated, one is amazed by the extent of difference between the two works. In *Fairyland*, caricatures are substituted for highly developed portrayals of human personages, and what amounts to a fairy tale is used in place of tragedy. Musically, the spectrum of *Fairyland* is as wide as that of *Mona* is narrow. Old fashioned, closed-form arias, ensemble numbers, religious choruses, drinking songs, soldiers' marches, and ballet--all exist alongside the newer dramatic techniques of leading motives, a modulating, opaque harmonic structure, and colorful orchestration. The diversity of styles within the work--its pageantry, lack of a truly convincing dramatic situation, and occasional sentimentality verging on salon music--suggest a *pièce d'occasion*. In fact, the work was tailored to meet the needs of a large, festive affair, the 1915 convention of the National Federation of Music Clubs held at Los Angeles.

With *Fairyland*, Parker intended to correct the "mistakes" of his earlier opera. His letters to Hertz following the production of *Mona* make evident his disappointment in its failure and his determination to do better if given another chance. Some of the changes in *Fairyland* are obviously attempts to overcome complaints that *Mona's* book lacked dramatic value, that the composer neglected melodic writing, and that he failed to draw upon his wide experience as a choral composer.

The Los Angeles production also helped to shape the final form of *Fairyland*. From the chronology of events, it seems probable that work on it was begun without a specific production in mind, but, at some point in its composition--perhaps even before the official announcement of the contest--the Los Angeles production must have become a specific goal for Parker and Hooker (see p. 65). Considerations of individual style then probably gave way to the demands of the occasion.

The nature of these requirements can be established by comparing the creation of *Fairyland* with that of another American opera, now almost forgotten, which was commissioned for a very similar occasion. On 29 August 1910, *Paoletta*, an opera in four acts with music by Pietro Floridia, was produced in Cincinnati for the Ohio Valley Exposition.[44] The composer was at the time a professor in the College of Music there. No evidence exists that Parker attended the performance or even knew of the work, yet the similarities in purpose and general structure between *Fairyland* and *Paoletta* suggest consensus on how festival operas should be written.

Floridia has described his goal as one which was "insisted upon" by the directors of the Cincinnati festival:

> The work should be a grand opera in the real sense of the word, it should be of such a character as to attract the generality of the public. "Popular" was the most insistent request; easy, melodious, accessible to everybody's understanding--nothing of what they called "high-brow" music, but at the same time nothing that could suggest musical comedy, or even light opera. In other words, a kind of "Aida," but in much more popular style.[45]

Parker's requirements, judging from contemporary accounts, were quite similar to those imposed on Floridia. The plot must be entertaining but dignified. Arias must be provided for the celebrated singers imported to sing the important roles. Most important, the music had to suit the capabilities of the various local choral organizations, the newly organized Los Angeles Symphony Orchestra, and the city's dance groups.[46]

Other similarities between *Fairyland* and *Paoletta* are apparent. The settings for both, medieval Europe, are remote. Principal characters for each opera are coloratura soprano, lyrical tenor, and dramatic bass. Choral composition dominates these operas, particularly in the finales to each Act. Paoletta's "Dove song" and Rosamund's aria, "In a garden," are both popular and lighter moments in each opera. Like Floridia, Parker found it necessary to regress stylistically to the nineteenth-century European grand opera tradition, but this imposed condition was at the same time in line with his own growing conviction to reach a broader public with his music.

Undoubtedly, Los Angeles' determination to have the convention and to stage an opera was motivated in part by the Panama-Pacific Exposition, commemorating the opening of the Panama Canal, which was held in the rival city of San Francisco during that same summer. Los Angeles wished to claim its share of the streams of visitors and attendant publicity that the West Coast was receiving. The West seized upon this opportunity to challenge the dominance of the East in cultural matters. That *Fairyland* became a part of this larger propaganda scheme is nowhere so evident as in the assertions of the production's impresario, F. W. Blanchard. Writing under headlines boldly proclaiming: "FAIRY-LAND WILL PLACE LOS ANGELES IN THE CENTER OF THE MUSICAL MAP," he boasted:

> I don't believe there is a city in the world that offers to the advancement of musical art such unparalleled and unequaled opportunities as does Los Angeles with its ideal surroundings and inspiration. . . . Not only will *Fairyland* make Los Angeles the new cradle of American Grand Opera, but it will make it a permanent home of Grand Opera because a new prize of $10,000 is to be offered by Los Angeles every four years as a prize for original American Grand Opera [a promise which remained unfulfilled].[47]

Coupled with praise of Los Angeles as the "cradle of American opera" were the inevitable efforts to give *Fairyland* an American theme. Conductor Alfred Hertz asserted: "I should liken Horatio Parker to the evangelist, John the Baptist, of biblical times--a prophet proclaiming a new school in a musical country awaiting the coming of ideals which would gradually create a following to be known as the disciples of American music."[48] Later, Hertz was more specific in describing *Fairyland's* "American" qualities as being more "tuneful" than *Mona*.[49] At a dinner of the California Yale alumni, he hailed both of Parker's operas as making the equivalent contribution to American music that those of Wagner had made to German music.

At the same meeting, librettist Brian Hooker offered his explanation of the "American" features of *Fairyland*:

> Prof. Parker . . . has given birth to a new school of music that is distinctly American--music that is both classic and easily popular. As your California fish, the sand dab, which is dug out of the depths of the ocean, is palatable to every man, so is the score of *Fairyland*, though embodying the deepest principles of art, a rare treat for those who pretend to hate classical music.[50]

Parker himself felt compelled to search for American qualities in his work. He expressed the hope that "some of the elasticity and optimism, which are the inevitable inheritance of American ancestry, running back nearly three hundred years, might find its way into the music."[51] He concluded:

> In time we must, and we shall have, a national music of our own, as broad and as richly varied as is our country itself. . . . Good music ought to reflect the character of the nation from whence it springs, as well as the individual who makes it. *Fairyland* is said to be cheerful, buoyant, and confident as the American character.[52]

The story takes place in the thirteenth century. The locale is a "hill" country in central Europe. A principal figure in the plot is Rosamund (coloratura soprano), an unwilling novice in an abbey supervised by Myriel (mezzo-soprano). Rosamund falls in love with Auburn (heroic tenor), the king of the local municipality, upon catching a glimpse of him as he rides by the abbey one day. Auburn is a religious man who frequently makes pilgrimages in search of a "Holy Land," and the dramatic substance of Act I consists of preparations for such a journey. Auburn vests his authority in Myriel while he is gone, a move which angers Auburn's ambitious brother, Corvain (bass). In the finale to Act I, the principality is transformed miraculously into a new land, a Fairyland, where Auburn and Rosamund meet and are crowned King and Queen. All of the peasants of the earthly principality including Robin (lyric tenor), their chief spokesman, now become the fairies of this Fairyland. Only Myriel and Corvain, the twin representatives of clerical and political control in the typical Medieval state, are absent.

Act II begins with a return to reality. Corvain and Myriel have become quite repressive and quarrel for control of the earthly municipality. Auburn returns unrecognized but fails to recognize Rosamund, who has been imprisoned by Myriel for breaking her novitiate, and by Corvain for not responding to his advances. In an effort to regain his crown, Auburn calls for the emblem of the rose on his tunic to "shine forth" as a sign that he can establish Fairyland here on earth. Instead the rose withers, and the act ends with the peasants deriding Auburn. The final act opens with Rosamund and Auburn chained to a stake awaiting execution. Suddenly, Auburn recognizes Rosamund as the queen of Fairyland. The plot is hinged on this act of recognition, for, at this instant, the peasants come pouring forth from a local tavern and are transformed once again into the fairies of Fairyland. The story ends in this abrupt fashion, with several loose strands of the plot left dangling.

The libretto to *Fairyland* was initially praised by the critics, who, after the fashion of *Mona*, then reversed themselves following the performances. Complaints ranged from its "fancifulness," and "lack of definiteness and purpose" to such prudish comments as "the admixture of the nuns and soldiers and fairies is absolutely irritating, but the idea of joining the drunken rowdies and fairies . . . savors of vandalism and beyond all argument is not of fairylore."[53]

Whatever the deficiencies of the libretto, it did afford Parker an opportunity to utilize his widest musical scope in composing since *Saint Christopher*, nearly two decades earlier. The music of *Fairyland* reflects his continuing preoccupation with the fusion of opera and oratorio. In *Saint Christopher, Morven and the Grail*, and other major choral works, he had tried to develop more dramatic emphasis within the bounds of the traditional oratorio; in *Fairyland*, he was concerned with the integration of architectonic choral elements into an operatic framework. *Fairyland* is foremost a choral opera.

Its second striking musical feature is the distinctly popular style of some of its arias and choruses. Up to this time, Parker had enjoyed a reputation as an intellectual composer. To quote critic Havra Hubbard: "The unexpected is that [*Fairyland*] contains several portions which are surprisingly and delightfully melodious, and such indulgences are not looked for in Parker's later writings."[54] On the other hand, Philip Greeley Clapp, in a pre-performance review of the work, was dismayed by what he considered Parker's "direct appeal to the public with a vengeance."[55] In order to gain popular acceptance, Parker was said to have sacrificed the unity of style which Clapp felt to be the admirable feature of *Mona*. He described the hymn-anthem of the nuns as "dangerously near eye-rolling sentimentalism"; Robin's solo, "Rose of the World," as "a bid for the favor of the musically unwashed"; and Rosamund's coloratura aria as "having no musical or dramatic justification . . . a bid for mid-act applause." Clapp's ascetic taste was not generally shared. Hertz maintained throughout the rehearsals and performances that *Fairyland* was superior to *Mona* because the latter "was less appealing and had not the value of melody. . . . Some of the melodies of *Fairyland* will be sung down the annals of time."[56] Many of the composer-delegates who attended the National Federation of Music Clubs' convention and the performances of *Fairyland*--Amy Beach, Charles Wakefield Cadman, Carl Busch, and Chadwick, among others--considered the variety of music in the opera to be an asset instead of a liability. They commented on Parker's rodigious technique and admired his versatility in drawing from a spectrum of styles bound on one end by the sentimental aria of the conventional operetta and on the other by the fluid motivic structure of the Wagnerian music drama.[57] *Fairyland* is the first work to incorporate stylistic elements from the composer's final period, a time during which he moved toward simplification in order to gain a broader appeal. If this goal was forced on Parker by the circumstances of the occasion, it soon acquired the rectitude of a philosophical conviction in the works that followed.

In turning to the composing of a more popularly based, conventional opera, Parker may have believed himself to be more attuned to the times. During his sabbatical leave of 1912-13, he had heard a great deal of opera abroad. Among the more contemporary works he listed in his diaries are the Strauss operas, *Feuersnot*, *Elektra*, *Der Rosenkavalier*, and *Ariadne auf Naxos*, Wolf-Ferrari's *Jewels of the Madonna*, and Puccini's *Manon Lescaut*. He was impressed especially with *Der Rosenkavalier*, which he heard several times both in Europe and in New York.[58] The popular Viennese music of that opera, particularly its waltzes, may have been the inspiration for his own waltz music in *Fairyland*.

The difference between the prelude to *Mona* and the overture to *Fairyland* is characteristic of the contrasting nature of Parker's operas. Although both use thematic material drawn from their respective works, the prelude to *Mona* is highly unified, with various motivic elements propelled to a strong climax and moving without pause into the first act. The overture to *Fairyland*, on the other hand, is a medley of leading themes with no evident dramatic purpose.

The quantity of choral writing in *Fairyland* (six choruses in Act I, three in Act II, and six in Act III), as well as their variety, is impressive. The pentatonic, modal melodies of the peasants' and soldiers' choruses convey a folksong quality which is nevertheless thwarted by relatively sophisticated harmonic and modulatory schemes. The chorus of peasants in Act I (Ex. 9-10) starts in D minor, but the first phrase cadences in C major (m. 4). The following phrase ends on a half-cadence in E-flat minor (m. 8).

Example 9-10. Peasants' chorus, Act I, *Fairyland*, Op. 77,
vc. sc., p. 17, mm. 1-9. Copyright 1915, 1942, G.
Schirmer, Inc. Used by permission.

The nuns' choruses, which occur frequently throughout, are
largely variants of the same melodic source material. Mostly
"ecclesiastical" in their conjunct motion and quietly flowing
rhythms, they occasionally approach the theatrical sentimentality
that Clapp mentioned in his review. For example, the climactic
drive of the first-act chorus is a succession of seventh chords and a
striking modulation from G-flat to the dominant seventh chord of D,
followed by short sequential patterns in G-flat emphasizing diminished and half-diminished seventh chords (Ex. 9-11).

This chorus is the most extended one in the opera (pp. 32-
46). A procession from the abbey winds onto the stage and inter-
rupts a lively dialogue between Robin and Corvain. Corvain continues to muse on his ambitions in an obbligato part to the opening
section of the chorus (pp. 34-35). Thus, the chorus is welded onto
the previous dramatic action and shows Parker to have been at the
peak of his skill in the setting of conflicting dramatic ideas.[59] Amy
Beach commented: "I know of no opera wherein this semi-reli-
gious, semi-dramatic and always entrancingly beautiful choral style
is maintained for so long a period and kept on such a high level."[60]

The finale to Act I contains three choruses associated with
Fairyland, all of which approach the lightness of operetta style. The
waltz theme of the first chorus and subsequent ballet is the most
outstanding (Ex. 9-12). The tune has grace and eloquence; furthermore, it is "catchy" enough, at least in the opening phrases, to be
easily remembered. Adorned as it is with chromatic harmony, a

Example 9-11. Nuns' chorus, Act I, *Fairyland*, Op. 77,
        vc. sc., p. 34, m. 1-p. 35, m. 1. Copyright 1915, 1942,
        G. Schirmer, Inc. Used by permission.

striking modulation up a major third (from E to G-sharp), and a
surprising amount of free canonic imitation in the inner parts, the
waltz meets the stipulation of being "popular," while at the same

time more "learned" than that of the usual light opera or musical
comedy.

Example 9-12. Fairies' chorus, Act I, *Fairyland*, Op. 77,
       vc. sc., p. 92, mm. 1-12. Copyright 1915, 1942, G.
       Schirmer, Inc. Used by permission.

Parker made little technical concession to amateur choral
singers. Although their melodic style is transparent enough, these
large choruses have a fairly complex harmonic-polyphonic and
modulatory structure. Technical problems are most extreme during
the second act. Here the peasants turn on Auburn in a declamatory,

derisive chorus (pp. 174-184) which is expanded into twelve separate parts, including those of the principals. The critics were awed
by such complexity but, at the same time, pleased with the importance of choral music to the opera. One remarked: "There is a new
vein which Mr. Parker has touched--a vein that is truly American,
especially so in the choral work."[61] Many applauded Parker's
return to what was considered his primary calling as a choral
composer.

The arias are the largest concession to popular taste. Those
given to the heroine, Rosamund, are the most numerous. In her
principal solo in the first act (pp. 52-55), she tells of glimpsing her
"King of Fairyland" from the abbey balcony. The fluid, through-
composed section is richly orchestrated and the vocal line reaches a
climactic high B-flat. Her solo from the second act, "In a garden"
(pp. 142-145), is more traditionally sectional. The orchestral introduction is followed by a simple, lyrical song accompanied by pizzicato string chords and delicate counter-figures in the oboe and
English horn (Ex. 9-13). At first, the quiet, reflective solo is a
welcome change from the preceding turbulent scene shared by
Rosamund and Corvain; however, the aria soon becomes a vehicle
for coloratura soprano, with roulades uncharacteristic of its composer. The number was a favorite with Los Angeles audiences and
critics in spite of Philip Greeley Clapp's disdain.

Example 9-13. Rosamund's aria, Act II, *Fairyland*, Op. 77,
    vc. sc., p. 143, mm. 3-6. Copyright 1915, 1942,
    G. Schirmer, Inc. Used by permission.

The three short solos based on the Rose motive (the rose is
the symbol of *Fairyland*) are the most significant portions in the

traditional aria style. They are assigned to different principals--
Robin, Auburn, and Rosamund--and occur as touchstones in the
finales to each act. They become the principal means of integrating
the entire opera. Both Robin's aria (pp. 106-108; Ex. 9-14), with its
relatively uncomplicated orchestra accompaniment, and that of
Rosamund (pp. 236-239; Ex. 9-15), with choral accompaniment
added to that of the orchestra, adhere closely to the descending
triadic pattern of the original motive and are quite simple in overall
structure. Auburn's version (pp. 170-173) is more artfully conceived, the Rose motive being but one of several (albeit the most
important) in the rich orchestral accompaniment. The motive is
heard in the cello (Ex. 9-16, m. 1) and is answered by one of the
Fairyland themes in the violin (m. 2). The aria reaches its climax
with a long-held high A by the tenor, yet another instance where
Parker discarded his earlier declamatory theories and returned to
more traditional emphasis on musical line and even virtuosity.

        Fairyland retains some of the dramatic-musical features of
Mona. Leading motives are used, but they have neither the frequency nor the structural importance of the earlier work. Large
sections of even the more dramatic segments are held together with
repeated, rhythmic accompaniments which lack any specific extra-
musical association. Such is the case with the dialogue between
Robin and Corvain in Act I (pp. 1 -33) in which a leading motive
only occasionally crosses a rhythmically patterned, non-motivic
accompaniment.

        The diversified style of *Fairyland* enabled the composer to
give his orchestra a highly varied expressive scope. Although the
score calls for the normal complement of woodwind and brass
(rather than the extra-large sections required for *Mona*), organ, steel
chimes, and a wind machine are added to the usual complement of
keyboard and percussion instruments. Admiration for the handling
of the orchestra was practically universal. Amy Beach reflected the
opinion of most American composers who attended the performances when she declared the orchestral writing to be the opera's
outstanding feature:

> It is in the orchestral score that much of the most poignant
> dramatic development is found. At each turn of the page a
> strong bit of melodic beauty is enhanced by some swift turn of
> harmony or modulation, that to follow this mood with the
> fascinating ballet music, in the greatest possible contrast, is a
> triumph of virtuosity.[62]

        In spite of Parker's attempts to write grand opera in a
manner more accessible to the general public, most critics' judgments are akin to those encountered for his earlier works. Hubbard

Example 9-14. Robin's rose aria, Act I, *Fairyland*, Op. 77,
    vc. sc., p. 106, mm. 1-8. Copyright 1915, 1942,
    G. Schirmer, Inc. Used by permission.

described the music as "scholarly," "complex," and "intellectual,"
rather than "inspirational," or "emotional," and concluded that the
"artificial" and "purposely sought" were more evident than the
"logical, direct, and simplest way of procedure."[63] The local critics
tended to compare *Fairyland* with a typical romantic opera and
found it wanting in several respects--among them the lack of sustained melody, the limited appeal of the musical style, the lack of
individual characterization, and, again, the tendency toward
"academic," "uninspired," "artificial" writing.[64]

　　At this late stage in his career, Parker could not shake off the
academic, intellectual image which had haunted him from the very
beginning. In view of what he had accomplished in *Fairyland*,
much of this criticism seems unfair, for some critics seem to have
leaned too heavily on their preconceptions about Parker rather than
the music before them. We are fortunate in having Amy Beach's
thoughtful and revealing commentary that *Fairyland* contains much

Example 9-15. Rosamund's rose aria, Act III, *Fairyland*,
   Op. 77, vc. sc., p. 236, mm. 1-5. Copyright 1915,
   1942, G. Schirmer, Inc. Used by permission.

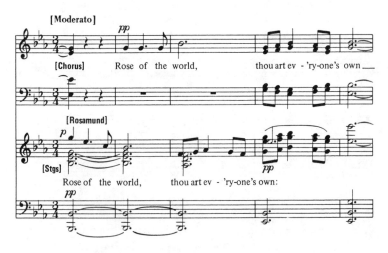

Example 9-16. Auburn's rose aria, Act II, *Fairyland*,
   Op. 77, vc. sc., p. 170. m. 10-p. 171, m. 2. Copyright
   1915, 1942, G. Schirmer, Inc. Used by permission.

interesting and well-made music. Perhaps Los Angeles critic Edwin
Schallert's overall description of *Fairyland* as "popular in the elevated sense of the term," and containing "even a bit of the splendor
of Meyerbeer" is its best assessment and a conclusion certainly
appropriate for a festival opera.

Cupid and Psyche

Parker's final work for the stage, the masque *Cupid and Psyche* (1916), cannot be considered as important or even highly individual, although it does contain some charming music.[65] Nor has the play by John Jay Chapman been considered as an important effort on the author's part. One of his leading biographers remarked: "What we have here is a twentieth-century prose writer imitating a Victorian versemaker's attempt to recapture a Renaissance treatment of a Greek myth!"[66] This historical hodgepodge is accountable in part to Chapman's conception of the production as a play within a play. The Prelude is a Renaissance setting, as guests are depicted gathering at the court of Lorenzo the Magnificent to watch the classic love story enacted after the late version in Apuleius. Turning to the music itself, we find that Parker added yet another historical dimension, for the deftly chiseled, easily singable melodies, the simplified, non-chromatic harmony, the steady rhythmic pulsation, and some of the structures of the pieces, are clearly modeled on the Baroque style.

The unpublished, 140-page manuscript calls for women's chorus, oboe, bells, harp, cembalo, and strings. The twenty-four musical segments consist of an overture in the French Baroque style, some choruses, a long dance scene, and shorter sections which underlie some of the spoken words.

The only musical association resembling the leading motive technique of the composer's operas and choral works is that representing Cupid (Ms score, p. 12). This leaping, rhythmically angular figure is expanded into a musical background for several melodramatic recitations by Cupid. It also is used as a signal by the oboe in assembling the sylvan inhabitants for a celebration. Finally, it appears as an English horn call during the ominous scene in Panthia's cave.

The writing for oboe is demanding but rewarding. Besides its use as a dramatic agent, the instrument functions as an obbligato in some of the choruses and as an expressive solo instrument with harp accompaniment for the scene in Psyche's bedchamber (p. 90). The harpsichord is usually written as a continuo instrument but occasionally has a solo part.

The principal choruses are a pastorale, dirge, drinking song, and final apotheosis. The dirge, sung as Psyche is condemned to marry a serpent, is set in D minor and unfolds in a simple, homophonic style (p. 36). The drinking song is largely in unison, its various segments drawn together by a lively refrain in the violins (p. 69). The concluding chorus is again a simple, homophonic structure; however, its majestic setting is reminiscent of Baroque grandeur.[67]

In one of the few commentaries on the work, Arthur Troostwyk found it "happy and pleasing . . . delightful and melodious."[68] Chapman commented that he thought the music better than his own work.[69] *Cupid and Psyche* shares with other pieces of the last style period--*The Dream of Mary*, *The Red Cross Spirit Speaks*, and *A.D.1919*--the common features of retrenchment to a less esoteric style. With *Cupid and Psyche*, we also have, as with *Six Old English Songs*, one of Parker's more successful attempts to recall the musical style of another era.

Chapter Ten

SECULAR MUSIC FOR SOLO VOICE

The Art Songs

Whereas Parker was considered the leading American oratorio and cantata composer of his time, he was but one of many well-known composers who made significant contributions to the American art song. Among the New England composers, he was overshadowed, particularly in output, by Arthur Foote and George Chadwick. Their works have been hailed as "the beginning of real artistry in American song" by William Treat Upton, whose survey *Art Song in America* is still the most encyclopedic in this area.[1]

The 1878 *Kate Greenaway Songs* are the composer's earliest. Their nursery-rhyme texts deal with such subjects as pets, toys, trips, parents, playmates, and many other childhood experiences. The simple one-stanza poems usually have no more than sixteen measures of musical setting divided into four-measure phrases with a few additional measures for a piano introduction, interlude, or postlude. The introductions often consist of the first half of the opening vocal phrase. The accompaniments are restricted to conventional rhythmic figures, which are sometimes replaced by block chords at climactic points. The melodies are nearly always diatonic, and the harmony, largely triadic, with occasional sevenths, ninths, and secondary dominants. *The Musical Times* and subsequent biographical sketches mention that the entire group of fifty songs was written in two days,[2] an incredible burst of composing after only slightly more than a year's music study. Parker considered them of sufficient merit to publish a few many years later in the *The Progressive Music Series* (1914-19).

Parker's first publication, an 1882 set entitled simply *Three Songs*, without opus number, is stylistically quite similar to the earlier *Kate Greenaway Songs*. His next set, a group of three songs published as Opus 10 in 1886, shortly after his return from Munich, merit more serious consideration for their composer as a maturing songwriter. Among these, "Night piece to Julia," with its evocation both of nocturnal mystery and of youthful love is the best. Its impassioned climaxes and sensitive accompaniment reveal an ardor that is missing in the composer's other music of the time.[3]

No other songs appeared until 1891 when the six songs of Opus 24[b] and three songs, Opus 23--"My love," "O waving trees," and "Violet"-- were published. These two sets are representative of two features of his 1890s style: strong emotional appeal and discursiveness in their compositional technique. Most modulate freely, have a variety of accompanying rhythmic patterns, and have a profusion of descriptive effects.

An example of such kaleidoscopic musical treatment can be found in "The light is fading down the sky," a passionate poem in spite of the peaceful suggestion of the opening line (Ex 10-1). The "horn-fifth" accompaniment of the first two lines establishes the outdoor setting of the song. The words, "thrushes' evening song," have their descriptive figure in the right hand, while the left hand introduces a restless mood with its syncopated rhythmic figure. A dramatic key change down one-half step from E-flat to D major underlines the words "But I have borne with toil and wrong." A chromatic "sigh" figure, resolving back to the dominant of E-flat, along with a sudden change in dynamics, accompanies the words "So long." Thus, the music reflects each change of mood in this brief stanza.

A more unified and harmonically daring song from the Opus 24 group is "Egyptian serenade" (Ex. 10-2). Parker provides an exquisite piece of musical craftsmanship for this simple lyric. The introduction is tonally nebulous with its interplay of B major and

Example 10-1. Opening, "The light is fading down the sky," Op. 24, No. 3, GS, 1891, p. 3, mm. 4-14.

shad - ows grow   and   mul - ti - ply,   I   hear   the thrush-e's ev-'ning

song,   But   I   have   borne   with ___

toil   and ___ wrong   So   long,   So   long!

F-sharp minor chords. The opening vocal phrase touches momentarily on E minor but pushes on to a C-sharp ninth chord (m. 5-6).
The following phrase establishes the dominant (B) key level (m. 7-
10), but, at the close of the stanza, Parker reaches up a major third
to D-sharp (m. 13). This opening section is then repeated a fifth
higher, and the remainder of the song glides gently down to E major
through intermediate cadences on G-sharp and F-sharp minor. The
ending is eloquently extended by means of a Neapolitan cadence.

Example 10-2. Beginning, "Egyptian serenade," Op. 24, No. 2, GS, 1891, p. 3, mm. 1-14.

Parker's accompaniments have many different textures. Upton commented: "Perhaps no other American songwriter of his time surpasses him in freedom and variety of the piano score."[4] The piano occasionally doubles or embellishes the melody, particularly at points of climax. Frequently the instrumental line anticipates that of the voice, as in the "Egyptian serenade" and "The light is fading from the sky" discussed above. These accompaniments resemble those of Alfred Pease and Homer Bartlett in their harmonic fullness, but their independence of melodic line suggests Chadwick's influence. If Parker's songs from this time lack stylistic unity to some degree, they amply repay the listener with the bountiful expressive detail found in their accompaniments. One is surprised to find the composer, who was rather conventional in his writing for solo piano, to have been so imaginative in the piano writing for his songs.

By 1896, Parker had published twenty-four secular and eight sacred songs. From 1896 to 1901 his energy was absorbed mostly by large works, but he did manage to write a few songs, among them, the gay *Spanish Cavalier's Song* (1896), with words by Isabella Parker; *Six Old English Songs*, Opus 47 (1899); and an assortment of songs to poems by Ella Higginson, Editha Ashmon Baker, and Isabella Parker grouped together as Opus 51.[5]

Among these, the *Six Old English Songs* gave the composer an opportunity to draw upon historical styles from the English lutenist-song composers to the eighteenth-century aria. The poems were taken from the works of Elizabethans Samuel Daniel and Thomas Campion; Stuart writers Thomas Carew, Charles Selby, and William Davenant; and one anonymous lyric. The songs have two verses each and are in modified strophic form, employing refrains in the English "fa-la-la" tradition and interludes in the manner of the Baroque *ritornello*. The bass lines are solidly contrapuntal and the harmonic progressions, with transient changes of key and mode at cadence points, suggest the lutenist-song composer style. Despite these seventeenth-century allusions, the writing is actually closer to the eighteenth century. In the more ambitious songs, the refrains, polarity of outer voices, and extended use of sequence are reminiscent of Handel, and the lighter songs suggest Thomas Arne.

In this set is found Parker's most popular song, "The lark now leaves his watery nest," which also enjoyed a great vogue in England as well as the United States at the turn of the century.[6] Audiences of the time must have admired the clever descriptive figures, the clear-cut, rhythmic sequential patterns, the transparent texture, and the virtuosic vocal line (Ex.10-3). The melismatic turns at the ends of several phrases, the variety of dramatic effects, and the brilliant ending, which sweeps to a high B-flat followed by a trill on the penultimate chord, make the song an extremely effective recital piece. Concerning "The lark," Upton remarked: "Its thoroughly objective character is peculiarly congenial to Parker's style, and the result is a song quite perfect of its type."[7] Upton also called the aria, "In a garden," from the opera, *Fairyland*, "austere in its harmonization." These characterizations make Parker appear to be a cool, reserved art-song composer. Rather, "The lark" is a buoyant song from a deliberately eclectic set, and "In a garden" is a charming showpiece in the operetta tradition of the early twentieth century. By using these atypical pieces as examples, Upton has overlooked the ardent romanticism of most of Parker's songs.

Example 10-3. Excerpt, "The lark now leaves his watery
    nest," Op. 47, No. 6, JC, 1899, p. 3, mm. 6-13.

The *Old English Songs* are permeated with allusions to other times and are not an accurate indication of Parker's style. They nevertheless represent an important point in his evolution as a songwriter, for their lightness of texture is increasingly evident in his songs of the twentieth century. The opulence of the earlier New York period thus gives way to a more intimate and terse style. Gone are the poems containing narratives or detailed descriptions, and, in their places, are texts expressing specific thoughts or feelings. These later songs come close to the economy found in the songs of Foote or MacDowell, and many of them maintain the ardor of Parker's earlier period.

Parker did not always exercise careful selectivity in choosing texts for his songs, a characteristic evident in the oddly-matched miscellanies for some of his song sets. Anthologies were sources for many of his texts, which explains in part the wide assortment of poets he used.[8] This criticism cannot be made about the group of seven songs comprising Opus 70 (1910), on poems by Brian Hooker, the very literary librettist for *Mona* and *Fairyland.* Brian Hooker's poetry, although strongly lyrical and directed toward the usual Romantic themes, is more contemporaneous in choice of words and syntax. The group is thematically unified in its treatment of the subject of love in a direct, forceful, even passionate manner.

Parker's choice of simpler musical forms is in keeping with the more decisive, singular sentiment of each song. A modified strophic form is most frequent with the accumulation of feeling swelling to a climax in the second or third stanza. Some songs such as "I shall come back" (No. 1), "A man's song" (No. 2), and "Only a little while" (No. 4), use a sustained cantilena. In others such as "A woman's song" (No. 3), and "Offerings" (No. 6), lyrical writing alternates with more angular and rhythmically fluctuating lines. A salient characteristic of the Brian Hooker songs is the interlocking of melody and harmony to create an intense but nonetheless restrained expressive unity. The melody of "I shall come back," with its numerous appoggiaturas, moves in an oscillating consonant-dissonant relationship to the harmony (Ex. 10-4). The piano part has no superfluous notes; it reinforces the vocal line and provides a sparse but refined harmony. The chromaticism of this later period becomes more fully integrated into the texture and does not stand out as do the clichés of earlier periods.

"Only a little while" is the finest in the set. The firmly etched pentatonic motive in E (Ex. 10-5A) becomes the basis of the refrain at the end of the first stanza, introduces the second stanza now in C (Ex. 10-5B), and finally is the principal motivic material for a splendid lyrical peak at the conclusion (Ex. 10-5C).

The coupling of poetry and music is best realized in the Brian Hooker set among all of Parker's art songs. Here Parker achieves what Donald Ivey has called "a true hybrid," in which both the music and poetic images are synthesized into an expressive whole.[9]

Among the songs which Parker published after 1910, the most notable is a set of three (1914) without opus number. The first, "Morning Song," and the last, "Nightfall," are short and direct, befitting their respective poems. The middle song, "Across the

Example 10-4. Excerpt, "I shall come back," Op. 70,
     No. 1, JC, 1910, p. 8, mm. 3-7.

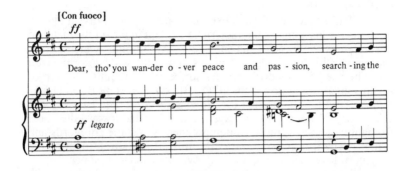

fields," is longer and more elaborate. The most distinctive song in this group is "Nightfall," with its tenuous beginning in B minor and concluding E minor chord.

Although Parker did not compose a large number of songs, their quality, by and large, is high. He always labored to make a distinctive and sometimes striking musical setting for each text. In spite of some elaborate piano parts to his earlier songs, he followed the general trend in American song writing, which Charles Hamm has identified as an emphasis on words and a subordinate piano accompaniment.[10] Parker's song's were written to appeal to a wide public, and, without being sentimental, express post-Romantic fervor. Their present neglect is unfortunate for they are both enjoyable in themselves and fine specimens of the *genre* for their time.

Example 10-5. Excerpt, "Only a little while," Op. 70.,
    No. 4, JC, 1910.

A. Headmotive, p. 26,   B. Beginning 2nd stanza,
    mm. 2-3.   p. 27, mm. 10-11.

C. Conclusion, p. 29, m. 6-end.

Music for Solo Voice and Orchestra

Two works--*Cáhal Mór of the Wine-Red Hand*, Opus 40, a rhapsody for baritone and orchestra (1895), and *Crépuscule*, Opus 62, a concert aria for mezzo-soprano and orchestra (1907)--are more closely related to Parker's efforts in the larger forms than to the art song. Philip Hale noted that *Cáhal Mór* can be described more accurately as "an orchestral rhapsody with baritone voice obbligato,"[11] a description that could, with the change of voice part, be extended to *Crépuscule*. In neither work, however, does the prominence of the orchestra obscure the lyrical and dramatic writing for voice.

When *Cáhal Mór* was finally published in 1910, *Musical America* gave the following description of the text:

> James Clarence Mangan's poem is a subject . . . to engross the attention of a composer with dramatic blood in his veins. It describes in expressive phrases the glory and prosperity that were Erin's while Cáhal Mór of the Wine-Red Hand ruled there with pomp and power. And then it speaks with potent forcefulness of the horror and desolation that followed his downfall--the whole thing being conceived *a la* Poe.[12]

By evoking thoughts of a splendid period in Ireland's history during the thirteenth century, the poem provided Parker with the prevailing theme of his student cantatas, the glorification of medieval chivalry. But the scope and intensity of Mangan's lyric far exceeds the lovelorn themes of *The Ballad of a Knight and His Daughter* and *King Trojan*.

Philip Hale also mentioned that Parker had originally intended to write a cantata on the subject of Cáhal Mór, a statement supported by several structural features of the piece which are also found in the composer's cantatas: the recapitulation of the music for the opening stanza in the final stanza, the importance of the orchestra in interludes and shorter connecting sections, and the unification of the work by means of a recurring motive.

In *Cáhal Mór*, the motive takes on a structural function quite similar to that of the cantata *Dream-King and His Love*, written two years previously. This principal motive is first heard in the long, florid, and tonally fluctuating introduction, its descending, pentatonic line being the distinguishing feature of later variants (Ex. 10-6). Its basic harmonic progression from tonic to dominant in D major is momentarily interrupted by a dominant-tonic chord progression in B-flat major. This interruption of one harmonic progression with another in a different, transient key is a device that Parker would use extensively over a decade later in his opera *Mona.*

Example 10-6. Principal motive, *Cáhal Mór,* Op. 40
(1895), vc. sc., HWG, 1910, p. 6, m. 14-p. 7, m. 1.

The main theme of the introduction to *Cáhal Mór* and those of the first and last stanzas evolve from this principal motive; however, the wide narrative gamut of the poem requires diversified material in the second through the fifth stanzas. The second stanza, concerning the military might of the Cáhal Mór's army, is dominated by a martial orchestral theme which serves as an accompaniment to an amorphous baritone solo (vocal score, pp. 7-9). The third stanza (pp. 9-12) describes the transformation from a present-day Irish rural scene to the splendid countryside that was Ireland during Cáhal Mór's reign. A motive depicting the magnificent dome of the palace extends upward in both the voice and orchestra, poised against a descending chromatic scale in the upper instruments of the orchestra (Ex. 10-7). The change from light to darkness, described in the fourth verse (pp. 14-16), is marked by a shift to the minor mode and a highly irregular rhythmic accompaniment alternating duple and triple eighth-note patterns. The dome theme reappears in an extended form and becomes the principal music supporting the declamatory voice part (pp. 14-17). The orchestral interlude between the fourth and fifth stanzas develops the majestic dome theme in different keys, first in inversion against itself (Ex. 10-8A), and then in rhythmic augmentation (Ex. 10-8B). With the climactic fifth stanza (pp. 17-18), text painting, which had been occasionally evident throughout the work, now becomes its most prominent feature. Broad, lyrical lines are now replaced by fragmented, contrasting phrases, as the destruction of Cáhal Mór's kingdom is described.

Example 10-7. Dome motive, *Cáhal Mór*, Op. 40 (1895),
vc. sc., HWG, 1910, p. 10, m. 6-p. 11, m. 1.

In the final stanza, the engulfing immediacy of the story fades back into the restrictive frame of remote history. Musically, a measure of equanimity is restored with a free recapitulation, both of the opening theme and of elements from the transformation scene.

Cáhal Mór, with its dramatic melody, expressive harmony, and ever-changing structure, is much more forward-looking than Parker's previous major work, *Hora Novissima*. Various reviews of the work are among the most favorable that Parker ever received. Following the first performance in 1895, Philip Hale was ecstatic:

> This Rhapsody is thus far in Mr. Parker's career the
> highest flight of his imagination. There is abandon that comes
> only from firm control of means. There is a keen sense of

dramatic values. There is splendor of thought. There is gor-
geousness of expression.[13]

Example 10-8. Transformation of dome motive, *Cáhal
Mór*, Op. 40 (1895), vc. sc., HWG, 1910.

A. p. 17, mm., 2-5.

B. p. 17, mm., 8-12.

Hale found the musical description of the dome to be the "highest
pitch of esthetic beauty . . . sumptuousness of instrumentation with
a touch of mysticism." Apthorp, on the other hand, expressed his
usual reserve toward a Parker composition: "To us his phrases
always bring the unexpected, and the unexpected in music is often
of a nature of disappointment." He could not decide whether Parker's "general melodic style" was one of "genuine originality" or "a
mere search after novelty."[14] In reviewing the 1910 publication of
the vocal score, *Musical America* called the work "one of the
landmarks in the progress of American vocal composition," saying
that "properly delivered, the song should produce an electrifying
effect."[15] The reviewer further commented that the principal motive
has the "genuine ring of Irish Folk Song, simply but powerfully
harmonized." In his notes for a 1926 Cleveland Orchestra performance, Arthur Farwell mentioned *Cáhal Mór*, along with *Harold
Harfager, The Norsemen's Raid, King Gorm the Grim,* and *North-*

ern Ballad, as evidence of Parker's deep and ineradicable Anglo-Saxon roots.[16]

The significance of *Cáhal Mór* lies in its opulent orchestration, its advanced tonal and harmonic writing, and its imaginative portrayal of the poem's dramatic incidents. A miniature in the grandiloquent style of Wagner's Walhalla music, this work stands between *Dream-King* of 1893 and *The Legend of Saint Christopher* of 1897 as a significant milestone on the path of Parker's evolution as a dramatic composer.

Parker's next work for solo voice and orchestra, *Crépuscule*, takes a middle position stylistically between the late Romantic French style as exemplified in Chausson's *Poème de l'amour et de la mer*, in which the voice part retains a lyrical line over a highly developed orchestral accompaniment, and more discursive vocal writing, as found in Delius's *Sea Drift*, in which the melodic line becomes subordinated to the atmospheric effects created by the harmony. Composed between the years 1904 and 1907,[17] *Créspuscule* is distinctive for its pervading chromaticism, which is also evident in the composer's symphonic poem *Vathek* from the same period. The writing for mezzo-soprano voice is quite varied, containing in some places the large contours of an opera aria and in other places the intimacy of an almost whispered declamatory section. The orchestra has extensive, independent interludes and elaborate motivic development as well as sonorous harmonies. Tone color changes frequently as melodic fragments pass from one instrument to another and is enriched at peaks when various instruments are brought together in a brilliant display of color. The oboe, an instrument for which Parker showed increasing partiality during his later years, has frequent incidental solos and often doubles the mezzo-soprano line.[18]

The tonal vacillation, chromaticism, and sensitive orchestration characteristic of the piece can all be found in Example 10-9, which is taken from the close of the first part. In the first four measures, the orchestra thrusts upward to a D major cadence (m. 4 of excerpt) which the solo voice resists with its sustained appoggiatura on E. By way of contrast, the next cadence on F-sharp minor is weak (m. 6), and the following sixth-chords in the woodwinds, which fall rapidly through major third intervals, eradicate any sense of tonality and become completely coloristic. The home key of E is reestablished momentarily (m. 9), but the piece moves on through chromatic motion to E-flat (m. 11).

In the middle section of the piece (vocal score, pp. 7-11), duple meter, faster pace, stronger pulse, and more traditional, recurring accompaniment figures replace the triple time, moderate pace, and fluid rhythms of the opening section. The lengthy final part is

Example 10-9. Excerpt, *Crépuscule*, Op. 62, vc. sc., GS, 1912, p. 6, mm. 3-13.

given over to an intensive symphonic development of materials introduced in the previous sections.

    Crépuscule's chromatic harmonies and elaborate orchestration relate it closely to the opera *Mona*, on which Parker began to work only a short time later.

Chapter Eleven

THE CHURCH MUSIC

Overview

Of the three aspects of Parker's career--composer, educator, and church musician--his service to the church was generally considered as the most significant during his lifetime. He was regarded as "the most representative church composer in America" by 1915.[1] The body of hymns, anthems, sacred songs, and service music that he composed is sizable, although he was not so prolific as his principal forerunner, Dudley Buck.

In addition to being a successful church organist and a composer of service music, Parker was highly respected for his views on church music. In the course of several addresses and newspaper interviews, he took a position about nearly every church music issue of his time, among which was the sweeping tide of secularization that had engulfed the Protestant church in America by the end of the nineteenth century. One of the most important writers of the period, William Dean Howells, commented about this change, using the erstwhile Puritan stronghold of Equity, New Hampshire, as an example:

> Religion . . . had largely ceased to be a fact of spiritual experience, and the visible church flourished on condition of providing for the social needs of the community.[2]

Religious activity and thought was broadened by such evolutionary concepts as the increasing perfection of humankind. George Santayana observed the American attitude as one in which religion "should be disentangled as much as possible from history and authority and metaphysics, and made to rest honestly upon one's own feelings, on one's indomitable optimism and trust in life."[3]

Religious music reflected this mitigation of dogma and increasing socialization of the church, and the music believed by many to be most suitable in fulfilling the needs of an increasingly wealthy, secular society was that of the quartet choir, a trained singer for each voice part. This small ensemble sometimes sang the musical portion of the service, but more often was the nucleus around which a volunteer choir was gathered. Nineteenth-century Protestantism, with its strong emphasis on social gospel and the creation of a beautiful service, welcomed the solo quartet in spite of its obvious secular trappings because it was capable of producing the sort of polished performances heard in concert halls.

A counterbalance to the quartet choir was the boy choir, a mainstay of earlier European church music, which was being revived in some in some Episcopal churches as a result of the Oxford Movement initiated by the Reverend John Keble, at Oxford, England, in 1833. The Movement appealed for a return to fundamental tenets and rituals of the historical church. Its musical features included not only the use of boy choirs, but also emphasis on choral services, vestments, processions, and a restricted choice of music.

The quartet choir, however, gained ascendancy in most American churches during the 1840s. The movement became so wide-spread "that almost all of the sacred music composed in America during the nineteenth century consisted of solos or duets with concluding quartet."[4] The presence of the solo quartet naturally led composers to create a music of technical complexity and expressive content equal to secular vocal music.

Parker's public statements show that he was unalterably opposed to this swelling secular influence in church music and was quite sympathetic to the tenets of the Oxford Movement. In his principal address on church music, he noted attitudes of "skepticism, agnosticism, and atheism" toward religion in his day and declared much of the church's music to be suitable "for ladies and children rather than for a full-grown male musician."[5]

His preference in church music was that of the Renaissance:

> The time I speak of, the late sixteenth century, seems to me the apex of the development of church music, it slopes in both directions from Palestrina very gradually toward the past, less gradually toward our own time.

He considered church music "weary waste . . . between Palestrina and Bach." Even in the case of the latter, he commented: "They [the cantatas, the passions, and the *B Minor Mass*] do not seem to me like church music, excepting only in so far as they are based upon church songs or chorales used as *canti firmi*." Beethoven and other Classical masters were said to manifest a sort of pantheistic devoutness which is just as evident in their instrumental music as in their liturgical settings. The church music of Liszt and Gounod was considered too "theatrical," and the oratorios of Mendelssohn, "sanctimonious," their thematic material "dull and sometimes vulgar." On the other hand, the "smaller church music" of Gounod was called "exquisite."

Parker had very definite ideas about the church service and the manner in which music was to be used in its enhancement. Concerning the service itself, he remarked:

> A liturgical form of service depends generally upon talk; it does not recommend itself to the seeker after abstract beauty--but there is an elevation, a holiness apparent in a simple, pure service in a great Gothic building which cannot but do a man good, regardless of religious convictions or lack of them.

Here is a suggestion that music as an art form should never intrude on the basic purpose of worship and, as a consequence, should remain subordinate to the liturgy.

Vocal music he thought to be more compatible with worship than instrumental music: "Religion seems the only concrete form of emotion which finds a natural expression in song." The "all-paid" mixed choir with four solo voices was Parker's practical choice for service music; however, if certain difficulties could be overcome, he considered the boy choir as more suitable:

> The personal element is what offends me most in connection with any service in church. . . . The boy choir . . . is so very impersonal . . . also decorative--but difficulty to sing in tune and lack of male altos does not make their growth likely.

He disparaged as an "abomination of desolation" that peculiarly American organization, the quartet choir. Unaccompanied choral singing he considered "the greatest good in church music, if well done. There is no danger of too much of it."[6]

At first, Parker was barely tolerant of using orchestras in the church service, preferring the organ instead.[7] By 1915, he had changed his mind and encouraged orchestral performance over that of the organ. Referring to the gallery orchestras of early America, he commented: "I cannot help think that our forefathers were on a more promising road than we are following at present."[8]

His preference in contemporary anthems was decidedly English; but even in this choice, he was mildly sardonic:

> To the conscientious choir-master, the English anthem
> is a great blessing. It is always easy, or the great publishing
> houses will not buy it. . . . What is so useful, so soothing, so
> inoffensive as a cool, grave English anthem?[9]

Parker's specific suggestions were Sir John Goss's *Oh Saviour of
the World*, Sir George Martin's *Holy Spirit*, George Elvey's *Come,
Holy Ghost*, and Sir John Stainer's *I saw the Lord*.[10]
There also exist some miscellaneous comments concerning
both anthems and church music in general which were excluded
from any of Parker's extant addresses.[11] They show even more
candidly the extent of his dissatisfaction with much of the religious
music of the day:

> What is a modern anthem?--Barnby, Sullivan, Stainer,
> [are] frankly Victorian. Barnby is the weakest, but I am per-
> plexed to say which is strongest. Stainer is more useful.
> Martin and Stanford are a fine pair for comparison: one,
> strong; the other, weak. But we find weakness more sympa-
> thetic than strength.

> One of the characteristics of our church music is that it
> is so yielding to fashion. . . . Perosi, in his oratorios (so-called)
> is the strongest illustration of modern fashionable methods
> applied to Church music. The result is the milkiest kind of
> lukewarm rubbish.

> The same things that make other kinds of music good
> will make church music the same--but nothing else. The same
> proper relation between material and form--the same respect for
> economy--the same discreet use of a suitable vocabulary of
> harmony.

His bias toward tradition is evident in his conclusion that "a promising feature of modern anthems is the great antiquity of some of
them. The older it is, the newer it sounds."
If Parker was severe in his opinions about anthems of the
time, he had, of necessity, a more compromising attitude as a practicing musician. A study of the principal anthems he used over a
three-year period at Trinity Church in Boston shows the most frequently performed piece to be M. B. Foster's *O for a Closer Walk
with God* (six times), hardly an anthem in the "severe" style.[12] The
representation of English composers is preponderant: sixteen performances among nine anthems for Stainer, nine performances
among seven anthems by Sullivan, twelve performances among
eight anthems by Barnby, and ten performances among four

anthems by Martin. Continental composers are represented with
nine performances among three anthems by Dvořák, thirteen performances among seven anthems by Gounod, and ten performances
among seven anthems by Mendelssohn. As for American composers, Parker used nine of his own anthems in seventeen performances, two by Chadwick, and one by Foote.

The Anthems

Parker wrote twenty-two published anthems (over two-thirds
of his total output) within the ten-year period immediately before
1900, another six during the first decade of the twentieth century,
and only one during the last ten years of his life. Some of his most
enduringly popular pieces--*Bow Down Thine Ear, The Lord Is My
Light, Give Unto The Lord, I Will Set His Dominion In The
Sea*--were written around the time of *Hora Novissima*.
Although anthem composing ceased to be a major concern
fairly early in his career, Parker continued to enjoy a reputation as
the leading American church composer throughout his life. In
1916, *The Lord Is My Light* was named the most frequently used
anthem in a symposium on sacred music conducted by *Diapason*.[13]
Eight years later, Harold W. Thompson made a survey of "what
anthems our leading Episcopal Church choirmasters find most
useful,"[14] and, although no single Parker anthem received first
place, his anthems as a whole were voted the most popular.[15] By
mid-twentieth century, he had dropped to twentieth place in a tabu-
lation of "anthems . . . used during one season between 1949 and
1953" by thirty-seven "leading choirs in this country," over half of
which were Episcopal.[16]
Those anthems from the period of *Hora Novissima* follow a
compositional formula rather standard for their time. The opening
section is written often in a major key and at a rapid tempo. The
melody is diatonic and rhythmically simple (Ex. 11-1). After the
opening choral statement, often a musical period in length, the
composer frequently divided the next musical period into antecedent-consequent phrases, alternating women's and men's voices.
The middle sections often call for solo, quartet, or semi-chorus.
The tempo is usually slower, and the meter, often compound. The
tonal relationship to the opening section varies, but the submediant
key, major or minor, is frequently used. The more secular style of
these middle sections is the result of greater emphasis on chromatic
harmony as well as melodic types which resemble popular music of
the period (Ex. 11-2). The remaining parts of these anthems are

treated more freely. A recapitulation is sometimes employed, with some extension of the opening melody plus a coda (*The Lord Is My Light* and *Give Unto The Lord*); however, a new closing theme is not uncommon (*Before The Heavens Were Spread Abroad*, and *I Will Set His Dominion In The Sea*).

Example 11-1. Opening, *I Will Set His Dominion in the Sea*, N, 1891, p. 1, mm. 5-12.

Example 11-2. Middle section, *I Will Set His Dominion*, N, 1891, p. 4, m. 17-p. 5, m. 1.

The anthems Parker wrote around the turn of the century are, on the whole, less exuberant and more lyrical than their predecessors. Homogeneity rather than variety is emphasized. Their rhythms and melodies are less closely related to secular types, and some begin with quietly flowing solos rather than the full, march-like, opening choruses of the earlier anthems. Such is the case for *In Heavenly Love Abiding* (Ex. 11-3). Overall structures of these later anthems are more varied, and the degree of chromaticism remains about the same for both earlier and later periods. Text-painting, so evident in the secular cantatas and most of the larger religious works, is infrequent.

Of two general characteristics concerning Parker's anthems, their simplicity and sensuous quality, the former is achieved through clear melodic and phrase structure, conventional harmonic progressions, and unequivocal tonal structures. Their sensuous impression is a result of melodic contour, occasionally striking

Example 11-3. *In Heavenly Love Abiding*, N, 1900, p. 1,
    mm. 12-20.

modulations, and chromatic embellishments to basically diatonic
chord progressions. These techniques at times seem to contradict
the stand against such writing which he took in his church music
addresses. For example, the chromatic embellishments of the
opening to one of his most popular anthems, *The Lord is My Light*
saps some strength from its diatonic vigor (Ex. 11-4). In the middle
section, the compound meter, the harmonization in thirds of the
opening portion of the melody and the appoggiatura chord on the
word "mercy," all make a rather unctuous impression (Example 11-
5). Some anthems have the dramatic features of Parker's more
ambitious choral works, such as the sudden modulation from A to C
major in Example 11-6. Such tendencies in Parker's writing have
caused some observers to use his anthems as exemplars of the
sentimental style of the time. Archibald Davison singled out the
composer's anthems for such criticism on four counts: frequency of
solo quartets, use of rhythms reminiscent of dance music, emphasis
on vocal virtuosity, and chromaticism.[17]

Example 11-4. Beginning, *The Lord Is My Light*, GS, 1890,
    p. 2, mm. 1-4.

Example 11-5. Middle section, *The Lord Is My Light*, GS,
    1890, p. 6, mm. 7-13.

Another critic of Parker's church music, Linda Jane Clark,
concluded, in her "case study" of Parker as organist and choirmaster
at Boston's Trinity Church, that he subordinated any inclinations he
may have had to produce a strong, distinctive church music to the
socially oriented sermons of pastors Phillips Brooks and Winchester
Donald.[18] We have Parker's own statement that he considered
music to be subordinate to the liturgy and perhaps the sermon, but,
at the same time, it is obvious that he did not envision a pronounced
difference between secular and sacred music writing that both
Davidson and Clark appear to demand. Clark explores this idea
further, to the point of splitting esthetic hairs, in her conclusion that
"Parker wrote and planned music for a liturgical event in which
[music's] place was secondary--an event in which the aesthetic
realm was *not* another mode of the interpretation of the Word of
God but merely a backdrop to the verbal interpretation of it."[19] This
thesis suggests that Parker deliberately wrote second-rate church
music, perhaps by making concessions to popular taste. But we also
find the same sensuous characteristics in Parker's most ambitious
music. If a significant difference between the composer's church

Example 11-6. Excerpt, *In Heavenly Love Abiding*, N, 1900,
    p. 3, mm. 9-16.

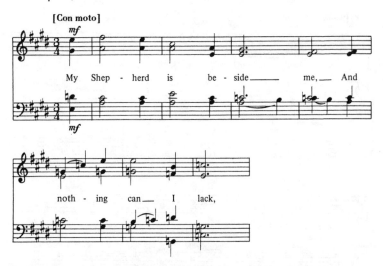

and secular music is to be observed, that distinction appears to be a matter of difficulty: the church music is accessible to most choirs, whereas the major religious works and secular music are more challenging.

Although Parker's high-minded principles, as expressed in his lectures, may appear to later generations as inconsistent with his own practice, compromise was probably necessary considering the strong secular pressure on the church of his time. As a leading church musician, he championed much of the Oxford Movement's efforts to develop a dignified, more impersonal service as a buffer to the erosion of religious values by secular ideas, but the full extent of the Movement had not yet affected deeply the substance of the music itself.

The Cantatas

Parker composed two multi-movement works which clearly belong under the discussion of church music rather than under that of larger choral works. These cantatas were undoubtedly intended to be sung by a church choir as a part of Christmas services rather than by a choral society, since their stylistic features are more nearly related to church music than the oratorios.

The first of these, *The Holy Child* (1893), for solo voices, chorus, and organ, was written at the time Parker left New York for his new post at Trinity Church in Boston. Aside from *Hora Novissima*, it is the only other large sacred work from the New York period. Undoubtedly it was written in order to meet the demand for a seasonal work, since it is little more than a group of anthems and sacred songs strung together. Isabella Parker fashioned the text from various sections of the Christmas story, and the whole is divided into two parts of four numbers each.

The second church cantata, *The Shepherds' Vision*, Opus 63, for solo voices, chorus, and organ, was written a few years after Parker had assumed the music post at Saint Nicholas in New York City in 1903. His aunt, Alice Jennings, translated the verse from the German of his good friend, Frank Van der Stucken.

Although *The Shepherds' Vision* is constructed with somewhat more artifice than *The Holy Child*, their purposes as occasional service music are identical. *The Shepherds' Vision* is shorter, having only five sections. The rather conventional first three parts relate the familiar Bible story: the picture of the shepherds in their fields is told in the opening homophonic chorus (with Parker's usual choice of a compound meter for a pastoral setting), the visit of the angel in the following soprano solo, and the journey of the shepherds to Bethlehem in an almost literal repeat of the opening chorus. The remainder of the text examines the story's implications in a colorful bass solo, and rejoicing is expressed in the final "Hallelujah" chorus. The music in these last two sections approaches the level of an oratorio in complexity.

Service Music

Parker wrote only two services: one in E major, Opus 18 (1892), and another in B-flat major, Opus 57 (1904). Both are quite similar in style. The earlier service remained the more popular throughout his life. Shortly after its publication, a church magazine reported that it was used "in at least two parishes other than his [Parker's] own."[20] At the time of Parker's death, an obituary noted that it was "constantly seen on the choral programs of England."[21]

These services illustrate Parker's ideals and those of the Oxford Movement for church music more completely than any of his other works. If his anthems generally follow his exhortation to compose "in the line of greater simplicity and directness," the liturgical settings reflect even more directly the corollary that "there are wonderful possibilities left in simple triads."[22]

Service in E shows unusual restraint.[23] The choral writing is predominantly four-part, and the organ is restricted to an accompanying role excepting a few short interludes. Only a somewhat constrained chromaticism is the principal concession made to the taste of the period. Most of the melodies are rhythmically placid, move conjunctly, and have simple harmonic support. Parker integrated the music for the various sections of the service to some degree with such devices as a recurring, ascending tetrachord, which dominates "Te Deum Laudamus" and is a prominent feature in the opening melody of "Jubilate Deo." Also, the middle part of the latter section has a melodic contour quite similar to the opening theme of the "Credo." If this service music does not reach the quality of Stanford's, it is nevertheless several steps above "triviality, sentiment, and sugary harmony," a characterization which has been made of the service music of Victorian composers such as Barnby, Sullivan, George Martin, and Stainer.[24]

Hymns

No composer had a greater respect for what he frequently called the "folkmusic" of the church, the hymn tune, than Parker. The preface to his own edition of The Hymnal (1903) contains the best exposition of his views:

> In more than twenty years' experience as choirmaster the editor has not observed that improvement in congregational singing which is so earnestly to be desired. A school of hymnody, which many call sentimental, has grown up and flourished during the past twenty years without improving, so far as we have observed, either the quantity or the quality of congregational singing. We may almost believe that our grandfathers had better church music for the people than we have. . . . But signs are now discernible of a desire for healthier, sturdier, more manly feeling in hymns and tunes. These signs are unmistakable and widespread, and are most gratifying evidences of the improvement of public taste. Lovers of hymnody no longer seek sensuous pleasure in rhythm and harmony, desired naturally enough by the very young, but look rather for convincing earnestness and sobriety of feeling. Clearly we need not more tunes, but better ones, attaining a higher standard of musical worth and dignity.[25]

Parker was quite intemperate in discussing hymn tunes used in the evangelical churches. Nowhere is his conviction concerning the effect of music on morality so evident as in the following statement from 1900:

> So is evil music as harmful to our sense of beauty, to our aesthetic sensitiveness, as these things are for our physical body. . . . People ask for bread and we give them sponge cake; for fish, and they are lucky if they get eels--sometimes real snakes, loathsome, wriggling, slimy moody and snakey [i. e., Rev. Dwight Moody and Ira Sankey] snakes--vulgar with the vulgarity of the streets and the music hall (great applause). If sentimentality is evil--and I think no one here will care to deny it--what shall we say of vulgarity? . . . Let the stuff be confined to the mission, where it may do good. Among people of any appreciable degree of refinement and culture it can only do harm.[26]

The composer was no more charitable toward the hymns of his own church. In an 1899 address, he created considerable indignation by calling the Episcopal Hymnal "a painful exhibition of vulgarity tempered by incompetency."[27] Its hymns were described as "the lowest form of music . . . just after the Anglican chant,"[28] which, in turn, is "a musical trilobite, scarcely to be distinguished from a vegetable."[29]

Parker's rhetoric set the standards for his own edition of *The Hymnal*, which came out in 1903. It was the fifth tune book to be published after the adoption of a revised and enlarged edition of *The Hymnal* at the General Convention of the Protestant Episcopal Church in 1892.[30] In his edition, Parker claimed to have discarded many of the "sentimental" hymns so prevalent in other hymnals; however, he admitted: "The editor's ideal of a Hymnal with music for congregations has not been fully attained. The quality of sentimentality cannot be quite eliminated."[31]

Parker stressed the purpose of *The Hymnal* to be congregational singing, noting that such activity "is best and heartiest in other than Episcopal churches." To achieve a situation in which both trained and untrained voices "join freely in the public worship," the following features of *The Hymnal* were enumerated:

> Alternate tunes, arrangements of other than churchly music, tunes for the choir in which the congregation cannot well join, as well as metronome marks and dynamic signs, have been avoided as much as possible, for all these seem rather to lessen than to add to the directness of choice and simplicity of expression which this book aims to encourage.

In an effort to include "the inheritance from our forefathers which we cannot afford to lose or neglect," the edition contains fewer new tunes than the other Protestant Episcopal hymnals. Also, by comparison, English hymnody--that of John Dykes, Henry Smart, Stainer, Myles Foster, and Sullivan was stressed more than that of Americans such as Lowell Mason. The result is a tune book representing Parker's musical tastes to a large degree. He was not able to reconcile his tendency to educate the congregation musically with his desire to promote congregational singing. The fact that he had not included enough "standards" that most congregations knew and loved did not go unnoticed in the church journals of the time.[32] Although the edition was highly praised for its lofty purposes, it did not achieve general popularity.

In *The Hymnal*, Parker used thirty of his own hymn tunes, set to thirty-four texts, representing most, if not all, of his hymn tune compositions up to that time. Five other tunes not found in his own edition are found in *The Hymnal* of 1918, which he assisted in editing.[33] Parker's tune's are invariably diatonic, and their harmonies have some chromatic embellishments. As might be expected, his harmonic progressions, while much more conventional than the large body of his work, nevertheless are more varied and striking than usual hymn-tune settings of this period.

Parker's hymn settings have elicited varying appraisals from critics. One of his contemporaries remarked: "Occasionally the composer reached out for organistic, less vocal harmonies . . . and showed . . . a fondness for pungent discordance."[34] At mid-century, Eric Routley described Parker's hymn tunes as a buttress against the post-Civil War flood of sentimentality which had engulfed hymn tune composition, an evaluation which undoubtedly would have pleased the composer, and named "Mount Zion" as an outstanding piece for its time.[35] However, Linda Clark fails to see Parker as anomalous among hymn-tune writers of his day, commenting: "Parker . . . was not able to eradicate that touch of sentimentality [in hymn-tunes] that is so often identified with late Victorian music."[36]

When compared to the overall contents of *The Hymnal*, Parker's hymn tunes are above average in difficulty. One minister, who had commissioned Parker to write some hymn tunes for a Methodist Sunday School hymnal, made the following comment along with his remittance: "I can assure you the tunes were sincerely admired by us all. The only criticism was they were--some of them--a little too 'mature,' a little beyond the grasp of our younger people."[37] Nevertheless, Parker's tunes were in demand for hymnals of all faiths. Requests for permission to publish them in at least twenty-eight different hymnals, from 1907 to 1919, are on file among the Parker papers at Yale.

Parker's hymn tune *Courage*, set to the text "Fight the good fight," is a bracing tune capable of being grasped quickly by the congregation (Ex. 11-7). Among its notable features are a melody which evolves continuously and effectively up to the final climactic period, part-writing more independent than most hymn settings, and imaginative harmonization, with transient dominant-tonic progressions to the mediant (mm. 7-8), the subdominant (mm. 11-12, 17-18), and the dominant keys (mm. 19-20). Two chromatic mannerisms typical of the period are evident in the half-step dip of the melody and supporting harmony at the end of the second verse (mm. 15-16) and in the diminished supertonic triad of the final cadence progression (m. 22). *Courage* indeed exemplifies Parker's ideal for a hymn tune somewhere between "the simplicity of our forefathers . . . [and] the mawkishness and platitudes of our modern hymnal."[38]

One leading Episcopal minister, Canon Winfred Douglas, went so far as to call Parker's hymns his greatest and most lasting contribution at the composer's memorial service in 1920:

> He alone among our composers attained an individual style which was a real contribution to the rich treasures of hymnody. These tunes, while keeping the personal characteristics distinctive of their composer, have achieved great popular success because they well express the feeling of our time and of our country.[39]

As with Parker's anthems, later generations have had difficulty in reconciling the statements of the composer and his contemporaries with the hymn tunes themselves. He avoided overt sentimentality, but there remains for us a suggestion of the sensuous style he professed to dislike. Although Parker did not manage to throw off completely the prevailingly secular characteristics of church music in his time, he was at least moderate in his use of them. The gulf between our concept of a suitable religious music and that of his generation is evident in the fact that the very principles of the Oxford Movement in which he believed were later used to discredit his own compositions.

Excerpt 11-7. Hymn "Fight the good fight," tune
"Courage," *Hymnal*, HWG, 1903, pp. 512-13.

Chapter Twelve

INSTRUMENTAL MUSIC

Introduction

The small quantity of Parker's instrumental music, relative to that of the other New England composers, is dispersed through several media, from piano and organ character pieces to a few large, symphonic works. He did not choose to concentrate enough on a particular instrumental *genre* to establish the kind of reputation which made MacDowell preeminent in the piano music and Foote and Chadwick important in symphonic and chamber music. Parker's lack of inspiration for purely instrumental composition is apparent particularly during his emerging years as a composer. Comparing two major student works, the cantata *King Trojan* with the *Symphony in C*, one finds that *King Trojan* approaches the technical complexity and expressive level of Dvořák's popular cantata *The Spectre's Bride*, whereas the *Symphony in C* is much more conservative in its allusions to Classical style.

As a young composer and church musician in New York during the late 1880s and 1890s, Parker turned to the writing of short, recital pieces for piano and organ which, on the whole, are not particularly distinctive. He also wrote a few longer chamber pieces and an overture for orchestra, *Count Robert of Paris*, which point toward his fully mature instrumental works, the *Organ Sonata*, the *Organ Concerto*, and the two symphonic poems, *A Northern Ballad* and *Vathek*.

These last-named orchestral works are Parker's highest level of achievement in a purely instrumental idiom. The expanded dynamic range and varied tone color of the orchestra seemed to suggest to him both an expressive melody and harmony and an imaginative counterpoint which begin to compare with his major choral works and operas. Following a performance of his tone poem *A Northern Ballad*, one observer wrote:

> The impression left by the whole is that if Mr. Parker would give up writing church music he has the stuff in him to turn out most effective secular material. His music is virile and fullbodied, and its eclecticism is not greater than that of most music now being written.[1]

Student Orchestral Compositions

Parker's earliest pieces, some short overtures for string orchestra, were written during that fruitful period of study under Chadwick (1881-82). Although they are student works and do not yet show distinctive characteristics of the composer's style, they are testimony to his prodigious production and rapid technical growth.

The four extant orchestral works from Parker's Munich study (1882-85) are *Concert Overture in E-flat*, *Regulus--Overture Heroique*, *Venetian Overture and Scherzo*, and the *Symphony in C*. The last three are more than merely student exercises. Parker thought enough of them to have them performed on a few orchestral programs shortly after his return to America; however, none had the importance for his career that "Rip Van Winkle" overture had for Chadwick's upon the latter's return to America.

Both *Regulus* and *Venetian Overture and Scherzo* show considerable development over the pre-Munich overtures in expressiveness, individuality of thematic material, and more variegated tone color. Another significant advance is the addition of development sections in both works. Although the *Venetian Overture and Scherzo* bears two consecutive numbers (Opuses 12-13), it probably was originally intended as a single work, the G minor *Scherzo* being the relative key to its preceding, B-flat major *Overture*. Furthermore, the surviving manuscript is continuously paginated from the beginning of the *Overture* to the end of the *Scherzo*. Parker evidently sanctioned its separation into two pieces, as the *Scherzo* was played alone on one of Van der Stucken's 1886 Novelty Concerts.[2] Since the composer's choral and chamber music from this period is more advanced, one is surprised that he allowed this piece, written in the style of a sprightly Haydn minuet, to be performed and thus considered as representative of his work.

Parker's single attempt at composing a symphony also lacks originality. In organization and style, it reveals a model no later than early Beethoven. After one or two performances of isolated movements upon his return to America, the composer allowed the work to lie dormant.

The Chamber Music

A few studies for string quartet, a violin sonata, a "Serenade" for violoncello and piano, and a piano trio are the extant chamber pieces from Parker's lessons with Chadwick (1881-82). As a group, they show more extensive contrapuntal treatment and motivic development than the orchestral overtures from the same period. Two student quartets (E minor and A major) from the Munich years also are extant. Parker wrote four mature chamber works: a string quartet and quintet, and two suites: one for piano, violin, and cello, and the other for violin and piano.

The *String Quartette in F Major* (1886) is Parker's most extensive instrumental writing up to that time. It is a substantial, four-movement work: a sonata-allegro movement, a lyrical "andante-lento" movement, a scherzo and trio, and an "allegro molto" finale. Mendelssohn or even Schumann, rather than Haydn and Beethoven, now appear to be his models. Following a Detroit performance in 1887, the *Evening Journal* commented:

> [The] work is a natural, modern in spirit and treatment. While some of its phrases were evidently written for their striking effects and not to follow out any distinct musical thought, the work is on the whole, graceful and melodious, though not in any way remarkable.[3]

Reaction of other Detroit critics was favorable but not enthusiastic. They were impressed by the "craftsmanship" and "cleverness," but uncertain about the "purposeful expression" of the work.

The *String Quintette in D Minor*, Opus 38, was first performed in 1895 on one of the Kneisel Quartet chamber music programs. Some discrepancy exists between Louis Elson's description of the piece and the parts-only holograph at Yale (two violins, one viola, and two cellos). Elson wrote of separate movements: the first, "free in form" with a "march-like theme"; the second, a "serenade-like" Andante; the third, a Scherzo composed of a "brisk" theme supported by a rapid figuration, pizzicato, and contrasted with intervening legato episodes; and the finale, "some broad work," with "a subsidiary theme of great beauty."[4] The holograph reveals the *Quintette* to be a continuous but sectional piece in which the principal theme undergoes transformation from a dirge-like opening through a spirited allegro, a cantabile, three-quarter time section, and the return of the principal theme in a lively finale. Its performance time is approximately eight minutes. Apparently these parts and the piece performed on the Kneisel concert are the same, although Elson's description applies closely only to the first and last movements. The Boston critics showed a wide range of opinion about its quality. Louis Elson was the most highly impressed, calling the composition "a noble work, and one which possibly indicates America's chief composer of the future."[5] Even Apthorp, who was usually the most reserved of the Boston writers towards Parker's music, compared the work favorably with the quintets of Boccherini, Schubert, and Brahms.[6] Only Philip Hale remained unimpressed: "I pay tribute to Mr. Parker's tunefulness and contrapuntal facility, but I cannot regard this quintet as one of his most inspired works."[7]

Both the *Quartette* and *Quintette* have had recent performances which show them to be vibrant works worthy of a place beside the chamber music of other late nineteenth-century American composers which is now being revived.[8]

Parker's two suites have the conservative cast of his piano music. The earlier *Suite for Piano, Violin, and Violoncello*, Opus 35 (1893), is a conventional, four-movement work: "Prelude," "Tempo di Minuetto," "Romance," and "Finale"; the *Suite for Violin and Pianoforte*, Opus 41 (1894), has a brief "Prelude Quasi Fantasia" followed by an untitled second movement, then a "Canzona," an "Intermezzo," and a "Finale."

Each of these movements has a prevailingly songlike quality; however, in some of the very places that Parker appeared to be achieving a truly uninhibited melodic expansiveness, he seemingly hastened to withdraw, almost apologetically. Consider the contrasting theme of the "Tempo di minuetto," Opus 35 (Ex. 12-1). After an introductory section in which the melody vacillates uncertainly between G minor and B-flat major, the piano establishes the major mode emphatically by leaping upwards to a high B-flat (m. 4) and descending in a long, two-octave scale emphasizing the subdominant (mm. 5-7). The gesture ends with a disappointingly weak cadence in the tonic key (m. 8).

For the most part, critics of the Boston performances of these works were respectful but not overly enthusiastic. Decorative adjectives such as "tuneful," "graceful," "melodious," and "fresh"--descriptions which were also applied to the *String Quartette* and the *Quintette*--are sprinkled throughout reviews of these suites as well.[9]

Parker's chamber works follow precedents laid down by both Arthur Foote and George Chadwick. Frequency of canonic

Example 12-1. Excerpt, "Tempo di minuetto," *Suite for Piano, Violin, and Violoncello*, Op. 35 (1893), GS, 1904, p. 18, mm. 1-8.

treatment and simultaneous presentation of leading themes in counterpoint, as found in Opus 35, show the influence of Chadwick. Similarities with Foote's style can be seen in Parker's cantabile themes and the alternating of lyrical with developmental areas. Sections of Parker's chamber music suggest that he may have been capable of equaling his associates had he given that medium more sustained attention.

The Piano Music

Parker's entire published output for piano includes but four sets of pieces and two short compositions written for an anthology of piano music, making a total of twenty pieces.[10] All appeared before 1900 and can be grouped within the romantic, character-piece *genre*. Their most characteristic form is a ternary design to which a coda is appended. The opening section is followed by a digression which becomes evident because of a change in one or more elements: melodic style, texture, key, mode, and/or tempo. The return to the opening section is usually modified by melodic ornamentation, a more complex rhythmic and harmonic pattern, and, sometimes, a carry-over of musical ideas from the middle section. In the coda, materials from the middle section are usually more heavily emphasized, making the formal structure A-B-A'-B'.

Within the sections themselves, musical ideas are worked out in a variety of ways. Sometimes, the theme of a particular section is developed so systematically and carefully that the section itself is quite unified and difficult to subdivide any further. Such is the case of the opening sections of "Elegie" (Opus 9, No. 1), "Ballad" (Opus 23, No. 2), and "Rondino" (Opus 23, No. 3). In other cases, individual sections fall into subsections which are, within themselves, three-part designs, as in the opening sections of "Scherzino" (Opus 19, No. 2) and "Novellete" (Opus 23, No. 6), or the contrasting section of "Rondino" (Opus 23, No. 3). Other sections are subdivided into a binary arrangement, such as the opening section of "Reverie" (Opus 23, No. 1) and the contrasting sections of "Ballad" (Opus 23, No. 2) and "Fairy tale" (Opus 23, No. 4).

Parker's piano pieces began to appear quite early on concert programs of some contemporary performers. William H. Sherwood used the "Impromptu" from Opus 9 in one of his Boston piano recitals during the 1887-88 season.[11] This piece, while neither difficult nor intense in feeling, is pianistic and immediately appealing. Little difference in esthetic purpose is found between "Impromptu" and another popular piano work, "Valse gracile" (Opus 49), which was on the celebrated recital of American piano music given by Josef Hofmann at Carnegie Hall on 23 January 1919. Critic Richard Aldrich found the "Valse" to be "swift, graceful, in the salon manner of Liszt or Moszkowski."[12]

Two other pieces from Parker's Opus 49 group (1899), "Conte sérieux" and "La Sauterelle," can be found in a modern edition, John Gillespie's *Nineteenth-Century American Piano Music*. They are very characteristic of Parker's composing for the piano. Gillespie finds the first piece "attractive" and the second "Parker at his charming best."[13]

Although much of Parker's piano music was popular and easily accessible, it was not showy or impassioned. Perhaps its inability to achieve wide popularity can be attributed, in part, to a certain restraint which Rupert Hughes described in the following manner:

> [Parker] has what you might call the narrative style. He follows his theme as an absorbing plot, engaging enough in itself, without gorgeous digressions and pendent pictures. His work has something of the Italian method. A melody or a theme, he seems to think, is only marred by abstruse harmony, and is endangered by diversions. One might almost say that a uniform lack of attention to color possibilities and a monotonous fidelity to a cool, gray tone characterize him.[14]

"Novelette" (Opus 23, No. 6) fits Hughes's description of Parker's piano music in its pursuit of a thematic idea, although the harmony is more imaginative than the writer suggests. Beginning in E major (Ex. 12-2A), Parker cadences in D-sharp minor at the end of the second period (Ex. 12-2B) and continues to run the melodic motive through a number of other keys before the piece concludes.

Nowhere is the general impression of Parker as a conservative composer more clearly suggested than in his piano music. His tonal schemes are quite conventional, although a few are unusual. For example, the "Étude mélodieuse" (Opus 19, No. 3), in G-flat major, modulates briefly to both F and G major, chromatically neighboring keys. Sectional forms, clearly structured melodies, chromatically tinged harmonies, and rhythmically gentle, flowing accompaniment figures are musical ingredients that he shared with his equally conservative fellow composers in this medium, Arthur Foote and Arthur Whiting.

The Organ Music

Parker had thirty-three recital pieces, a sonata, and a concerto for organ published. Two juvenile duets for organ and an *Introduction and Fugue in E minor* (1916) are also among Parker's manuscripts at Yale.[15] This output is indeed small when one remembers that Parker's teacher, Rheinberger, had written numerous miscellaneous pieces for organ in addition to twenty sonatas and two concertos.

Example 12-2. Excerpts, "Novelette," *Six Lyrics for the Piano without Octaves*, Op. 23, No. 6, GS, 1891.

A. mm. 1-4.

B. mm. 13-16.

At the time of Parker's death, Hope Leroy Baumgartner made an assessment of the composer's organ compositions, placing them into three periods.[16] The first he framed chronologically, from 1890 to 1896, and deemed "eminently melodious, brimful of youthful enthusiasm." The second period is described as contrapuntal, tending to follow "the ponderous idiom of Rheinberger." No dates are given, but examples representing the second period were published at the same time (1890-93) as those Baumgartner had designated as the first period. Baumgartner ignored the *Organ Concerto* (1902) and grouped the *Sonata* (1908) and the last two sets of character pieces (1908-10) into a third period. Although he made no stylistic comments pertaining to the third period itself, his remarks about the individual pieces suggest that he regarded it as a successful blending of both polyphonic and poetic styles.

Baumgartner's classification needs some revision. Parker's periods of organ composition can be described as follows: 1880-96, 1902 (i.e., the *Organ Concerto*), and 1908-10. The first and last periods cannot be defined by texture but rather contain both contrapuntal and character pieces. Although no radical style changes are evident, the two periods follow the pattern of changes in Parker's other compositions, with the first-period pieces having exuberance, even flamboyance in some cases, and the last, integration and economy. Parker's reluctance to compose for the organ actually came from several, strongly held, personal beliefs. In an address before a chapter meeting of the American Guild of Organists around 1898,[17] he spoke about "the nature and limitations of the instrument" being "incompatible" with the "intense Romanticism of the present day." Furthermore, the example of Bach's immense genius gave him a feeling of futility in composing for the instrument:

> But so long as we have our Bach, whose music is drawn from the whole soul of the instrument, and fitly expressive as nothing else is, of its whole character, no one may call us poor. Let us be content with Bach and measure or test all subsequent organ music by it. Most of it will drop to pieces.

Aside from the sonatas of Mendelssohn (which were described as "shiny from much use"), those of Rheinberger and Gustav Merkel, and the symphonies of Widor, were called "fragmentary," and "limited," along with other post-Bach literature.

Turning to Parker's own compositions, we should distinguish between those written in one of the polyphonic forms and those that resemble the style of the nineteenth-century character piece. Among the recital pieces of the 1890-96 group, most are character pieces. They are organized like the piano pieces in a ternary form plus coda.

Two from the early Opus 17 group are unpretentious. A few idiomatic devices are evident, such as the use of pedal point in "Impromptu," Opus 17, No. 2, (Ex. 12-3), and a rhythmic effect in "Romanza," Opus 17, No. 3: a block-chord, quarter-note melody on one manual echoed as eighth-note afterbeats on the other. The meandering, opening theme of the "Impromptu" has a rhythmic pattern easily adapted to sequences which occur frequently in the earlier organ compositions (Ex. 12-3, mm. 5-7).

Some early pieces have more linear writing. In the most ornate, "Andante religioso," Opus 17, No. 4 (Ex. 12-4), each manual and the pedal part has its distinctive line. The middle section of the piece is much more sprightly than the outer ones because of staccato articulations and an angular, short rhythmic motive. Rupert Hughes considered the work "much better as a gay pastorale than as a devotional exercise."[18] Two other pieces, "Wedding song," Opus 20, No. 1, and "Pastoral," Opus 28, No. 3, also have strong emphasis on contrapuntal writing within the frame of the character piece.

Versatility in handling thematic material is evident in "Canzonetta" and "Eclogue," Opus 36, Nos. 1 and 4, which have

Example 12-3. Opening, "Impromptu," *Four Compositions for the Organ*, Op. 17, No. 2, GS, 1890.

Example 12-4. Opening, "Andante religioso," *Four Compositions for the Organ*, Op. 17, No. 4, GS, 1890.

flowing, wide-ranging melodies evolving from short rhythmic-melodic motives. In both, homophonic texture is prevalent; however, "Eclogue" also depends upon polyphony for part of its structure, containing a canon at the distance of one measure and the interval of one octave.

Among the polyphonic pieces from the early period, "Fughetta," Opus 20, No. 2, of 1890, is a misnomer, for the formal structure and working-out of this piece are as thorough as expected in a full-fledged fugue. Another polyphonic composition from the Opus 20 set, called "Fantaisie," No. 4, has homophonic writing as well. In several ways, "Fantaisie" could be considered a study in compositional procedures later used in *Hora Novissima* and other major choral pieces: the broad chordal opening serves as a repository from which ideas are drawn to be used during the course of the piece; themes which are initially presented in separate sections are later combined; the contrapuntal writing shifts constantly from free to imitative; chromatically-based harmonies are present alongside diatonic; and, finally, some thematic evolution is apparent.

Among the polyphonic numbers in Opus 36, the "Fugue in C minor," No. 3, is an example worthy of the reputation that the composer had gained as one of Rheinberger's best students. Parker may have followed the pattern of the fugue from Rheinberger's *Sonata No. 1*, Opus 27, which is also in C minor, for both are double fugues in which the subjects are announced consecutively and then worked out in combination.

A period of fifteen years separates the earlier organ pieces (concluding with the three pieces in Dudley Buck's *Vox Organi* of 1895) from Parker's last efforts in this medium, the Opus 67 and the Opus 68 groups of 1910. Two pieces in each of these sets can be categorized as character pieces, and both reveal the change that the composer's style had undergone during the intervening years.

"Revery," Opus 67, No. 2 (Ex. 12-5), is constructed in the usual form for the character piece, A-B abbreviated A-Coda; however, the melody no longer grows from short motivic figures treated sequentially. The opening phrase is, in fact, six measures in length and employs only one sequential repetition. Much more highly developed, freely flowing contrapuntal lines in the lower voices replace either the usual homophonic setting or the rather conventional polyphonic devices of the earlier pieces. The pedal part is also drawn into the contrapuntal activity at the end of the phrase, and even some imitation occurs in the upper parts.

Other features of Parker's mature style found in these later works include freer-flowing melodies and a richer harmonic palatte. Fewer chromatic mannerisms of the earlier compositions are evident, and some harmonic progressions are more striking because of the use of chords such as the Neapolitan sixth at climactic points. Counterpoint is less strict and thus does not have the "textbook" aspect of the earlier polyphonic pieces. The writing for organ has fewer orchestral effects, an occasional feature of the earlier compositions, to mar the distinctiveness of the instrument's sound.

A few pieces, such as "Concert piece," Opus 17, and "Concert piece no. 2," Opus 28, do not fit readily into either the polyphonic or character piece categories. In the first "Concert piece," exposition and recapitulation occur without an intervening development in a sonatina structure. Its two principal themes are quite similar: legato, full-breathed, and admirably suited to the

Example 12-5. Opening, "Revery," *Four Compositions for Organ*, Op. 67, No. 2, GS, 1910.

sonority of the organ. The second "Concert piece," with its imitative sections, has a more varied texture than its homophonic predecessor. Its themes show greater contrast, and the minor-mode middle section has a folklike quality, with its principal theme and parallel-third harmonization resembling Brahms's *Hungarian Dances* or Dvořák's *Slavonic Dances*.

Two other pieces in the miscellaneous category are "Triumphal march," Opus 28, No. 1, and a "Festival prelude," Opus 67, No. 1. Both attempt to capture the brilliance and virtuosity of the French school of organ playing that Parker so admired. The opening to "Festival prelude" is illustrative of the full registration, fanfare themes, and driving rhythms found in these pieces (Ex. 12-6).

The last three movements of the *Sonata in E-flat for Organ*, Opus 65 (1908), the composer's largest solo essay for organ, are the apotheosis of various ideas that Parker had used in his smaller pieces for organ. The first movement, "Allegro moderato," in E-flat minor, is a standard sonata form. The middle two movements, however, remind one of the song forms of the character pieces. The second movement, an "Andante" in B major, has a quiet, lyrical character, and the third movement, an "Allegretto" in B-flat minor, is playful and rhythmic. The final movement is an extensive, four-voiced fugue in E-flat major employing all of the polyphonic devices at which the composer was adept.

One of the principal, present-day objections to much organ music from the turn of the century is that composers tried to emulate orchestral tone color to a large extent. From Parker's own

Example 12-6. Opening, "Festival prelude," *Four Compositions for Organ*, Op. 67, No. 1, GS, 1910.

comments on the subject, one would surmise that he objected to the use of the organ as a symphonic substitute,[19] but his own organ music shows no such unequivocal position. Some of the pieces seem designed to illustrate the power, massiveness, and weight characteristic of the organ, and others show the influence of the French coloristic school with numerous suggestions for the use of stops and technical figures more suited to orchestral color and style.

As in the case of his church music, much of Parker's organ writing contains mannerisms of the time which are no longer fashionable. Some of the character pieces appear to be utilitarian rather than artistic. Nevertheless, the polyphonic pieces, the brilliant concert pieces, and the outside movements of the *Sonata* stress musical ideas which have remained popular. This part of Parker's repertory for organ should be revived today. Certainly the *Concerto for Organ and Orchestra* should also be heard again. It not only contains his best writing for organ but is also perhaps his finest purely instrumental achievement. It is discussed under orchestral music below.

Compositions for Orchestra

Parker's six mature orchestral works span twenty-five years, from 1890 to 1915. The two overtures--*Count Robert of Paris*, presented at the first public Manuscript Society Concert in New York in 1890, and *Collegiate Overture*, Opus 72, commissioned for the Norfolk Festival of 1911--use sonata-form procedures, as do the tone poems, *Northern Ballad*, Opus 46, composed for a Boston

Symphony Orchestra concert in 1899, and *Vathek*, Opus 56, written in 1903. *Fairyland Suite*, consisting of the overture, intermezzo, and ballet music from the opera, was written in 1915 for the New Haven Symphony Orchestra. The *Concerto for Organ and Orchestra*, Opus 55, written for Parker's performances with the Boston Symphony Orchestra and the Chicago Orchestra during the winter of 1902-03, combines the composer's intimate knowledge of his major performing instrument with his considerable facility in handling the orchestra.

Parker was able to match most of his contemporaries in interesting, highly varied tone color. Chadwick, however, may have been more imaginative in his treatment of musical ideas, particularly with *Symphonic Sketches* and *Tam O'Shanter*, and was able to reach an individuality in his orchestral writing that Parker never achieved. Even Parker's mature orchestral music has traces of the stiffness apparent in the early instrumental works: a somewhat rigid manipulation of thematic material and preoccupation with structure. Had he relied more on the more fluid techniques he had worked out for the orchestral interludes of his major choral works, the orchestral pieces might have been more notable. In spite of his concern for structure, he did not achieve the clarity of design and consistent style that distinguish both Chadwick's and Foote's instrumental music. Although Parker had Foote's gift for lyrical writing, he was less critical in choosing his ideas. A sometimes jarring juxtaposition of sentimental and severely academic styles occurs in Parker's orchestral compositions, just as it does in his other music. Nevertheless, his orchestral compositions were significant works in their time and add an important dimension to an understanding of his career.

Count Robert of Paris. Parker's first instrumental work after his student days, *Count Robert of Paris*, took the *New York Times* critic somewhat by surprise at the first public concert sponsored by the Manuscript Society of New York in 1890. The brevity of the review and the diffidence displayed by the writer suggest that Parker was still relatively unknown:

> Mr. Parker's "Count Robert of Paris" can hardly be
> given fair judgement from want of knowledge of his aims, but
> his music is muscular, symmetrical, and sonorously scored. He
> is evidently a man of some ability.[20]

This overture is a major development over his earlier, classically-oriented *Symphony in C*. Its broad, lyrical, principal themes become the basis of extensive motivic development throughout the work, and its harmony and orchestration show the more progressive influence of Wagner rather than reminders of Haydn, Beethoven, or Mendelssohn found in earlier works. Particularly notable are the large climaxes, fluidity of movement between sections, and effective thematic transformations.

Count Robert of Paris appears to have grown in favor with critics as Parker became a more prominent composer. Five years after the Manuscript Society performance of 1890, a New York Philharmonic presentation in New Haven elicited several favorable comments, such as a "dignified piece . . . modern in style, vigorous, with every climax well worked out." A "thorough command of orchestration" was said to be evident in "some brilliant and effective passages" for the strings and in "the bold treatment of the brass."[21]

A Northern Ballad and Vathek.

A Northern Ballad was written at a time of continuing controversy over the importance and manner of nationalism in music, a legacy of Dvořák's statements made during his term as Director of the National Conservatory of Music in New York. Both its title and content suggest another step in Parker's move away from German influences, a process begun a few years earlier with his setting of the Irish legend, *Cáhal Mór of the Wine-Red Hand*, in 1895.

The theme of the introduction to *A Northern Ballad* has been described as "of the folk-song variety."[22] Simplicity is evident in emphasis on pentatonic movement, tonic and dominant pitches, short two-measure phrases, and recurring rhythmic patterns (Ex. 12-7). Perhaps the title also caused reviewers to assume nationalistic influence on the piece, although Parker made no such implication, but they could not agree as to origin. Following a performance by the New York Philharmonic in February of 1901, Henry Krehbiel described the piece as "Celtic rather than distinctively Norse,"[23] and the *New York Mail and Express* noted the use of "Scotch melodies and instrumental coloring."[24]

A Northern Ballad also shows the influence of Tchaikovsky's, *Romeo and Juliet Overture*, particularly with the woodwind-choir orchestration of the introductory theme (Ex. 12-7) and the accompaniment of the D-flat coda theme with harp arpeggios (12-10). *Vathek* reveals yet another model, that of Richard Strauss, with its use of solo violin (as in *Ein Heldenleben*), colorful woodwind orchestration, chromaticism, and large climaxes. Parker's own characteristic style: his melodic turns, harmonic progressions, and manner of working out themes are nevertheless clearly evident throughout these symphonic poems and particularly in the subsidiary theme areas (Ex. 12-9 and Ex. 12-12).

In both pieces, Parker develops germinal motives extensively, using various devices from diminuitive woodwind figurations to broad brass chorales. *A Northern Ballad* (Ex. 12-7) is exemplary of such treatment, for both "Allegro non troppo" themes (Ex. 12-8A and B) are developed from introductory theme motives (marked a, b, and c; see Ex. 12-7). Also, the subsidiary theme of the exposition (Ex. 12-9) begins with an inversion of the perfect fourth interval of the "a" motive and moves immediately to a version of the "b" motive. Finally, the D-flat theme of the coda (Ex. 12-10) begins with a rhythmic augmentation of the "b1" motive.

Example 12-7. Introductory theme, *A Northern Ballad*, Op. 46, ms. fl. sc., NH, 1899, p. 1, mm. 1-11, from the Horatio Parker Papers in the Music Library at Yale University. Used by permission.

Example 12-8. Excerpts, 1st theme area (E minor), *A Northern Ballad*, Op. 46, ms. fl. sc., NH, 1899, from the Horatio Parker Papers in the Music Library at Yale University. Used by permission.

A. p. 4, mm. 8-13.

B. p. 5, mm. 2-6.

Example 12-9. Subsidiary theme, *A Northern Ballad*, Op. 46, ms. fl. sc., NH, 1899, p. 13, mm. 2-7, from the Horatio Parker Papers in the Music Library at Yale University. Used by permission.

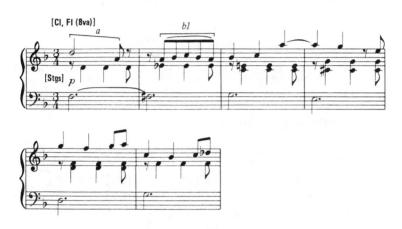

Example 12-10. Coda theme, *A Northern Ballad*, Op. 46, ms. fl. sc., NH, 1899, p. 42, m. 8-p. 44, m. 7, from the Horatio Parker Papers in the Music Library at Yale University, Used by permission.

At the beginning of *Vathek*, the antecedent phrase, consisting of a prominent half-step turn in the second measure, and the consequent phrase, a pentatonic, chorale-like woodwind motive (Ex. 12-11A), are ideas which are later developed. Example 12-11B shows one of several versions of the opening motive, now

Example 12-11. Opening theme, *Vathek*, Op. 57, ms. fl.
   sc., NH, 1907, from the Horatio Parker Papers in
   the Music Library at Yale University. Used by
   Permission.

A. p. 1, m. 3-p. 2, m. 1.

B. Derived motive, p. 2, m. 10-p. 3, m. 3.

heard in the lower strings, in which the half-step figure is preceded
by a rising, wide-leaping span.

It is quite surprising that *Vathek* apparently had no performances during Parker's lifetime. Its motivic treatment is even more
daring than that of *A Northern Ballad*. Some of Parker's most
beautiful and characteristic chromatic writing can be found in the
second theme (Ex. 12-12). The rhapsodic first-half of the middle
section, with its extensive, highly embellished incidental solos for
several instruments, has no counterpart in any of his other works.
Such a limpid chromatic line as the opening motive and its supporting coloristic harmonies will not be heard again until *Crépuscule*
and *Mona*, nearly five years later.

Parker's symphonic poems have not been so neglected as his
other music. Both pieces can be heard on modern recordings performed by Karl Krueger and the Society for the Preservation of the
American Musical Heritage, and a performance of *A Northern
Ballad* by the Albany Symphony Orchestra has been released recently by New World Records.

Collegiate Overture. In his Opus 72, *Collegiate Overture*,
Parker used several college songs then popular at Yale as thematic
material for a full-blown sonata-form movement, thereby creating
an American counterpart to Brahms's *Academic Festival Overture*.
One of Parker's rare ventures in a lighter musical vein, the piece

Example 12-12. Second theme, *Vathek*, Op. 57, ms. fl. sc., NH, 1907, p. 2, m. 10-p. 3, m. 3, from the Horatio Parker Papers in the Music Library at Yale University. Used by permission.

was inspired by Carl Stoeckel, the director of the Norfolk Festival "who, in a genial, expansive mood after last year's [1910] festival suggested the idea to the composer."[25]

Although the overture has its serious moments, humor is the prevailing mood.[26] The tunes include the "Undertaker's song," "Boolah" (which Parker noted sounds "quite as well upside-down"), "Eli Yale," "Amici," and the orchestra is assisted by a male chorus with "Integer vitae," "Gaudeamus igitur," and "Here's to good old Yale." The construction for this potpourri of songs is far more intricate than a simple medley; rather, it is a model of contrapuntal craftsmanship in which complexity adds to the humor.

Concerto for Organ and Orchestra

Parker's organ concerto is the largest and most impressive of his instrumental works. It was the third of his pieces premiered by the Boston Symphony (*Cáhal Mór* was performed in 1895, and *A Northern Ballad*, in 1899). Contemporaneous newspaper reviews suggest that conductor Wilhelm Gericke requested Parker to appear in a dual role as composer and performer.

Parker was well acquainted with Rheinberger's two organ concertos; in fact, he had been the soloist for the premiere of the

earlier one, Opus 137, as a student in Munich. In his own work, he
was to follow his teacher's example and eliminate the woodwinds
from the orchestration. Thus, the work is scored for four horns, two
trumpets, three trombones, tuba, timpani, harp, strings, and organ
solo. With this three-movement work, Parker handled the task of
contrasting and balancing two large masses of sound, that of the
organ and the orchestra, in several different ways. The opening
half of the first movement, the outside sections of the scherzo-like
second movement, and the final movement all have concerted writing between the organ and strings and/or brass.[27] In the last half of
the opening movement, the organ is reduced to an accompanying
role for solo violin, solo horn, and strings; however, in the trio of
the second movement, the organ plays alone in the manner of a
character piece. The finale contains traditional fugal writing and a
pedal cadenza, completing the display of the instrument's resource-
fulness.

Thematic expansion from motivic cells, a technique Parker
used in both his chamber works and symphonic poems, is also
apparent here. In the *Allegro* (the first part of the opening movement), the rhythmic pattern--dotted quarter note, eighth note, quarter note--which is at first inconspicuous in the broad, upsweeping
motion of the E-flat minor opening theme (Ex. 12-13A, m. 5)--
becomes more prominent in the section that immediately follows
(Ex. 12-13B). First the strings and then the brass carry this rhythmic figure to an effective climax (full score, p. 5). In the subsequent A major theme, the motive is telescoped into a hemiola pattern (Ex. 12-14). Another motivic cell, the eighth-note pattern in
the D major theme (Ex. 12-15, m. 6), is used in the following
developmental area (pp. 10-12). The concluding theme for the
Allegro section, returning to E-flat minor, becomes a composite of
eighth-note and dotted-note motives (Ex. 12-16). These motives are
carried over from the first movement into the second, where they
figure prominently as a part of its principal theme (Ex. 12-17A, B,
and C).

Yet another motive, a rather unpromising, unctuous half-
note progression which opens the last half of the first movement,
Andante, nevertheless leads to one of Parker's most effective
themes, a rhapsodic violin solo soaring over the organ's descending
thirds (Ex. 12-18). The half-note rhythmic motive, recurring at the
opening of the first fugue subject in the finale (Ex. 12-19), and the
eighth-note motive, now the basis of the second fugue subject (Ex.
12-19, beg. m. 5) are developed in the final movement. Although
the finale is a vast contrapuntal edifice, Parker interpolated a lyrical
theme (Ex. 12-20) at several points, thus providing a sharp contrast
to the more austere fugal sections.

Example 12-13. Themes, 1st subject area. 1st mov.,
Organ Concerto, Op. 55, fl. sc., N, 1903.

A. p. 1, mm. 1-10.

B. p. 3, mm. 7-13.

The reaction of the critics was mixed following the Boston premiere of 1902. William Apthorp objected to the idea of the piece itself, expounding on its uselessness, describing the organ as "semi-articulate" and "tongue-tied," and concluding that only an organ player would be interested in the work.[28] Howard Ticknor did not become sidetracked by the novelty of the piece's instrumen-

Example 12-14. A̲ major theme, 1st mov., *Organ Concerto*, Op. 55, fl. sc., N, 1903, p. 6, m. 9-p. 7, m. 3.

Example 12-15. D̲ major theme, 1st mov., *Organ Concerto*, Op. 55, fl. sc., N, 1903, p. 8, m. 9-p. 9, m. 9.

Example 12-16. E-flat minor theme, 1st mov., *Organ Concerto*, Op. 55, fl. sc., N, 1903, p. 13, mm. 3-8.

tation but rather attended to its quality, calling it "dignified and beautiful."[29] Louis Elson was also favorably impressed, concluding with a characteristically Brahmin notion that restraint shown in virtuosity, registration, and orchestration, is the piece's outstanding feature.[30]

The enthusiasm of the Chicago critics after the Chicago performance a week later made up for any disappointment Parker

Example 12-17. Themes, 2nd mov., *Organ Concerto*, Op. 55, fl, sc., N. 1903.

A. p. 28, mm. 1-5.

B. p. 28, mm. 5-8.

C. p. 28, mm. 8-13.

may have had in the Boston reviews. The *Chicago Record-Herald* reviewer commented: "Professor Parker has certainly coped successfully with the difficult problem [organ with orchestra] and blends the tone so that, instead of a clash, there are beautiful symphonic effects."[31] The *Tribune* critic enthused: "The organ stands out brilliantly, and yet he has made interesting all that he has given the orchestra to do." Although the *Chicago Inter-Ocean* writer found the work "attention-compelling rather than awakening a delighted interest," the *Chicago Evening Post* reviewer apparently found Parker capable of both qualities: "He has imagination and ideas as well as technical knowledge, and there is emotion in what he writes . . . an imposing and brilliant composition."

The few performances the *Organ Concerto* received during the remainder of Parker's life failed to generate sufficient enthusiasm to secure for it a permanent place in the concert repertory. For its day, the *Organ Concerto* was experimental in its exploration of

Example 12-18. Principal theme, Andante, 1st mov.,
     Organ Concerto, Op. 55, fl. sc., N, 1903, p. 19,
     mm. 1-6.

Example 12-19. Fugue subject, 3rd mov., *Organ Concerto*,
     Op. 55, fl. sc., N, 1903, p. 39. m 27-p. 40, m. 8.

the tonal and technical possibilities of organ and orchestra. In spite
of its novelty and generally high quality, it has been largely
ignored. A revival on 25 January 1976 by organist Bradley Hull
and the Collegium Musicum under the direction of Fritz Rikko at
the Church of the Holy Rest in New York City has given us a

Example 12-20. Contrasting theme, 3rd mov., *Organ Concerto*, Op. 55, fl. sc., N, 1903, p. 41, mm. 17-21

reminder of its historical interest and intrinsic worth. Its unusual structure, strength of musical ideas, inventiveness shown in their development, and excellence of idiomatic writing for organ and orchestra make this piece Parker's most important creative effort in instrumental music and one worthy of a permanent place in the living repertory of American orchestral music.

Chapter Thirteen

AN EVALUATION

A musical life as diversified as Horatio Parker's cannot be reduced to a few obvious conclusions, but certain facts are apparent. He was indisputably the foremost American choral composer of his generation and a patriarchal figure among America's Protestant church musicians and choral societies. Many of his oratorios, cantatas, glees, anthems, and hymns were sung throughout this country and, for an appreciable time, in England. But his role as a composer extended into other fields: his two grand operas won prestigious prizes; his chamber music and songs were highly regarded; and his few symphonic works were performed by major orchestras of the day.

His work in areas of music other than composition was equally important to his contemporaries. He was quite prominent as both an organist and conductor throughout his career. For twenty-five years, he led the music department of one of our most important universities, and his influence on music education generally, through his work as editor, speaker and writer, extended down even to the elementary school. As a frequent lecturer, he spoke, sometimes with humor but always with authority, on nearly every musical issue of the day. He was an important liaison with the European fount of our musical culture, and, drawing on his frequent trips to England and the continent, he offered the American public his gleanings from the musical vanguard there.

This study has challenged certain generalizations about Parker's life and music found in many histories. His often-touted austere and churchly compositional style describes only a part of his work. To categorize him simply as a conservative and backward-looking composer is to ignore his innovations in opera and choral music and to misconstrue how he was viewed by critics of his day. To describe his personality as pedantic and rigid fails to account for discontent with the status quo that he showed throughout his career in his writings and compositions.

Although Parker played many musical roles in his time, he thought of himself primarily as a composer, and it is to this aspect of his career that most observers turn. Writing shortly after mid-century, Roger Sessions, a student whom Parker held in high regard, summarized then-prevailing views about the composer: that he was second only to MacDowell in importance at the turn of the century, that he was both musical and highly skilled, but that he lacked originality.[1] Other writers have stressed the matter of nationalism and have considered Parker an important representative of the German wing of American music which inhibited the growth of an indigenous style.[2] Aaron Copland has addressed yet another issue by delving into the personalities and social conditions of Parker's generation and concluding that they were "overgentlemanly, too well-mannered, and [that] their culture reflected a certain museum-like propriety and bourgeois solidity."[3] Even such a staunch admirer of Copland's view of American music history as Alan H. Levy objected to this evaluation:

> *Hora Novissima* is an oratorio of terrific passion. More importantly, Chadwick, Parker, and Paine were simply damn good composers, irrespective of style. Their absence from the twentieth-century concert stage reflects extramusical prejudices over which a late-nineteenth-century composer could not possibly have exerted any control. Paine, Parker, et al. were indeed members of the social elite and for this seem "overgentlemanly." Given their time and station they had little choice. The hard lines of social distinction were insurmountable for any mere composer who did not wish to commit professional suicide.[4]

Copland's dismissal of Parker's generation is a part of a long-standing general criticism of New England's role in American culture. For example, George Santayana also thought that New-England intellectuals were too complacent:

> About the middle of the nineteenth century, in the quiet sunshine of provincial prosperity, New England had an Indian summer of the mind; and an agreeable reflective literature showed how brilliant that russet and yellow season could be. There were poets, historians, orators, preachers, most of whom had studied foreign literatures and travelled; they demurely kept up with the times; they were universal humanists.[5]

Although Santayana was writing about the generation before Parker's, his criticism has not only been extended to those that followed but also deepened to include an accusation of moral indifference as well. Writing slightly more than a decade after Parker's death, Edward Robinson attacked the composer for betraying his cultural leadership by writing music completely divorced from the social issues of the day:

> How incongruous that, in a period characterized by such things as the Pullman and Homestead strikes, the bellicose adventures of the White Squadron, and the historic march of Coxey's Army, an artist should look for musical inspiration in the words: "City of high renown, Home of the saints alone, Built in the heaven!" [from *Hora Novissima*].[6]

Most observers, however, do not take such a radical position of restricting art to the categorical demand that it respond to some real or supposed cultural malaise. But such a personal attack on Parker shows that he had become a representative cultural figure for his generation.

On the other hand, Parker has not been without his champions. During the period between the world wars, his strongest supporters were A. Walter Kramer and Paul Rosenfeld. In a tribute to Parker, written on the tenth anniversary of his death, Kramer lashed out at "the rising generation of composers in this country" who no longer valued Parker's "seriousness of purpose, dignity of style and masterly workmanship."[7] During World War II, Rosenfeld appealed to a broader sense of national tradition which he thought Parker's music exemplified and which he found missing in the overtly nationalistic writing of the time: "For lack of Parker, we of the musical house forego the self-assurance which the perception not only of his relation to ourselves but his representation of American life [affords]."[8] Rosenfeld believed that we could best attain a musical maturity by writing an American music inclusive of its past and fostering an attitude which sees that past as valuable in itself.

The qualities that Kramer found in Parker's music and Rosenfeld's faith in tradition were values more commonly accepted in Parker's time than later. Parker and his generation were thoroughly imbued with the concepts of continuity and progress, and thought of themselves as the seedbed from which the "Great American Composer" would spring. Such horticultural metaphors are found repeatedly in writing about American music, from John S. Van Cleve's comment at the turn of the century--"There must indeed be much good writing before a genius of the first order can find a mellow leaf-loam deep enough for the ramifying amplitude of his mighty thoughts,"[9]--to Paul Henry Lang's description, nearly half a century later, of Parker and MacDowell as "springing from a musical soil hardly tilled, yet equalling the feats of those who had behind them the unbroken past of c nturies of great music."[10]

Parker would certainly have agreed with Van Cleve and have been gratified by Lang's remark. On the few occasions when he appraised his own music, Parker did not go further than Wilfrid Mellers's conclusion that it contained "a truth that preserves a modest vitality."[11]

It is ironic that the "Great American Composer," whom Parker and his colleagues envisioned as a phenomenon of the distant future, should have studied, unrecognized as such, under his very tutelage at Yale in the person of Charles Ives. As Ives's reputation has continued to grow throughout the twentieth century, his reminiscences about Parker, particularly as interpreted by others, have been increasingly damaging to Parker's reputation, both as composer and teacher. Although Parker hardly remembered Ives as a student,[12] Ives's recollections of Parker were most vivid. They come down to us as off-hand comments which we nevertheless must consider carefully.[13] The anecdotes he related to Henry and Sidney Cowell and others were often critical, but Ives also described Parker as a good teacher as well as a kindly and, at times, perhaps indulgent man. In the final analysis, his opinion of Parker seems to have been ambivalent.

Frank Rossiter has attributed Parker's apparent neglect of Ives to the fact that Ives was not committed to becoming a professional musician.[14] A more cogent reason may be that Ives's school years (1894-98) coincided with the busiest part of Parker's career. At that time he was preoccupied with organizing the music department at Yale, preparing his courses, continuing his previous occupation as organist-choirmaster at Trinity Church in Boston, taking on additional obligations as conductor of the New Haven Symphony and choral societies in the area, and, perhaps most important, solidifying his own composing career, which had been given a boost with the premiere of *Hora Novissima* in 1893. The beginning of their teacher-pupil relationship must have been rocky, for Ives had already covered and was probably bored with the instruction that Parker offered in the basic music courses. The sudden death of Ives's father during his freshman year created further tensions, since Ives might have then looked up to Parker as a father-figure.[15]

Ives's occasional remarks have been developed by some writers into the image of Parker as an unfeeling, inhibiting pedant.[16] Rosalie Sandra Perry, who has looked beyond Ives's comments and into his actual music education under Parker, offers a view which balances somewhat this lopsided interpretation of their relationship.[17] Even more recently, J. Peter Burkholder has also concluded that Parker actually played a positive role in Ives's education, not only in the development of his craft but also in his esthetic growth as a classical-music composer:

Parker offered Ives a means to free his music from the limitations of both aspiration and genre imposed by Danbury's cultural life . . . an ideal of music as an abstract art. . . . Here is
where Parker exercised his most profound and enduring influence."[18]

The basic issue separating Parker and Ives is not simply that
of clashing personalities, a teacher's neglect, or a student's rebel-
liousness, but the differences in their musical Americas. Parker's
was that of the Musical Establishment, from the amateur community chorus to such high-art citadels as the Metropolitan Opera. On
the other hand, Ives's world was not like Parker's, a pressing reality
with which he had constantly to deal, but one of nostalgic remem-
brances and isolated experimentation.

Although their immediate environments and careers caused
them to write quite different kinds of music, Ives and Parker did
share broader philosophic concepts: faith in social progress and
belief in the ethical basis of art.[19] Progress was the key idea of the
late nineteenth century. The American philosopher John Fiske drew
on Darwinian evolutionary theory and Herbert Spencer's belief in
the inevitability of progress to suggest that achieving a perfect
society was not only possible but would occur, perhaps within a few
generations.[20] Parker's own writings show his enthusiasm for such
ideas. As early as his eighteenth year, he made an ambitious New
Year's resolution (1882) to work ceaselessly for progress,[21] a theme
he continued to emphasize in lectures and public statements
throughout his life.

This sense of social mission was an outgrowth of the Puri-
tanical-Transcendentalist-Victorian heritage that Parker shared with
his generation. Moral values were cited as reasons for almost all
activity. At Harvard, Charles Eliot Norton taught ethically based
esthetics in his art history course, causing critic Van Wyck Brooks
to comment that "He preached [taste] as his forebears preached
salvation."[22] Writer Arlo Bates also twitted his fellow Bostonians
for their propensity "toward the ethical and the supernatural so
strong that we have to have these things served up even in our
amusements."[23] Parker's own lectures and addresses constantly
linked ethics with esthetics. He admonished his students in the
opening lecture of his History of Music course to avoid using music
as a self-indulgence, and he mistrusted music that, to him, gratified
only the senses.[24] Although fond of insisting that music should
have deeper, more abiding values, he never attempted a critical
assessment of these; undoubtedly, he believed them to be as self-
evident to others as they were to him.

In a society of established values, pressure for social, intellectual, and artistic conformity was great. As a result, Parker and

his colleagues produced a body of music which, from today's vantage point, seems quite similar in structure, content, subject, style, and purpose. They also enjoyed a comradeship which enabled them to share many musical ideas. Thus, the reciprocal influences of Parker, Foote, Arthur Whiting, Chadwick, and others can be traced from their most ambitious compositions down to their functional music for choir loft and student recitals.

Nevertheless, each person was distinctive, and five characteristics are frequently mentioned in writing about Parker that serve to mark him as an individual: his personality, his identification with choral and religious music, his reputation as a composer of academic and elevated music, his eclecticism, and his position regarding an American idiom.

First, his personality and intellectual bearing elicited considerable comment in his day. His Yale colleague and eminent writer William Lyons Phelps once remarked: "I have never heard any one speak English with more beautiful enunciation or more correctly and yet without one shade of affectation or pedantry."[25] At the 1915 production of Parker's opera *Fairyland* at Los Angeles, local reporter Grace Wilcox found his appearance to be anomalous amid the ballyhoo there:

> [He is] neat, well groomed, cultured, terse, polite--but
> reserved. . . . Looking at the man and listening to him talking
> in his concise, grammatical manner with a set poise . . . in an
> exclusive atmosphere created entirely by himself--Horatio
> Parker might be a librarian, a pedagogue, a student of archeology--a student of anything.[26]

Historian John Tasker Howard was sufficiently impressed with Parker's aura of intellectuality to comment on it at some length in his overview of the composer's career:

> Parker was quite the man of the world. Fastidious, immaculate,
> he commanded a social standing often denied musicians of his
> time. He had for his friends artists, writers, and men from the
> several professions. . . . He was at ease talking on any subject;
> he could hold his own in prolonged discussions on topics far
> removed from music.[27]

Parker's bearing is all the more remarkable when one considers the casualness of his schooling, indeed, the lack of any formal training in higher education aside from the conservatory. He was largely self-taught, acquiring varying proficiencies in Classical literature, Greek, Latin, French, Italian, and, of course, German. His daughter

Isabel Semler remarked that he often read and studied late into the night.[28]

Although Parker may have demonstrated intellectual breadth in his relations with others, his addresses and essays incline toward a lack of rigorous structure, an unwillingness to explore ideas in great depth, and a tendency toward premature generalization. Possibly the pattern of his thinking might have been different had his education been more systematic and leisurely rather than grasped hastily between intervals of composing.

Parker also showed the impatience of other self-made intellectuals with culturally broadening courses in the university curriculum. As we have observed earlier, he was the most emphatic among the music educators of his time in stressing technical training exclusively. He evidently believed that his students could acquire a liberal education on their own as he had done.

A second distinctive feature is Parker's pre-eminence in choral and religious music which were then such a major part of America's cultural activity.[29] At one time or another, Parker conducted over a half-dozen singing societies in New England and the mid-Atlantic region. In addition, his diaries and scrapbooks record his work as a guest conductor at many choral concerts and festivals throughout the country.

While these societies helped him to gain recognition and provided a portion of his livelihood, they also imposed limitations. These groups were composed mostly of amateurs whose technical deficiencies undoubtedly fell short of his aspirations. Performances were frequently given with only piano or organ accompaniment, while orchestras, when used, were often hastily prepared. Yet choral organizations were an extremely important part of turn-of-the-century American culture. Some time after their prime, Olin Downes eloquently described their role:

> Today [1931] they are not quite the same as they were. In the nineties there was deeper and truer music enthusiasm. The choruses, always recruited from local ranks, were profoundly in earnest in their work, and they were the true mainstay and inspiration of the festivals. The orchestra, the solo singers, were indispensable features and box office attractions. But the festival spirit, the essence of the festivals . . . was the chorus, and the musical energy of the community which it represented. . . . But if it is said that such models and such scores were not a part of American music, then American music is misunderstood and misrepresented. This spirit was devotional, earnest, high-minded. It embodied high living and thinking, a deep love of music in its simpler and less complex

manifestations and a reliance upon it for solace and inspiration.[30]

The fact that Parker was so closely identified with choral music is a factor in his diminished popularity today. Several of his cantatas and oratorios owe their existence to such festivals as Downes described, and his reputation has ebbed accordingly as they have been curtailed or have disappeared altogether. Yet another notable factor about Parker is his reputation as a scholarly composer of lofty music that many concertgoers of his time had difficulty in understanding. We have seen that this opinion was shared by both critics and lay persons and extended from his most ambitious works down to even his humblest hymn settings. Actually, this generalization not only oversimplifies but also distorts the complexity of his career. It did not unfold in such an orderly and predictable manner, but alternated between established and newly emerging styles. Summarizing its course would be useful at this point.

Only the early oratorio, *Hora Novissima*, and the choral music written after its style support the commonly held view of Parker as a conservative composer. He established his reputation as a choral and church composer in the early nineties with this music and thereafter sustained a traditionalist cast for the next two decades with such works as *Adstant Angelorum Chori*, with its allusions to Renaissance polyphony; *A Wanderer's Psalm*, the diminutive restatement of *Hora Novissima*; *Hymnos Andron*, employing ancient Greek theoretical concepts; and the ceremonial works, *Union and Liberty*, *Spirit of Beauty*, and *A Song of Times*. This evocation of the past pleased those who were eager to find an American music equal to that of Europe with esthetic goals that had been clearly established since the mid-19th century. This music abounds in pleasing melody, sensuous harmony, colorful orchestration, and stirring counterpoint. Important critics of the time, such as William Apthorp, H. E. Krehbiel, Philip Hale, and William Henderson, praised much of this music and were influential in Parker's own self-appraisal as a conservative. Had Parker confined himself to this style, his generation might have considered him more accessible.

Other compositions follow a different line of thought and suggest that Parker was not altogether happy with his conservative reputation. These pieces, composed concurrently with the more traditional ones, indicate considerable striving for newness. Although the difference between these two types may not be so evident to us, the more progressive pieces were considered at least novel, and sometimes radical, for their time. *Cáhal Mór of the Wine-Red Hand* (1895) and *Crépuscule* (1911) are harmonically progressive pieces for solo voice and orchestra. Structurally, both *A Star Song* (1902) and the *Organ Concerto* (1902) were so unique that they puzzled both critics and audiences. But Parker's first opera, *Mona* (1911), remains his most ambitious work among this group. Because it contradicted his church-choral image so completely, it must be considered his supreme act of professional courage. In the face of general expectation that he would conform to prevailing conservatism, he wrote his most progressive work. It marks the high tide in his use of pervading chromaticism, vacillating tonality, and angular melody, all of which are also apparent in his concert aria of the same time, *Crépuscule* (1912).

This zigzagging between conservative and progressive styles is only part of the reason that Parker perplexed his contemporaries. Just as surprising to them was his change, late in career, from the church-choral milieu to opera. From studying his addresses and other commentaries and re-examining some of his compositions predating *Mona*, we now realize that his intense interest in dramatic music and his confidence that he could do something new and worthwhile in that field certainly did not bud at middle age. Well over a decade before *Mona*, his second oratorio, *Saint Christopher* (1897), shows a well-developed leading-motive structure, and, in *King Gorm the Grim* (1908), a single pathetic idea is effectively sustained for the duration of the cantata. Parker's most advanced writing and progressive dramatic principles converge in *Mona*, thus making it doubly difficult for his contemporaries to understand. His second opera, *Fairyland*, was, in part, a concession to conservative popular taste, but he continued to explore dramatic possibilities with the Parsifal-like oratorio, *Morven and the Grail* (1915) and the tableau-structured *Dream of Mary* (1918). These compositions, infused as they are with the spirit of contemporaneous musical drama, may seem less important to us than the *Hora Novissima* group, but they nevertheless occupied the major part of his creative activity from the mid-nineties to the end of his career.

Parker's disappointment over *Mona's* failure appears to have crystallized his growing concern to communicate more directly with a wider public. Although he did not abandon his interest in dramatic music, a change in his musical style is clearly apparent: a return to largely diatonic harmony with fewer chromatic embellishments, more traditional key relationships, balanced structures, simpler melody, and, for some pieces, reduced orchestration. *Morven and the Grail* and *Fairyland* only partially show this change, but the later major works, *Cupid and Psyche* (1916), *The Red Cross Spirit Speaks* (1918), *The Dream of Mary* (1918) and *A.D. 1919*, are simplified to such a degree that they constitute a third and final style.

In summarizing his accomplishments, the critics of his day failed to note their variety. Louis Elson found Parker "less impassioned than MacDowell, less poetically melodic and dramatic than Chadwick," his special niche being the writing of "dignified contrapuntal works."[31] Arthur Farwell and W. Dermot Darby found him "scholarly but somewhat ascetic," and his style to be one of "self-contained and poised loftiness."[32] W. L. Hubbard called Parker's work "scientific and undramatic . . . not generally popular."[33] Like his student Roger Sessions, Parker appears to have gained more respect than enthusiasm for the body of his works. Only his elaborate counterpoint was fully appreciated, and it enhanced his prevailing image as an ecclesiastical composer who wrote the kind of music that appealed to "the conscious minds of cultivated Americans,"[34] rather than the dramatic composer who quickened their emotions.

Another distinguishing and frequently mentioned characteristic is the degree of Parker's eclecticism. Not only was he probably the most facile composer of his day, but he also seems to have been the most susceptible to other composers' mannerisms. Those most frequently cited as his models are Mendelssohn, Franck, Liszt, Gounod, Brahms, Wagner, and Dvořák. For today's listener, some of Parker's borrowings are astonishing and seem to border on plagiarism. Why would he use short phrases from such well-known works as Mendelssohn's "Wedding March," Franck's *Symphony in D Minor*, and Wagner's *Der Fliegende Holländer* with no apparent reason to quote such passages deliberately? The question remains unanswered. A few of his contemporaries objected to such reminiscences, but most did not seem unduly disturbed. Aside from Parker's few literal quotations, his eclectic writing was not only tolerated, but even received with enthusiasm--especially when he evoked the polyphonic splendor of earlier times. Drawing on ideas from different historical periods was an esthetic value in itself during the 1890s and was prevalent throughout all of the arts. Nowhere is this condition more evident than in the profusion of architectural styles that constitute the White City buildings of the 1893 Chicago World's Fair, *the* symbolic event of the time. The center attraction, Richard Morris Hunt's Administration Building, could be ridiculed as a hodgepodge of disparate parts with its Roman dome rising over Greek columns, but most visitors found these same elements fusing into a monumental architecture of striking, unified projection. The components of *Hora Novissima* and their integration into an oratorio of singular beauty reveal this esthetic in music, perhaps more completely than any other composition of the time.

The fifth issue which recurs frequently in writings about Parker is his relation to musical nationalism. At first glance, he appears to be not at all nationalistic, but, in fact, he did have a strong concern for his identity as an American composer. Just as others of his persuasion composed some pieces with vernacular melodies (MacDowell's *Indian Suite*), or, at least, texts from New World sources (Foote's *Farewell to Hiawatha*), so Parker contributed his share. Among his larger works, *A Northern Ballad* has an Anglo-American idiom, and *Union and Liberty* and *A. D. 1919* have characteristic music to enhance their stirring, patriotic texts.

Nationalism was but one idea, and certainly not the most important, in Parker's work. We have seen that his thinking about it parallels the more publicized remarks of MacDowell, who was wary and even disdainful of being categorized as an American composer. Nevertheless, the times in which Parker lived compelled him to deal with the subject in a variety of ways which deserve further analysis here.

Much historical writing today describes Parker's generation as German-dominated, a classification which is oversimplified and somewhat inaccurate. Joseph A. Mussulman has designated the cultural stance of late nineteenth-century America more precisely as cosmopolitan nationalism:

> As a result of its dedication to the pursuit and dissemination of Culture in the name of progress, the educated class was faced with the opportunity and the impulse to shape the form and character of American civilization and especially to clarify its relationships with its European heritage. Confronted on the one hand with a widespread antagonism toward Europeans, their ideas, and their products, and on the other with a clear need for the continued assimilation of the best of the European heritage, the only reasonable course for the Culture-guardians to pursue was a temperate nationalism balanced by an objective, discriminating cosmopolitanism.[35]

Here we have the dilemma of American composers at the turn of the century: having to master a full-blown tradition nurtured elsewhere and, in addition, having to assert their own cultural identity. The ideas and accomplishments of German composers certainly dominated cosmopolitan thinking and composing, but we have seen in this study that Parker was eager to maintain a separateness from German composition and pedagogy.

When pressed on the matter of writing an American music, composers such as MacDowell and Parker frequently resorted to connecting nationality with emotional traits. Thus, Parker referred to his opera *Fairyland* as being "cheerful, bouyant, and confident as the American character."[36] He found it distasteful to push further and adopt Dvořák's suggestion to use plantation songs, spirituals, and Indian melodies as musical content.

Although Parker rejected Dvořák's ideas, he did not ignore the subject of ethnic tradition entirely. We have noted that he chose what he called the Anglo-Saxon tradition over the German as the path for American music to follow. McDonald Smith Moore has explored this idea recently in his examination of the careers of New Englanders Daniel Gregory Mason and Charles Ives.[37] As the argument about ethnic strains in American music intensified following World War I, composers Daniel Gregory Mason and John Powell took over Parker's position and became leading proponents of the Anglo-American point of view. With the New-England group, nationalism was never restricted to pure ethnicity itself but rather focused on the esthetic and ethical qualities of the ethnic group and the role that serious music played in symbolizing these qualities. Moore finds that composers, from Paine and Parker through Mason and Ives, shared a belief "that great music communicated a transcendental experience whose substance was essentially religious," and that such music was "redemptive" in counteracting both commercial and sensual aspects of American society.[38]

Both Moore and Barbara Zuck, in her *A History of Musical Americanism*, have shown that this abstract ideal, centering largely in New England, lost ground following World War I to a concept of American art music derived from vernacular traditions much more broadly based than the Anglo-American alone.[39] Cowboy songs, Appalachian ballads, Afro-American and Native-American music come to mind when one thinks of the high tide of Americanist influence during the first half of the twentieth century, and Parker used none of these.

But Parker did draw on one vernacular source, not particularly ethnic in origin, which has a clearly American identity. We have observed earlier how he occasionally used melodic contours and chromatic harmony reminiscent of hymn settings and popular songs of his day even in his most ambitious compositions. At times, his music has the very sentimental mannerisms found in the extremely popular songs of such composers as Reginald de Koven ("Oh, promise me," 1889), Ethelbert Nevin ("The Rosary," 1898), Charles Wakefield Cadman ("At Dawning," 1906), and Thurlow Lieurance ("By the Waters of Minnetonka," 1919), all of whom mediated between popular and serious music.[40] Public attitude toward this style of writing has undergone a drastic change since World War I. Once considered sophisticated, it is now frequently described as maudlin. But such a reversal of taste does not alter its historical importance.

More recently, Barbara Tischler, in *An American Music*,[41] and Nicholas Tawa, in *Serenading the Reluctant Eagle*,[42] have offered varying theses about musical nationalism which revive the arguments of Parker's generation. Each supports a different side of what Mussulman has called cosmopolitan nationalism for the late nineteenth century. Tischler addresses the cosmopolitan side in her account of the waning interest in nationalism following World War II. She notes that the recent development of the "international language of musical modernism" has put American composers on a par with their European counterparts because both have labored in the development of this radically new style. On the other hand, the older Romantic tradition, which composers such as Parker had to assimilate, was created nearly single-handedly by the Europeans and seemingly required Americans to do something extra or different in order to assert their own identity and worth. According to Tishler, the sharing in the building of the international modernist movement practically eliminates the need for an identifiable nationalism. By confining the definition of American music simply to that written by an American, regardless of content or style, Tishler comes very close to the cosmopolitan attitude of Parker and many of his generation.

Tawa, however, warns us that overemphasis on international modernism has led to today's deep cleavage between composers and the public.[43] He finds that the nationalistic 1920s-40s period of American art music was beneficent because it emphasized communication with a larger public through compositions that are both accessible and moving. In the last decade of his life, Parker faced the problems that Tawa outlined when he turned from the esoteric style of *Mona* to write a more generally appealing music, some of it in the patriotic spirit of that time.

Achieving the balance between individuality and the need to communicate, often through national idioms, not only changes from generation to generation but also within a composer's lifetime. We have seen how Parker began as the cosmopolitan composer of the oratorio *Hora Novissima*, moved to a temperate Anglo-American nationalism with the tone poem *Northern Ballad*, and ended his career with the cantata *A. D. 1919*, one of his most accessible and overtly nationalistic pieces. His own career reflects the course of his country, from the eclectic nineties through a feeling of strong national identity brought on by World War I.

Today Parker's music lingers on by means of a few anthems and hymns, some songs such as "The lark now leaves his watery nest," and *Hora Novissima*. As important as they are, these pieces give us as limited perspective of his achievement, as if we were to confine our view of Sibelius to *Finlandia*, *Valse Triste*, and the *Symphony No. 1*. If we are to recapture the breadth and vision of serious music before World War I, we need to hear with fresh ears at least parts of Parker's monumental operas, *Mona* and *Fairyland*, which have their distinctive places in American music, and some of the post-*Hora Novissima* choral music, much of which contains

novel dramatic ideas. The very size of some of these works makes
their production formidable, but much of Parker's music, even short
sections of the longer works, can be given meaningful and satisfying performances.[44]
     These pieces are historically significant, but they should be
heard again for yet another, more important, reason. Parker's music
shows sufficient craft, complexity of design, and, at times, sheer
beauty of sound to be its own reward for performing and listening.
Although he was among our most eclectic composers, his distinctive voice can be heard in nearly all of his music. Many of his
smaller and lesser known works, such as his art songs and his
chamber and instrumental music, can also bear revival. In the
appendix listing Parker's works, I have marked with double asterisks the compositions which I believe provide a good idea of his
attainment and which may have both significance and pleasure for
us.
     Parker bore the responsibilities of being a commanding
figure in America's musical life from his late twenties, the time of
Hora Novissima, until his death at the age of fifty-six. Although, in
seeking our own cultural aspirations we did not follow directly the
path he cleared, many of his ideals are still an important part of our
thinking. To become better acquainted with Parker's music and that
of other important composers from his generation can do more than
engender an affectionate remembrance for and an understanding of
our past. By opening our minds to this music, we will expand our
esthetic sensitivity and grasp an appreciation for its intrinsic beauty.

PART III:
CHAPTER NOTES

CHAPTER NOTES

Chapter One--THE FORMATIVE YEARS

1. Horatio Newton Parker, *Some Descendants of Six Pioneers from Great Britain to America* (privately printed, 1940), p. 7.

2. Isabel Parker Semler, *Horatio Parker, A Memoir For His Grandchildren Compiled From Letters and Papers* (New York: G. P. Putnam's Sons, 1942; reprinted., New York: Da Capo Press, 1973), p. 22.

3. George W. Chadwick, *Horatio Parker [Address] Delivered Before the American Academy of Arts and Letters, July 25, 1920* (New Haven: Yale University Press, 1921), p. 6.

4. Semler, p. 303. His father's ancestors arrived in New England in 1635; his mother's ancestors settled in Virginia in 1683.

5. Ibid., p. 29.

6. Letter to writer from Helen L. Beede, Recorder, Lasell Junior College, Auburndale, Massachusetts, 12 October 1961.

7. "Horatio Parker," *Musical Times* 43 (1 Sept. 1902): 587; Ruth Hopkins Spooner, *Lasell's First Century, 1851-1951* (Boston: Abbey Press, 1951), p. 53.

8. Horatio Newton Parker, p. 6.

9. Ibid., p. 7.

10. Semler, pp. 53, 61.

11. Letter dated 11 December 1890, postmarked Auburndale, "Horatio Parker Papers," MSS 36 (hereafter cited as HP Papers), Yale University Music Library Archival Collection, compiled by Adrienne Nesnow, II (correspondence), E (family).

12. Semler, p. 22.

13. Letter to writer from Fred Alexander, Chairman of the Historical Research Committee, Jackson Homestead, Newton, MA, 11 Nov. 1961. In addition to checking the roles of schools, Mr. Alexander conversed with C. W. Blood, a son of one of Parker's teachers, and Anne Bunker, the daughter of a friend of Isabella Parker.

14. *Musical Times* 43 (1 Sept. 1902): 587.

15. Ibid.

16. Semler, p. 33.

17. *Musical Times* 43 (1 Sept. 1902): 587.

18. Clipping, n. d. [ca. 1893], HP Papers, IV (clippings), E (scrapbooks), 3 (misc. scrapbook).

19. Letter to writer from Marion K. Conant, Assistant Librarian, Dedham Historical Society, 20 September 1961.

20. Clipping, n.d. [ca. 1893], *Boston Journal*, HP Papers, IV E 6 (misc. scrapbook). A similar anecdote is found in Semler, p. 34.

21. Ibid.

22. Ibid.

23. Chadwick, pp. 7-8.

24. HP Papers, II A (Parker correspondence to others) and B (others to Parker), contain 23 letters exchanged between Parker and the Chadwicks (George and Ida May). Semler has published 11 of these letters.

25. Semler, p. 40.

26. Ibid., pp. 39-40. Probably Willard Burr, Jr.

27. Ibid., Chap. 2 passim.

28. Ibid., p. 40.

29. Victor Yellin, *The Life and Operatic Works of George W. Chadwick*, Ph. D. thesis, Harvard University, 1957, pp. 45-46.

30. Semler, Chap. 2 passim.

31. *Jahresbericht Der Königliche Musikhochschule in München*, 9-11 (1882-1885), p. 10 of each issue.

32. Semler, p. 61.

33. Letter from Isabella Parker to Alice Jennings, 24 September 1884, HP Papers, II E. This letter also documents the fact that Parker's setting of Psalm 23 was written in Munich and not at an earlier period as Chadwick has suggested (Chadwick, p. 8).

34. Letter from Isabella Parker to Alice Jennings, 29 June 1885, HP Papers, II E.

35. Unidentified clipping found in "Biographies of Musicians," Vol. I, p. 196, Allen A. Brown Collection, Boston Public Library (hereafter cited as BpBr).

36. Clipping labeled "Boston Transcript, Aug. 12, 1885," among Arthur Whiting papers, Music Division, New York Public Library, Astor, Lenox and Tilden Foundations (hereafter cited as NYPL for the main library).

37. Chadwick, p. 9.

38. David Stanley Smith, "Horatio Parker," *Musical Quarterly* 16 (April 1930): 154-55.

39. Mabel Daniels, *An American Girl in Munich* (Boston: Little, Brown, and Company, 1905), pp. 73, 276-77.

40. Biographical sketch from *Metropolitan Magazine*, 11 June 1911, "Horatio Parker," clipping file, Music Division, NYPL.

41. Clipping from *Boston Evening Transcript*, 27 September 1899, HP Papers, IV E 6.

42. Such comments appear in approximately twenty periodicals and text-books dating back as far as 1893.

43. Unidentified clipping, n. d. (ca. 1893), HP Papers, IV E 3.

44. Semler, p. 68. Also, the *Jahresbericht* for 1885 does not list Parker as having received the "absolutorialzeugnis" [graduation certificate].

45. Van Wyck Brooks, *New England: Indian Summer (1865-1915)* (New York: E. P. Dutton, 1940), p. 191.

Chapter Two--THE EARLY PROFESSIONAL YEARS

1. Brooks, p. 331.

2. File, "Cathedral School of St. Paul," NYPL.

3. Parker nevertheless continued to record in his diary weekly trips to Garden City for private teaching until 1891, long after he had moved to Manhattan. His resignation from Saint Paul's on 4 February 1891 is noted in his diary.

4. Catalogues, 1885-1890, file, "Cathedral School of St. Mary," NYPL.

5. Letter, BpBr. The Boston performance did not occur (Semler, p. 84).

6. Clippings from the *Detroit Free Press*, *Detroit Evening Journal*, and *Detroit Tribune*, 30 November 1887 , HP Papers, IV A (Parker's Works and Performances).

7. H. E. Krehbiel,*Review of the New York Musical Season 1885-86* (London & New York: Novello, Ewer, & Co., 1886), p. xix.

8. G. H. Wilson, *Boston Musical Yearbook* 5, 1887-88 (Boston: G. Ellis [printer], 1888), p. 34.

9. Unidentified newspaper clipping dated 1887 and pasted in back of the vocal score for *King Trojan*, BpBr.

10. Clipping marked "Boston Journal, Sept. 27, 1899," HP Papers, IV E 6.

11. The performances of *King Trojan* and the *Ballad* given here and below are recorded in Wilson, *Yearbook*, vols. 4, 5, and 10.

12. Conversation, writer with Isabel Parker Semler, New Canaan, Connecticut, 18 September 1961. See also Semler, p. 71.

13. *Trow's New York City Directory* lists their address at 79 East 125th St. (New York: Trow Directory, Printing, and Bookbinding Co., 1887), p. 102.

14. Semler passim, and HP Papers, II E.

15. Information about St. Andrew's during Parker's time there can be found in *Yearbook for Saint Andrew's Church*, 1887 and 1888 (New York: Advent Press, 1887) and in Rev. George B. Draper, D. D., and Milm

P. Bayton, Esq., *History of St. Andrew's Church (Harlem) in Two Chapters: A. D. 1829-1889* (New York: [private printing], 1889).

16. *Yearbook of the Church of the Holy Trinity; 1888* (New York: Medical Abstract Press, n. d.). On inside page facing back of cover, Parker is listed as "Organist and Choirmaster."

17. Semler, p. 81.

18. *Souvenir of the Dedication Festival and Founder's Day of Saint James' Church, January 29, 1928* (New York: Rudge, n. d.). This short pamphlet has a brief description of the parent church, Holy Trinity, at the beginning.

19. Henry Steele Commager, *The American Mind* (New Haven: Yale University Press, 1950; paperback ed., 1959), Chapter 9, "Religious Thought and Practice" passim.

20. Semler, p. 81.

21. Letter from Rev. James Elliot Lindsley, Rector of St. Stephen's Church and author of a history of St. James' Church, 3 October 1961.

22. *Yearbook, Holy Trinity.*

23. Unidentified clipping, n. d. (ca. 1893), HP Papers, IV E 3.

24. HP Papers, V (Writings), A (Diaries and Jottings), diary, 1890. Draper and Bayton, p. 6, give $2,000 as the amount recommended by the board of St. Andrew's for both choirmaster and surpliced choir.

25. HP Papers, III (Programs).

26. See Sumner Salter, "Early Encouragements to American Composers," *Musical Quarterly* 18 (Jan. 1932): 76-105, for a discussion of the activities of such groups. See also Martha Furman Schleifer, *William Wallace Gilchrist* (Metuchan, New Jersey: The Scarecrow Press, Inc. 1985), Chapter VI, for a discussion of the Manuscript Society of Philadelphia, which was organized in 1892, shortly after the New York group.

27. A *New York Times* article (7 December 1890, p. 4) gives the founding year of the Manuscript Society as 1888; however, the program for the public meeting on 3 December 1896 lists the founding date as 26 August 1889. I am grateful to Margery Lowens for providing me with some Parker compositions and dates performed at Manuscript Society meetings.

28. File, "Manuscript Society," NYPL.

29. Title page, published vocal score (London: Novello, 1891).

30. Wilson, *The Musical Yearbook* 9 (1891-92), p. 25.

31. "Report of the Standing Committee of the Board of Trustees, 1 June 1892," *Proceedings of the General Theological Seminary* 6 (1 October 1884 to 23 May 1893): 642.

32. Letter to writer from Ray F. Brown, Director of Music, General Theological Seminary, 15 February 1963.

33. "National Conservatory of Music," *Harper's Weekly*, 13 December 1890, pp. 969-70.

34. *Grove's Dictionary of Music and Musicians; American Supplement*, ed. Waldo Selden Pratt (London: Macmillan, 1920, enlarged 1928), p. 306.

35. Letter from Mrs. Frederick Pier to Parker, 17 October 1907, asking for advice on selecting a church hymnal and identifying herself as a former pupil in Parker's harmony class at the National Conservatory (HP Papers, II A); letter from Williams Arms Fisher (representing the Oliver Ditson Co.) to Parker, 5 May 1911, in which Fisher commented: "The days when I worked with you in canon and fugue seem far away, but I have not forgotten them" (HP Papers II D).

36. *New York Times*, 26 October 1892, p. 4.

37. Alec Robertson, *Dvořák* (New York: Collier Books, 1962), p.80. Originally published under same title as part of the Master Musician Series (New York: Farrar, Straus & Cudahy, 1943).

38. File, "National Conservatory of Music," Music Division, NYPL.

39. Clipping from *Boston Journal*, n. d. (ca. 1893-94), pasted into back of score for *Hora Novissima*, BpBr. Several writers maintain that *Hora Novissima* was also submitted to the National Conservatory composition contest but that *Dream-King* was found more acceptable. See George Chadwick ("American Composers," *History of American Music*, vol. 4, *The American History and Encyclopedia of Music*, general ed. W. L. Hubbard [New York: Irving Squire, 1908-10], p. 5), David Stanley Smith ("Horatio Parker," p. 156), and John Tasker Howard (*Our American Music*, [New York: Thomas Y. Crowell, 1931], p. 339).

40. The erroneous statement that Richard Henry Warren, leader of the Church Choral Society, conducted the first performance is found in several pub-

lished biographical sketches. All periodical accounts of the time state that Parker was the conductor.

41. Clipping, *Saint James' Choir Journal*, March 1893, HP Papers, IV E 3.

42. Theodore Thomas, *A Musical Autobiography*, ed. Georg P. Upton, 2 vols. (Chicago: McClurg, 1905; repr. with a new introduction by Leon Stein, New York: Da Capo, 1964), vol. 2, p. 175.

43. Clipping from the *Boston Journal*, n. d. (ca. Fall, 1893), HP Papers, IV E 6.

44. Clipping dated "May 6, 1893," HP Papers, IV E 6.

45. *New York Times*, 4 May 1893, p. 5.

46. Unidentified clipping , HP Papers, IV E 3.

47. *The Musical Times* 34 (1893): 586. Both the *Times* and *Hora Novissima* were published by Novello.

48. Clipping, 5 February 1894, in back of score to *Hora Novissima*, BpBr.

49. Clipping, *Boston Journal*, 5 February 1894, in back of score to *Hora Novissima*, BpBr.

50. Clipping from *Saint James' Choir Journal*, March, 1893, HP Papers, IV E 3.

51. Ibid.

52. Commager, *The American Mind*, p. 58.

53. "Music in America," HP Papers, V, C (Papers, Addresses, Essays), 36/2, p. 2.

54. Clippings from *Saint James' Choir Journal*, March, 1893, *Boston Journal*, n. d., and *Springfield Union*, 5 October 1895, HP Papers, IV E 3.

55. Trinity Church in the City of Boston, Massachusetts 1733-1933 (Boston: [private printing], 1933), p. 101. This portion of the church history was written by William H. Dewart, asst. minister, 1893-1902.

56. Diary, 10 November, and 13 December 1983, HP Papers, V A.

57. Clippings from various Boston papers, HP Papers, IV E 6. See also the *Boston Evening Transcript*, 29 and 30 January 1894, pp. 1.

58. Clippings from *Milwaukee Sentinal*, 18 May 1894, and *Milwaukee Journal*, 24 February 1896, HP Papers, IV E 6.

59. George Wilson Pierson, *Yale College 1871-1921* (New Haven: Yale University Press, 1952), Chap. I passim.

60. Rollin Osterweis, *Three Centuries of New Haven* (New Haven: Yale University Press, 1953), p. 371.

Chapter Three--THE EDUCATOR

1. Pierson, p.58.

2. Ibid., p. 52.

3. David Stanley Smith, *Gustave J. Stoeckel, Yale Pioneer in Music* (New Haven: Yale University Press, 1939), p. 4.

4. Ibid, p. 6.

5. Walter Raymond Spalding, *Music at Harvard* (New York: Coward-McCann, 1935), Chap. 4 passim, and John C. Schmidt, *The Life and Works of John Knowles Paine* (Ann Arbor: UMI Research Press, 1980), Chaps. 3-5 passim.

6. Luther Noss, *A History of the Yale School of Music, 1855-1970* (New Haven: [private printing], 1984). In the "Prologue" is found the most complete published account of the organization of the Yale Music Department and the generosity of the Battell family which made this possible.

7. Noss, pp. 27, 291-292.

8. *Report Of the President of Yale University* (New Haven: private printing, 1890-1920), 1893-94, p. 9.

9. Noss suggests that Samuel Sanford, a pianist and teacher of excellent reputation from Bridgeport, Connecticut, was first offered the Battell professorship but turned it down, recommending Parker instead (p. 31).

10. *Catalogue, Department of Music [School of Music]*, (New Haven: private printing, 1890-1920), 1894. Reprinted in Noss, pp. 296-297.

11. David M. Thompson, *A History of Harmonic Theory in the United States* (Kent, Ohio: Kent State University Press, 1980), pp. 74-79.

12. *Report of the President*, 1906, p. 164.

13. Conversation, writer with Parker's son-in-law, Ralph Semler, New Canaan, Connecticut, 18 September 1961, who took the course as an undergraduate.

14. "The history of music," HP Papers, V B (Lectures), Lecture 1, p. 6. Hereafter lecture and page numbers are designated in the text.

15. "Music at Yale,", HP Papers, V C 35/23, p. 3.

16. Ralph Waldo Emerson, "The Conduct of Life," in Percy Miller, ed., *The American Transcendentalists* (New York: Doubleday Anchor Books, 1957), p.184.

17. "Music at Yale," p. 3.

18. *Catalogue*, 1902-03, 1913-14.

19. Edward MacDowell, *Critical and Historical Essays* (Boston: A. P. Schmidt, 1912; reprint ed., with a new introduction by Irving Lowens, New York: Da Capo Press, 1969,) Chaps. I, II, XX, XXI passim.

20. "Music at Yale," p. 5.

21. Ibid., p. 4.

22. *Report of the President*, 1909, p. 226; 1916-17, p. 234.

23. See Semler, p. 270, for Douglas Moore's reminiscence.

24. Conversations with Bruce Simonds, New Haven, Connecticut, 8 September 1961 and 24 September 1962.

25. Semler, pp. 69-73.

26. Charles E. Ives, *Memos*, ed. John Kirkpatrick (New York: Norton, 1972), p. 181.

27. Letter from Edwin Arthur Kraft, 20 April 1962, Cleveland, Ohio.

28. Gertrude Norman and Miriam Lubell Shrifte, *Letters of Composers* (New York: A. A. Knopf, 1946; pbk. ed., Grosset & Dunlap, n. d.), p. 318.

29. "Music as a University Course," *The American Monthly Review of Reviews* 14 (July 1896): 87. Pratt, who is also quoted below, was a leading music historian and educator who taught at Hartford Theological Seminary and Smith College at that time.

30. "The Proper Place of Musical Study in Universities and Colleges," *New York Times*, 14 February 1904, p. 22.

31. Lecture subtitled "for the Connecticut school teachers," n. d., HP Papers, V C 36/4.

32. "Music at Yale," p. 15.

33. Horatio Parker *et al.*,eds., *The Progressive Music Series For Basal Use in Primary, Intermediate, and Grammar Grades*, 8 vols. (Boston and New York: Silver-Burdett and Co., 1914-1919). See also Polly Carder [Silver Burdett music education consultant], *American Music in the Publications of the Silver Burdett Company*, booklet printed for the annual meeting of the Sonneck Society, Tallahassee, Florida, 7-10 March 1985, for an index to the first four volumes.

34. Letter from Charles E. Griffith, Norwich, Vermont, to George A. Booker, Tallahassee, Florida, 16 November 1959.

35. Letter from W. Otto Miessner, Connersville, Indiana, to George A. Booker, Tallahassee, Florida, 24 Nov. 1959.

36. The diaries for these years list contacts with Cyril Scott, Wolf-Ferrari, Delius, Van der Stucken, Bruch, Humperdinck, Percy Grainger, Stanford, Debussy, Pierné, Widor, Reger, Julius Röntgen, Amy Beach, Robert Heger, Sibelius, Moszkowski, D'Indy, and R. Strauss (HP Papers, V A).

37. Alternate title, *Music and Public Entertainment*, Vol. 9 of *The Young Folks Library: Vocations*, ed.-in-chief, William DeWitt Hyde, 10 vols. (Boston: Locke and Hall, 1911; reprint ed., New York: AMS Press, 1980.)

38. Letter from William De Witt Hyde to Parker [c. 1910], HP Papers, II B.

39. Noss, pp. 57-58.

40. Noss lists Parker and Sanford as cochairmen of the Department of Music until 1904, when Parker became Dean. The designation "Department of Music" is used in most catalogues; however, *Catalogue*, 1902-03, carries a subtitle, "Yale

Music School," and *Catalogue*, 1914-15, "School of Music." After 1914 the administrative complex for music was presumably known as a "School" rather than a "Department."

41. The season of 1904 was typical of the number and variety of musical events. There were six symphony concerts (New Haven Symphony Orchestra), two artists's recitals (Guilmant and Hofmann), two oratorio performances, seven chamber concerts (including three by the Kneisel Quartet and one by the Adamowski Quartet), thirteen organ recitals, four student concerts, and one People's Choral Union concert. *Report of the President*, 1903-04, p. 242.

42. One lecture series included some of the most eminent men in American music: H. E. Krehbiel on "Folksong"; W. F. Apthorp, "The function of criticism and the critic"; Edgar S. Kelley, "Oriental music"; W. J. Henderson, "The Classic and Romantic in Music"; and Horatio Parker, "Church music." *Report of the President*, 1899-1900, p. 71.

43. Ibid., 1900-01, p. 98.

44. Noss, pp. 73-74.

45. Ann Whelan, "The History of the New Haven Symphony Orchestra," *The Connecticut Times*, 16 March 1921, p. 3.

46. *Catalogue*, 1896-97, p. 6.

47. Clipping dated 20 October 1895, HP Papers, IV E 3.

48. The programs of concerts from 1895 to 1918 list such well-known artists as Pablo Casals, Fritz Kreisler, Efrem Zimbalist, Harold Bauer, Rudolph Ganz, Marcella Craft, Albert Spalding, Francis Rogers, Herbert Witherspoon, Leo Ornstein, and Alma Gluck.

49. *Report of the President*, 1917, p. 327.

50. *Report of the President*, 1903-04, p. 171.

51. Louis C. Elson, *The History of American Music* (New York: Macmillan, 1904; rev. to 1925 by Arthur Elson; reprinted, New York: Franklin, 1971), p. 178.

52. *Report of the President*, 1904-05, p. 180.

53. "Music at Yale," p. 11.

Chapter Four--NATIONAL AND INTERNATIONAL RECOGNITION

1. Clipping from *Springfield Republican*, 5 October 1894, HP Papers, IV E 6.

2. Clippings from the New Haven papers: *Leader, Register, Journal-Courier,* and *Palladium* (ca. 1896), HP Papers, IV E 3.

3. Clipping dated 9 December 1896, HP Papers, IV E 3.

4. These include "French opera" and "Organ music" at Atlanta, Georgia (Diary, 21 Oct. 1895, HP Papers, V A); and "Lasting qualities in music," for the New England Chapter of the American Guild of Organists (Samuel A. Baldwin, *The Story of the American Guild of Organists* [New York: H. W. Gray Co., 1946], p. 46). In addition, Parker published an article outlining some of his ideas on music education ("Music as a University Course," *Music* 10/2 [June 1896], 181-85). He also wrote a set of lectures called "Church music" (HP Papers, V C) which he gave as a part of a Department of Music lecture series in 1899 and subsequently each year at the Yale Divinity School.

5. HP Papers, V C 36/2.

6. Unidentified clipping, HP Papers, IV E 3.

7. Unidentified clipping, HP Papers, IV E 3.

8. Clipping, n. d., HP Papers, IV E 3.

9. Diary, July 1898, HP Papers, V A.

10. Diary, 1899, HP Papers, V A; clippings from New Haven papers, 8 April 1899, HP Papers, IV E 3. Wilhelm Gericke and the Boston Symphony performed *A Northern Ballad* 29 and 30 December 1899 (clippings from the Boston papers, 30 December 1899, HP Papers, IV E 3) as did Theodore Thomas, to whom the work was dedicated, with both the Chicago Orchestra, 9 February 1900, and the Cincinnati Orchestra, 12 May 1900 (*Programs*, Chicago Symphony Orchestra, 1899-1900, and program for the Cincinnati Festival concert, HP Papers, III [Programs]). Additional performances were given by the New York Philharmonic Society in 1901 (Clipping from the *New Haven Register* 18 February 1901, HP Papers, IV E 3), and at the 1904 Saint Louis World's Fair and the 1915 Panama-Pacific Exposition in San Francisco (Diaries, 23 June 1904 and 1 August 1915, HP Papers, V A).

11. *A Quaker Singer's Recollections* (New York: Macmillan, 1920), p. 209.

12. Vol. 34 (1893): 587.

13. Clippings from the *Musical Standard* (London), 22 July 1893, and *Musical Record* (London), 1 January 1894, HP Papers, IV E 3.

14. Clipping from *Boston Journal*, n. d. (ca. 1893), HP Papers, IV E 3.

15. Clipping, 26 August 1899, HP Papers, IV E 5.

16. Clipping, 7 September 1899, HP Papers, IV E 5.

17. Clipping from the London *Athenaeum*, 23 September 1899, HP Papers, IV E 5.

18. Clipping from London *Daily News*, 15 September 1899, HP Papers, IV E 5.

19. Clipping, 15 September 1899, HP Papers, IV E 5.

20. Unidentified clipping, n. d., HP Papers, IV E 5.

21. Diary, 16 February 1900, HP Papers, V A: "Sent away Cantus Peregrinus," the subtitle.

22. Clippings from the *Musical Times*, the *Birmingham Post*, the *Chestershire Observer*,the *Manchester Courier* and the *Manchester Guardian*, HP Papers, IV E 5. Observations about the Chester Festival are drawn from these sources.

23. Clipping from *Hereford Times*, 15 September 1900, HP Papers,IV E 5.

24. Clippings from Hereford and London papers, HP Papers, IV E 5.

25. Clippings from *Boston Journal* and *Boston Herald*, HP Papers, IV E 3.

26. In a letter to Parker, 14 February 1900, Atkins speaks of using the *Service in E* (Semler, p. 122).

27. Unidentified clipping, HP Papers, IV E 5.

28. Semler, p. 139.

29. Diaries, 1901-02, HP Papers, V A.

30. Letter from C. V. Stanford to Parker, 7 December 1901, HP Papers II (correspondence), C (topics: Cambridge degree).

31. Letter from Jebb to Stanford, 3 March 1902, HP Papers, II C.

32. Unidentified clipping, n. d., found in score to a *A Star Song*, BpBr.

33. Clipping from *New Music Review*, January, 1919, p. 58, HP Papers, IV E 5.

34. HP Papers, VII (misc. items), A 2 (royalty statements), John Church Co.

35. "Address before the National Institute of Arts and Letters." HP Papers, V C 35/3. The quotations below are taken from this source.

36. Margery Morgan Lowens, *The New York Years of Edward MacDowell*, unpublished Ph. D. dissertation, Ann Arbor, University of Michigan, 1971, p. 221.

37. See Semler, p.155-65, for the entire paper; p. 175, for a description of "The Club," to which Parker spoke.

38. "Essay on Beauty," included in Percy Miller, ed., *The American Transcendentalists*, p. 176.

39. "Concerning contemporary music," HP Papers, V C 35/10, pp.12-13. This address is published in *Proceedings [of the] American Academy of Arts and Letters* (1909-1910), pp. 36-43.

40. "Miscellaneous notes for addresses," n.p., HP Papers, V C 36/14.

41. Ibid.

42. "Concerning contemporary music," p. 13.

43. Clipping from *Boston Herald*, 28 December 1902, found in back of score to Horatio Parker, *Concerto for Organ and Orchestra*, BpBr.

44. Clippings, 3 January 1903, HP Papers, IV E 6.

45. Edwin H. Lemare, noted concert organist, performed the work with the Pittsburgh Symphony Orchestra, 27-28 February 1903 (HP Papers, II [Correspondence] B). Parker performed it again with the Boston Symphony Orchestra at a benefit performance in New Haven, 22 March 1904 (Programs of the New Haven Symphony Orch., 1903-04, Yale Music Library), and at a concert of the Church Choral Society, St. Bartholomew's Church, New York City (clipping

from New York *Sun*, 22 April 1904, HP Papers, IV E 3). Albert Spalding, well-known American violinist and Army officer stationed in Rome in 1918, wrote to Parker telling him of a pending performance there (letter dated 31 December 1918, HP Papers, II B).

46. Diary, 14 July 1904: "Finished sketch of Crépuscule," HP Papers, V A.

47. At end of MS full score: "Tapper's barn, 19 September 1907." HP Papers, I C L/op 62.

48. Letter from Mr. Charles D. Davis to Parker, 28 May 1903, HP Papers II B.

49. Diary, 1904, HP Papers V A.

50. Leo T. Molley, *Tercentenary Pictorial and History of the Lower Nangatuck Valley, Containing a History of Derby* (Ansonia, Connecticut: Emerson Bros. 1935). p. 63.

51. Letter from E. M. Chied, Treasurer of Derby Choral Club, Derby, Connecticut, to Parker, 4 March 1914; diaries after 1903, HP Papers, V A and II C (topics: choral societies).

52. Letter from James M. Helfeustein, New York City, to Winchell Donald, Boston, 4 Mar. 1902, HP Papers II B.

53. No known connection with the composer of the same name.

54. *The New York City Guide* (New York: Random House, 1946), p. 688.

55. Letter from Donald to Parker, 6 March 1903, HP Papers, II V B.

56. Diary, HP Papers, V A.

57. Letter from Isabella Parker, Auburndale, MA, to Horatio Parker, 16 May 190[2?], HP Papers, II E 2.

58. *The Century: 1847-1946* (New York: The Century Association, 1947) provides a history of the organization.

59. MacDowell was elected on 7 January 1905. *In Memoriam, a Book of Records Concerning Former Members of the American Academy of Arts and Letters* (New York: private printing, n. d.), p. 4.

60. *Program of the Inaugural Grand Concerts* (Washington, D. C.: private printing, 1905).

61. Clipping from *Buffalo Express*, 1 June 1905, HP Papers, IV E 2.

62. *Dramatic Compositions Copyrighted in the United States, 1890-1916*, Library of Congress, Copyright Office, 12 June 1902, 20 September 1903, D:2050. I am indebted to the late Miss Eva J. O'Meara, former librarian of the School of Music at Yale University, who responded so generously to my inquiry concerning *The Eternal Feminine*.

63. *Yale Alumni Weekly*, 12 October 1904.

64. *New York Times*, 25 September 1906, p. 9.

65. Letter from Carl Stoeckel, Norfolk, Connecticut, 23 May 1902, to Parker, HP Papers, II B.

66. Semler, p. 196-198.

67. Diary, 17 May 1907, HP Papers, V A. The date of his selection is given as 20 May 1907 in the official history of the club: Robert R. Robins, Arthur Church *et al.*, *A History of the Orpheus Club of Philadelphia: 1872-1936* (Philadelphia: private printing, 1936), p. 46.

68. Robert A. Gerson, *Music In Philadelphia* (Philadelphia: Theodore Presser Co., 1940), p. 258.

69. Gerson, p. 142.

70. Clipping, n. d., HP Papers, IV E 1.

71. Bispham, p. 337.

72. Gerson, p. 260.

73. Gerson, p. 260; Robins, p. 68.

74. See Semler, pp. 217-23, for a more extensive description of life at Blue Hill.

Chapter Five--THE FINAL YEARS

1. Henry E. Krehbiel, *More Chapters on Opera* (New York: Henry Holt, 1919), pp. 169-171.

2. Clipping from *Ansonia Evening Sentinal*, 13 March 1912, HP Papers, IV E 1.

3. Semler, pp. 188-91.

4. Clipping dated 4 May 1911, HP Papers, IV E 1. Only Mildenberg made public at that time the fact that he was a contestant. He brought suit against the Metropolitan Opera Association, claiming that it had lost part of his score. Edward E. Hipsher, *American Opera and Its Composers* (Philadelphia: Theodore Presser Co., 1927), p. 322.

5. Clipping from the *New York Herald*, 4 May 1911, HP Papers, IV E 1.

6. Clipping from the *New York Sun*, 23 May 1911, HP Papers, IV E 1.

7. Clipping from *Boston Herald*, n. d., in back of score to *Mona*, BpBr.

8. Clipping from *Musical Leader*, n. d., HP Papers, IV E 1.

9. Clipping dated 3 May 1911, HP Papers, IV E 1.

10. Clipping dated 4 May 1911, HP Papers, IV E 1.

11. Clipping from the *New York Press*, 3 May 1911, HP Papers, IV E 1.

12. As quoted in *Musical Courier*, 6 March 1912, "Horatio Parker," clipping file, Music Division, NYPL,

13. *Musical Courier* 64 (6 March 1912): 23.

14. *Musical America*, 15 (9 March 1912): 7.

15. Letters from Parker to Hertz, 15 May 1911, HP Papers, II A.

16. Ibid., 15 July 1911.

17. Ibid., 3 Sept. 1911.

18. Ibid., 16 Dec. 1911.

19. Ibid.

20. *Musical America*, 15 (27 Jan. 1912): 9.

21. 15 March 1912, p. 13, col. 1.

22. Clipping dated 6 March 1912, "Horatio Parker," clipping file, Music Division, NYPL.

23. *Musical America* 15 (16 March 1912): 2.

24. As quoted in the *New York Sun*, 10 March 1912, HP Papers, IV E 1.

25. A complete account of the first performance was carried in major New York and Boston newspapers on 15 March 1912. Clippings for the performance are in Bp, NYPL, and at Yale.

26. William H. Seltsam, *Metropolitan Opera Annals* (New York: Wilson, 1947), p. 237.

27. HP Papers, V A. The diaries show that Parker began receiving parts of the libretto from Hooker during the fall of 1912: Act I on October 12, and part of Act II on November 15.

28. Letter postmarked Munich, 29 December 1912, HP Papers, II A.

29. Clipping from *Musical Courier*, 14 July 1915, p. 23, HP Papers, IV E 4.

30. Clipping from *Musical America*, 24 October 1913, HP Papers, IV E 4.

31. Ibid.

32. Clipping from *Los Angeles Examiner*, 8 November 1914, HP Papers, IV E 4.

33. Letters from Parker to Blanchard, 22 October and 22 November 1914, HP Papers, II A.

34. Ibid., 22 March 1915.

35. Letter dated 17 March 1915, HP Papers, II B.

36. Clipping from *Los Angeles Examiner*, 18 June 1915, HP Papers, IV E 4.

37. Unidentified clipping, n.d., HP Papers, IV E 4.

38. Clipping from *Los Angeles Herald*, 21 May 1915, HP Papers, IV E 4.

39. Clipping from *Musical Courier*, 14 July 1915, p. 23, HP Papers, IV E 4.

40. HP Papers, V C 35/4.

41. HP Papers, V C 35/9

42. Unidentified clipping, n.d., HP Papers, IV E 4.

43. Clippings from Boston papers, HP Papers, IV E 4.

44. Diary, 5 Apr. 1916: "Received notice of J. Chapman's play," HP Papers, V A. Program from 20 October 1916 performance, "Parker, memorabilia," Yale Room, Sterling Memorial Library, Yale University.

45. Clipping from *Boston Herald*, n.d., HP Papers, IV E 4.

46. HP Papers, V C 36/14 (miscellaneous notes), n.p.

47. HP Papers, V C 35/4. Quoted material found on pp. 8 and 3.

48. Clipping from the Washington, D. C., *Evening Star*, 20 May 1916, HP Papers, IV E 4.

49. *Yale Review* 7 (July 1918): 777-88. Typescript, HP Papers, V C 36/8, p. 3.

50. Semler, p. 279.

51. *Report of the President of Yale University*, 1917, p. 329.

52. Semler, p. 294.

53. Letter from Parker to Oscar Sonneck, 10 December 1917, HP Papers, II A.

54. Semler, p. 282.

55. Letter from William Arms Fisher to John Finley, Boston, 19 September 1917, HP Papers, II D. Fisher quotes Parker as writing: "All possible profit and benefit I desire to go to the Red Cross."

56. Diary, 5 May 1918, HP Papers, V A.

57. *New Music Review and Church Music Review* 19 (May 1920): 192.

58. HP Papers, II B.

59. Letter from Chapman to Parker, n.d., HP Papers, II B.

60. Unidentified clipping, n. d., "Parker, memorabilia," Sterling Memorial Library, Yale Room, Yale University.

61. Letter from Hooker to Parker, n.d., HP Papers, II B.

62. Letter from Stokes to Parker, 9 April 1919, HP Papers, II B.

63. Semler, p. 299.

64. Diary, 1919, HP Papers, V A.

65. Semler, p. 300.

66. *Boston Evening Transcript*, 18 December 1919, p. 13.

67. *The New England Conservatory of Music Bulletin* 1 (January 1920): 4. The pallbearers included President Hadley of Yale, W. S. Kendell, Dean of the Art School, Professors Harold Arnold, Bernadotte Perrin, and John Adams. Musical associates included George Chadwick, Frederick Converse, Wallace Goodrich, Carl Stoeckel, Henry Krehbiel, and David Stanley Smith.

68. *Boston Evening Transcript*, 18 December 1919, p.13.

69. Semler, p. 305.

70. *New York Sun*, 21 December 1919, section 8, p. 4, col. 2.

71. *New York Tribune*, 19 December 1919. Pt. IV, p. 12, col. 1.

72. Clipping, 30 December 1919, HP Papers, IV C (obituaries).

73. Clipping dated 25 December 1919, "Parker, memorabilia," Sterling Memorial Library, Yale Room, Yale University.

74. Clipping dated 20 December 1919, HP Papers, IV C.

75. Clipping dated 19 December 1919, HP Papers, IV C.

76. Clipping, n.d., HP Papers, IV C.

Chapter Six--SECULAR CHORAL MUSIC

1. A sales account from the publisher, the John Church Co., shows that 691 copies were sold up to 1903, exceeding even the American sales of Parker's most popular song for solo voice, "The lark now leaves his watery nest" (HP Papers, II D [publishers]).

2. The cantatas with German texts had to be given English settings in order to have any commercial value in America, and the composer's mother Isabella Parker, in most cases, performed this function as a lyrical but somewhat flowery versemaker. For *The Norsemen's Raid*, the English translation was done by Emily Whitney.

3. Wilson, *Yearbook*, 1892-93, p. 207.

4. *Boston Evening Transcript*, 1 April 1893, p. 7.

5. Clipping, n. d., Arthur Whiting papers, Music Division, NYPL.

6. Clipping, *New York Tribune*, 25 November 1887, HP Papers, IV B 6.

7. Clipping, 27 September 1899, in back of score, BpBr.

Chapter Seven--THE CEREMONIAL MUSIC

1. Miscellaneous unidentified writings, HP Papers, V C 36/14.

2. Vocal score. English translation by Isabella Parker.

3. Clipping from *Boston Herald*, n. d., HP Papers, IV E 4.

4. Semler, p. 299.

5. Ibid., p. 300.

6. Clipping from an unidentified Philadelphia newspaper, n. d., HP Papers, IV A.

7. George P. Upton, *The Standard Cantatas* (Chicago: A. C. McClurg, 1888)88), p. 286.

8. *New York Tribune*, 20 October 1901, p. 9.

Chapter Eight--THE LARGE SACRED CHORAL WORKS

1. Schleifer, *William Wallace Gilchrist*, p. 55.

2. Saint Louis Symphony; Gunther Schuller, conductor; New World Records, 262/63 (1978).

3. Unidentified clipping, "Biographies of Musicians," I, p. 196, BpBr.

4. Letter to Alice Jennings, 25 June 1885, HP Papers, II E 3.

5. Parts of this translation appear in many of the hymnals of the time under such titles as "The World is Very Evil," "Brief Life is Here Our Portion," "Jerusalem, the Golden," and "For Thee, O Dear, Dear Country."

6. Chadwick, p. 10.

7. Clipping from *Boston Journal*, n. d., BpBr.

8. "Horatio Parker," clipping file, *Concert Goer*, No. 202, p. 2, Music Division, NYPL.

9. Clipping from *Boston Journal*, 5 February 1894, BpBr.

10. *New York Times*, 4 May 1893, p. 5; Robert Stevenson, *Protestant Church Music in America* (New York: Norton, 1966), p. 116, fn. 291.

11. George P. Upton, *The Standard Oratorios* (Chicago: A. C. McClurg, 1890), p. 109.

12. *New York Times*, 4 May 1893, p. 5.

13. This and following quotations taken from clippings in back of score to *Hora Novissima*, BpBr.

14. *Musical Times* 34 (1893): 587.

15. Clipping, 14 September 1899, BpBr.

16. Yellin, p. 291.

17. Clipping, *Musical Courier*, 22 July 1893, and following quotations taken from clippings in back of score to *Hora Novissima*, BpBr.

18. "Horatio Parker," clipping file, Music Division, NYPL.

19. Clipping, *Boston Evening Transcript*, 18 Feb. 1918, BpBr.

20. Chase, p. 377.

21. Clipping, *Pall Mall Gazette*, BpBr.

22. *Musical Courier* 36 (20 Apr. 1898): 12.

23. Henderson quotation, *New York Times*, 16 Apr. 1898, p. 7; Apthorp, *Boston Evening Transcript*, 7 December 1899, p. 10.

24. Unidentified clipping, HP Papers IV E 3, also in Elson, *The History of American Music*, 1925, p. 180.

25. Chadwick, p. 15.

26. Semler, p. 100.

27. Clipping from *The London Times*, 15 September 1899, HP Papers, IV E 5.

28. Letter from Atkins to HP, 1 February 1902, HP Papers, II B.

29. Both clippings from back of *Saint Christopher* score, BpBr.

30. *Monthly Musical Record* 11 (April 1899): 160.

31. Clippings from *New York Sun* (11 April 1899, p. 4) and New York *Tribune*, *Times*, and *Herald* (all 17 March 1899), HP Papers, IV E 3.

32. Clipping dated 14 September 1900, HP Papers, IV E 5.

33. Clipping from *New York Tribune*, 16 September 1900, HP Papers, IV E 5.

34. Clippings from HP Papers, IV E 5.

35. Clipping from *Boston Journal*, 18 December 1900, HP Papers, IV E 3.

36. Clipping from *Music Review*, ca. 1900, HP Papers, IV E 3.

37. Semler, p. 125.

38. Diary, 3 June 1902, HP Papers, V A; on 19 March 1908, Parker wrote "Gerontius, good performance" for New Haven Oratorio Society presentation which he conducted.

39. This and following quotes from clippings in score to *A Star Song*, BpBr.

40. Both quotations from *New York Times*, 9 November 1902, p. 14.

41. Clippings for this and following on *Morven* dated 14 April 1915, HP Papers, IV E 4.

42. Chadwick, pp. 18-19.

43. *Philadelphia Public Ledger*, 31 December 1911, p. 7.

44. Perhaps unaware of Goepp's work, Herbert Sanders praised the unusual features of Parker's cantata, calling it "something different." *American Organist* 2 (1919): 197-198.

45. See p. 73 above for a description of the staging.

46. Sanders, *American Organist* 2 (1919): 197-198.

Chapter Nine--MUSIC FOR THE STAGE

1. C. L. Graves, *Hubert Parry: His Life and Works*, 2 vols. (London: Macmillan and Co., 1928), II:213.

2. Clipping from *Pall Mall Gazette*, 8 October 1899, in back of score to *Hora Novissima*, BpBr.

3. Semler, p. 164.

4. *The Theatre* 6 (November 1906).

5. "French opera," HP Papers, V C 35/11, for quotations in this paragraph.

6. "Contemporary music," HP Papers, V C S/C7, for this and following quotations on pp. 147-48.

7. "French Opera," p. 3.

8. Clipping from *Boston Herald*, n. d., BpBr.

9. Clipping dated 6 May 1911, HP Papers, IV E 1.

10. *Boston Evening Transcript*, 3 May 1911, p. 26.

11. As reported in the *Albany Independent* clipping dated 3 May 1911, HP Papers, IV E 1.

12. Clippings from various New York newspapers, HP Papers, IV E 1. See also *Twenty-Five Years After With Yale, 1902* (Newburgh, New York: The Moore Printing Co., 1927), p. 271. After 1921, Hooker turned to a lighter vein, writing musical comedies. His most notable success was *The Vagabond King* of 1925. His translation of *Cyrano De Bergerac*, done for Walter Hampden, had an extended New York run in 1924.

13. Brian Hooker, *Mona* (New York: Dodd, Mead and Co., 1911) ix.

14. Jack Lindsay, *The Romans Were Here* (London: Frederick Muller, 1956), pp. 72-81.

15. Clipping from *New York Tribune*, 21 May 1911, HP Papers, IV E 1.

16. Clippings from *Boston Mirror*, 20 December 1911; *New York Tribune*, n. d.; and *Boston Evening Transcript*, 23 September, 1911--all from BpBr.

17. Clipping from *Boston Herald*, 23 October, 1911, BpBr.

18. *New York Tribune*, 15 March 1912, p. 7; *Boston Evening Transcript*, 15 March 1912, p.13; *New York Times*, 17 March 1912, Pt. 7, p. 7.

19. Clipping from *New York American*, 15 March 1912, HP Papers, IV E 1.

20. Hooker, p. 26.

21. Ibid., p. 27.

22. Both Frederick Converse's *The Pipe of Desire* and Victor Herbert's *Natoma* were mentioned by several critics as having poor librettos.

23. Semler, p. 235.

24. Clipping from *New York World*, ca. 1911, HP Papers, IV E 1.

25. Henry E. Krehbiel, *More Chapters of Opera* (New York: Henry Holt, 1919), p. 265.

26. *New York Tribune*, 15 March 1912, p. 7.

27. Unidentified clipping, HP Papers, IV E 1.

28. Clipping from *New York Sun*, 15 March 1912, HP Papers, IV E 1.

29. Clipping from *New York American*, 15 March 1912, HP Papers, IV E 1.

30. See Krehbiel, p. 263, for a matter-of-fact assumption on the use of leading motives.

31. *Musical America* 15 (23 March 1912): 1.

32. Ibid., (27 January 1912): 9.

33. In an article on leading motive treatment ("Mona, a Thematic Analysis," *Musical Observer* 6 [April 1912]: 22-28), J. van Broekhoven listed twenty-four. I have used Broekhoven's identification wherever possible and have made additional identifications when necessary.

34. Parker considered Debussy's use of "the six-tone scale" and the "augmented triad . . . a definite negation of tonality" ("Contemporary Music," p. 7, HP Papers, V C S/C7).

35. *Musical America* 15 (27 January 1912): 9.

36. The Roman army motive, p. 20, m. 10, and slavery motive, pp. 104-11, are illustrative of bitonality.

37. *Boston Evening Transcript*, 15 March 1912, p. 13.

38. Quoted in *Musical America* 15 (23 March 1912): 4.

39. Review of prelude and love duet from *Mona*, performed by the Orchestra of America, Richard Korn conducting, New York, 22 February 1961 (*Opera News* 125 [1 Apr 1961]: 33).

40. Clipping from *Boston Evening Transcript*, 9 March 1912, sec. 2, p.8.

41. Unidentified clipping, "Horatio Parker," clipping file, Music Division, NYPL.

42. Clipping from *New York Tribune*, 24 March 1912, HP Papers, IV E 1.

43. [A. Walter Kramer]. "Mefisto's Musings," *Musical America* 54 (10 March 1934): 9; Paul Rosenfeld, "The Fate of 'Mona,'" *Musical Chronicle (1917-1923)* (New York: Harcourt, Brace & Co., 1923), 54-60.

44. Act I was given in New York in March 1920. In 1930, *Paoletta* earned for its composer the David Bispham medal of the American Opera Society of Chicago. Bispham had created the principal role of Gomarez in the Cincinnati

production (Edward E. Hipsher, *American Opera and Its Composers* (Philadelphia: Theodore Presser Co., 1927, p. 180).

45. As quoted in Hipsher, p. 180.

46. Parker continued to meet the exigencies of the production after he had arrived in Los Angeles right up to the last minute. Just before the performance he composed a special number for the well-known ballerina Albertina Rasch, who was hired practically at the eleventh hour to coordinate the efforts of the amateur ballet corps. (Clippings from the Los Angeles papers, June 1915, HP Papers, IV E 4.)

47. Clipping from *Los Angeles Examiner*, 14 June 1915, HP Papers, IV E 4.

48. Clipping from *Los Angeles Examiner,*, 20 June 1915, HP Papers, IV E 4.

49. Clipping from *Los Angeles Graphic*, 3 July 1915, HP Papers, IV E 4.

50. Clipping from *Los Angeles Examiner*, 18 June 1915, HP Papers, IV E 4.

51. Clipping from *Los Angeles Daily Times*, 1 July 1915, HP Papers, IV E 4.

52. Ibid. Parker's opinions concerning the qualities of American music are representative of the established composers of the time. Edward MacDowell stipulated the following: "What we must arrive at is the youthful optimistic vitality and the undaunted tenacity of spirit that characterizes the American man. This is what I hope to see echoed in American music." (As quoted from a lecture on "Folkmusic" in Lawrence Gilman, *Edward MacDowell* [New York and London: John Lane, 1921], p. 83.)

53. Clippings from Los Angeles papers, HP Papers, IV A; the final quotation: *The Musical Leader* 30 (8 July 1915): 33.

54. *Boston Evening Transcript*, 15 September 1915, p. 23.

55. *Boston Evening Transcript*, 13 March 1915, sec. 3, p. 6.

56. Clipping from *Los Angeles Graphic*, 3 July 1915, HP Papers, IV E 4.

57. Clipping from *Los Angeles Daily Times*, 2 July 1915, HP Papers, IV E 4.

58. Three entries in diaries: 6 Oct. 1912: "Rosenkavalier"; 15 January 1913: "Anna gave me tickets to Rosenkavalier, 1st row. Fine performance, good fun"; 4 June 1913: "Rosenkavalier"; HP Papers, V A.

59. A similar antiphonal section is found in the second act of *Saint Christopher* (1897). Here the male chorus representing Satan's legions is juxtaposed with a women's "ecclesiastical" chorus (vocal score, pp. 70-74).

60. Clipping from *Los Angeles Daily Times*, 2 July 1915, HP Papers, IV E 4.

61. Clipping from *Los Angeles Herald*, 2 July 1915, HP Papers, IV E 4.

62. Clipping from *Los Angeles Daily Times*, 2 July 1915, HP Papers, IV E 4.

63. *Boston Evening Transcript*, 15 September 1915, p. 23.

64. HP Papers, IV E 4. These include Edwin Schallert, *Los Angeles Daily Times*; Otheman Stevens, *Los Angeles Examiner*; Joseph P. Dupuy, *Los Angeles Herald*; W. Francis Gate, *Los Angeles Graphic*; Bruce Bliven, *Los Angeles Outlook*. All are dated 2 July 1915.

65. George W. Chadwick, about the same time or shortly thereafter, was working on his own pastoral opera *Love's Sacrifice*, which parallels "Cupid and Psyche" in mythological plot and eclectic idiom. Chadwick evidently did not attach great importance to his work, for he had it orchestrated by his New England Conservatory class. (Yellin, p. 285.)

66. Richard B. Hovey, *John Jay Chapman: An American Mind* (New York: Columbia University Press, 1959), p. 239.

67. The chorus for one of the performances consisted of only twelve voices (HP Papers III, program to 20 Oct. 1916 production at Yale.).

68. *Musical America*, 21 (24 June 1916): 34.

69. Hovey, p. 239.

Chapter Ten--SECULAR MUSIC FOR SOLO VOICE

1. William T. Upton, *The Art Song in America* (Boston: Oliver Ditson Co.), p. 113.

2. *The Musical Times* 43 (1 September 1902): 588.

3. An excerpt from this song can be found in Rupert Hughes, *American Composers* (Boston: Page, 1900), p. 180.

4. Upton, p. 132.

5. A Victor recording of "Love in May" (Op. 51, No. 1) was made on 18 May 1908 by soprano Emma Eames and has been reissued by New World Records (NW 247).

6. Accounts of the John Church Company show 1,621 copies sold in England and 630 copies in this country up to 1903 (HP Papers, VII [Miscellaneous Items], A 2 [Royalty statements]). A Victor recording of "The lark," was made on 18 May 1908 by baritone Emilio Gogorza and has been reissued by New World Records (NW247).

7. Upton, p. 132.

8. Conversation with Mrs. Isabel Parker Semler, New Canaan, Connecticut, 18 September 1961.

9. Donald Ivey, *Song: Anatomy, Imagery and Styles* (New York: Free Press, 1970), p. 24.

10. Charles Hamm, *Music in the New World* (New York: Norton, 1983), pp. 454-56.

11. Clipping from *Boston Journal*, 30 March 1895, HP Papers, IV E 3.

12. *Musical America* 13 (13 November 1910): 28.

13. Clipping from *Boston Journal*, 30 March 1895, HP Papers, IV E 3.

14. *Boston Evening Transcript*, 1 April 1895, p. 5.

15. *Musical America* 13 (13 November 1910): 28.

16. Program notes for Cleveland Symphony Orchestra concerts, 11 March 1926.

17. Entries in diaries between 1904 and 1907.

18. The oboe is an important solo instrument in both of the operas. It is also the solo woodwind instrument for the church cantata *The Shepherds' Vision*, the masque *Cupid and Psyche*, and the part-song set for women's chorus *Seven Greek Pastoral Scenes*.

Chapter Eleven--THE CHURCH MUSIC

1. Arthur Farwell and W. D. Darby, eds., *Music in America*, vol. 4 of *The Art of Music*, ed. Daniel Gregory Mason, 13 vols. (New York: The National Society of Music, 1915-16), p. 357.

2. Quoted from *A Modern Instance*, p. 27, in Commager, *The American Mind*, pp. 167-68.

3. Quoted in Commager, *The American Mind*, p. 168.

4. Leonard Ellinwood, *The History of American Church Music* (New York: Morehouse-Gorham, 1953), p. 74.

5. "Church music," HP Papers, V C 35/7. This address, from which the quotations on pp. 193-194 are taken, is 38 pages long in its most complete version. It was the basis of his annual lectures to the Yale Divinity School student body as well as occasional lectures throughout the country.

6. "Address before the American Guild of Organists," HP Papers, V C 35/1 (paginated from 45 through 57), p. 54.

7. "Church music," p. 17.

8. "Church music since Bach," (California, 1915; supplement to "Church Music"), HP Papers, V C 35/9, p. 7.

9. "Church music," p. 13.

10. Ibid., p. 14.

11. "Miscellaneous notes for addresses." n. p., HP Papers, V C 36/14.

12. *Music List, Trinity Church in the City of Boston, October 1895 - June, 1898.* (Boston: private printing, 1898).

13. Clippings from *Musical America*, 12 June 1916, and the *Rochester Express*, 21 June 1916, "Horatio Parker," clipping file, Music Division, NYPL.

14. As reported in Ellinwood, pp. 134-35. Complete information on this survey is found in *The Diapason*, 14 (September, 1923): 9, and (December 1923): 4.

15. His two most popular anthems, *In Heavenly Love Abiding* (1900) and *The Lord Is My Light* (1890), placed only seventh and eighth, respectively, on the listing of individual anthems receiving the most votes.

16. Ellinwood, pp. 137-39. See Linda Jane Clark, *Music in Trinity Church, Boston, 1890-1900: A Case-Study in the Relationship Between Worship and Culture*, Doctor of Sacred Music Thesis, Union Theological Seminary, 1973, for extensive analyses of two Parker anthems *Bow Down Thine Ear* and *Light's Glittering Morn Bedecks The Skies* (pp. 288-304).

17. Archibald Davidson, *Protestant Church Music in America* (Boston: E. C. Schirmer, 1933), pp. 8, 102, 117, and 128.

18. Linda Jane Clark, *Music in Trinity Church*, p. 312.

19. Ibid., p. 314.

20. Clipping from *The Church Standard*, Philadelphia, February 1893, HP Papers, IV E 3.

21. *New Music Review and Church Music Review* 19 (January 1920): 59.

22. HP, "Church music," p. 15.

23. See Linda Clark's extensive analysis of the *Service in E* (*Music in Trinity Church*, pp. 240-63). She declares that harmony is Parker's principal conceptual approach, with other compositional elements subordinate. To her, the *Service* is lacking in purely musical interest and the "music is subservient to the text" (p. 263).

24. Edmund Fellowes, *Cathedral Music from Edward VI To Edward VII*, 4th ed., (London: Methuen & Co. 1948), p. 225.

25. Horatio Parker, *The Hymnal* (New York: H. W. Gray, 1903), Preface.

26. "Address before The American Guild of Organists," p. 49.

27. Clipping from *The Churchman*, 16 Feb. 1899, HP Papers, IV E 3.

28. Clipping from *The Illustrated Farmer*, 9 Feb. 1899, HP Papers, IV E 3.

29. Clipping from *The Churchman*, 16 Feb. 1899, HP Papers, IV E 3.

30. *Grove's American Supplement*, p. 251. The earlier tune books were published in 1893, 1894, 1894, and 1897.

31. Parker, *The Hymnal*, Preface. This and following quotations on pp. 203-204 are taken from the Preface.

32. Clippings from *Southern Churchman* 30, p. 1; and *The Church Standard*, 19 September 1903, p. 613, HP Papers, IV E 6..

33. *The Hymnal* (New York: H. W. Gray, 1918). Parker also assisted the Rev. Charles L. Hutchins with the latter's *The Church Hymnal* (Boston: Parish Choir, 1914), an enlarged edition of the Episcopal hymnal (852 pp.) for church organists. In 1907, Parker and Harry B. Jepson edited *University Hymns* (New York: A. S. Barnes, 1907) for use in Battell Chapel at Yale University. This substantial hymnal (331 pp.) includes three hymns by Parker: No. 431 (Auburndale) "Christ is Our Cornerstone," No. 269 (Courage) "Fight the Good Fight," and No. 343 (Pro patria) "God of Our Fathers, Whose Almighty Hand."

34. Hamilton C. MacDougall, "The Hymn-tunes of Horatio Parker," *Diapason* 11/7 (June 1920): 16.

35. Eric Routley, *The Music of Christian Hymnody: A Study in the Development of the Hymn Tune* (London: Independent Press, 1957, p. 166.

36. *Music in Trinity Church*, p. 231. Clark argues that "Mount Zion" is not a rhythmically unified tune and is difficult to sing successfully at one given tempo (p. 239).

37. Letter from J. R. Van Pelt, Cornell College, Mt. Vernon, Iowa, to HP, 28 April 1911. In the same letter, Van Pelt quoted Peter Lutkin as informing him personally that Parker "is the very best composer in America."

38. HP is quoted in a clipping from *The Illustrated Farmer*, 9 February 1899, HP Papers, IV E 3.

39. Semler, p. 309.

Chapter Twelve--INSTRUMENTAL MUSIC

1. As quoted from the *New York Commercial Advertiser* in a clipping from the *New Haven Register*, 18 Feb. 1901, HP Papers, IV E 6.

2. Krehbiel, *Review of the New York Musical Season: 1885-86*, p. xix.

3. All clippings from Detroit papers are dated 30 November 1887, HP Papers, IV A.

4. Clipping from the *Boston Traveller*, 22 January 1895, HP Papers, IV E 3.

5. Ibid.

6. *Boston Evening Transcript*, 22 January 1895, p. 4.

7. Clipping from *Boston Journal*, 22 January 1895, HP Papers, IV E 3.

8. The *Quartette* was performed on 2 July 1975, and *Quintette*, on 5 April 1985, both at the University of Colorado, Boulder.

9. Clippings from Boston papers, 22 January 1895, HP Papers, IV E 3.

10. A juvenile work, *Valses Caprises*, evidently for piano, comes from the period of Parker's study with Chadwick.

11. Wilson, *The Musical Yearbook of the United States*, Vol. V (1887-88), p. 23.

12. Richard Aldrich, *Concert Life in New York: 1902-1923* (New York: G. P. Putnam's Sons, 1941), p. 589. "Valse gracile" can be heard in a performance by Malcolm Frager on New World Records (NW 206).

13. John Gillespie, ed., *Nineteenth-Century American Piano Music* (New York: Dover, 1978), xix.

14. Hughes, p. 178.

15. One duet has been edited by William Osborne and published as *Quick March: Duet for Two Organists* (Carol Stream, Illinois: Hope Publishing Co., 1975). Parker also arranged and transcribed for organ a volume of twenty-one compositions by famous composers.

16. Hope Leroy Baumgartner, "The Organ Works of Horatio Parker," *The American Organist* 2 (December 1919): 487-89.

17. "Address before the American Guild of Organists," HP Papers, V C 35/1.

18. Hughes, p. 181.

19. "Address before the American Guild of Organists," p. 52.

20. *New York Times*, 11 December 1890, p. 4.

21. Clipping from *New Haven Register*, c. 1895, HP Papers, IV E 3.

22. As quoted in the program for the thirteenth pair of concerts, Chicago Symphony Orchestra, February 10-11, 1900.

23. As quoted in a clipping from the *New Haven Register*, 18 February 1901 HP Papers, IV E 6.

24. Ibid.

25. HP Papers, III Programs 30/4. This file contains a typewritten copy of what appears to be a program note by the composer from which this quotation is taken.

26. The exaggerated pictorial detail of "Cavalry Song" (Opus 24, No. 1) and *The Leap of Roushan Beg* (Opus 75) are similarly whimsical.

27. A review of the Chicago performance described the opening as ineffective because the string melody could not be heard over the sustained organ sound. Clipping from the *Chicago Evening Post*, 3 January 1903, HP Papers, IV E 6.

28. *Boston Evening Transcript*, 28 December 1902, p. 9.

29. Clipping from *Boston Herald*, 28 December 1902, BpBr.

30. Clipping from *Boston Advertiser*, 28 December 1902.

31. This and following quotations from Chicago papers are taken from clippings dated 3 January 1903, HP Papers, IV E 6.

Chapter Thirteen--AN EVALUATION

1. Roger Sessions, *Reflections on the Musical Life in the United States* (New York: Merlin Press, 1956), p. 142.

2. Alan Howard Levy, Chapter I, "The German Orthodoxy," *Musical Nationalism: American Composers' Search for Identity* (Westport, Connecticut: Greenwood Press, 1983), pp. 3-13.

3. Aaron Copland, *Music and Imagination*; The Charles Eliot Norton Lectures, 1951-52 (New York: Mentor Books, 1959), p. 109.

4. Levy, *Musical Nationalism*, p. 6.

5. George Santayana, *Character and Opinion in the United States* (New York: G. Scribner's Sons, 1921), p. 1.

6. Edward Robinson, "Horatio Parker," *The American Mercury* 22 (April 1931): 499.

7. A. Walter Kramer, "Horatio Parker--Ten Years After--An Appreciation," *Musical America* 49 (25 December 1929): 22. Extensive excerpts in Semler, pp. 252-254.

8. Paul Rosenfeld, "Horatio Parker, One of the Parents," *Modern Music* 19 (May-June 1942): 217.

9. John S. Van Cleve, "Americanism in Music," *The American Monthly Review of Reviews* 19 (January 1899): 96.

10. Paul Henry Lang, *History of Music in Western Civilization* (New York: Norton, 1941), p. 938.

11. Wilfrid Mellers, *Music in a New Found Land* (London: Barrie and Rockliff, 1966), p. 25.

12. David Wooldridge, *From the Steeples and the Mountains* (New York: Knopf, 1974), p. 206. Wooldridge's biography of Ives contains two letters from Parker to English musicologist H. E. Wooldridge, one of which refers to Ives: "There was a Charles Ives in my class when I came to Yale" (4 October 1910). This is Parker's only extant written comment about Ives known to me.

13. Charles E. Ives, *Memos*, pp. 39, 51, 86, 99, 181, 183-84, and 258. Editor John Kirkpatrick has also described the music curriculum at Yale together with the number of students registered for courses while Ives was a student there (p.182). See also Henry and Sidney Cowell, *Charles Ives and His Music* (New York: Oxford University Press, 1955; paperback ed. 1969), pp. 31, 34, and 67.

14. Frank R. Rossiter, *Charles Ives and His America* (New York: Liverright, 1975), p. 84.

15. *Charles E. Ives Memos*, p. 258.

16. See Wooldridge, pp. 4-10; also *An Ives Celebration: Papers and Panels of the Charles Ives Centennial Festival-Conference, 1974*, eds. H. Wiley Hitchcock and Vivian Perlis (Urbana, Illinois: University of Illinois Press, 1977), p. 251; and Theodor Timreck, *A Good Dissonance Like a Man* (New York: Foundation for the Arts, 1976), a film based on the life and music of Ives.

17. Rosalie Sandra Perry, *Charles Ives and the American Mind* (Kent, Ohio: Kent State University Press, 1974), pp. 6-12.

18. J. Peter Burkholder, *Charles Ives: the Ideas behind the Music* (New Haven: Yale University Press, 1985), p. 64. Pages 59-66 deal with Ives's study with Horatio Parker at Yale.

19. MacDonald Smith Moore, *Yankee Blues: Musical Culture and American Identity* (Bloomington: University of Indiana Press, 1985), Part I, "New England's Musical Mission" passim.

20. Henry Steele Commager, *The American Mind*, pp. 83-85. Among the popular Utopian novels of the day, Edward Bellamy's *Looking Backward* (1888; reprint, New York: Signet Classics, 1960) set the year 2,000, A. D., as the time and Boston as the place for the realization of a perfect society.

21. Semler, *Horatio Parker*, p. xx.

22. Van Wyck Brooks, *New England: Indian Summer*, p. 251.

23. Brooks, *New England: Indian Summer*, p. 414.

24. HP Papers, V B, p. 6.

25. Semler, p. 94.

26. HP Papers, IV E 4.

27. Howard, *Our American Music*, p. 337.

28. Conversation with writer, 18 September 1961.

29. Arthur Foote noted "the mighty influence" of choral groups, "especially in New England" (*Arthur Foote, 1853-1937: An Autobiography* [Norwood, Massachusetts: Plimpton Press, 1946], p. 38).

30. *New York Times*, 12 April 1931, sect. X, p. 7.

31. Elson, *The History of American Music*, p. 178.

32. Farwell and Darby, *Music in America*, p. 341.

33. W. L. Hubbard, ed., *The History of American Music*, p. 295.

34. Santayana, *Character and Opinion*, pp. 1-2.

35. Joseph A. Mussulman, *Music in the Cultured Generation: A Social History of Music in America, 1870-1900* (Evanston: Northwestern University Press, 1971), p. 32.

36. Clipping from *Los Angeles Daily Times*, 1 July 1915, HP Papers, IV E 4.

37. Moore, *Yankee Blues*.

38. Ibid., p. 22.

39. Barbara Zuck, *A History of Musical Americanism* (Ann Arbor: UMI Research Press, 1980), pp. 69-86.

40. Hamm, *Music in the New World*, pp. 454-59.

41. Barbara L. Tischler, *An American Music: The Search for an American Musical Identity* (New York: Oxford University Press, 1986),

42. Nicholas E. Tawa, *Serenading the Reluctant Eagle: American Musical Life, 1925-1945* (New York: Schirmer Books, 1985).

43. Tawa writes: "In the fifties, the fructifying union between composer and public ended. The composer wrote as if the approval of listeners did not matter; national characteristics disappeared from American compositions; internationalism took hold" (Ibid., p. 217).

44. For example, the "Gloria" chorus from Act 3 of *The Legend of Saint Christopher* makes an excellent ten-minute concert segment. I have pointed out numerous other examples throughout the text.

PART IV:
APPENDICES

APPENDIX A: LIST OF WORKS

The following information has been compiled for the purpose of giving an overview of Parker's published music, manuscript sources, writings, and recordings. It is based on previous listings, the most extensive of which are those of Oliver Strunk (1930), William Kearns (1965), and Adrienne Nesnow (1981). Nearly all of Parker's music, writings, letters, and memorabilia are found in the Yale Music Library, and Nesnow's listing is a complete inventory of this collection. Other sources include the Library of Congress, the New York Public Library, the Boston Public Library, and the New England Conservatory Library. The Fleischer Collection at the Philadelphia Free Library has several of Parker's major works which are out of print and are available on loan for study or performance.

The compositions are listed chronologically under the following categories: Choral Works, Music for the Stage, Music for Solo Voice, Church Music (Anthems, Service Music, Hymns), Instrumental Music (Keyboard, Chamber, Orchestral), Arrangements-Transcriptions-Editing, and Writing-Addresses-Editing-Interviews. The order for each entry includes (1) the opus number or year of composition in the left margin, (2) the title, preceded by a single asterisk (*) if the composition was an important one in its time or by a double asterisk (**) if the work is worthy of revival, and followed by date of composition for those works with opus number, (3) timing for works worthy of revival, (4) source of text if any, (5) information about the most important complete or nearly complete manuscripts, including number of pages in score and availability of parts, (6) information about publication including reprints, and (7) information about first performances of major works.

As noted in the Preface all complete works, published or unpublished, are indicated in italics; parts of composite works are marked by quotation marks.

Choral Works

Opus no.
or year

2   *Five Part Songs.* 1882. Listed in Sk as "MS, 1882," lost.

1883   *Zwei Gesänge für Gemischten Chor*: 1. "In der Früh, wenn die Sonne
         kommen will," 2. "Ist der Himmel davor so blau." Ms lost. Premiere:
         Munich, 23 June 1883, (listed in *Jahresbericht der Königliche Hoch-
         schule in München* 9 [1882-83]: 37).

1   *Mountain Shepherd's Song*, TTBB w. pf. 1883. (Uhland). Ho: *Des
         Knaben Berglied*, 9 pp.(inc), NH. Pub: 15 pp., RB, 1883.

3   *The Lord is My Shepherd* [Psalm 23], S solo, women's chorus,
         organ, harp. 1884. Ho: *Psalm für Soprano Solo, Frauenchor, Orgel u.
         Harfe*, 13 pp. NH. Pub: fl sc, 23 pp., GS, 1904; vc sc, 12 pp., arr. David
         S. Smith, GS, 1904.

6   *The Ballad of a Knight and His Daughter*, chorus, orch. 1885. (F. L.
         Stolberg). Ho: *Ballade für Chor und Orchester in F moll*, 35 pp. +
         parts, NH & PHf. Pub: vc sc, 23 pp., GS, 1891.

8   **King Trojan*, T & Bar. soli, chorus, orch. 1885. (Alfred Muth). 28
         min. Hos: 164 pp., text in Ger. (König Trojan), 164 pp. text in Eng. +
         parts, NH; vc sc, 88 pp., Wc. Pub: vc sc, 71 pp., APS, 1886. 1st perf:
         Munich, 15 July 1885.

15   *Idylle*, T & B soli, SATB, orch. 1886. (Goethe, *Dem festlichen Tage
         begegnet mit Kränzen.*). Hos: 32 pp., text in Ger. (1886); 31 pp., text in
         Eng. (1891), NH. Pub: vc sc, 19 pp., Eng. & Ger., GS, 1891.

14   *Blow, Blow, Thou Winter Wind*, TTBB & piano. 1888. (Shakespeare).
         Ho: 8 pp., NH. Pub: 11 pp., wo. op. #, GS, 1892.

16   **The Norsemen's Raid*, TTBB & orch. 1888. 11 min. Hos: *Norman-
         nenzug* (H. Lingg), 28 pp., text in Ger. (1888); vc sc, "The Voyage of the
         Normans," 25 pp., (1892), NH. Pub: vc sc, 34 pp., Eng. & Ger., Eng.
         trans. by Emily Whitney, JC, 1911.

1889   *Ecclesia*, SATB soli, SATB chorus, SSA boys' chorus, keyboard. Eng.
         text. Ho: 64 pp., NH.

1890   *Twelve Christmas Carols for Children*, see under Songs.

21   **The Kobolds*, SATB & orch. 1890. (Arlo Bates, from his *Albrecht*).
        Ho: 34 pp. NH. Pub: vc sc, 23 pp., NE, 1891. 1st perf: dedicated to the
        Hampden County (MA) Musical Assn. & perf. at their annual festival, 7
        May 1891.

26   **Harold Harfager*, SATB & orch. 1891. Ho: 32 pp., NH. Pub: vc sc,
        15 pp., GS, 1891. 1st perf: 30 Apr. 1891, American Composers' Choral
        Assn. concert, NY.

31   ***Dream-King and His Love*, T solo, chorus, orch. 1891. (E. Geibel,
        "Traumkönig und sein Lieb"; Eng. trans., Emily H. Whitney). 19 min.
        Ho: 40 pp., NH. Pub: vc sc, 32 pp., GS, 1893. Winner of prize in
        cantata classification offered by National Conservatory of Music; 1st
        perf., 30 Mar 1893, NY.

27   *Two Choruses for Women* or *Two Part-Songs* [Sk & Ks], S solo, SATB,
        piano; 1. "The fisher" (Goethe, Eng. trans., Charles T. Brooks) 2. "The
        water fay" (Heine, Eng. trans., Charles G. Leland). 1892. Pub: 11 pp. &
        8 pp., GS & BMC, 1892.

30   ***Hora Novissima*, SATB soli, SATB chorus, orch. (Bernard de Mor-
        laix, from *De contemptu mundi*; Eng. trans., Isabella Parker). 1891-92.
        63 min. Mss: ho, 204 pp., Wc; ms, 204 pp., NH. Pub: vc sc, 167 pp.,
        NE, 1893 [reprint, Be, 1976]; full sc, NE, 1900 [reprint, DC, 1972]; no.
        5 "O bona patria" ("O country bright and fair"), Be, 1952; no. 8 "Stant
        Syon atria" ("There stand those halls on high"), HWG, n.d. (in *Church
        Music Review*, no. 1248, pp. 80-109); no. 10 "Urbs syon unica" ("City of
        high renown"), ed. Leonard Van Camp, Ga, 1975. 1st perf: Church
        Choral Society of NY, 3 May 1893.

33   [Choruses for men's voices] or *Six Part-Songs* in Sk [not listed individu-
        ally; only 3 songs accounted for], TTBB, unac. 1. "Three words" (Wil-
        liam B. Dunham) 2. "My love" (Langdon E. Mitchell) 3. "Valentine"
        (Charles B. Blanden). Pub: GS, 1893.

37   *The Holy Child, A Cantata for Christmastide*, STB soli, SATB chorus,
        keyboard. 1893. (Isabella Parker, from Bible). Ho: 46 pp, NH. Pub: 48
        pp., GS, 1893, 1927; "Night in Bethlehem" from *The Holy Child*, for
        SSAA & org., arr. H. Harold Geer, 15 pp., GS, 1937.

39   [4 choruses for men's voices] or *4 Part-Songs* [Sk], TTBB, unac.
        1. "Behold, how good and joyful," 2. "Softly now the light of day,"
        3. "Lord, dismiss us with Thy blessing," 4. "Blest are the departed."
        1893. Ho: 12 pp., NH. Pub: GS, 1894.

42   *Ode for Commencement Day*, TTBB, orch. 1895. (Edmund C.
        Stedman). Ho: 32 pp., text inc. + parts, NH. Pub: vc sc, 16 pp., GS,
        1895.

1897   *In May*, SSAA & orch. Ho: 13 pp., + parts, NH. Pub: vc sc, 8 pp., GS,
        1897.

1898   *Laus Artium*: "a cantata by Artium Laudator" [pseud.], soli, chorus,
        orch. Hos: 40 pp., inc.; vc sc, 107 pp., NH.

43   **The Legend of Saint Christopher* soli, chorus, orch. 1898. (Isabella
        Parker). 70 min. MS: full sc. + wnd. pts, Be; Ho: vc sc, 5, 152 pp., inc.,
        NH. Pub: vc sc, 188 pp. NE, 1898; hymn from Act III, scene 2: "Jam
        sol recedit igneus" ("Now sinks the sun"), SATB, unac., 8 pp., NE:
        Novello's Octavo Anthems, no. 673, 1900, & *Church Music Review*, no.
        1457, 1928. Pub. orch. & vocal parts at Wc.; wind pts. only, Be. 1st
        perf: New York Oratorio Society, 15 Apr 1898.

45   ***Adstant Angelorum Chori*, 2 SATB choruses, unac. 1899. (Thomas à
        Kempis; Eng. trans., Isabella Parker). 15 min. Pub: 47 pp., GS. 1st
        perf: awarded 1st prize in competition sponsored by Musical Art Society
        of NY; and premiered by that group 16 Mar 1899.

63   *The Shepherds' Vision*, Christmas cantata, S or T, B soli, SATB
        chorus, org. (ob., stgs., hp., ad lib). 1900. (Alice C. Jennings, Eng.
        trans. from Ger. of Fank van de Stucken). Ms. fl sc, Be; Ho: 27 pp.
        NYp. Pub: 31 pp., HWG, 1906.

48   [Choruses for men's voices] or *Three Part Songs* [Sk & Ks], TTBB,
        unac., **1. "The lamp in the west" (Ella Higginson) 2:30 min., 2.
        "Awake, my lady sweetlips" (Higginson), 3. "The night has a thousand
        eyes" (Francis Bourdillon). 1901. Pub: JC, 1901.

50   * *Wanderer's Psalm, A*, soli, chorus, orch. 1900. (Based on Psalm 107).
        Ms: fl sc + wnd pts, Be; Ho: vc sc, 121 pp. NH. Pub: vc sc, 112 pp.,
        NE. Pub.orch. parts at Wc. 1st perf: Three Choirs Festival, Hereford,
        England, 13 Sept. 1900.

1901   *An Even Song*, women's chorus. (C. Thaxter). Pub: NE. Listed in Sk.

53   **Hymnos Andron*, or *Greek Festival Hymn*, T & Bar soli, TTBB
        chorus, orch. 1901. Ho: 114 pp., + parts, NH. (Greek text, Thomas D.
        Goodell; Eng. trans., Isabella Parker). Pub: vc sc, 40 pp., GS, 1901. 1st
        perf: 23 Oct 1901, Yale University, 200th anniversary celebration of
        founding of school.

54   *A Star Song, lyric rhapsody for SATB soli, SATB chorus, orch. 1901.
        (Henry B. Carpenter). Ms: vc sc, 59 pp., NH. Pub: full score, 97 pp.,
        JC, 1901. Awarded prize in cantata category, Paderewski Fund, 1901.
        1st perf: 23 Oct 1901, Norwich, England.

54b   Come Away, SATB, unac. 1901. (John Dowland). Pub: 11 pp., NE.

1902   "The robbers," chorus & piano. Pub: The Laurel Song Book, ed. W. L.
        Tomlins, pp. 86-90.

1903   "Forget-me-nots," SATB, unac. Copyright, Hinds & Noble, 1903; pub:
        The Most Popular Love Songs, ed. G. C. Noble, HNE, 1906, p. 48.

60   Union and Liberty, SATB, band or orch. 1905. (Oliver W. Holmes).
        Hos: 45 pp. + pts. (band), 45 pp. + pts. (orch), NH. Pub: vc sc, 16 pp.,
        GS. 1st perf: inaugural activities for the second term of President
        Theodore Roosevelt, 6 Mar. 1905.

61   Spirit of Beauty, TTBB, band. 1905. (Arthur Detmers). Ho: 54 pp.,
        NH. Pub: vc sc, 24 pp. GS. 1st perf.: dedication of Albright Art Gal-
        lery, Buffalo, NY, 31 May 1905.

64   **King Gorm the Grim, ballad, SATB, orch. 1907. (Theodore Fontana;
        Eng. trans, Marion P. Whitney). 18 min. Ho: 66 pp., + pts., NH; 73 pp.,
        Wc. Pub: fl sc, 71 pp., GS, 1910; vc sc, 28 pp., GS, 1910. 1st perf.:
        Annual Festival of Litchfield County Choral Union, Norfolk, CT, 4 June
        1908.

1907   **The Lark Now Leaves His Watery Nest, song arr. for SATB, piano.
        1:50 min. Pub: 11 pp., JC., 1907,08. See Six Old English Songs, op.
        47, no. 6, under Songs.

1908   Piscatrix, TTBB, unac. (D. H. Holmes). Ho: 7 pp., NH. Pub: 7 pp.,
        GS.

66   School Songs, title in Sk. 1911. 1. unidentified. 2. "Springtime revel-
        ries" (Nixon Waterman), SATB & piano, pub: 12 pp., SB, 1912. 3.
        "The storm" (Nixon Waterman), pub: High School Song Book, Gertrude
        Parsons, ed, SB, 1919. 4. "Freedom, our queen" (Oliver W. Holmes),
        pub: 10 pp., SB, 1911. Nos. 2 & 4 in The Beacon Series of Vocal Selec-
        tions for Schools, Classes, and Choruses. No. 4 reprinted, 8 pp., The
        New Beacon Octavo, no. 601, SB, 1920.

1911   **"Song of the swords," from opera Mona. 4 min. Pub: vc sc, 13 pp.,
        Schirmer's Collection of Part-Songs and Choruses for Mixed Voices,
        GS.

1911   [Trios for Parker's daughters]: 1. "I remember the black wharfs and
       ships" (Longfellow), 2. "September gale" (C. H. Crandall), 3. "Rollick-
       ing robin" (Lucy Larcom). Ho: 2, 2, 2 pp., NH. Pub: #1, SSA & p., *A
       Book of Choruses for High Schools and Choral Societies*, SB, 1923.

72   *Collegiate Overture*, orch., male chorus. See Instrumental Music.

73   *A Song of Times*, cantata, S solo, SATB, bugle corps, band or orch., org.
       1911. (John L. Long). Pub: vc sc, 28 pp., GS. 1st perf: dedication of
       the new Wanamaker Dept. Store, Philadelphia, PA, 1 Dec 1911.

1912   *Song of a Pilgrim Soul*, SSA & piano. (Henry Van Dyke). Pub: 3 pp.,
       private printing, NH.

74   **Seven Greek Pastoral Scenes*, SA soli, SSAA, ob, hp, piano. 1908-
       12. 17 min. (Text after Meleager and Argentarius). Ho: vc scs 12, 3, 8,
       4, 4, 4, 8 pp., NH; Ms: #2 "Heliodore," voice, ob, piano, 5 pp., NYp.
       Pub: vc sc, 32 pp., GS.

75   *The Leap of Roushan Beg*, ballad, T solo, TTBB, orch. 1913. (Henry
       W. Longfellow). 1913. Pub: vc sc, 27 pp., GS. 1st perf: Orpheus Club
       of Philadelphia, second concert of 1913-14 season.

76   **Alice Brand*, cantata, T & Bar or S & mS soli, women's chorus, piano.
       1913. 18 min. (Sir Walter Scott). Pub: 32 pp., GS.

1915   *Gloriosa Patria*, patriotic hymn, SATB. (Helene H. Boll). Pub: 3 pp.,
       Schirmer's Secular Choruses, no. 6183, GS.

79   **Morven and the Grail*, oratorio, SATBar soli, SATB, orch. 1915.
       (Brian Hooker). Pub: vc sc, 204 pp., BMC. 1st perf: 100th anniversary
       of the founding of the Handel and Haydn Society, Boston, 13 Apr 1915.

1915   **"Ave virgo glorioso," from opera *Fairyland*, arr. S solo, SSAA, piano.
       7 min. (Latin & Eng., trans. Eva J. O'Meara, Arthur Men del). Pub: 16
       pp., GS.

1916   [Two carols]: "Have you heard the wondrous story," Easter carol, 2
       pts. for boys and girls, piano, 1 p., n. 136; "All my heart this night re-
       joices," Christmas carol, SATB, 1 p., n. 324 (P. Gerhardt, 1656; trans.,
       C. Winkworth). Pub: *Carols Old and New*, ed. Charles L. Hutchins,
       Boston: The Parish Choir.

81   *An Allegory of War and Peace*, chorus, band. See Music for the Stage.

82   *The Dream of Mary*, morality , spoken pts., S1,2,A,B soli, SATB, chil-
        dren's chorus, congregation, w orch. or organ. 1918. (John J. Chap-
        man). Ms: fl sc + pts, Be; Pub: vc sc, 124 pp., HWG. 1st perf: annual
        festival of Litchfield County Choral Union, Norfolk, CT, 4 June 1918.

1918   *The Red Cross Spirit Speaks*, SATB, SSAA, & TTBB, piano. (John
        Finley). Pub: 12 pp. each, HWG. See also under Songs.

1919   "Triumphal march," SATB, piano. (David K. Stevens). Pub: *High
        School Song Book*, ed. Gertrude Parsons, SB. See also organ piece
        Opus 66, no. 1.

84   *A. D. 1919*, S solo, SATB, orch. 1919. (Brian Hooker). Ho: 67 pp.,
        NH. Pub: vc sc, 37 pp., YUP. 1st perf: commemorative honoring Yale
        students and alumni killed in World War I, 15 June 1919.

1941   *The Despairing Lover*, TTBB, unac. (William Walsh). Pub: 12 pp., Ga.

Music For The Stage

1904   *The Eternal Feminine*, incidental music for the play, chorus and orch.
        (F. Nathan). Music lost: 14 orch. pieces w several women's choruses
        (*Yale Alumni Weekly*, 14 [12 Oct 1904]). 1st perf: [?] New Haven, 7
        Nov 1904.

1905   *The Prince of India*, incidental music for the play, T solo, chorus, orch.
        (J. I. C. Clarke, from novel by Lew Wallace). Ho: 291 pp., NH. 1st
        perf: Broadway Theatre, New York, 24 Sept 1906.

71   *Mona*, opera in three acts, soli, chorus, orch. 1909-11. (Brian Hooker).
        Hos: 3 vols., 906 pp.; vc sc, 321 pp., + parts, NH. Pub: vc sc, 273 pp.;
        **"Song of the swords," chorus arr. (see Choral Music), GS, 1911.
        Winner of Metropolitan Opera contest for an opera in English written by
        a native-born American, 1911. 1st perf: Metropolitan Opera, NY, 12
        Mar 1912.

77   *Fairyland*, opera in three acts, soli, chorus, orch. 1914. (Brian Hook-
        er). Ho: 3 vols., 560 pp., + parts; **"Prelude, Intermezzo and Ballet"
        (see Instrumental Music: Orchestra), NH. Pub: vc sc, 250 pp.; **"Ave
        virgo glorioso," (see Choral Music); **"In a garden," **"A rose song,"
        (see Secular Music for Solo Voice), GS, 1915. Winner of prize offered
        by the National Federation of Music Clubs (NFMC) and city of Los

Angeles, 1914. 1st perf: biennial convention of National Federation of
Music Clubs, Los Angeles, 1 July 1915.

80   *Cupid and Psyche*, masque in 3 acts, SSA chorus, oboe, strings, harp,
piano, harpsichord. 1916. (John J. Chapman). Ho: 143 pp.; piano arr.,
minus choral numbers, 47 pp., NH. 1st perf: New Haven, 16 June 1916,
commemorating the 50th anniversary of the founding of the School of
Fine Arts, Yale University.

81   *An Allegory of War and Peace*, SATB chorus, band. 1916. (Francis
Hartman Markoe). Ho: vc sc, 46 pp. NH. 1st perf: second musical
interlude from the Yale pageant celebrating 200th anniversary of the
establishment of Yale University at New Haven, performed in Yale
Bowl, 21 Oct 1916.

Music For Solo Voice

1878   *Kate Greenaway Songs*, voice and piano (Songs marked with * are
published in *The Progressive Music Series*): 1."Under the window," 2.
"Will you be my little wife?" 3. "You see merry Phyllis," 4. "As I went
out to hear the news," 5. "Three tabbies," 6. "Little Fanny wears a hat,"
6b. "Beneath the lillies*," 8. "Margery Brown," 9. "Little wind blow on
the hill top," 10. "Indeed it is time*," 11. "School is over," 12. "Little
Polly will you go?" 13. "As I was walking up the street," 14. "Five little
sisters," 15. "In go-cart so tiny," 16. "Some geese went out a-walking,"
17. "You're going out to tea," 18. "Poor Picky's dead," 19. "Up you go
shuttle-cocks," 20. "Look over the wall," 20b. "Little boys and girls," 22.
"Tommy was a silly boy," 23. "Higgledy-piggledy*," 23b "Which is the
way to Somewhere Town?" 25. "The boat sails away," 26. "Pipe thee
high," 27. "Polly's, Pen's, and Poppety's mama was kind and good,"
28. "Bowl away," 29. "For what are you longing you three little boys?"
30. "O ring the bells," 31. "Then ring the bells" (a free inversion of
No. 30), 31b. "This little fat goblin*," 33. "I saw a ship that sailed the
sea," 34. "Yes that's the girl," 35. "It was Tommy who said," 36. "Shall I
sing? Says the lark," 37. "Little Miss Patty and Master Paul*," 38. "Yes
it is sad of them," 39. "Now all of you give heed," 40. "What is Tommy
running for?" 55. "A butcher's boy met a baker's boy," 42. "The twelve
miss Pelicoes," 43. "Little baby if I threw," 44. "The finest biggest fish,"
[45] "Prince Finnikin and his mama*," 46. "High ho! Time creeps but
slow," 47. "My house is red," 48. "Three little girls were sitting on a
rail," 49. "What has the old man come for?" 50. "Ring the bells! Ring."
Ho: 75 pp., NH.

1879   *La Coquette*. Ho: 3 pp., NH.

1881   [3 songs] 1. "Slumber song," 2. "Wedding song," 3."Goldilocks." Ho: 4
        pp., Wc. Pub: 5 pp., APS, 1882.

1886   [2 songs] 1. "Why so pale and wan fond lover?" 2. "Hi ho! A ho!"
        [listed as "A ho! A ho!" in Nw]. Ho: 1 p., 3 pp., NH.

10   *Three love songs for tenor*: 1. "Love's chase" (Thomas L. Beddoes),
        **2. "Night piece to Julia" (Robert Heink [Robert Herrick]) 1:45 min., 3.
        "Orsame's song" (Sir John Suckling). 1886. Ho: 10 pp., NH; Ms: Wc,
        1. 5pp., 2. 3pp., 3. 2pp. Pub: APS.

1886   *Devotion*, for Bar/T & piano. (F. L. Humphreys). Pub: 7 pp. WAP.

1890   [2 sacred songs]: 1. "Rest," 2. "There is a land of pure delight," (Isaac
        Watts). Ho: 4 pp., 5 pp., Wc. Pub: 5 pp., 7 pp., APS.

22   *Three Sacred Songs*, for S/T (Bar): 1. "Morning," 2. "Evening,"
        3. "Heaven's hope." 1891. Pub: GS.

23   [3 songs]: 1 & 2. *Two Love Songs*: "My love," "O waving trees,"
        3. "Violet." 1891. Hos: #3, 4 pp., 5 pp., NH. Pub: wo op. #, high and
        low voice, GS. Listed as Op. 25 in Sk.

24[b]   **Six Songs* : 1."Cavalry song" (Edmund C. Stedman), Bar; 2."Egyptian
        serenade" (George W. Curtis), mS/Bar; 3. "The light is fading down the
        sky" (Elizabeth A. Allen), mS/Bar or S/T; 4. "O ask me not" (Hans
        Hopfen), S/T; 5. "Pack, clouds away!" (Thomas Heywood), mS/Bar;
        6. "Spring song," (George W. Curtis), S/T. 1891. Pub: GS.

1893   *Come see the place where Jesus lay*. (Thomas Kelly). Pub: 9 pp., GS.
        See Church Music for anthem arr.

34   *Three Songs*: 1."I know a little rose," ST; 2. "My lady love," ST; 3. "On
        the lake," mS/Bar. 1893. Pub: GS.

1893   *In Glad Weather*. (Charles Buxton-Going). Pub: 5 pp., ES.

1893   "A rose song." (Richard H. Stoddard). Pub: *Novello's School Songs*,
        No. 644, pp. 20-22. Tonic sol-fa notation beneath text.

1893   [2 songs]: 1. "Love is a rover," S (Samuel M. Peck); 2. "A song of three
        little birds." Hos: #1, 4 pp.; #2, 4 pp., NH. Pub: 5 pp., 7 pp., GBJ.

1893   [2 songs]: 1. "Fickle love" (Louise C. Moulton), 2. "Uncertainty"
        (Charles Swain). Pub: 5 pp., 7 pp., HBS.

1894   *Divine Care* (Alice Jennings). Pub: HBS. Listed in Sk; not at NH.

1894   *Two Shakespeare Songs* 1. "A poor soul sat sighing," 2."It was a lover
        and his lass." Pub: HBS. Listed in Sk; not at NH.

40   **Cáhal Mór of the Wine-Red Hand*, rhapsody for Bar, orch. (James C.
        Mangan). 1893. 13 min. Hos: 61 pp.; vc sc, 22 pp. (1900) at Bc; vc sc,
        David Bispham papers, NYp; sc, 61 pp., + pts, Phf. Pub: 23 pp., HWG,
        1910. 1st perf: Boston Symphony Orch.; Max Heinrich, soloist, 29
        March 1895.

1895   *Salva Regina*, Bar/A. (Eng. & Lat.). Pub: 7 pp., GS.

1896   *Spanish Cavalier's Song*. (Isabella Parker). Pub., 7 pp., HBS.

47   **Six Old English Songs*: 1. "Love is a sickness full of woes" (Samuel
        Daniel), 2. "Come, o come, my life's delight" (Thomas Campion),
        3. "He that loves a rosy cheek" (Thomas Carew), 4. "Once I loved a
        maiden fair" (Old English), 5. "The Complacent Lover" (Sir Charles
        Selby), **6. "The lark now leaves his watery nest" (Sir William
        Davenant), 1:50 min. 1897-99. Ho: #6, 4 pp.; 2 pp., acc. arr. for orch.,
        NH. Pub: editions for both high and low voice, JC, 1899; No. 3 publ.
        wo op. #, *The Music of the Modern World*, D. Appelton, 1897.

1900   *The Green is on the Grass again*. Ho: 3 pp., NH.

51   *Four Songs*: **1. "Love in May" (Ella Higginson), 1:20 min, 2. "June
        night" (Ella Higginson), 3. "A spinning song" (Isabella Parker), 4. "At
        twilight" (Edith A. Baker). 1893-1901. Hos for #1-3, 4 pp., 3 pp., 5 pp.,
        NH; #1 & 2, American Academy of Arts and Letters. Pub: JC, 1901.

1903   *Hapless Doom of Women*. Ho: 3 pp., NH.

1903   *Shame upon You, Robin*. Ho: 4 pp., NH.

1903-16 [the Toedt songs], for S, violin, piano unless otherwise indicated:
        1. "Come, little leaves," 1903; 2. "The sea princess," 1904; 3. "Where do
        all the daisies go?" 1905; 4. "Only one," 1906; 5. "The south wind,"
        1907; 6. "A hush song," 1908; 7. "A summer lullaby" (E. L. Bumstead),
        1909; 8. "Deep in the heart of a rose," 1910; 9. "When I walk with you"
        (Fred A. Bowles), 1911; 10. "Wohl über Nacht" (August Sturm), 1912;
        11. "The charm of spring," 1913; 12. "Winter songs," 1914; 13. "It was a
        lover and his lass" (Shakespeare), SS, vln, & p., 1915; 14. "The flower

wind" (Alfred Hyatt), S & p., 1916. Microfilm of holographs, NH. Pub: #5, arr. S & p., 7 pp., Ga, 1939. These songs were Christmas presents to concert tenor Theodore Toedt, his wife Ella, who sang the first perf. of *Hora Novissima*, and their children. The Mss were in the possession of H. W. Mortimer, Larchmont, New York.

59   *Four Songs*: 1. "Songs" (Robert L. Stevenson), 2. "Serenade" (Nathan H. Dole, 3. "The blackbird" (William E. Henley), 4. "Good-bye" (Christina Rossetti). 1903. Hos: #1, 3 pp.; #3, 3 pp.; #4, 3 pp., NH. Pub: GS, 1904.

1904   *My Heart Was Winterbound until I Heard You Sing.* Ho: 4 pp., NH.

1904   *Two Songs from Tennyson's "Queen Mary,"*, med. v. & p.: 1. "Milkmaid's song," 2. "Lute song." Pub: 5, 5 pp., GS.

58   *Three Sacred Songs*, settings of medieval hymns, org. acc.: 1. "Come, Holy Ghost/Nunc sancte nobis spiritus" (St. Ambrose), 2. "Lo, now the shades of night/Ecce jam noctis tenvatur umbra" (St. Gregory), 3. "Declining now, the sun's bright wheel/Labente jam solis rota" (Charles Coffin); Eng. trans. by Rev. John Anketell. 1903-05. Hos: #1, S, 4 pp.; #2, A, 4 pp.; #3, Bar, 4 pp., NH. Pub: NE, 1905.

1905   *Springtime of Love*, med. v. (Frank D. Sherman). Ms: 4 pp., NH. Pub: 5 pp., GS.

1906   *The Garden Pirate.* (Gertrude Rogers). Ho: 2 pp., NH.

1906   *Last Night the Nightingale Waked Me.* (Théophile Marzials) opus 24b Ho: 5 pp., NH.

1906   *The Reason Why . . .* "a song for Isabel and Grace [HP's daughters] with their Mama at Christmas," SS. Ho: 6 pp., NH.

1906-08 *Three Songs*: 1. "Morning song" (Martin Schütze), 2. "Across the fields" (Walter Crane), 3. "Nightfall" (Martin Schütze). Ho: #2 , 6 pp., 1906; Ho: #s 1 & 3, "Mood Pictures," 6 pp., "for Mollin Sawyer [Mrs. Homer E.] at Christmastide 1908," NH. Pub: BMC, 1914.

62   **Crépuscule/Twilight*, concert aria for mS, orch. 1907. (Vicomte J. de Beaufort; Eng. trans., Emily Whitney). 12 min. Ho: 54 pp., NH; sc, 54 pp., + pts, Phf. Pub: vc sc, 19 pp., GS, 1912. 1st prize in voice-with-orchestra category, National Federation of Music Clubs Contest, 1911; 1st perf: Philadelphia Orch., 27 Mar 1911.

1907   *The First Christmas*, 4 S & p. Ho: 10 pp., NH.

1908   *The Wandering Knight's Song*, Spanish ballad of 1555. (trans., Lock-
        hart). Pub: 5 pp., JC.

1909   *Thy Kiss, Beloved.* (trans. Govenour Morris). Ho: 4 pp., NH.

1909   *O I Will Walk with You, My Lad*, Ho: sketch, 3 pp., NH.

1909   *On the Hillside.* Ho: 5 pp., NH.

1909   *Thy Presence Dwells among the Starlit Places.* Ho: 3 pp., NH.

1910   "Morning song." (George Darley). Pub: *Modern Music and Musicians
        for Vocalists*, v. 3, pp. 502-507 and their *International Library of Music
        for Vocalists*, v. 3, copyright, The University Society, Inc.

70   **Seven Songs*: 1. "I shall come back," 2. "A man's song," 3. "A
        woman's song," 4. "Only a little while," 5. "A robin's song," 6 "Offer-
        ings," 7. "Together." 1909. (Brian Hooker). 15 min. Several holo-
        graphs for each song, NH. Pub: for high and low voice, JC, 1910.

1911   *Rollicking Robin.* (Lucy Larcom). Ho: 2 pp., NH.

1911   "A Christmas song," voice, ob., hp. or piano. (J. G. Holland). Ho:
        5 pp., NH. Pub: arr. v. & p., *Century Illustrated Monthly Magazine* 61
        (Dec 1911): 303-04.

1912   *Two Songs*: 1. "A perfect love" (Alfred H. Hyatt), 2. "Her cheek is like a
        tinted rose" (Florence E. Coates). Hos: #1, 4pp., 5 pp., NH; #s 1 & 2,
        4 pp. each, Wc. Ded. to Mrs. Homer E. Sawyer. Pub: 5 pp. each, APS,
        1914.

78   *The Progressive Music Series for Basal Use in Primary, Intermediate,
        and Grammar Grades.* Eds. Horatio Parker, Osbourne McConathy,
        Edward B. Birge, & W. Otto Meisner. Boston & New York: Silver
        Burdett Co.: 4 vols, 1914; *Teacher's Manual*, 1915; *One-Book Course*,
        1917; *Primary Book for Sight Reading*, 1919. Contains 53 songs by
        Parker. See Ks and Carder for song listings.

1915   *Tomorrow.* (Florence E. Coates). Ho: 7 pp., "for Mollin Sawyer," NH.

1916   *The Pearl.* (Alfred H. Hyatt). Ho: 7 pp., "for Mollin Sawyer," NH;
        Pub: 5 pp., Ga, 1939.

83   **The Red Cross Spirit Speaks*, mS & orch. (John Finley). Ho: 20 pp., F
        minor; Ms: 20 pp., G minor, + pts for both versions, NH; vc, 6 pp., Bc;
        Pub: vc, 7pp., HWG, 1918. Written for Louise Homer.

1918   *Hymn for the Victorious Dead*, solo voice & pf. accom. (Hermann
        Hagedorn). Ho: 6 pp., NH. Pub: *The Outlook* 120 (18 Dec.1918):
        [625]-27.

Church Music

Anthems and Service Music

> Anthems and service music are SATB, organ, unless otherwise
> indicated. Solo parts are indicated. All publications are at NH
> unless otherwise indicated.

1889   *Christ Our Passover* (Easter anthem). Ho: 12 pp., NH. Pub: 10 pp.,
        AMC, 1890; 7 pp., HWG, 1908.

1890   *Bow Down Thine Ear* (Psalm 86, 1-5). Pub: 8 pp., GS.

1890   **The Lord Is My Light* (Psalm 27, 1-3, 8, 11). 4 min. Pub: 15 pp, GS;
        JF, 1967. Parker's most popular anthem.

1890   *Magnificat and Nunc Dimittis in E-flat* (English text). Pub: 8 pp., 7 pp.,
        GS.

1890   *There Is A Land of Pure Delight* (Isaac Watts). Pub: 7 pp., GS. Not at
        NH.

1890   *Deus Misereatur in E* (Psalm 67). Pub: 7 pp., GS.

1890   **Give Unto the Lord*. S solo. Pub: 15 pp., NE.

1891   **I Will Set His Dominion in the Sea*. Pub: 12 pp., NE.

1891   *The Riven Tomb*. Pub: *New York Herald*, 29 Mar., p. 11.

1891   *Te Deum in A* (English text). Pub: 11 pp., GS.

1891   *Who Shall Roll Us Away the Stone?*. S solo. Pub: ML. Listed in Sk; not
        at NH.

1891   *Twelve Christmas Carols for Children*: 1. "Mountains bow your heads
        majestic," 2. "Legends of the infancy," 3. "The morning star," 4. "The
        shepherds went their hasty way," 5. "Emmanuel, God with us,"

6. "Hymn for Christmas day," 7. "The Incarnation," 8. "The moon shone bright," 9. "A cradle song of the Blessed Virgin," 10. "Sleep, Holy Babe," 11. "When I view the mother holding," 12. "A Child this day is born." Unison chorus and pf. Pub: GS.

1892   *Let Us Rise Up and Build.* S & Bar, chorus, brasses, hp, timpani, org. (Nehemiah ii, 18,20; Deuteronomy xxxi, 6). Ho: 28 pp. + pts, NH. Composed for the laying of the cornerstone of the Cathedral of St. John the Divine, NY, 27 Dec.

18   *The Morning and Evening Service in E, together with the Office for the Holy Communion.* Ho: 100 pp. (lacking pp. 18-19); #14, "Magnificat" & #15 "Nunc Dimittis," arr. for orch., 14 pp., 1892, NH. Pub: 77 pp., NE, 1892.

1893   *Before the Heavens Were Spread Abroad.* T solo. (Christmas anthem). Pub: 8 pp., N; 8 pp., HWG.

1893   *Come, See the Place Where Jesus Lay.* (Easter anthem). Pub: 8 pp., GS.

34b   *Magnificat and Nunc Dimittis in E-flat.* Pub: 12 pp., N, 1893.

1893   *Te Deum laudamus.* (English). Pub: 12 pp., GS.

1894   *Light's Glittering Morn Bedecks the Sky.* B solo.(Easter anthem; St. Ambrose, trans. J. M. Neale). Ho: 14 pp., NH. Pub: 15 pp. GS; CTW 1976.

1894   *Rejoice in the Lord* (Revs. Charles Wesley, John Taylor); *Look, Ye Saints; The Sight Is Glorious.* (Thomas Kelly). Hymns for ascensiontide. Pub: 4 pp., OD; CTW, 1976.

1896   *Far from the World, O Lord, I Flee,* S/T solo. Pub: 7 pp., CSE; 8 pp., N, 1901.

1897   *O Lord, I Will Exalt Thee.* SATB soli. Ho: 12 pp., n.d., NH. Pub: 12 pp., GS.

1898   *Grant, We Beseech Thee, Merciful Lord.* Unaccom. Pub: 3 pp., BMC.

1898   *Calm on the Listening Ear of the Night.* S /T solo. (Rev. E. H. Sears; Christmas Anthem). Ho: 6 pp., NH. Pub: *The Churchman* 78 (10 Dec. 1898): 871-874; 8 pp., N.

1899   *Behold, Ye Despisers.* B solo. (Acts 13:41, St. Luke 20:38, I Corinthians 15:52, 54-57; Easter anthem). Pub: 11 pp., NE.

1900   **Now Sinks the Sun*. ("Jam sol recedit," vespers hymn from *The Legend of St. Christopher*). 3 min. Unaccompanied. Pub: 8 pp., N.

1900   *In Heavenly Love Abiding*, S solo. (Anna L. Waring). Pub: 8 pp., N.

1900   *While We Have Time*. Pub: 6 pp., N. Not at NH.

1901   *Thou Shalt Remember*. Bar solo. Pub. 12 pp., NE. Composed for the 150th anniversary of establishment of church in Auburndale, MA.

1903   *God That Madest Earth and Heaven*. (Reginald Heber, Richard Whatley). Pub: N.; *The Bicentennial Collection of American Choral Music*, ed. Mason Martens (Dayton: McAfee Music Corp., 1975), pp 133-36.

1903   *Come, Gentles, Rise*, unison chorus. (David Evans). Pub: GS in *The Churchman* 87 (1903): 885-86; 3 pp., single ed., 1905.

1904   *Brightest and Best*, S solo. (Bishop Reginald Heber, Christmas anthem). Ho: 12 pp., NH. Pub: GS.

57   *The Office for the Holy Communion in Bb*, S solo. Pub: 27 pp., N., 1904.

1904   *It Came Upon a Midnight Clear*, vln, hp, ad. lib. (Edmund H. Sears). Pub: 11 pp., OD.

1905   *I Shall Not Die but Live*, Bar solo. (Easter anthem). Pub. 13 pp., OD.

1909   *To Whom Then Will Ye Liken God*, T solo. (Isaiah 11). Pub. 11 pp.; arr. T solo, TTBB, 9 pp., HWG.

1916   *The Voice that Breathed o'er Eden*, v & keyboard. Ho: 2 pp., NH. "Epithalanium for Isabel's [daughter] wedding, Feb. 12, 1916."

1919   *He Faileth Not*, S solo. (Frances R. Havergal). Pub: 11 pp., HWG.

1923   *Come Earth's Latest Hour*. (Opening chorus from *Hora Novissima*). Pub: 16 pp., HWG.

n.d.   *He Who Hath Led*. S solo. Ho: 9 pp., NH.

n.d.   *Magnificat and Nunc Dimittis in E*. Pub: 16 pp. HWG

n.d.   *O 'Twas a Joyful Sound*, unaccompanied. Pub: 5 pp., OD.

Not located: *The Day of Praise, Jerusalem*, both mentioned in *Music Review*, 1
(Dec. 1891): 62.

Hymns

The following selected list of Parker hymn tunes (arranged alphabetically) is compiled from four hymnals, for the first three of which the composer was editor or a member of the editorial staff. The fourth source is the 1940 Episcopal hymnal. These hymnals contain the majority of hymn tunes written by Parker. A complete listing would require a much more extensive inventory, as he contributed to hymnals of many different denominations. See Katherine Diehl, *Hymns and Tunes -- an Index* (New York: The Scarecrow Press, 1966), for the location of hymns marked with asterisks in twenty-three contemporary hymnals. The four hymnals, together with their symbols as used in the list, are as follows:

P   Parker, Horatio, ed. *The Hymnal, Revised and En-larged. As Adopted by the General Convention of the Protestant Episcopal Church in the United States of America in the Year of Our Lord, 1892.* New York: Novello, Ewer and Co., 1903.

U   Parker, Horatio and Harry B. Jepson, eds. *University Hymns for Use in the Battell Chapel at Yale with Tunes arranged for Male Voices.* New York: A. S. Barnes and Co., 1907.

H18   *The Hymnal as Authorized and Approved for Use by the General Convention of the Protestant Episcopal Church in the United States of America in the Year of our Lord, 1916.* New York: The Church Pension Fund, 1918.

H40   *The Hymnal of the Protestant Episcopal Church in the United States of America.* New York: The Church Pension Fund, 1943.

Hymn Tune	Text	Hymnal and Hymn no.
Alleluia	Lord of the harvest, it is right and meet	P:262
Ancient of days*	Ancient of days, who sittest throned in glory	P:311 H18:519

Auburndale*	Christ is our cornerstone	P:294 U:341 H18:458
Brannenburg	More love to Thee, O Christ	P:654
Bude	Thou who with dying lips	P:277
Clovelly*	O Lord, be with us when we sail	P:305
Courage*	Fight the good fight	P:505 U:269 H18:113(2)
Foundation*	Tho' faint, yet pursuing How firm a foundation	P:628 P:636 H18:212(2)
Garden City*	Our day of praise is done The day is past and over	P:23 P:645
Gray	We come, Lord to thy feet My times are in the hand	P:536 P:626
Holy day*	Come, let us all with one accord	P:26
Ilkley	Jesu, Thou joy of loving hearts	P:430
Jesu Pastor	Jesus, tender shepherd, hear me	P:534
Jubilate*	Rejoice the Lord is King	H40:350
Keswick	For all thy saints, O Lord	P:181
Kilbeck	Lord of the harvest, Thee we hail	P:190
King of Glory*	In loud exalted strains	P:482
Litany, No. 6	By the gracious saving call	P:529
Mission*	Go forward Christian soldiers	H18:535
Mt. Zion*	Oh, 'twas a joyful sound to hear	P:493 H18:307 H40:390

Parker*	The royal banners forward go	H40:63
Pax Ventalis	God of the nations	H18:442
Pixham	Forth in thy name, O Lord I go	P:99
	Almighty God, whose only son	P:639
	Father in Heaven	H18:367
	Faith in Thy name, O Lord	H40:150
Pro Patria*	God of our fathers, whose almighty hand	P:343
		H18:430(2)
Rothenburg	Glory be to God the Father	P:617
St. Mary	Hail to the Lord who comes	P:154
Spes Vitae	Laboring and heavy laden	P:436
Stella*	All my heart this night rejoices	P:538
		H18:545(2)
Veni Sancte Spiritus	Come Thou Holy Spirit, come	P:378
Venit Angelus	The angel sped on wings of light	P:156
Venite	The Spirit, in our hearts	P:596
Vexilla Regis	The royal banners forward go	P:94
		H18:144(2)
Victor's Crown*	Look ye saints	H18:185(2)
Vision	O wondrous type! O vision fair	P:157
Vox Aeterna*	Hark! the voice eternal	P:35
		H18:518
Whittingham*	Jerusalum! high tower thy glorious walls	H18:543(2)

Instrumental Music

Keyboard Music

1881   *Geschwindmarsch für zwei Orgelspielern.* Ho: 15 pp., NH. Pub: as
        Quick March, ed. William Osborne, HP, 1975.

1881   *Polonaise.* Piano. Ho: 2 pp., NH.

1882   *Duetto for Two Organs.* Ho: 11 pp., NH.

1882   *Concert Stücke*, for 2 pianos. Ho: sc, 27 pp. + 1 pt. 11 pp., NH.

1882   *Overture*, A major. Orch., arr. for piano. Ho: 12 pp., NH.

[1882-85] *Fantaisie*, two pianos. Ho: 16 pp. [3 - 18], NH. A set of variations
        numbered 34-59. This student composition may have been music to
        which Parker referred, "Sixty-eight variations on a familiar theme," in an
        interview, ca. 1893 (HP Papers, IV E 3). See also "Thema mit varia-
        tiones" (1882-85) under Chamber Music.

9   *Morceaux caractéristiques pour piano.* 1885-86. 1. "Elegie," 2. "Scher-
        zo," 3. "Impromptu," 4. "Caprice," 5. "Gavotte." Ho: #1, 4 pp.; #s3 &
        2 [pagination in this order], 9 pp.; #4, 4 pp.; #5, 5 pp.; Wc. #5, 2 pp.,
        NH. Pub: APS, 1886 wo op #.

17   *Four Compositions for the Organ.* 1890. 1. "Concert piece,"
        2. "Impromptu," 3. "Romanza," 4. "Andante religioso." Pub: GS.
        Dedicated to S. B. Whitney, organist, Church of the Advent, Boston.

19   *Four Sketches for Piano.* 1890. 1. "Romanza," 2. "Scherzino,"
        3. "Étude mélodieuse," 4. "Nocturne." Ho: 18 pp., Wc; #4, 3 pp.,
        NH. Pub: APS.

20   *Four Compositions for the Organ.* 1891. 1. "Wedding song,"
        2. "Fughetta," 3. "Melody and intermezzo," 4. "Fantaisie." Pub: GS.

23[b]   *Six Lyrics for the Piano without Octaves.* 1891. 1. "Reverie,"
        2. "Ballad," 3. "Rondino," 4. "Fairy tale," 5. "Barcarolle," 6."No-
        vellete." Pub: GS as op. 25. Listed in Nw as op.25; in Sk as op. 23.

28   *Four Compositions for the Organ.* 1891. 1. "Triumphal march," 2.
        "Largetto," 3. "Pastorale," 4. "Concert piece no. 2." Pub: GS.

32   *Five Sketches for Organ.* 1893. 1. "Prelude," 2. "Vision," 3. "Scherzo,"
        4. "Pastoral interlude," 5. "Nocturne." Pub: NE.

36   *Four Pieces for the Organ.* 1893. 1. "Canzonetta," 2. "Canon," **3.
        "Fugue in C minor," 3:40 min., 4. "Eclogue." Pub: GS.

36[b]   *Meditation.* Ho: 4 pp., marked as op. 36 and dated 27 Apr. 1893, NH.

1894   [Two compositions for piano]. 1. "Capricietto," 2. "Dialogue." Ho:
        4 pp. each, Bp. Pub: *Famous Composers and Their Works*, vol. 13, eds.
        Theodore Thomas, John Knowles Paine, and Karl Klauser (Boston: J.
        B. Millet Co., 1895), pp.1097-1106.

1896   **Three Compositions for Organ.* 1. "Postlude," 2. "Melody,"
        3. "Marcia religiosa." 8:00 min. Ho: #2, 4pp.; #3, 6 pp., Bp. Pub: *Vox
        Organi*, ed. Dudley Buck (Boston: J. B. Millet, 1896): #1 in vol. 2, pp.
        141-47; #2 in vol. 3, pp. 262-68; #3 in vol. 4, pp. 385-91. According to
        Sk, 1 & 3 are reprinted in *The American Organist* (TP, 1918).

49   **Trois morceaux caractéristiques pour le piano.* 1899. 1. "Conte
        sérieux," 2. "La sauterelle," 3. "Valse gracile." 7:00 min. Pub: JC; #1
        & 2, Nineteenth-Century American Piano Music, ed. John Gillespie
        (New York: Dover Publications, Inc., 1978), 278-285.

1899   *Northern Ballad.* For orch., arr. for p., 4 hands. Ho: 18 pp., NH.

1902   *Lento*, E minor. Orch., arr. for p., 4 hands. Ho: 20 pp., NH.

1902   *Vathek.* Orch., arr. for p., 4 hands. Hos: 24 pp.; 22 pp. (1903), NH.

1906   *Praesentir Marsch.* Piano, 4 hands. Ho: 6 pp., NH.

65   **Sonata in E-flat for Organ.* 1908. Ho: 42 pp., NH. Pub: G. S.
        Dedicated to Samuel P. Warren.

67   *Four Compositions for the Organ.* 1910. 1. "Festival prelude," 2.
        "Revery," 3. "Scherzino," 4. "Postlude." Pub: as op. 66 in *Recital
        Pieces: A Collection of Twenty-one Original Compositions for the
        Organ by Horatio Parker*, GS, #s1-4. The remaining compositions had
        been previously published and include op. 17, #s 1-3; op. 20, #s 1, 3, 4;
        op. 28, #s 1,2; op. 36, #1,3,4; the "Allegretto" from the *Sonata*, op. 65;
        and op. 68, #s 1-5.

68   *Five Short Pieces for Organ.* 1908. 1. "Canon in the fifth," 2. "Slumber
        song," 3. "Novelette," 4. "Arietta," 5. "Risoluto." Pub: GS.

1911   *Collegiate Overture.* TTBB & orch., arr.for piano, 4 hands. Ho: 33 pp.,
        NH.

1916   *Introduction and Fugue in E Minor.* Ho: 11 pp., NH.

Chamber Music

1881   *Scherzo*, G major (trio in C maj.). String quartet. Ho: 6 pp., "Mar. 29,"
        NH.

1881   *Scherzo*, G major (trio in D maj.). String quartet. Ho: 4 pp., "Nov.2,"
        NH.

1881   *Quartet*, D major. Ho: "Grave-Allegro Molto," 15 pp.; "Romanza,"
        6 pp.; "Scherzo," 4 pp.; "Finale," 12 pp., Nov.-Dec., at NH.

1882   *Trio*, C minor. Piano, vln., vc. Ho: dated "February," I, 25 pp.; II
        "Adagio," 12 pp.; III "Scherzo," 17 pp.; IV "Finale," 17 pp. + pts., 8 pp.
        each, Feb., at NH.

[1882-85] *Thema mit Variationes*, stg. quartet. Ho: 12 pp. NH. Ten-measure
        theme followed by numbered variations, 1 - 27. Var. 28-33 are unnum-
        bered; var 33 inc. This composition excercise may have been the music
        Parker referred to in an interview (ca. 1893) as an early work, "Sixty-
        eight variations on a familiar theme" (HP Papers IV E 3). See also
        "Fantaisie," (1882-1885) 2 pianos, under Keyboard Music.

[1882-85] *Quartet*, E minor. Theme, variations, and fugal finale. Ho: 12 pp.,
        n.d., NH.

11   **String Quartette in F Major.* 1885. 20 min. Ho: inc. sc + complete
        pts, NYv; inc. sc., NH. 1st perf. Detroit, MI, 29 Nov. 1887.

35   *Suite for Piano, Violin, and Violoncello.* 1893. Pub: sc, 36 pp. + 2 pts.,
        GS, 1904. 1st perf: Manuscript Society, NYC, 3 Mar. 1893.

38   **String Quintette in D Minor.* 2 vln, 1 va, 2 vc. [1880s?]. 10 min. Ms:
        pts., 7 pp. each, NH; Pub: *Three Centuries of American Music*, ed. John
        Graziano, Garland Publishing, forthcoming. 1st perf: Kneisel Quartet,
        Boston, 21 Jan. 1895.

41   **Suite for Violin and Pianoforte.* 1894. "Prelude," "Quasi fantasi,"
        "Canzone," "Intermezzo," "Finale." Ho: sc, "Apr. 10," 37 pp. + vln. pt.,
        NH. 1st perf: Timothée Adamowski, vln., and Arthur Whiting, piano,
        Boston, 15 Jan. 1895.

Theme and Variations in G minor. Vln, va, vc, piano. 1902. Ms: sc., 9
pp., "Yale University, Fall 1902," Cn.

Orchestra Music

Approximately a dozen works in incomplete form can be found
at NH. These date largely from Parker's pre-Munich study with
Chadwick (1881-1882). Only complete works are listed below.
Unless otherwise indicated, the orchestration is for the normal
complement of winds, percussion, and strings.

1881   [Unidentified piece, orch., C major]. Ho: 44 pp., "Jul 16-21," NH.

[188-] *Allegro non troppo*, stg. orch. Ho: 14 pp., NH.

1882-83 *Scherzo*, D minor, string orch. Ho: sc., 7 pp.,,+ pts., NH. Listed in
        Jahresbericht, Königliche Musikhochschule [Munich] 9 (1882-83): 31,
        as a composition by Parker.

4   *Concert Overture in E-flat.* 1884. Ho: sc, 46 pp. + pts., NH; sc & pts,
        Phf. 1st perf: Royal Conservatory, Munich, 7 July 1884.

5   *Regulus, Overture Heroique.* 1884. Ho: 43 pp. + pts., NH; sc & pts.,
        Phf. Early perf: Brooklyn, 1888, acc. to unidentified clipping, BpBr.

12   *Venetian Overture.* 1884. Ho: 29 pp., [bound w op. 13] + pts., NH; sc
        + pts., Phf.

13   *Scherzo*, G minor. 1884. Ho: 30 pp., [bound w/ op. 12] + pts., NH; sc +
        pts., Phf. Early perf: Van der Stucken Orchestra, Steinway Hall, NYC,
        30 Jan. 1886.

7   *Symphony in C.* 1884. Ho: 140 pp. + pts., NH; sc + pts, Phf. 1st perf:
        Royal Conservatory, Munich, 11 May 1885.

24   *Count Robert of Paris*, overture. 1890. Hos: 47 pp., NH; 48 pp., Bc;
        sc + pts., Phf. 1st perf: Manuscript Society, NYC, 10 Dec. 1890.

46   **Northern Ballad*, symphonic poem. 1899. 13.30 min. Hos: 59 pp.,
        Bc; 52 pp., NH; sc + pts., NH & Phf. See arr. piano, 4 hands, under
        Keyboard. 1st perf: New Haven Symphony, 7 Apr. 1899. Therafter
        performed by most major orchestras. Parker's most frequently per-
        formed orchestra piece. See 4-hand piano arr. under Keyboard.

55   **Concerto for Organ and Orchestra. 1902. 22 min. Ho: 93 pp., Wc;
      Ms sc, 89 pp., Bp; Ms sc, 90 pp. + pts, NH; sc + pts., Phf. Pub: fl sc.,
      67 pp., N. 1st perf: Boston Symphony Orchestra, Parker as soloist, 26
      Dec. 1902. See arrangement for organ solo under Arrangements of
      Parker's Music.

56   **Vathek, symphonic poem. 1902-03. 14 min. Based on William
      Beckford's tale). Ho: 56 pp., 1903, NH; sc + pts., Phf. Pub: facsimile
      ed., Garland Publishing, forthcoming. See 4-hand piano arr. under
      Keyboard.

72   Collegiate Overture, TTBB & orch. Hos: 84 pp., Br, 84 pp. + pts., NH;
      sc + pts., Phf. 1st perf: Lichtfield County Choral Union, Norfolk, CT, 7
      June 1911. See 4-hand piano arr. under Keyboard.

77d   **Suite from Fairyland. 1915. 15 min. Prelude, Intermezzo, and Ballet
      from the opera. Ho: 33, 9, 79 pp.+ pts., NH.

Arrangements, Transcriptions, Editing

Part Songs For Mixed Chorus

1895   The Battle Hymn of the Republic. Unac. 5 pp., GS.

1895   My Country, 'Tis of Thee. Unac. 2 pp., GS.

1895   The Star Spangled Banner, John S. Smith. Unac. 4 pp., GS.

Part Songs For Male Chorus

1895   In einem Kühlen Grunde, Friedrich Silcher. German, J. von Eichen-
        dorff; Eng.trans., Theodore Baker. Unac., 7 pp., GS.

1895   Die Lorelie, Franz Schubert. German, Heinrich Heine; Eng. trans.,
        Theodore Baker. Unac., 7 pp., GS.

1908   Cossack War Song. Eng. version, H. E. Krehbiel. Pf accom., 8 pp., GS.
        Perf: Orpheus Club, Phila., 1908-09 season.

1908   *Three Irish Folk Songs*: 1. "The Shan Van Voght," 2. "At the mid-hour
        of night," 3. "Kitty Magee." Unac., GS. Perf: Orpheus Club, Phila.,
        1910-11 season.

1908   *Two Minnelieder*: 1. "Moonrise," 2. "Three Roses." Eng. trans., Emily
        H. Whitney. Pf. accom. 11 pp., GS.

Excerpts From Larger Choral Works

1907   *The Rainbow*, quartet from *The Deluge* (Le Déluge), C. St. Saëns. SATB
        w/ org. accom., arr. from orch. Eng. Pub: 7 pp., GS.

1908   Two Choruses from *Stabat Mater*, Mme. M. F. C. Grandval: 1."Power
        Eternal, Judge and Father," SATB w/ org. accom., 11 pp.;
        2. "Guide Us, Father," SAT w/ org. accom., 7 pp., GS.

1908   *The Valley of the Espingo* (Das Thal des Espingo), Joseph Rheinberger.
        (Paul Heyse, trans. Alice C. Jennings). Male chorus, piano, arr. from
        orch. Pub: 36 pp., GS.

Solo Voice

1892   *A Recruiting Song for Times of Peace and Times of Sacrifice*, Lt. C. A.
        L. Trotten. (New Haven: Our Race Publishing Co.). Author acknowl-
        edged help from Parker.

1912   *German, French and Italian Song Classics*, 4 vols. JC. Original text w
        Eng.translation. Music edited by Parker.

Piano

1892   *Vorspiel zum Ersten Akt des Lyrischen Dramas "Vlasda"*, Frank Van der
        Stucken. Pub: Berlin: Friedrich Luckhardt; GS. Arr. four hands from
        orch.

Orchestration

[ca. 1903] *The Quest*, Ethelbert Nevin. Orchestration for the cantata by Parker.
        See John T. Howard, *Ethelbert Nevin* (New York: Crowell, 1935),
        p. 336.

Organ

1895   *A Collection of Arrangements and Transcriptions for the Organ*: Rheinberger, "Melodie"; St.-Saens, "Le cynge" and "Prelude to Le deluge"; Domenico Scarlatti, "Siciliano"; Schumann, "Canon," "Message," "Northern Song," "Romanza," op. 28, no. 2; Volkmann, "The Song of a Hero"; and Wagner, "Albumleaf." Pub: 72 pp., GS.

Hymnals

1903   *The Hymnal*, Revised and enlarged: as adopted by the general convention of the Protestant Episcopal Church. Pub: 751 pp., NE. Ed. Horatio Parker. See also Church Music: Hymns.

1907   *University Hymns for Use in Battell Chapel at Yale.* Pub: 331 pp., ASB. Tunes arr. for male voices by Parker and Harry B. Jepson. See also Church Music: Hymns.

1914   *The Church Hymnal*, as adopted by the general convention of the Protestant Episcopal Church in the United States. Ed. Rev. Charles L. Hutchins (New York: The Parish Choir). "The editor is under special obligation for advice and critical assistance to Mr. Horatio Parker [among others]."

1918   *The Hymnal* [Episcopal Church]. Parker was a member of the commission charged with choosing the hymn tunes. See also Church Music: Hymns.

Public School Music

1914-19 *The Progressive Music Series.* See Music for Solo Voice. Parker was an editor as well as a contributor.

Arrangements of Parker's Music

1903   *Concerto for Organ*, op. 55. Arr. as organ solo by David S. Smith. Pub: 28 pp., N.

1955   "Finale," from oratorio *Hora Novissima*. Abridged and arr. by Denes Agay. Pub: *Panorama of American Classics*, TP, pp. 25-27.

Writings, Addresses, Editing, Interviews

Practically all of this material is found in the HP archives at
Yale. I have given the principal and have not listed duplicate
or alternate versions of holographs and manuscripts.

1881,1890-1919 [Diaries] [1894 missing]. HP Papers, V A. Pocket-sized books
for keeping appointments, accounts, etc.

[1893]   "Organ loft hearings" [interview: early training, music profession].
Unidentified clipping, HP Papers, IV E 3.

1894-1919 *Report of the President of Yale University.* New Haven: Private Printing. Yale, Sterling Library. HP wrote those sections dealing with the
School of Music.

1894-1919 *Catalogue for the School of Music.* New Haven: Private Printing.
NH. HP & Samuel Sanford (1894-1904), HP (1905-1919).

1895-1919 New Haven Symphony Orchestra. Programs. New Haven: Private
Printing, NH.

1895-1898 *Music List, Trinity Church in the City of Boston, Oct. 1895--June,
1898* (Boston: private printing, 1898). This listing (a copy at Bp) includes all music performed at services. HP was organist and choirmaster.

1896   "Music in Yale University." Ts: 6 pp., HP Papers, V, C, NH. Pub:
"Music as a University Course," *Music* 10 (June 1896): 181-85; abstract
in *Review of Reviews* 14 (July 1896): 87.

[1897]-1916 [Church Music]. 1. "Church music," TS: 19 pp., n.d.; 2. "Church
music," Ts: 38 pp., n.d.; 3. "A paper for the Clerical Club in Massachusetts" [1898], TS: 11 pp.; 4. "Church music," TS: 15pp., [27 Oct 1904];
5. "Church music since Bach, California, 1916," Ts: 10 pp.; 6. "Church
music [sketches]," HO: 8 pp.,-- all HP Papers, V C.1 and/or 2 may be
drafts of a lecture HP was invited to give on 29 Mar. 1897 in New York
City as part of a Columbia Lecture Series in cooperation with Carnegie
Hall.

[1899]   [Interview with English critic Vernon Blackburn on HP's music and that
of other composers]. Unidentified clipping, HP Papers, IV E 5.

1899-1901 "The modern orchestra," "for New Haven, April 7, 1988; delivered
Feb. 27, 1901." Ho: 28 pp., HP Papers, V C.

1899   "Hymns for the church," a paper for the Episcopal Club of Massachu
        setts, "Jan. 12." Ho: 20 pp., HP Papers, V C. Excerpts in Semler, 73-76.

1899   "Professor Parker on English Executive Musicians," *The Musical Times*
        40 (1899): 661-662.

1899   [The Worcester Festival: greetings]. Ho: 3 pp., HP Papers, V C.

1900   "For the National Institute of Arts and Letters, January 25, 1900." Ts:
        5 pp., HP Papers, V C.

1900   "Address before the American Guild of Organists, May 16, 1900." Ts:
        13 pp. HP Papers, V C. Nw gives date as Nov 2 (p. 123).

[190-]-1907 "The history of music," lectures for HP's music history course at
        Yale. Two sets: 1st , Ho: 19 lectures; 2nd, Ts 21 lectures [2-4 inc., 7
        missing], 1907-08, HP Papers, V B. The following lecture titles are
        taken from the 2nd set excepting the missing chapters 2-4, 7, which are
        taken from the 1st set. 1. [Intro., general remarks, emphasis on listen-
        ing], 7 pp. 2. "Ancient music: Chinese, Japanese, and Hindu," 5 pp. 3.
        "Ancient music: Egyptian, Arabic, Turkish, Hebrew," 15 pp. 4. "An-
        cient music: the Greeks," 26 pp. 5. [Roman music through Gregorian
        chant], 8 pp. 6. "Organum, discantus, faux bourdon, Guido" 7 pp. 7.
        Medieval music: organum, discantus, faux bourdon, Guido's composi-
        tion, troubadours, minnesinger," 14 pp. 8. "Contemporaries of
        Palestrina," 9 pp. 9. "Successors of Palestrina to Bach," 11 pp. 10.
        "Bach," 8 pp. 11. "Handel," 11 pp. 12. "Instrumental music," 9 pp. 13.
        "Haydn," 6 pp. 14. "Opera and Gluck," 9 pp. 15. "Mozart," 9 pp. 16.
        "Beethoven," 14 pp. 17. "Schubert," 9 pp.; "Weber," 5 pp. 18.
        "Schumann," 7 pp.; "Chopin," 3 pp. 19. "Mendelssohn," 6 pp.; "Liszt,"
        5 pp. 20. "Wagner," 7 pp. "Final 1908: a review," 10 pp.

1901   "George Frederick Handel," *Century Library of Music*. Ed. Ignace Jan
        Paderewski et al. (New York: Century Co.), Vol. 12: 377-393.

[1902] "Impressions of a year in Europe," address to "The Club," New Haven.
        Ho: 15 pp., HP Papers, V C. Excerpts in Semler, 155-165.

1903-07 Church service list for Church of St. Nicholas, New York. HO: note-
        book, 53 pp., HP Papers, V A.

[1907] "Music at Yale." Ts: 15 pp., HP Papers, V C.

[1907] "Music in America." Ts: 17 pp., HP Papers, V C.

1908   Address at Norfolk Festival, Litchfield County Choral Union on the
        occasion of the premiere of HP's *King Gorm the Grim*. Ts: 4 pp., HP
        Papers, V C. Excerpts in Semler, 198-201.

1909   "Contemporary music" [address for the American Academy of Arts and
        Letters, 14 Dec.]. Ts: 18 pp., HP Papers, V C; "Concerning contempo-
        rary music," *Proceedings of the American Academy of Arts and Letters* 1
        (1909-10): 36-43; *North American Review* 191 (Apr. 1910): 517-526;
        and *Musicians' Practical Instructor*, Vol. 12, *University Musical Ency-
        clopedia*, ed. Louis C. Elson (New York: The University Society, 1914),
        pp. 796-810.

1911   "Introduction" and ed., *Music and Drama*, also called *Music and Public
        Entertainment*, Vol. 9, *Young Folks Library: Vocations.* 10 vols. Ed.
        William Dewitt Hyde (Boston: Hall and Locke, 1911; reprint ed., New
        York: AMS Press, [1978]) pp. xiii-xxii.

1911   [Mona], address at Norfolk, CT, 1911. TS: 6 pp, HP Papers, V C. Ex
        cerpts in Semler, pp. 234-237.

1912   [Mona], address to the MacDowell Club, New York, 10 Jan. Ts: 16 pp.,
        HP Papers, V C. Semler, pp. 237-240. *Musical America* 15/12 (23 Jan.
        1912): 9.

1912   [Mona], address before the Metropolitan Opera Association, 23 Mar. Ts:
        5 pp., HP Papers, V C. Excerpts in Semler, pp. 243-245.

1914-19 *The Progressive Music Series for Basal Use in Primary, Intermediate,
        and Grammar Grades.* 8 vols. plus teacher's manual. Eds. Horatio
        Parker, Osbourne McConathy, W. Otto Meisner, and Edward Bailey
        Birge, (Boston and New York: Silver-Burdett & Co.).

1915   "Talk on 'Fairyland' before Tuesday Musical Club of Salt Lake City,
        Utah." Ho: 12 pp. + Tss, HP Papers, V C.

1915   "The art of listening" [address delivered before the fifth convention of
        the Music Teachers' Association of California, 12 July]. Ts: 14 pp., HP
        Papers, V C. See also *Musical America*, 22/12: 2, for a brief reference to
        this address.

1915   "Music in our public schools: [Address] to the Connecticut School
        Teachers [Music Teachers' Association, 1915]." Ts: 13 pp., HP Pa-
        pers, V C.

1916   "Address to the Music Teachers' National Association (sic.) [American
        Federation of the Arts?], Washington May 19, 1916." Ts: 7 pp, HP

Papers, V C. Subject: American music. MTNA proceedings for 1916 contain no such address. The pencil addition at the head of the Ts gives the date and erroneous title. See clipping, *Washington Evening Star*, 20 May 1916, HP Papers, V E 6, which identifies the American Federation of Arts as the audience for this address.

1916   "French opera, for Springfield, Mass., Jan. 6, 1916." Ts: 10 pp. + Ho: 2 pp., HP Papers, V C.

1916   "Music in Colleges," *The Art World* 1/2 (Nov. 1916): 101-103.

1917   "Some Orchestral Conditions." Ts: 14 pp., HP Papers, V C. *Atlantic Monthly* 119 (Apr. 1917): 485-490.

1917   "Our Taste in Music." Tss: 7-16 pp., HP Papers, V C. At top of one copy: "Delivered at dedication of Sprague Hall 1917." Pub: *The Yale Review* 7 (1918): 777-788.

n.d.   "Modern French orchestral music." Ts: 8 pp. (p.7 missing), HP Papers, V C.

n.d.   [Germany]. Ho: 6 pp., HP Papers, V C.

n.d.   "Great songs." Ts: 7 pp., HP Papers, V C.

n.d.   [Hymn tunes]. Ts: 3 pp., HP Papers, V C.

n.d.   "Music as a vocation." Ho: 13 pp., HP Papers, V C.

n.d.   "Music festivals." Ho: 6 pp., HP Papers, V C.

n.d.   [Music in universities]. Ho: HP Papers, V C.

n.d.   "Oratorio." Ho: 3 pp., HP Papers, V C.

--   [Misc. unidentified writings by HP]. HP Papers, V C.

APPENDIX B: DISCOGRAPHY

This discography is a listing of private and commercial recordings. I am especially indebted to Ellen S. Johnson, librarian of the Archive of Recorded Sound at Groton Music Library, University of Kansas, for her help in identifying early commercial recordings.

A. D. 1919, Opus 84. Performance, Feb. 1958, Yale University, Nancy Savin, soprano soloist, the Connecticut College Choir, the Yale Glee Club, and the Yale University Orchestra, Fenno Heath, director. Carillon Productions, K80P-6126, side two, private recording.

Concerto for Organ and Orchestra, Opus 55. Performance, 25 Jan. 1976, Church of the Heavenly Rest, 5th Ave. at 90th St., New York City; Bradley Hull, organist, and the Collegium Musicum, Fritz Rikko, musical director. Deryck Waring Recordings, PE6-0878, side 4, private recording, 25 W. 43rd St., New York, NY 10036.

"Fugue in C Minor," *Four Pieces for Organ*, Opus 36, No. 3. Richard Morris, organist. New World Records, NW 280 (1976).

Hora Novissima, Opus 30. Gertrude Hopf, S; E. Wein, A; Edward Kent, T; Walter Berry, B; the American Recording Society Orchestra, William Strickland, conductor. American Recording Society, ARS335, 3 sides, (1953); reissued by Desto, D ST6413 (1965) [Vienna Symphony Orchestra listed].

_____. Washington and Cathedral Choral Societies, Paul Callaway, director, and the Glee Clubs of the National Cathedral School for Girls and St. Albans School for Boys, Richard Dirksen, director. Recorded Publications Co., Camden, NJ, A32M-69681-84, four sides, private rec.

_____. Performance, 25 Jan. 1976, Church of the Heavenly Rest, 5th Ave. at 90th St., New York City. Jennifer Barron, S; Cynthia Munzer, A; Leo Goeke, T; Richard Anderson, Bar; the Canterbury Choral Society, Charles Dodsley Walker, conductor, and The Collegium Musicum, Fritz

Rikko, musical director. Derick Waring Recordings, PE6-0878, three sides, private recording, 25 W. 43rd St., New York, NY 10036.

"Jam sol recedit igneus," *The Legend of Saint Christopher*, Opus 43. Washington Cathedral Choir, Paul Galloway, cond. Vanguard, VRS- 1036 (LP), VRS-2021 (LP stereo) (1958).

"The lamp in the west," *Three Part Songs*, Opus 48, No. 1. University of Kansas Glee Club, Justus H. Fugate, student cond. Columbia 691-D (1926).

_____. Columbia Stellar Quartette. Columbia A 1871.

_____. Wesleyan Glee Club, Calvin Kuhl, cond. Brunswick 3158-BA.

_____. Syracuse University Glee Club, Birger M. Beausang, cond. Brunswick 3158-BA

"The lark now leaves his watery nest," *Six Old English Songs*, Opus 47, No. 6. Horatio Connell, Bar; accom. unidentified, Columbia, 29975 (1906).

_____. Emilio de Gorza, Bar; accom. unidentified, Victor, 74118 (1908); reissued, New World Recordings, NW 247 (1976).

_____. Agnes Nicholls, S; accom. unidentified, His Master's Voice, 3837 (1909).

"Love in May," *Four Songs*, Opus 51, No. 1. Emma Eames, S; accom. unidentified, Victor, 88131 (1908); reissued, New World Records, NW 247 (1976).

Mona, "Prelude," Eastman Rochester Symphony Orchestra, Haward Hanson, cond. Mercury, SR90524 (1970).

_____. "Interlude," Philharmonia Orchestra, Richard Korn, cond. Allegro-Elite, 3150-A; Concord, 3007 (1955).

_____. "Suite" [Prelude and love duet]. Performance, 22 Feb. 1961, Orchestra of America, Richard Korn, cond. Arlene Saunders, S; Enrico Di giuseppe, T; Unidentified private recording, two sides.

A Northern Ballad, Opus 46. Royal Philharmonic Orchestra of London, Karl Krueger, cond. Society for the Preservation of the American Musical Heritage, MIA 132, one side, (1966).

_____. Albany Symphony Orchestra, Julius Hegyi, cond. New World Records, NW 339 digital (1986).

"The Shan Van Vogt," No. 1, *Three Irish Folk-Songs*, arr. male chorus. Columbia University Glee Club, Bailey Harvey, cond. Carillon 117 (LP).

Sonata in E Flat for Organ, Opus 65. William Osborne, organist. Orion Master Recordings, ORS 78309.

"Valse gracile," *Trois morceaux caractéristiques pour le piano*, Opus 49, No. 3. Malcolm Frager,pianist, New World Records, NW 206 (1978).

Vathek, Opus 56. Royal Philharmonic Orchestra of London, Karl Krueger, cond. Society for the Preservation of the American Musical Heritage, MIA 138 (1967).

APPENDIX C: BIBLIOGRAPHY

Books and Monographs

Aldrich, Richard. *Concert Life in New York: 1902-1923*. New York: Putnam's Sons, 1941.

American Academy of Arts and Letters. *In Memoriam, A Book of Records Concerning Former Members of the American Academy of Arts and Letters*. New York: private printing, n. d.

Baldwin, Samuel A. *The Story of the American Guild of Organists*. New York: H. W. Gray Co., 1946.

Bellamy, Edward. *Looking Backward*. 1888, reprint ed., New York: Signet Classics, 1960.

Bispham, David. *A Quaker Singer's Recollections*. New York: H. W. Gray Co., 1946.

Brooks, Van Wyck. *New England Indian Summer (1865-1915)*. New York: E. P. Dutton, 1940.

Burkholder, J. Peter. *Charles Ives: the Ideas behind the Music*. New Haven: Yale University Press, 1985.

Century Association. *The Century: 1847 - 1946*. New York: The Century Association, 1947.

Chadwick, George. "American Composers," *History of American Music*, vol. 4 of *The American Encyclopedia and History of Music*. See Hubbard, W. L., ed., for main entry.

_____. *Horatio Parker* [Address] *Delivered before the American Academy of Arts and Letters, July 25, 1920*. New Haven: Yale University Press, 1921.

323

Chase, Gilbert. *America's Music*. 2nd ed. New York: McGraw-Hill, 1966.

Clark, Linda. *Music in Trinity Church, Boston, 1890-1900: A Case-Study in the Relationship Between Worship and Culture*. Doctor of Sacred Music thesis, Union Theological Seminary, 1973.

Commager, Henry Steele. *The American Mind*. New Haven: Yale University Press, 1950; paperback ed., 1959.

Copland, Aaron. *Music and Imagination*; The Charles Eliot Norton Lectures, 1951-52, Harvard University (New York: Mentor Books, 1959.

Cowell, Henry and Sydney. *Charles Ives and His Music*. New York: Oxford University Press, 1955; paperback ed., 1969.

Daniels, Mabel. *An American Girl in Munich*. Cambridge: University Press, 1905.

Davidson, Archibald. *Protestant Church Music in America*. Boston: E. C. Schirmer Music Co., 1933.

Draper, Rev. George B., and Bayton, Milm P., Esq. *History of St. Andrew's Church [Harlem] in Two Chapters: A. D. 1829-1889*. New York: private printing, 1889.

Ellinwood, Leonard. *The History of American Church Music*. New York: Morehouse-Gorham, 1953.

Elson, Louis C. *The History of American Music*. New York: Macmillan, 1904; revised 1925, Arthur Elson; reprint ed., New York: Franklin, 1971.

Farwell, Arthur, and Darby, W. D., eds. *Music in America*, vol. 4 of *The Art of Music*. Ed. Daniel Gregory Mason. 13 vols. New York: The National Society of Music, 1915-16.

Fellowes, Edmund. *Cathedral Music from Edward VI to Edward VII*. 4th ed. London: Methuen and Co., Ltd., 1948.

Foote, Arthur. *Arthur Foote, 1853-1937: An Autobiography*. Norwood MA: Plimpton Press, 1946.

Gerson, Robert. *Music in Philadelphia*. Philadelphia: Theodore Presser, 1940; reprint ed., Westport, CT: Greenwood Press, [1976].

Gillespie, John. *Nineteenth-Century American Piano Music*. New York: Dover, 1978.

Gilman, Lawrence. *Edward MacDowell*. New York and London: John Lane, 1921.

Graves, C. L. *Hubert Parry: His Life and Works*. 2 vols. London: Macmillan and Co., 1928

Hamm, Charles. *Music in the New World*. New York: Norton, 1983.

Hipsher, Edward E. *American Opera and Its Composers*. Philadelphia: Theodore Presser, 1927.

Hitchcock, H. Wiley, and Perlis, Vivian, eds. *An Ives Celebration: Papers and Panels of the Charles Ives Centennial Festival-Conference, 1974*. Urbana: University of Illinois Press, 1977.

Hooker, Brian. *Mona*. New York: Dodd, Mead, 1911.

Hovey, Richard. *John Jay Chapman--An American Mind*. New York: Columbia University Press, 1959.

Howard, John Tasker. *Our American Music*. 3rd ed. New York: Thomas Y. Crowell, 1946.

Hubbard, W. L., ed. *The History of American Music*, vol. 4 of *The American History and Encyclopedia of Music*. 12 vols. New York: Irving Squire, 1908-10.

Hughes, Rupert. *Contemporary American Composers*. Boston: Page, 1900.

Hutchins, Rev. Charles L. *The Church Hymnal*. Boston: Parish Choir, 1914.

Hymnal, The [Episcopal]. New York: H. W. Gray, 1918.

Ives, Charles E. *Memos*. Edited by John Kirkpatrick. New York: W. W. Norton, 1972.

Ivey, Donald. *Song: Anatomy, Imagery, and Style*. New York: Free Press, 1970.

Krehbiel, Henry E. *More Chapters of Opera*. New York: Henry Holt, 1919.

Lang, Paul Henry. *History of Music in Western Civilization*. New York: W. W. Norton, 1941.

Levy, Alan Howard. *Musical Nationalism: American Composers' Search for Identity*. Westport, CT: Greenwood Press, 1983.

Lindsay, Jack. *The Romans Were Here*. London: Frederick Muller, 1956.

Lowens, Margery Morgan. *The New York Years of Edward MacDowell*. Ph. D. dissertation, University of Michigan, 1971.

MacDowell, Edward. *Critical and Historical Essays*. Boston: A. P. Schmidt, 1912; reprint ed. with a new introduction by Irving Lowens, New York: Da Capo, 1969.

Mellers, Wilfrid. *Music in a New Found Land*. London: Barrie and Rockliff, 1964.

Miller, Percy, ed.. *The American Transcendentalists*. Garden City, New York: Doubleday Anchor Book, 1957.

Molley, Leo T. *Tercentary Pictorial and History of the Lower Nangatuck Valley, Containing a History of Derby*. Ansonia, CT: Emerson Brothers, 1935.

Moore, MacDonald Smith. *Yankee Blues: Musical Culture and American Identity*. Bloomington: University of Indiana Press, 1985.

Mussulman, Joseph A. *Music in the Cultured Generation: A Social History of Music in America, 1870-1900*. Evanston: Northwestern University Press.

Norman, Gertrude, and Shrifte, Miriam Lubell. *Letters of Composers*. New York: A. A. Knopf, 1946; paperback ed., Grosset and Dunlap. n.d.

Noss, Luther. *A History of the Yale School of Music, 1855-1970*. New Haven: private printing, 1984.

Osterweis, Rollin. *Three Centuries of New Haven*. New Haven: Yale University Press, 1953.

Parker, Horatio Newton. *Some Descendents of Six Pioneers from Great Britain to America*. Privately printed, 1940.

Parker, Horatio W., ed. *The Hymnal*. New York: H. W. Gray, 1903.

_____, et al., eds. *The Progressive Music Series For Basal Use in Primary, Intermediate, and Grammar Grades*. 8 vols. Boston and New York: Silver-Burdett, 1914-1919.

_____, ed. and introduction. *Music and Drama [Music and Public Enter-
    tainment]*. Vol. 9 of *Young Folks Library: Vocations*, 10 vols. Edited
    by William DeWitt Hyde. Boston: Hall and Locke, 1911; reprint, New
    York, AMS Press, 1980.

_____, and Jepson, Harry B., eds. *University Hymns*. New York: A. S.
    Barnes, 1907.

Perry, Rosalie Sandra. *Charles Ives and the American Mind*. Kent, OH: Kent
    State University Press, 1974.

Pierson, George Wilson. *Yale College 1871 - 1921*. New Haven: Yale
    University Press, 1952.

Pratt, Waldo Selden, ed. *American Supplement* to *Grove's Dictionary of Music
    and Musicians*. London: Macmillan, 1928.

Robertson, Alec. *Dvořák*. New York: Farrar, Straus, and Cudahy, Inc., 1943;
    paperback ed., New York: Collier Books, 1962.

Robins, Robert P., and Church, Arthur, et al. *A History of the Orpheus Club of
    Philadelphia: 1872 - 1936*. Philadelphia: private printing, 1936.

Rosenfeld, Paul. *Musical Chronicle (1917-1923)*. New York: Harcourt, Brace
    and Co., 1923.

Rossiter, Frank R. *Charles Ives and His America*. New York: Liverright, 1975.

Routley, Eric. *The Music of Christian Hymnody: A Study in the Development of
    the Hymn Tune*. London: Independent Press, 1957.

Saint James' Church, New York City. *Souvenir of the Dedication Festival and
    Founder's Day of Saint James' Church, January 29, 1928*. New York:
    Rudge, n.d.

Santayana, George. *Character and Opinion in the United States*. New York: C.
    Scribner's Sons, 1921.

Schleiffer, Martha Furman. *William Wallace Gilchrist (1846-1916): a Moving
    Force in the Musical Life of Philadelphia*. Metuchen, NJ: The Scare-
    crow Press, 1985.

Schmidt, John C. *The Life and Works of John Knowles Paine*. Ann Arbor: UMI
    Research Press, 1980.

Semler, Isabel Parker. *Horatio Parker: A Memoir for His Grand-children Compiled from Letters and Papers*. New York: G. P. Putnam's Sons, 1942; reprint, New York: Da Capo, 1973.

Sessions, Roger. *Reflections on the Musical Life in the United States*. New York: Merlin Press, 1956.

Smith, David Stanley. *Gustave J. Stoeckel, Yale Pioneer in Music*. New Haven: Yale University Press, 1939.

Spalding, Walter Raymond. *Music at Harvard*. New York: Coward-McCann, 1935.

Spooner, Ruth Hopkins. *Lasall's First Century, 1851-1951*. Boston: The Abbey Press, 1951.

Stevenson, Robert. *Protestant Church Music in America*. New York: W. W. Norton, 1966.

Tawa, Nicholas. *Serenading the Reluctant Eagle: American Musical Life, 1925-1945*. New York: Schirmer Books, 1985.

Thompson, David M. *A History of Harmonic Theory in the United States*. Kent, OH: Kent State University Press, 1980.

Tischler, Barbara. *An American Music: The Search for an American Musical Identity*. New York: Oxford University Press, 1986.

Trinity Church in the City of Boston, Massachusetts 1733 - 1933. Boston: private printing, 1933.

Twenty-five Years After with Yale, 1902. Newburgh, NY: The Moore Printing Co., 1927.

Upton, George. *The Standard Cantatas*. Chicago: McClurg, 1888.

_____. *The Standard Oratorios*. Chicago: McClurg, 1896.

Upton, William Treat. *Art Song in America*. Boston: Oliver Ditson, 1930.

Wooldridge, David. *From the Steeples and the Mountains*. New York: Knopf, 1974.

Yellin, Victor. *The Life and Operatic Works of George W. Chadwick*. Ph. D. thesis, Harvard University, 1957.

Zuck, Barbara. *A History of Musical Americanism*. Ann Arbor: UMI Research Press, 1980.

Articles and Periodicals

Baumgartner, Hope Leroy. "The Organ Works of Horatio Parker," *The American Organist* 2 (Dec. 1919): 487-489.

Boston Evening Transcript. 1893-1919.

Foote, Arthur. "A Bostonian Remembers." *Musical Quarterly* 23 (Jan. 1937): 37-44.

"Horatio Parker." *The Musical Times* 43 (1 Sept. 1902): 586-92.

Kramer, A. Walter. "Horatio Parker--Ten Years After--An Appreciation." *Musical America* 49 (25 Dec. 1929): 22.

_____. "Mefisto's Musings," *Musical America* 54 (10 March 1934): 9.

MacDougall, Hamilton C. "The Hymn-tunes of Horatio Parker," *Diapason* 11 (June 1920): 16.

"Mona, A Step in Advance." *Musical Courier* 64 (20 March 1912): 21.

The Monthly Musical Record. London. 1899.

"Music as a University Course." *The American Monthly Review of Reviews* 14 (July 1896): 87.

Musical America. New York. 1898-1916.

The Musical Courier. New York. 1893-1915.

The Musical Leader. Chicago. 1915.

The Musical Times. London. 1893-1905.

"The National Conservatory of Music." *Harper's Weekly* 34 (13 Dec. 1890): 969-970.

New England Conservatory of Music Bulletin. 1 (Jan. 1920): 4.

New Music Review and Church Music Review. 19 (May 1920): 192.

New York Sun. 1919.

New York Times. 1890-1931.

New York Tribune. 1901-1919.

Opera News: 125 (1 Apr. 1961).

Parker, Horatio W. "Concerning Contemporary Music." *Proceedings of the American Academy of Arts and Letters.* 1 (1909-10): 36-43.

_____. "Our Taste in Music." *Yale Review.* 7 (July 1918): 777-788.

_____. "Some Orchestral Conditions." *Atlantic Monthly* 119 (April 1917): 485-490.

Philadelphia Public Ledger. 1911.

"The Proper Place of Music Study in Universities and Colleges." *New York Times*, 14 Feb. 1904, p. 22.

Robinson, Edward. "Horatio Parker." *American Mercury* 22 (April 1931): 497-501.

Rosenfeld, Paul. "One of the Parents." *Modern Music* 19 (May-June) 1942): 215-331.

Salter, Sumner. "Early Encouragements to American Composers." *Musical Quarterly* 18 (Jan. 1932): 76-105.

Smith, David Stanley. "Horatio Parker." *Musical Quarterly* 16 (Apr. 1930): 153-169.

Van Broekhoven, John. "Mona, A Thematic Analysis." *Musical Observer* 6 (Apr. 1912): 22-28.

Van Cleve, John S. "Americanism in Music." (from *Music*, ed., W. S. B. Mathews) *The American Monthly Review of Reviews* 19 (Jan. 1899): 96.

Wheelan, Ann. "The History of the New Haven Symphony Orchestra." *The Connecticut Times*, 16 March 1921, p. 3.

Yale Alumni Review. 18 (1894).

Yale Alumni Weekly. 14 (12 Oct. 1904).

Proceedings, Reports, Yearbooks, Catalogues, Programs and Directories.

The Boston Directory. 1886-1895.

Boston Symphony Orchestra. Programmes, 1895-1902.

Carder, Polly. *American Music in the Publications of Silver Burdett Co.*, Booklet printed for annual meeting of Sonneck Society, Tallahassee, FL, March 7-10, 1985.

Cathedral School of Saint Mary. Catalogues, 1885-90.

Cathedral School of Saint Paul. Circulars, 1886, 1888.

The Chicago Symphony Orchestra. Programs, 1901-02.

Church of the Holy Trinity, New York. *Yearbook: 1888.* New York: Medical Abstract Press.

Cleveland Orchestra. Programs, 1926.

Dramatic Compositions Copyrighted in the United States, 1890-1916. Washington, D. C. Library of Congress. Copyright Office.

General Theological Seminary, New York. *Proceedings of the General Theological Seminary.* 6 (1884-93).

Kearns, William Kay. "Index of Works," *Horatio Parker, 1863-1919: A Study of His Life and Music.* Ph.D. Dissertation, University of Illinois, 1965, pp. 703-728.

Krehbiel, H. E. *Review of the New York Musical Season.* 5 vols. New York: Novello, Ewer and Co., 1885-1890.

Munich Music Conservatory. *Jahresbericht der Königliche Musikhochschule in München* 9-11 (1882-85).

Nesnow, Adrienne. *Horatio Parker Papers.* Yale University Music Library Archival Collection. New Haven, CT.: 1981.

New Haven Symphony Orchestra. Programs. 1895-1919.

The New York City Guide. New York: Random House, 1946.

New York Philharmonic Society. Programs. 1901-02.

Newton, MA, English and Classical School. *An Illustrated Biographical Cata-
logue of the Principals, Teachers, and Students of the West Newton
English and Classical School, 1854-1893.* Boston: Rand Avery Supply
Co., 1895.

Philadelphia Orchestra. Programs, 1911.

Roosevelt, Theodore. *Program for Inaugural Concerts.* Washington, D. C.,
private printing, 1905.

Saint Andrew's Church, New York. *Yearbook: 1887-1888.* New York: The
Advent Press.

Seltsam, William H. *Metropolitan Opera Annals* New York: Wilson, 1947.

Strunk, Oliver. "Works of Horatio W. Parker," *Musical Quarterly* 16 (April
1930): 164-169.

Trinity Church, Boston. *Music List, Trinity Church in the City of Boston, Oct.
1895-June 1898.* Boston: private printing, 1898.

Trow's New York City Directory. 1887-1894. New York: Trow Directory, Printing, and Bookbinding Co.

Upton, George, ed. *Concert Programmes*, vol. 2 of *Theodore Thomas: A Musical Autobiography.* 2 vols. Chicago: McClurg and Co., 1905.

Wilson, George H. *The Boston Musical Year Book.* 10 vols. Vols. 1 & 2, title as
above; vol. 3, *The Boston Musical Year Book and Musical Year in the
United States*; vols. 4-10, *The Musical Yearbook of the United States.*
Vols. 1-4, Boston: G. Ellis, 1884-87; vols. 5-7, Boston: Alfred Mudge
and Son, 1887-1890; vols. 8-9, Worcester, MA: Charles Hamilton,
1890-1892; vol. 10, Chicago, Clayton F. Summy, 1892-93.

Yale University. *Catalogue of the Officers and Graduates of Yale University in
New Haven, Connecticut 1701-1924.* New Haven: Private Printing,
1924.

_____. *Catalogue for the School of Music.* 30 vols. (title varies). 1890-1921.

_____. *Report of the President of Yale University*. New Haven: private, annual printings, 1890-1921.

Libraries

Boston Public Library. Music Room. Scrapbooks of clippings, programs, and other material by Allen A. Brown, Arthur Foote, and Philip Hale. Clippings pasted on inside covers of scores donated to library by Allen A. Brown.

Library of Congress. Washington, D. C. Horatio Parker correspondence and music manuscripts.

New England Conservatory of Music. Boston. Library. Horatio Parker manuscripts.

New York Public Library. Astor, Lenox and Tilden Foundations. Fifth Ave. and Forty-second Street: files on Saint Mary's and Saint Paul's Cathedral Schools.

_____. Music Division of the Performing Arts Research Center Amsterdam Avenue: "Horatio Parker," clipping file; Manuscript Society file; Arthur Whiting papers.

Newberry Library. Chicago. Theodore Thomas papers.

Yale University. Library of the School of Music. Horatio Parker Papers inc. nearly all music in manuscript and published, extensive correspondence, programs, clippings and scrapbooks, writings, biographical material, and miscellaneous items.

_____. Sterling Memorial Library, "Memorabilia."

Letters and Interviews

Alexander, Fred. Chairman, Historical Research Committee, Jackson Homestead, Newton, MA. Letter to writer, 11 Nov. 1961.

Bailey, Parker. Brooklyn, NY. Nephew of Horatio Parker. Interviews and correspondence with writer, 1961-70.

Beede, Helen L. Recorder, Lasell Junior College, Auburndale, MA. Letter to writer, 12 Oct. 1961.

Brown, Ray. Director of Music, General Theological Seminary, New York City. Letter to writer, 15 Feb. 1963.

Conant, Marion K. Asst. Librarian, Dedham [MA] Historical Society. Letter to writer, 20 Sept. 1961.

Griffeth, Charles. E. Associate of Horatio Parker. Letter to George A. Booker, Tallahassee, Fl, 16 Nov. 1969.

Köllner, Marie Louise. Munich, Germany. Letter to writer, 2 Dec. 1962.

Kraft, Edwin. Organist, Trinity Church, Cleveland, OH. Letter to writer, 20 Apr. 1962.

Lindsley, Rev. James Elliot, Rector of St. Steven's Church, New York City. Letter to writer, 3 Oct. 1961.

Messner, W. Otto. Connersville, IN. Letter to George A. Booker, Tallahassee, FL, 24 Nov. 1959.

O'Meara, Eva J. Former librarian and curator of Horatio Parker materials, School of Music, Yale University. Interviews and correspondence with writer, 1960-1972.

Orpheus Club, Philadelphia. Interviews with members, 21 March 1964.

Semler, George. New York, NY. Great nephew of Horatio Parker. Correspondence with writer, 1972-present.

Semler, Isabel Parker. New Canaan, CT. Horatio Parker's daughter. Interview and correspondence with writer, 1960-67.

Semler, Ralph. New Canaan, CT. Horatio Parker's son-in-law. Interview with writer, 18 Sept. 1961.

Shepard, Brooks. Librarian of the School of Music, Yale University. Interviews and correspondence with writer, 1960-68.

Simonds, Bruce. New Haven, CT. Interviews with writer, 8 Sept. 1961, 24 Sept. 1962

Film

Timrock, Theodor. *A Good Dissonance is Like a Man.* (the life and music of
Charles Ives). New York: Foundation for the Arts, 1976.

INDEX

Anglo-Saxon music, 49-51, 190,
221, 243
Church music, 193-194, 203
Composition, 28, 37, 50-51, 147
French music, 9, 49
French opera, 138
German music, 49
Music esthetics, 26, 71, 236
Music education, 30-32
Music history, 25-28
Music listening, 70
Nationalism, 241-244, see also
opinions on American music
Opera, 143
Professional activities:
Administration, 34-35, 61
Choral music, 238-239
Church positions, 5, 13, 14, 39,
53, 61, 253 n.24
Conducting, 35-39, 41-42, 45-46,
57, 61
Editing, 202-204, 313-314, 316
Music courses taught, 25-29
Organist, 8, 14, 39, 51-52, 54, 61
Teaching positions, 11-12, 16-17,
22, 68 68-69, 137, 139
Writings:
Catalogue, Yale School of Music,
314
Church service list for Church of
St. Nicholas (New York), 315
Diaries (20) passim, 314
"George Frederick Handel," 315
Miscellaneous, 317
Music and Drama, 316
"Music as a University Course,
260 n.4
"Music in Colleges," 317
Music List, Trinity Church
(Boston), 314
New Haven Symphony Orchestra
Programs, 314
"Our Taste in Music," 317
Report of the President of Yale,
314

"Some Orchestral Conditions,"
317
Parker, J. C. D., 103
Parry, Charles Hubert Hastings, 26,
79, 143
Parsifal, Wagner, 45
Passion According To Saint Matthew,
Bach, 37
Pax Triumphans, Van der Stucken,
133, 135
Peabody Institute, 40, 59
Pease, Alfred, 181
Pelléas et Mélisande, Debussy, 147,
149, 151
Penn Athletic Club (Philadelphia), 57
People's Choral Union (New Haven,
CT), 39, 259 n.41
People's Temple (Boston), 45
Pergolesi, Giovanni Battista, 115
Perosi, Dom Lorenzo, 195
Perry, Rosalie Sandra, 235
Phelps, William Lyons, 237
Philadelphia Orchestra, 52, 300
Pierné, Gabriel, 258 n.36
Pipe of Desire, The, Converse, 60,
273 n.22
Ploessl, Anna, see Parker family
Poème de l' amour et de la mer,
Chausson, 190
Pohlig, Karl, 52
Powell, John, 243
Powers, Francis Fisher, 14
Pratt, Silas Gamaliel, 15
Pratt, Waldo Selden, 30 258 n. 29
Prince of India, Wallace-Clarke, 144
Progressive Music Series, The, 32
Public School Music Curriculum
(Yale), 33-34
Puccini, Giacomo, 143, 167

---- Q ----

Quartet choir, 193, 194
Queen's Hall (London), 44

354   Index

---- R ----

Raff, Joseph Joachim, 7
Randolph, Harold, 58
Rasch, Albertina, 275 n.46
Redemption, Gounod, 37, 106
Redemption Hymn (J. C. D. Parker),
    103
Redford, Robert, 47
Reger, Max, 258 n.36
Reiger, William H., 22
Reiss, Albert, 154
Requiem, Verdi, 37, 111, 114
Rheinberger, Josef, 5, 7, 8-9, 14, 39,
    79, 118, 123, 213, 215, 217, 225
Richter, Hans, 14, 42
Rikko, Fritz, 230
Rip Van Winkle, Chadwick, 208
Robinson, Edward, 234
Rockstro, William Smyth, 26
Rogers, Francis, 259 n.48
Roi d'Ys, Le, Lalo, 46
Romeo and Juliet Overture, Tchaikov-
    sky, 221
Roosevelt, Theodore, 53, 94-95, 293
Rosenfeld, Paul, 162, 234
Rosenkavalier, Der, R. Strauss, 167,
    275 n.58
Rossini, Gioacchino, 106, 115
Rossiter, Frank, 235
Routley, Eric, 204
Rowbotham, Rev. John Frederick, 26
Royal Conservatory (Munich), see
    Königliche Musikhochschule
Röntgen, Julius, 258 n.36
Rubinstein, Anton, 131

---- S ----

St. Andrew's Church (New York), 13-
    14
St. Anne, hymn tune, 39
St. Botolph Club, Boston, 22
St. John (J. C. D. Parker), 103
St. John's Church, Roxbury (MA), 6

St. Louis World's Fair, 41, 260 n.10
St. Luke's Church, Brooklyn, 13
St. Mary's Cathedral School, Garden
    City, Long Island, 12
St. Nicholas Church of New York, 57,
    61, 201
St. Paul's Church, Dedham, MA, 5, 6
St. Paul's Cathedral School, Garden
    City, Long Island, 11, 12, 83
St. Peter, John Knowles Paine, 104
Saint-Saëns, Camille, 46
Salome, R. Stauss, 147, 149
Samson et Dalila, Saint-Saëns, 46
San Francisco Symphony Orchestra,
    67
Sandberger, Adolf, 46
Sanders, Herbert, 141, 272 n.44
Sanford, Samuel Simmons, 25, 42, 61
    256 n. 9, 258 n.40
Sankey, Ira, 203
Santayana George, 192, 233
Sapio, Romualdo, 17
Sawyer, Mrs. H. E., 22
Schallert, Edwin, 174
Schmidt, Arthur Paul, 6
Schubert, Franz, 210
Schumann, Robert, 209
Scott, Cyril, 209 n.36
Scott, Walter, 90
Sea Drift, Delius, 190
Seidl, Anton, 18
Selby, Charles, 181
Semler, Grace Parker., 13, 75, 299
Semler, Isabel Parker, 13, 14, 18, 29,
    56, 74-75, 238, 299
Semler, Ralph, 257 n.13
Sessions, Roger Huntington, 36, 233,
    241
Shelly, Harry Rowe, 15
Sherwood, William H, 212
Sibelius, Jean, 244, 258 n.36
Sibley, Churchill, 44
Siegfried, Wagner, 46
Simonds, Bruce, 9, 29, 257 n.24
Slavonic Dances, Dvořák, 218
Smart, Henry, 204

356